ORGANISATIONAL CHANGE

ORGANISATIONAL CHANGE

Barbara Senior

FINANCIAL TIMES
PITMAN PUBLISHING

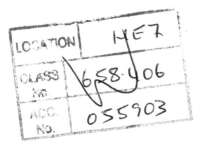

FINANCIAL TIMES

MANAGEMENT

LONDON • SAN FRANCISCO
KUALA LUMPUR • JOHANNESBURG

Financial Times Management delivers the knowledge,
skills and understanding that enable students,
managers and organisations to achieve their ambitions,
whatever their needs, wherever they are.

London Office:
128 Long Acre, London WC2E 9AN
Tel: +44 (0)171 447 2000
Fax: +44 (0)171 240 5771
Website: www.ftmanagement.com

A Division of Financial Times Professional Limited

First published in Great Britain in 1997

© Barbara Senior 1997

The right of Barbara Senior to be identified as author
of this work has been asserted by her in accordance
with the Copyright, Designs, and Patents Act 1988.

ISBN 0 273 62491 1

British Library Cataloguing in Publication Data
A CIP catalogue record for this book can be obtained from the British Library.

10 9 8 7 6 5 4 3 2

Typeset by Tek Art, Croydon, Surrey
Printed and bound in Great Britain by Clays Ltd, St Ives plc

The Publishers' policy is to use paper manufactured from sustainable forests.

Contents

About this Book

Introduction

All people in all organisations are concerned and involved with change, whether of the small-scale variety, such as adopting an updated version of a computer program, or of the large-scale variety, such as a change of strategy with subsequent changes in structure and operations. Consequently, no study of organisational life is complete without complementary studies of the way change affects it and how that change can be managed. In a world of constantly fluctuating demand and supply, of changing customer needs as well as the wider concerns brought about by the legitimate expectations of employees, change is essential. The impetus for writing this book comes from the belief that organisations and change must live comfortably together or else they will perish. Its content derives from many years of experience in helping meet the learning needs of students of business and management with respect to the way people in organisations approach and deal with change.

The aim of this book

The overall aim of this book is to provide a discussion of change in relation to the complexities of organisational life. The text takes both a theoretical and practical approach to the issue of organisational change in seeking to meet both the academic and applied aims of most business and management courses.

More specifically this text aims to be:

- *Comprehensive* in its coverage of the significant ideas and issues associated with change at all levels of organisational activity from the strategic to the operational. Change is also examined in terms of its effects at the individual, group, organisational, and societal levels.
- *Conceptual* in the way it explores and critiques theory and research with respect of organisations and change.
- *Practical* in its provision of descriptions and worked examples of different approaches to 'doing' change.
- *Challenging* through asking readers to undertake activities including responding to discussion questions. The text in each chapter is interspersed with activities intended to personalise ideas from the text and to reinforce learning. End of chapter discussion questions ask for longer and more detailed responses.
- *Balanced* in its use of case studies and examples which are drawn from various types of organisations – public and private sector, small and large.

Who should use this book?

This book is intended for all who are interested in exploring, in some detail, issues associated with organisational change and how to deal with it. Specifically:

- *Undergraduate students* on Business Studies, modular or joint degrees should find it sufficiently structured to provide an understandable route through the subject.
- *MBA students* should find the blend of theory and practice appropriate to the academic and applied demands of their courses. Requirements to relate theory and research to their own situations should prove useful in their day to day organisational activities.
- *Postgraduate students* on other specialist taught masters programmes should find sufficient practical examples in the text to illustrate theory even if they have little practical experience of management and business themselves.
- *Students on professional courses* which include elements relating to the management of change.
- *Practising middle and senior managers* who wish to delve more deeply into theoretical discussions of change and its complexity in relation to organisational functioning. In addition, or alternatively, they could benefit from study of the various change models described in the book as they apply to different change situations.

Readers of the book will benefit if they have some prior knowledge of the subject area of organisational behaviour. However, the book is written so as to be understandable to those with no such prior knowledge.

Distinctive features

- *Clear structure.* The book is structured into three parts. The first part considers the nature of organisations operating in complex environments and responding to the 'winds of change'. It includes some detailed discussion of the causes of change. Theoretical perspectives are introduced with a discussion of the nature of change. Part One of the book acts as an introduction to Part Two which 'opens up' the organisation to expand on a number of issues which are crucial to an understanding of organisational change and how it happens. Finally, Part Three moves firmly into addressing the more practical considerations of designing, planning and implementing change. It concludes with a chapter which revises and extends a number of themes discussed in the book as they suggest pointers to understanding and managing change successfully.

- *Chapter summaries and learning objectives.* Each chapter begins with a short summary of the chapter content. This is followed by a list of learning objectives. On completion of each chapter, readers can check their learning against these objectives.

- *Boxed illustrations and activities.* Illustrations which expand or give examples of points made in the text are used throughout the chapters. These might be quotations from writings referred to in the text or further explanations of theories, research or other points made. They include small case studies and extracts from relevant newspaper articles. The text in the illustration boxes is simply for reading.

On the other hand, the 35 activity boxes, typically, ask the reader to carry out an activity or piece of research or actively apply some ideas from the text to their own experience.

- *End of chapter discussion questions.* Each chapter ends with questions which are intended to promote a more lengthy consideration of issues raised in the text. Many of the questions are set in 'examination' type terms and can be used as preparation for such tests as might be associated with a particular course.

- *Academic sources and references.* In line with the academic requirements of most courses, discussion of issues is supported by numerous references to other people's work in this subject area. Full details of references in the text can be found easily by consulting the alphabetical listings at the end of each chapter and through the author index at the end of the book.

- *Lecturer's Guide.* A Lecturer's Guide is available to those lecturers adopting this textbook. It includes commentaries on each chapter, in particular how to use the activities and the kind of responses to be expected from students' carrying out the activities and answering the discussion questions. Additional class work is suggested.

How to use this book

The book has a simple structure. Readers new to the subject of organisational change will find the chapters in Part One essential. If they have no knowledge of organisational behaviour, Part Two is especially important. For those who have already studied organisational theory and behaviour, Part Two offers some revision, but with additional discussion of how change interacts with these aspects of organisational life. For those who need advice on how to plan and implement change, Part Three does this.

Distributed throughout all the chapters except the last, are a series of activities which are intended to extend learning brought about by reading. Sometimes they ask for reflection of points made. At other times they ask for application of concepts and ideas to situations familiar to the reader. In the main, the activities are formulated to help readers apply knowledge to practice. A useful strategy is to read through a chapter quickly first. Then, on a second reading, carry out the activities.

The discussion questions at the end of Chapters 1–8 offer opportunities for readers to write at some length on issues associated with organisational change. They are particularly useful as preparation for completing qualification assignments and examinations.

About the Author

Barbara Senior is Principal Lecturer in Management at Nene University College Northampton. Previously she was a Regional Manager for the Open College, Team Leader of the Work and Unemployment programme at the Open University and Senior Lecturer in Human Resource Management at Liverpool Polytechnic (now John Moores University).

Leaving school at 16 years of age, she worked initially in administration in a large catering establishment and then in the gas industry before setting up a dressmaking and tailoring business. Meanwhile, she studied, as a mature student, with the Open University to gain a first class honours degree in psychology and organisational systems studies. During this time, she also gained a master's degree in Organisational Psychology from Lancaster University. She is a Chartered Occupational Psychologist and Member of the Institute of Personnel and Development.

She is the author (with John Naylor) of two previous books on the subjects of work and unemployment. She has published a number of articles and conference papers based on her research interests in the areas of teamworking and cross-cultural management. She lectures in the subject areas of organisational behaviour and change to MBA and other postgraduate students on management and business courses and has a particular interest in promoting creative thinking and innovation as part of this.

Acknowledgements

My very special thanks go to my husband Gerry. I thank him for his tolerance of my many absences from family life, as well as his practical and moral support throughout the writing period. My two children, Jayne and David have given good advice and kind words when needed.

A particular acknowledgement goes to those MBA and other masters students who were asked to read the draft chapters as part of their studies, and who gave me valuable comments which helped to improve the final version. I am touched by their willingness to share their organisational experiences with me, some of which appear (in disguise) at various times in the book. My colleagues at Nene University College Northampton have shown great forbearance at my chattering when I needed someone to talk to. This book would not have happened without the encouragement of Penelope Woolf at Financial Times Management. My thanks also go to Michelle Graham who steered the book into production.

Finally, I have tried to be true to the large amount of research and work already accomplished in the subject area of organisational change. Every effort has been made to trace and acknowledge ownership of copyright. The publishers will be glad to hear from any copyright holders whom it has not been possible to contact.

Part One

THE CONTEXT AND MEANING OF CHANGE

Introduction to Part One

Change in organisations does not happen in a vacuum. If nothing happened to disturb organisational life, change would be very slow and, perhaps, merely accidental. However, many commentators on organisational life warn that the pace of change is accelerating and all organisations must be prepared to respond to, and even anticipate change.

Part One of this book examines what is meant by organisational change and the reasons that it happens. Chapter 1 begins this process by proposing a model of organisation which recognises the fact that organisational life is influenced by many factors, mainly those originating outside the organisation. A metaphor of the 'winds of change' is used to show how organisational activities are the outcomes of historical developments as well as the results of the day-by-day vagaries of political, economic, technological and socio-cultural influences.

The second chapter of Part One explores further the environments in which organisations operate and which influence their operation. Chapter 2 also investigates the different forms that change in organisations can take.

Part One therefore sets the scene for the more detailed discussion of organisations and change in Part Two.

CHAPTER 1

Organisations and their changing environments

In this chapter, organisations are defined as systems comprising elements of formal organisational management and operations as well as elements of more informal aspects of organisational life. The organisational systems, themselves, are conceptualised as operating in three types of environments. These are the temporal, external and internal environments whose elements interact with each other to form the 'triggers' of change which are significant in bringing about organisational changes.

Objectives

To:

- describe the general characteristics of organisations and their essential components;

- say how different methods of wealth creation, viewed from a historical perspective, have influenced present-day organisational strategies and focus;

- discuss the concept of organisations as systems operating in multi-dimensional environments and its implications for understanding the causes of organisational change.

A VIEW OF ORGANISATIONS

It is sometimes difficult to track down a comprehensive definition of what is meant by 'an organisation'. Many books on management, decision-making, even organisational design, do not give a straightforward definition of what organisation means. Some, however, have been attempted. The following are two of these.

> Organizations are social arrangements for the controlled performance of collective goals. (Huczynski and Buchanan, 1991, p. 7.)

> Organization: a group of people brought together for the purpose of achieving certain objectives. As the basic unit of an organization is the role rather than the person in it the organization is maintained in existence, sometimes over a long period of time, despite many changes of members. (Statt, 1991, p. 102.)

Even though the second of these definitions appears more complex than the first, they both have the same theme – that of *people interacting* in order to achieve some defined *purpose*. However, as might be deduced, the interactions of people, as members of an organisation, need some kind of *managing*, that is there will be elements of *co-ordination and control* of these activities. In organisations of above ten or so people in size, this implies some kind of *structuring* of these people's activities which picks up the idea of *organisational roles* mentioned in Statt's definition. In addition, the activities of individual organisational members and their interactions with one another imply a *process* through which work gets done in order to achieve the organisation's purposes or goals. Above all, there is the requirement for *decision-taking* about the processes (the means) by which the goals (the ends) are achieved. Illustration 1.1 encapsulates most of this but adds the idea of a boundary which prescribes which people belong to the organisation and which do not.

Illustration 1.1
THE MEANING OF ORGANISATION

A typical working definition of an organization might say it is: (1) a social entity that (2) has a purpose, (3) has a boundary, so that some participants are considered inside while others are considered outside, and (4) patterns the activities of participants into a recognizable structure (Daft 1989). Although organizations are real in their consequences, both for their participants and for their environments, they are essentially abstractions. . . . The hospital, the firm, or the school will have physical aspects to them, the buildings, the plant and equipment and the like, but to understand how organizations work we need to go further than this. The factory has something real and physical about it but this is not the organization; people are doing tasks to which there is a pattern, raw materials are taken in, converted, and distributed to markets; capital is provided by banks and other financial institutions; systems provide information for decision-making and co-ordination; people are talking about matters which do not necessarily appear to have anything to do with the job, some people remote from the physical plant, perhaps a continent away, are making decisions critical to our factory.

Source: Butler, R. (1991), *Designing Organizations. A Decision-Making Perspective* (London, Routledge, pp. 1–2).

The example of the factory given by Butler (1991) draws attention to the fact that organisations cut across geographical boundaries and, therefore, organisational boundaries are, in Butler's words, also 'abstractions'. Yet, the notion of an organisational boundary is very real in that it draws attention to the concept of an organisation's environment. By this is meant all those influences which may act to disturb organisational life but which are not considered directly as a part of it. The mention of capital provided by some kind of financial institution is a recognition that organisations are connected to wider systems which form part of the environment – such as those which supply finance and other resources, not least human resources.

This view of organisations draws on the concept of an organisation as a system of interacting sub-systems and components set within wider systems and environments which provide inputs to the system and which receive its outputs.

This is shown in Figure 1.1 which identifies the main elements of most organisations and their functioning. These are grouped into two main sub-systems – the formal and informal sub-systems. Thus elements of the formal sub-system include the organisation's strategy, whether this is devised by a single person, as in the case of a very small owner-manager company, or by the board of directors and top management group in a large multi-divisional organisation. Other components

Figure 1.1

The organisation as a system

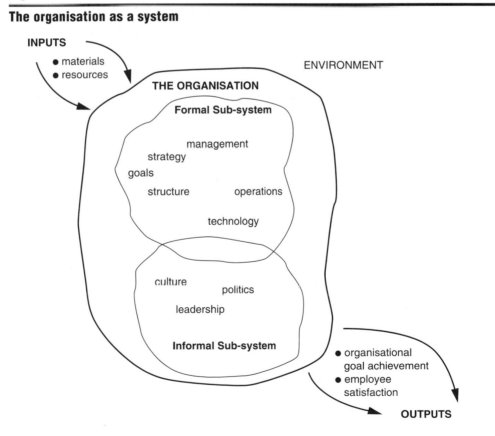

include the organisation's goals and the means of achieving these through operational activities such as the production of goods or provision of services. In addition, there is a service component which is that set of activities which help and facilitate the core operational activities to happen. Examples are the personnel departments, accounting and finance, information technology services and clerical and administrative support. Management, as the formal decision-making and control element is also evident in all organisations, whether this involves a few people or is spread throughout the organisation.

It is clear, from any examination of complex systems such as organisations, that some kind of structuring of activities is required if chaos is not to ensue. Thus the concept of organisational structure is central to that of organisational systems. However, over 20 years ago, Child (1973) drew attention to other more intangible elements of organisational life such as the political behaviour of organisational members. A more recent example is Nadler's (1988) inclusion of the informal organisation (patterns of communication, power and influence, values and norms) in his systems model of organisational behaviour. Stacey (1996) has coined the phrase 'shadow system' to describe these less predictable and more intangible aspects of organisational life. Thus, the idea of the 'informal sub-system' encapsulates the more hidden elements of organisational culture and politics and the rather less hidden element of leadership – including those who are led.

These relatively stable sub-systems and elements of organisational functioning interact with each other in some kind of transformation process. This means taking inputs such as materials and other resources from the organisation's environment and transforming them into outputs which are received back into the environment by customers and clients. However, while these outputs can be thought of as the legitimate reason for the organisation's existence, an output that is relevant, in particular, to the informal sub-system is employees' behaviour and their satisfaction with their jobs.

Finally, the concept of organisational systems as *open* systems is an important one. As mentioned above, all organisations receive inputs from their environments and provide outputs back into that environment. The boundaries of organisational systems are, therefore, permeable. This means that they are also significantly influenced in their strategies and activities by both historical and contemporary environmental demands, opportunities and constraints. The next section traces some historical trends which have influenced organisational strategies and processes through time. This tracing of history acts as a prelude to a consideration of the more immediate environment of organisations today and as they might present themselves in the future.

THE HISTORICAL CONTEXT FOR CHANGE

The forces which operate to bring about change in organisations can be thought of as winds which are many and varied – from small summer breezes which merely disturb a few papers to mighty howling gales which cause devastation to structures and operations causing consequent re-orientation of purpose and re-building. Sometimes, however, the winds die down to give periods of relative calm, periods of relative organisational stability. Such a period was the agricultural age which Goodman (1995) maintains prevailed in the UK until the early 1700s. During this period, wealth was created in the context of an agriculturally based society influenced mainly by local markets (both customer and labour) and factors outside people's control such as the weather. During this time, people could fairly well predict the cycle of activities required to maintain life, even if that life might be at little more than subsistence level.

To maintain the meteorological metaphor, stronger winds of change blew to bring in the industrial revolution and the industrial age. Again, according to Goodman, this lasted until around 1945. It was characterised by a series of inventions and innovations which reduced the number of people needed to work the land and, in turn, provided the means of mass producing hitherto rarely obtainable artefacts; for organisations, supplying these in ever increasing numbers became the aim. To a large extent, demand and supply were predictable, enabling companies to structure their organisations along what Burns and Stalker (1966) described as mechanistic lines, that is as systems of strict hierarchical structures and firm means of control.

This situation prevailed for some time after the Second World War, with demand still coming mainly from the domestic market and organisations striving to fill the 'supply gap'. Thus, the most disturbing environmental influence on organisations of this time was the demand for products which outstripped supply. The (supposed) saying by Henry Ford that, 'You can have any colour of car so long as it is black', gives a flavour of the supply-led state of the market. Apart from any technical difficulties of producing different colours of cars, Ford did not have to worry about customers' colour preferences: he could sell all that he made.

Figure 1.2 characterises organisations of this period as 'task-oriented', with effort being put into increasing production through more effective and efficient production processes.

The push, during this period, for ever-increasing efficiency of production supported the continuing application of the earlier ideas of Taylor (1911) and scientific management allied to Fordism which was derived from Henry Ford's ideas on assembly-line production (see Wood, 1989). This was a period mainly of command and control, of bureaucratic structures and the belief that there was 'one best way' of structuring organisations for efficient production. However, as time passed, this favourable period for organisations began to wane as people became more discriminating in the goods and services they wished to buy and as technological advancements brought about increased productivity so that supply overtook demand. In addition, companies began, increasingly, to look abroad for additional markets.

At the same time, they faced more intensive competition from abroad for their own

Figure 1.2

Market factors impacting on operations of Western organisations

Source: Goodman, M. (1995), *Creative Management* (Hemel Hempstead, Prentice-Hall, p. 38).

Illustration 1.2
VALUE-ORIENTED TIME

Customers

As competition becomes more severe and markets over-supplied, organisations must find products and services which are differentiated not only by purpose and form but by the 'added-value' which attaches to them. This means identifying potential customer expectations and then exceeding them. In other words, organisations must constantly increase customers' perceived value for money.

As the life-cycle of a product shortens, organisations must be under constant pressure to introduce new product offerings. This implies a continuing striving for innovation in terms of both products and the services associated with them. Innovation is, however, not only associated with the product itself but also with ways of supplying and marketing it. What may differentiate one product offering from another is not the product itself but the innovative production techniques, quality and relationship marketing – skills which are difficult for the competition to copy.

Production

About the production processes of the future, Goodman (1995, p. 49) says:

On the supply side, production will continue to get leaner and more responsive to customer demand. Lean production appears to do the impossible. It delivers the great product variety once associated with craft production at costs that are often less than those associated with mass production. Furthermore these benefits are provided together with products of high quality by sophisticated networking processes.

Human brainpower

The economies of the West can no longer rely on mass production processes. Ideas and brainpower have become an increasingly important component of modern product and service packages. It is through people's intelligence and creative thinking that organisations will improve competitiveness. Information technology and information systems are of more importance than the mass production systems which gave competitive advantage in the past. People in organisations will become their most important asset as it is only people who have the brainpower to focus on identifying and solving complex problems. To quote Goodman (1995, pp. 49–50):

The successful product packages of the future will result from the exposure of creativity to complex, curvilinear, messy, fuzzy logic-type problems. As demand grows for such value packages, so individuals will respond by having ingenious ideas. This will challenge organisations, with their liking for structure and order, as intensive creativity usually arises out of chaos and disorder conditions. . . . Thus, old mind-sets and rule books will have to give way to new organisational patterns that continuously encourage individuals to have ideas.

products and services. In the West, this development has been accompanied by a shift in focus from manufacturing to service, whether this merely adds value to manufactured products or whether it is service in its own right; for instance financial services, help in selling houses, the services of doctors and solicitors or taking part in education and training. In the neo-industrial age of the advanced countries, the emphasis is moving towards adding *value* to goods and services – what Goodman calls the value-oriented time (*see* Illustration 1.2) as contrasted with the task-oriented, products/services-oriented and systems-oriented times of the past and current periods. Table 1.1 lists the organisational responses, in terms of marketing, production and people, to the different time periods.

Change throughout the ages is encapsulated in the comments of Jones, Palmer, Osterweil and Whitehead (1996) when they say:

> As we approach the 21st century the pace and scale of the change demanded of organisations and those who work within them are enormous. Global competition and the advent of the information age, where knowledge is the key resource, have thrown the world of work into disarray. Just as we had to shed the processes, skills and systems of the agricultural era to meet the demands of the industrial era, so we are now having to shed ways of working honed for the industrial era to take advantage of the opportunities offered by the information age. . . . Organisations are attempting to recreate themselves and move from the traditional structure to a dynamic new model where people can contribute their creativity, energy and foresight in return for being nurtured, developed and enthused.

Table 1.1
Key organisational responses in the United Kingdom 1994–1995

Key organisational responses	Task-oriented time	Product/service design time	Systems/process-oriented time	Value-oriented time
Marketing	Seller's market. Focus on increasing sales.	Development of market segments. Positioning and targeting. *Niche marketing*	Strategic marketing. Increasing importance of single customer focus.	Relationship marketing. Value-added marketing.
Production	Supplying volume. Reducing costs.	Automation. Work study.	Statistical process control. Quality/service chain. Just in time.	Lean systems. Information management. Autonomous units. Improving response times. Networking.
People	Compliance. Work study. Problems caused by growth and functionalisms.	Manpower. Planning. Human resources. Management. Team working.	Quality (systems). Kaizen. Problem solving.	Task/project focused teams. Cross-functional teams. Information management. Proliferation of messy problems.

Source: Goodman, M. (1995), *Creative Management* (Hemel Hempstead, Prentice-Hall, p. 40).

Table 1.2
Russia and China: very different countries

Sectoral structure of employment (% of total)	Russia 1990	Russia 1994	China 1978	China 1994
Industry	42	38	15	18
Agriculture	13	15	71	58
Services	45	47	14	25
Total	100	100	100	100
Employment in the state sector	90	44	19	18

Source: Walker, T. (1996), 'China leads the pack – so far', *Financial Times*, 28 June, p. 4.

Jones *et al.* are probably realistic as they predict these developments for Western advanced societies. However, it must be remembered that not all parts of the world are at this stage of development in terms of the move from agriculture to industry to services. Table 1.2 illustrates the numbers of people working in the agricultural, industrial and services sectors of the economy in China compared to Russia which is, itself, way behind Western countries in the proportion of its economic activity devoted to services. China is still predominantly an agricultural society, particularly when compared to the United Kingdom where only 3.5 per cent of people work in the primary and utilities sector – which includes workers in the gas, electric and water industries as well as agriculture (Department for Education and Employment, 1996). Yet the article in the *Financial Times* (Walker, 1996) from which the statistics given in Table 1.2 are taken, indicates that China is quickly moving towards an industry and services dominated period. The winds of change are blowing strongly for countries such as Russia and China. Their progress through the agricultural, industrial and services periods will be swift in comparison with the time it took the more advanced Western countries to reach the same stage.

Activity 1.1

Consider how you would describe an organisation with which you are familiar in terms of its wealth-creating capacity. For instance, try answering the following questions.

- *With which sector of the economy (agricultural, manufacturing, services) are its outputs mainly associated?*

- *What type of market does it have? Use the categories given in Table 1.1 as a guide.*

- *Does it supply domestic or foreign markets – or both?*

- *Is it into volume production, automation of products/services or group/autonomous unit production?*

- *Does it practise Just-In-Time (JIT) delivery with an emphasis on quality service?*

- *What type of people does it employ – unskilled, skilled, professional?*

- *Are people easily attracted to work in the organisation?*

- *How much autonomy do employees have with regard to the work they choose to do and the way they do it?*

- *Is decision-taking devolved to the lowest level possible or kept within the hands of top management?*

AN UNCERTAIN FUTURE

Some responses to Activity 1.1 may give a sense of an organisation operating in a fairly predictable environment and with a sense of security for the future. Other responses may suggest a sense of uncertainty about markets, demand, the ability to attract the type of labour required and whether employment will increase or decrease. If creativity and innovation, working in teams to solve complex problems are indicative of the organisation analysed in Activity 1.1, it has quite likely already moved into value-oriented time.

Most people asked about organisational life today agree that it is becoming ever more uncertain as the pace of change quickens and the future becomes more unpredictable. This is echoed by academics and business people alike. For instance, looking ahead to the future, Drucker, writing in 1988, maintained that 20 years hence (i.e. about the year 2008) organisations would be almost wholly information based and that they would resemble more a symphony orchestra than the command and control, managed structures prevalent in the last decade (*see* Illustration 1.3).

With this as one example of the way organisations might change in the future, Drucker predicted the demise of middle management and the rise of organisations staffed almost exclusively with high-grade, specialist staff. The view that middle management will no longer be required is debatable and would certainly not be

---

Illustration 1.3
ORGANISATIONS AS SYMPHONY ORCHESTRAS

Writing about the way that information technology is transforming business enterprises, Drucker says:

A large symphony orchestra is even more instructive, since for some works there may be a few hundred musicians on stage playing together. According to organization theory then, there should be several group vice president conductors and perhaps a half-dozen division VP conductors. But that's not how it works. There is only the conductor-CEO – and every one of the musicians plays directly to that person without an intermediary. And each is a high-grade specialist, indeed an artist.

Source: Drucker. P. F. (1988), 'The Coming of the New Organization', *Harvard Business Review*, January–February, p. 48.

subscribed to by everyone (e.g. Eccles, 1996). However, the projected growth in the numbers of professionals and knowledge-based workers and the decrease in numbers of lower skilled workers is supported by the latest figures and trends, published by the Institute for Employment Research (1995) (*see* Illustration 1.4).

Since the industrialisation of production, the more recent rise of ever more service industries and the information technology explosion, the pace of change in the environment in which organisations operate has quickened to such an extent that writers such as Clarke (1994) maintain that: 'The last decade has brought with it a time of totally unprecedented change. In every direction businesses are in turmoil, from computing to financial services, from telecommunications to health care. Change is an accelerating constant' (p. 1). This view is broadly confirmed by Dawson (1994) in his discussion of a 'new bias for organizational action' (pp. 1–2), by which he means the need for managers to be leaders of change or else, in an increasingly competitive environment, their organizations will cease to exist.

The somewhat dramatic tone of these pronouncements appears to be supported by Handy (1991) when he says we are entering the 'Age of Unreason'. However, Handy qualifies this by saying, 'Change, after all, is only another word for growth, another

Illustration 1.4
HIGHER-LEVEL OCCUPATIONS GROWING FASTEST . . .

A continuing and substantial shift of employment towards the Managerial, Professional and Technical occupations is taking place, across all sectors, and is projected to continue. In 1994 these high level occupations accounted for about 36% of total employment. By 2001 they are projected to account for almost 2 in every 5 jobs (39%).

Non-manual jobs below this level will also show substantial growth, due almost entirely to the major increase in Personal and Protective Service jobs. Clerical occupations will actually decrease slightly, and Sales occupations will grow but at a slightly lower rate than total employment. The share of manual jobs will continue in steady decline, although at a rate rather slower than in previous years. Overall new jobs are most likely to arise in skill-intensive knowledge-based occupations. An increase in higher-level qualifications and skills will be needed to match the occupational change.

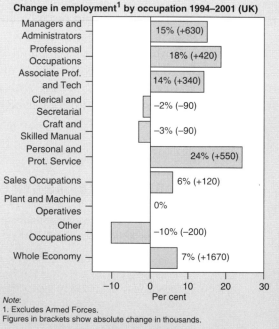

Change in employment[1] by occupation 1994–2001 (UK)

Note:
1. Excludes Armed Forces.
Figures in brackets show absolute change in thousands.
Source: Institute for Employment Research 1995.

Source: Department for Education and Employment, *Meeting the National Skills Challenge. A Summary of 'Labour Market and Skill Trends 1996/97'*, SEN 267, Crown Copyright 1996, p. 3.

synonym for learning. We can all do it and enjoy it, if we want to.' (pp. 270–1). Given this, he also warns that continuous, incremental change has now become discontinuous change and that, in contrast to the past, changes are no longer predictable. Consequently, it is crucial that organisational managers and decision-makers are aware of, and understand, more about the environmental winds which are blowing to disturb organisational life; in other words to be able to analyse the factors which trigger organisational change.

ORGANISATIONS TODAY – ENVIRONMENTAL TRIGGERS OF CHANGE

Activity 1.2

List (ideally by brainstorming) as many factors as possible which you think could affect what an organisation produces or sells, the markets for its goods or services, the methods of organising the way work gets done or the attitudes and performance of its members. Keep your list for later use.

Figure 1.1 depicts an organisation as a system receiving inputs from its environment and releasing outputs back into it. The previous section discussed how social and technological changes have, in the past, impacted on the products and services offered by organisations and the way they operate. A number of writers have been mentioned, who predict ever more 'turbulent' (Emery and Trist, 1967) environments – ever more stormy winds.

The view of organisations existing as systems of interrelated elements operating in multi-dimensional environments has a number of supporters. The work of Checkland (1972), for instance, is well known for the development of the soft systems model – an approach designed specifically for analysing and designing change in what Checkland terms 'human activity systems', most frequently, organisational systems. Nadler (1988) has proposed a systems model applied to organisational behaviour and other authors such as Stacey (1996) use systems concepts in their discussion of organisations and change. Most writers on organisations stress the importance of the nature of the environment for organisational management and decision-making. The following lists some of the elements of an organisation's environment which might have emerged from completing Activity 1.2:

- an organisation's markets (clients or customers)
- suppliers
- governmental and regulatory bodies
- trade union organisations
- competitors
- financial institutions
- labour supply
- levels of unemployment
- economic climate
- technological advances
- computing and information systems developments

An organisation's environment will also include broader influences such as the internationalisation of trade, the prevailing political ideology, attitudes to trade unions, changes from public to private ownership or vice versa, demographic changes and changes in family structure and differences between the rich and the poor. Thus, Nadler and Tushman (1988) summarise the environment as, 'All factors, including institutions, groups, individuals, events and so on, that are outside the organization being analyzed, but that have a potential impact on that organization'.

This view of the organisation as a system operating in, and being influenced by, changes in its environment, is not without its critics (Silverman, 1970) who object to the associated ideas that organisations have goals and that the organisational system operates to achieve these. The charges are that this reifies the organisation and denies the view that individuals act in accordance with their own idiosyncratic view of the organisation – or more likely, their particular part of it. Critics of the systems approach to understanding organisations maintain that individuals and groups within organisations have their own goals and perceptions of their organisational role which may not coincide with that of higher management or other individuals and groupings. Therefore, this view, which has been termed the 'social action' approach to understanding organisational life, maintains there is no one system but a multitude of different co-existing systems, each of which has its own reality.

Even so, logic implies that at least some of the environmental factors mentioned above influence the way organisations operate. What is more, changes in one or more of these environmental factors are likely to trigger consequent changes in some or all of the ways an organisation and its constituent components operate.

The impact of PETS

Some analysts have found it useful to group different environmental factors into categories under the mnemonics PEST (Johnson and Scholes, 1993) and STEP (Goodman, 1995), both of which refer to the Political, Economic, Technological and Socio-cultural factors which influence organisations, their strategies, structures and means of operating, including their human resource practices. The mnemonic PETS could as easily be used. In addition, it is a useful metaphor to distinguish different aspects of the organisational environment and their specific relationship to organisations as triggers of change. Illustration 1.5 uses the metaphor of a cat's behaviour to give an example of how changes in the technological environment, which were ignored as triggers for change, caused devastation to a once proud industry.

Figure 1.3 illustrates the factors which exist as part of an organisation's environment. All, at some time, will impact upon an organisation's formal and informal sub-systems and their components as well as which products or services it offers and in which markets.

An example of far-reaching changes as a result of a change of leaders is given in Illustration 1.6. A change of government is analogous to the advent of a new lion king in a pride of lions in that the behaviour of government leaders is not far removed from that of the new lion king such is the force with which they seek to expunge previous ideologies and their effects.

Illustration 1.5
A CLEVER CAT

Picture the scene of a group of birds pecking away trying to find worms, with some confidence in the safety of numbers, heads down busying themselves about their own immediate purpose. A young cat, using relatively new skills, might easily pounce to catch one or more birds. Being inexperienced, the cat has only limited success. So the birds re-form and continue as if uninterrupted. Meanwhile the cat goes away and practises and gets some more experience of hunting and returns to mount a much more skilful attack with far more resulting damage.

This analogy sheds light on the case of the British motor-cycle industry when faced with Japanese competition. Early Japanese motor-cycle models made few inroads into the traditional British motor-cycle markets and, heads down, confident in a product and a process which had always been successful, the industry ignored the threat of the Japanese. However, like the older, wiser cat, the Japanese returned, pounced and dealt wounding blows from which the British motor-cycle industry has never recovered. Thus, the British motor-cycle industry paid the price for not changing in the face of developing technologies which allowed its competitors to forge ahead.

Figure 1.3

PETS factors and organisational change

- Government legislation
- Government ideology
- International law
- Universal rights
- Wars
- Local regulations
- Taxation
- Trades union activities

- Competitors
- Suppliers
- Currency exchange rates
- Employment rates
- Wage rates
- Government economic policies
- Other countries' economic policies
- Lending policies of financial institutions
- Changes from public to private ownership

Political factors

Economic factors

ORGANISATION

Socio-cultural factors

Technological factors

- Demographic trends
  (customers and employees)
- Lifestyle changes
- Skills availability
- Attitudes to work and employment
- Attitudes to minority groups
- Gender issues
- Willingness and ability to move
- Concern for the environment
- Business ethics

- Information technology/the Internet
- New production processes
- Computerisation of processes
- Changes in transport technology

> **Illustration 1.6**
> ## A NEW LION KING
>
> A single lion will typically head a group of lionesses with their young, just as a prime minister will head a reigning government and parliament. When the lion grows old, he is prey to the attacks of younger lions looking to take over the 'harem' in the same way that a long-serving prime minister is prey to being usurped by those who want to take over power. If the younger lion is successful in driving the old one out, the younger lion will then proceed to kill all the existing young cubs in order to destroy the old lion's gene pool and introduce his own.
>
> In such a way do new prime ministers and their governments act. For the old lion's gene pool, substitute the ideology of the old government and for the new lion's gene pool substitute the new government's ideology. The result is that the new government denounces and downgrades all that the previous government achieved; what was good then is no longer celebrated now. Within a short time, in the same way that the new lion's genes are established in the new generation of young lions, so do the acts of the new government become the only ones which matter.

The story of the new lion king may be stretching a point in assuming lions as PETS. However, just as the new lion king 'cleansed' the pride of lions of the old king's genes and thus caused a change in the characteristics and behaviour of the new generation of lions, so will a change in political ideology bring requirements for new behaviours in organisations because of the changed constraints and opportunities within which they must operate. In addition, not only do changes in the political environment influence organisations directly, they also interact with changes in the economic environment – for instance, the government-inspired privatisation of previously publicly owned institutions (e.g. in the UK, electricity, gas, the railways), or the co-operation of different countries to form economic trading blocs (e.g. the European Community or the ASEAN-4 Group). As Illustration 1.7 shows, changes coming from one sector of the environment are compounded by their interaction with influencing factors from other sectors of the environment – a clear demonstration that environmental triggers for change rarely act as single influences.

An example of changes in the socio-cultural environment triggering other changes elsewhere are social expectations for continuous increases in the standard of living which must, however, be set against fewer opportunities for permanent secure employment; demographic changes causing 'gluts' or shortages in the numbers of young people coming into the labour market; changes in family structures where men as well as women may wish to stay home to look after children.

An article in the *Financial Times* (20 September 1996), by Kate Bevan, comments on the increase in the numbers of single men and women living alone (from 933 000 in 1971 to 1 705 000 in 1991 projected to 3 154 000 in 2011) in addition to the increase in single widowed people (from 1.6 million in 1971 to a projected 2.5 million in 2011) in the context of the changing role of housing associations which currently provide social housing for more than 900 000 tenants. A new law, the Housing Act of 1988, required housing associations to seek funds from the private sector to replace partially funds which were hitherto provided through government. The ability to raise

---

Illustration 1.7

BIGGER ROLE FOR GOVERNMENTS WILL BE IN FASHION NEXT YEAR

The revitalisation of the state to make the long-term development of the global economy more effective is the main theme of next year's World Bank development report. A draft outline of the report indicates a shift in thinking at the World Bank over the role of government in economic policy making.

The document says that 'an effective – not a larger – state is needed to create the institutional infrastructure for markets to flourish'.

The World Bank believes that 'the great (and false) debate between state and market for now seems to be over. Fiscal crises, the inflexibility of planning and the problems of public enterprises have shown the limits of the state'.

But it adds: 'the key objective is to show that the state and market are institutionally intertwined' and one must not dominate the other. . . . A significant role for the state in the 21st century will be in providing a framework under which the trade-off between market-based growth and escalating environmental problems are resolved. . . .

It [the report] calls for 'good governments' which it says concerns 'creating an environment for the positive interplay between state, private and civil society institutions' . . .

'Competition for investment and jobs accelerates the shift towards better government discipline and business orientation'.

The report intends to look at how the state's interaction with the market and its own citizens can 'best be improved to achieve more sustainable economic development.' This – it believes – can be achieved through greater decentralisation, delegation and participation, 'bringing the state closer to the people'.

Source: Taylor, R. (1996), 'Bigger role for governments will be in fashion next year', *Financial Times*, 28 June, p. 4.

---

money in this way has meant that, as well as providing social housing, associations have moved into provision of accommodation for other groups such as medical staff (on behalf of health authorities) and students, thus encompassing profit and not-for-profit activities.

This widening of their scope also extends beyond the provision of housing (for which they were originally set up) to provision of community facilities such as meals on wheels and community alarm systems. However, a statement at the end of the article shows how the changes they have made in response to a change in the law and their funding base is beginning to distort their fundamental purpose of care and support of people who could be termed 'disadvantaged':

> **The biggest issue . . . is the way in which care provision and housing are funded. At present, about 35 per cent of turnover and three out of five staff are dedicated to care and support work. With a shift for focusing funds for social housing to just providing the bricks and mortar, housing associations are going to be limited in their ability to support tenants.** (Bevan, 1996.)

A conclusion from this example is that housing associations are being significantly affected by a combination of legislative, economic and socio-cultural changes in the environment.

Activity 1.3

Take the list you made as a result of carrying out Activity 1.2 and categorise each factor identified there according to whether you consider it to stem from the political, economic, technological or socio-cultural sectors of the environment.

Carrying out Activity 1.3 may show that some factors can be categorised in more than one way. This is not unusual and simply illustrates the fact that aspects of the organisational environment are interrelated and operate in a complex way to trigger change within organisations. In fact, some factors may not be able to be categorised, in a strict sense, as *environmental* triggers for change. For instance, as well as the triggers for change that come from the PETS environment, there are also forces for change operating within organisations themselves, and these also need to be managed. A number of writers (e.g. Huczynski and Buchanan, 1991, Johnson and Scholes, 1993, McCalman and Paton, 1992, and Stewart, 1991) are in agreement in identifying these as internal triggers or sources of change. Consequently, organisations must cope with not only a plethora of external forces for change, but also internal forces for change. Illustration 1.8 gives an indicative list of such factors.

Illustration 1.8
EXAMPLES OF INTERNAL TRIGGERS FOR CHANGE

- An organisation becoming unionised or de-unionised
- A new chief executive or other senior manager
- A revision of the administrative structures
- The re-design of a group of jobs
- The re-design of a factory or office layout
- The purchase of new IT equipment
- A new marketing strategy
- A cut in overtime working
- Staff redundancies

ORGANISATIONAL RESPONSES TO CHANGE

The discussion above suggests that organisations operate in at least three types of environment, which together make up the total 'operating environment' (Sadler, 1989, p. 174) of an organisation. The first consists of the historical developments bringing changes over time. These range from those activities which are mainly industry focused to those which rely more on knowledge and brainpower – what Handy (1994) calls 'focused intelligence', that is the ability to acquire and apply knowledge and know how. This can be summarised in the term *temporal environment*. This is an environment which influences organisations in at least two ways. The first is in a general way, through the cycles of industry-based innovation which move organisations through major series of developments such as are shown in Figure 1.2. The second is in a more specific way through the life cycle of the organisation itself. This includes its particular history built up from its founder days through periods of expansion and decline, all of which is instrumental in helping to explain an organisation's 'idiosyncrasies' of strategy and structure, culture, politics and leadership style.

The second type of environment is the *external environment* which includes the political (including legal), economic, technological and socio-cultural environment as well as those factors which are pushing for globalisation and an increasing concern with the physical environment (the PETS environment). The third environment is the organisation's *internal environment* (*see* Illustration 1.8) which, to some extent, consists of those organisational changes which are the first-line responses to changes in the external and temporal environments. Figure 1.4 is a stylised depiction of the concept of organisations as systems operating in multi-dimensional environments, with all that this means for organisations and change.

Figure 1.4

The organisational system operating in multi-dimensional environments

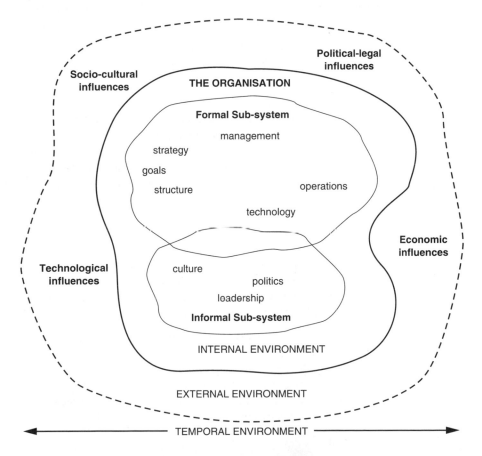

It is not difficult to speculate on the effects that the many and interacting influences referred to in Figure 1.3 can have on organisational life and many organisations' abilities to survive and prosper. The key task, for organisations, is to manage these – in Schein's (1988, p. 94) words, organisations have continually to achieve 'external adaption and internal integration'. The purpose and focus of efforts to do so are, essentially, what managing organisational change is all about. This means understanding more fully how the formal aspects of organisational life respond to pressures from the internal, external and temporal environments – that is how change is leveraged through strategy, structure and operational processes. In addition, it means understanding the more informal processes such as power, politics and conflict, culture and leadership.

This chapter has commented on the winds of change as they blow variably and, to a degree, unpredictably. This proposition is taken further in Chapter 2 which explores the multi-dimensionality of the causes of organisational change and the nature of change itself.

DISCUSSION QUESTIONS AND ACTIVITIES

1 Give examples of environmental forces for change which are likely to affect, significantly, the way organisations operate in 10 years' time. Justify your choices.

2 Carry out an 'environmental scan' of an organisation which you know well. The following steps should help as well as access to large sheets of paper!

(a) Using the PETS framework, the results from Activities 1.2 and 1.3, and the suggestions in Figure 1.3, list those factors which you consider could affect the future performance of the organisation and/or the way it operates. Concentrate on those factors which are external to the organisation.

(b) Take this list and indicate where there are linkages between some factors and others. Doing this diagrammatically, using lines and arrows, helps. You could use a plus sign to show where the effects combine to reinforce each other and a minus sign to indicate where one factor might help negate another.

(c) Mark with a star those factors which are critically important to the organisation. Consider whether these originate mostly in the political-legal, economic, technological or socio-cultural parts of the PETS environment. Are they also linked to the general movement of organisations into value-oriented time?

(d) Finally, list the starred factors and rank them according to the volatility of the external environment. Consider whether this volatility provides an opportunity or a threat to the organisation and its future performance.

Through carrying out this process you may have realised how much you know about the organisation's environment but also how much you do not know! The outcome of this activity may, therefore, be not only an increased understanding of the environmental forces facing the organisation, but also a realisation that environmental scanning requires continuous vigilance and collection of information which must then be used creatively to help predict necessary changes within the organisation itself.

REFERENCES

Bevan, K. (1996), 'The challenge of coping with change', *Financial Times*, 20 September.

Burns, T., and Stalker, G. M. (1966), *The Management of Innovation*, London, Tavistock Publications.

Butler, R. (1991), *Designing Organizations. A Decision-Making Perspective*, London, Routledge, pp. 1–2.

Checkland, P. B. (1972), 'Towards a System-based Methodology for Real-world Problem Solving', *Journal of Systems Engineering*, Vol. 3, No. 2.

Child, J. (1973), 'Organization: a choice for man', in Child, J. (ed.), *Man and Organization*, London, George Allen & Unwin.

Clarke, L. (1994), *The Essence of Change*, Hemel Hempstead, Prentice-Hall, p. 1.

Daft, R. L. (1989), *Organization Theory and Design*, 2nd edn., St. Paul, MN, West Publishing Co.

Dawson, P. (1994), *Organizational Change. A Processual Approach*, London, P.C.P., pp. 1–2.

Department for Education and Employment (1996a), *Meeting the National Skills Challenge. A Summary of 'Labour Market and Skill Trends 1996/97'*, Skills and Enterprise Network 267, Crown Copyright, London, Department for Education and Employment, p. 3.

Department for Education and Employment (1996b), *Labour Market and Skill Trends 1996/1997*, Skills and Enterprise Network 266, Crown Copyright, London, Department for Education and Employment.

Drucker, P. F. (1988), 'The Coming of the New Organization', *Harvard Business Review*, January–February, pp. 45–53.

Eccles, T. (1996) 'Management power and strategic change', *Financial Times*, 12 July.

Emery, F. E., and Trist, E. L. (1967), 'The Next 30 Years: Concepts, Methods and Anticipations', *Human Relations*, 20.

Goodman, M. (1995), *Creative Management*, Hemel Hempstead, Prentice-Hall.

Handy, C. (1991), 'The Age of Unreason', in Henry, J. (ed.), *Creative Management*, London, Sage, pp. 270–1.

Handy, C. (1994), *The Empty Raincoat*, London, Hutchinson.

Huczynski, A., and Buchanan, D. (1991), *Organizational Behaviour*, Hemel Hempstead, Prentice-Hall, p. 7.

Institute for Employment Research (1995), University of Warwick, Coventry.

Johnson, G., and Scholes, K. (1993), *Exploring Corporate Strategy Text and Cases* (3rd edn.), London, Prentice-Hall, pp. 37–8.

Jones, P., Palmer, J., Osterweil, C., and Whitehead, D. (1996), *Delivering Exceptional Performance: Aligning the Potential of Organisations, Teams and Individuals*, London, Pitman.

McCalman, J., and Paton, R. (1992), *Change Management: Guide to Effective Implementation*, London, P.C.P., p. 7.

Nadler, D. A. (1988), 'Concepts for the Management of Organizational Change', in Tushman, M. L., and Moore, W. L. (eds.), *Readings in the Management of Innovation*, New York, Ballinger Publishing Company, pp. 718–32.

Nadler, D. A., and Tushman, M. L. (1988), 'A Model for Diagnosing Organizational Behavior', in Tushman, M. L., and Moore, W. L. (eds.), *Readings in the Management of Innovation*, New York, Ballinger Publishing Company, pp. 148–63.

Sadler, P. (1989), 'Management Development', in Sisson, K. (ed.), *Personnel Management in Britain* (2nd edn.), Oxford, Blackwell, p. 174.

Schein, E. H. (1988), 'Coming to a New Awareness of Organisational Culture', *Sloan Management Review*, Vol. 25, No. 1, p. 94.

Silverman, D. (1970), *The Theory of Organisations*, London, Heinemann Educational Books.

Stacey, R. D. (1996), *Strategic Management and Organisational Dynamics* (2nd edn.), London, Pitman Publishing.

Statt, D. A. (1991), *The Concise Dictionary of Management*, London, Routledge, p. 102.

Stewart, J. (1991), *Managing Change Through Training and Development*, London, Kogan Page, pp. 118–20.

Taylor, F. W. (1911), *Principles of Scientific Management*, New York, Harper & Row.

Taylor, R. (1996), 'Bigger role for governments will be in fashion next year', *Financial Times*, 28 June, p. 4.

Walker, T. (1996), 'China leads the pack – so far', *Financial Times*, 28 June, p. 4.

Wood, S. (1989), 'The Transformation of Work?', in Wood, S. (ed.), *The Transformation of Work*, London, Unwin Hyman, Chapter 1.

CHAPTER 2

The nature and causes
of change

This chapter elaborates further on the causes of change – in particular the multi-dimensionality of causes and the way one interacts with another. The nature of change, including different types of change, is then discussed. A basic distinction can be made between convergent, incremental types of change and transformational change which is organisation wide and is characterised by radical shifts in strategy, mission and values as well as suitable changes of structures and systems. The chapter concludes with an examination of the different change situations which organisations experience and provides an appreciation of their relationship to the way change might be designed and implemented. The chapter, which concludes Part One, loops forward to link to Part Three, where different methodologies for change are discussed in more detail.

Objectives

To:

- identify the multiple causes of change and the possible relationships between them;

- discuss the nature of change as a multi-dimensional concept;

- analyse change situations in order to choose appropriate methods of managing and implementing change;

- recognise that there are limitations to the 'common-sense' approach to managing change because of cultural, political and leadership influences.

THE MULTIPLE CAUSES OF CHANGE

Identifying the causes of change

In the previous chapter, three aspects of an organisation's environment were identified which act as triggers for organisational change. First, there was what was termed the temporal environment, which encompasses the longer-term historical influences, such as the changes from an agricultural economy to one based on machines. This has evolved to the current situation, which is characterised by the predominance of service industries and predictions of increasing reliance on knowledge and information as a way of creating wealth. Second, the external environment was discussed in terms of the PETS analogy, that is factors associated with political/legal, economic, technological and socio-cultural change. Third, internal triggers for change were identified, for instance, changes in people (attitudes, beliefs, skills), scale of activities and organisational tasks, organisational strategy and structure, products or services, reward systems or use of technology.

Clearly, as Dawson (1994) maintains, internal and external triggers for change are often interdependent. For instance, at the time of writing, government policy is resulting in a reduction in financial resources for higher education, which in turn might lead to staff redundancies and consequent restructuring of teaching and research activities – an example of changes in part of the external environment (the political environment) triggering a change in the internal environment (financial budgeting) which in turn triggers another internal change (possible staff redundancies and/or restructuring of essential activities).

Forces for change within an organisation are frequently the result of some external force. It is also certain that organisations that do not respond to triggers such as increasing competition, new legislation or the expectations of customers will soon decline and may cease to exist. However, in addition to bringing about change in the internal environment, organisational personnel can, to some extent, influence factors external to the organisation. For instance, to follow on with the example of government policy towards higher education, the setting up of a government committee to consider the shape and future of higher education gives an opportunity for managers of universities and other interested organisations to lobby committee members, politicians, the media and others and thus influence the committee's findings on the future and form of their organisations. This process is shown in Figure 2.1.

Figure 2.1 is an example of the use of the control model concept to depict the inputs to and outputs from an organisational (or, in this case, an organisational sector) process. In this case, it illustrates how information on the effects of the outputs is fed back to be compared against the goals of the process owners (in this case the higher education sector organisations). The results of this comparison are then used to modify the inputs to the process which in turn change the outputs to bring them more in line with the achievement of the goals.

Figure 2.1

Control model of a process for influencing government policy towards higher education

---

Illustration 2.1

MULTIPLE CAUSES OF A CHANGE OF STRATEGY AT SHELL

Shell may face fresh pressure over Nigerian oil discovery

by Robert Corzine in London and Paul Adams in Lagos

Shell, the Anglo-Dutch oil group which has come under international pressure to withdraw from Nigeria, is believed to have made a big oil discovery off the coast of the west African country.

If the find is confirmed, it could rekindle international criticism of Shell's role in Nigeria under military rule. The company is the largest foreign oil producer in the country, accounting for about half the total output.

The company said yesterday it was conducting production tests at a well in the Bonga One exploration area in deep water off Nigeria.

Shell said it was too early to assess the potential of the well.

But oil industry observers in Lagos, Nigeria's commercial capital, say the company's operations at the site suggest that it has made a major discovery.

A Shell spokesman in Lagos said, 'We are doing reservoir tests now, and it can take several months to determine the size of the discovery.

'This is a whole new drilling environment, not like the [continental] shelf where the oil is being produced.'

Most of the company's Nigerian fields are onshore in the Niger delta, close to poor communities where resentment at the lack of local benefit from the oil industry has led to direct confrontation with Shell and other operators.

This resulted in clashes with the Ogoni movement led

by the late Ken Saro-Wiwa who was executed last November after being convicted of the murder of rival Ogoni chiefs. The executions brought international criticism of Shell.

Shell has resisted demands that it withdraw from Nigeria, and it recently confirmed that it is to go ahead with a multi-billion dollar natural gas project in the country.

But the problems associated with onshore production have caused Shell and other large oil companies operating in Nigeria to look offshore for future developments.

The deep water exploration blocks are seen as vital to the future of Shell and the oil industry as a whole in Nigeria.

In recent years, Shell has failed to replace its annual production with new discoveries. Its exploration division has been drawn to Nigeria because the geology of the deep water areas is similar to that of the US Gulf of Mexico, where a series of finds have been made by Shell recently.

Bonga One is the third well drilled in the new deep water blocks since international oil groups signed production-sharing contracts with the Nigerian government in 1993. The blocks are operated by Snepco, a different Shell subsidiary to the operator which is already producing nearly 1m barrels of oil a day, about half Nigeria's output.

Source: Financial Times, 8 March 1996, p. 1.

Building models of organisational processes such as these, and presenting them in diagrammatic form, helps analyse the dynamic nature of change.

In this case there is a clear indication of the multiple causes of change and the way they interact. Illustration 2.1 gives a further example of this, taken from the private sector. It shows again how the temporal, external and internal environmental influences combine to force change.

Analysing the causes of change

Situations of change, such as the ones described above, draw attention to the complexity of the change environment. However, it is not sufficient merely to *identify* these triggers for change. Analysing the relationships between them – in other words, their systemic nature – is even more important. Figure 2.2 is an attempt to do this with a simple model of the change situation which is described in Illustration 2.1.

Multiple-cause diagrams such as that in Figure 2.2 have the power to capture the complex dynamics of change situations. They help bring about a deeper understanding of how interventions in one variable can have far-reaching effects in other parts of the situation. They act, therefore, not only in a descriptive mode, but also as an analytical tool for understanding and managing change.

Figure 2.2

The multiple causes of the situation faced by Shell

Renewed criticism of Shell's role in Nigeria → Demands for Shell to withdraw from Nigeria ← International criticism of Shell's role in Nigeria

Successful experience in discovering oil in similar geological conditions in the USA

Shell's new oil discovery

Boycott of Shell petrol ← Execution of Ogoni leader

Shell's failure to keep up new discoveries → Shell looks for alternative offshore possibilities in Nigeria

Clashes between government and the Ogoni people

Importance of oil industry to Nigeria

Resentment and direct confrontation with Shell

Nigerian government's wish to exploit its natural resources → Shell as largest foreign oil producer in Nigeria (mostly onshore production)

Little benefit from oil money in nearby communities

It is clear from the account in Illustration 2.1 and the multiple-cause diagram of these in Figure 2.2 that Shell's activities are driven by economic imperatives, that is the need to make a profit and satisfy shareholders. However, other interacting influences from Shell's operating environment can be identified, all of which, apparently, resulted in Shell's change of strategy and operations. The following are just some of the multiple causes of the changes in Shell's operations illustrated in the diagram.

- *Interaction of political and economic aspects of the external environment.* The Nigerian government's political imperatives mean it must bring trade to the country in order to improve its economic standing. One important way is to exploit its natural oil resources. This implies contracting with large oil companies to do this, as shown by the arrows in the bottom left corner of the diagram.
- *Interaction of temporal (historic) and external (socio-cultural) environments.* The oil exploitation policy of the Nigerian government has not benefited one section of its people – the Ogoni community who protested that the oil extraction was ruining their traditional way of living and means of subsistence while not bringing any material or other advantage.
- *Interaction of different external triggers for change, e.g. socio-cultural, economic and political influences.* The resulting confrontation between the Ogoni and the Nigerian government led to one of the Ogoni leaders being executed in spite of international condemnation, with some people refusing to buy Shell petrol.
- *Interaction of external triggers for change (political and economic) with influences from Shell's own internal environment.* Shell's successful experience in the USA, coupled with its need to reverse failures to keep up with new oil discoveries, influenced its move to offshore exploration in Nigeria, (presumably) encouraged by the Nigerian government's continuing political and economic needs.

The above shows the complex situation surrounding Shell and its activities and the way a variety and number of triggers for change interact systemically – that is a change in one influencing factor will have 'knock on' effects on many other influencing factors. One can also speculate that changes in the technology used to extract oil, process and transport it might also influence Shell's strategy and way work is organised.

An example of the far-reaching effects of a different but dominant developing technology in another context is given in Illustration 2.2. This is a summary of a newspaper article on how the growth of the Internet technology is influencing the business environment.

In the article reproduced in Illustration 2.2, Kehoe and Taylor show that, what was unimaginable a few years ago, is now with us and with far-reaching implications for life generally and business in particular. However, although the article is predominantly about change in the technological environment of organisations, it is also about economic imperatives and, not least, the impact this development will have on people's lifestyles including their social interactions, expectations and cultural norms.

Illustration 2.2

HOW THE GROWTH OF THE INTERNET IS REVOLUTIONISING THE COMPETITIVE ENVIRONMENT FOR BUSINESS

The authors of this article argue that, while the growth of the Internet is bringing online information services to millions of businesses and individuals, it may not spell instant benefit to all. On the one hand, the Internet may spell opportunity, but for others, it could undermine long-established business patterns.

One example is that research papers may now be published (free?) on the Internet, threatening the academic journal publishers. This may, indeed, be welcomed by financially stressed libraries who struggle to keep up with their journal subscription payments.

If the technology to hold voice conversations over the Internet improves (with charging at local call rate only), it will challenge companies such as AT&T in the USA and British Telecommunications who charge on the basis of time and distance.

Other challenges to financial institutions and information-based services identified by the authors are the establishment of Internet banking services, the development of online securities trading with almost instant confirmation of share and options trades, and the provision of cut-price and increasingly secure delivery of all types of information.

As well as challenges such as these, the authors mention the opportunities the Internet poses for expansion and increased operating efficiency for many businesses. Figures of Internet users quoted are 56 million world-wide with a prediction of 200 million by 1999. These provide a potentially enormous market.

The authors observe that, 'So far, the biggest "winners" have been companies providing software, computer equipment and access services that form the infrastructure of the global network. Chief amongst these is Netscape Communications, the software company that burst on to the market last year with its Network browser which provides an easy way to find information on the Internet'. They quote Jim Barksdale, Netscape president and chief executive, as saying, 'Bill [Gates, chairman and chief executive of Microsoft] didn't see this coming. Larry [Ellison, chairman and chief executive of Oracle] didn't see this coming'. And they say, 'Now two of the world's largest software companies are trying to catch up with a company that was formed less than two years ago.' It is clear that the IT industry itself could do very well out of the Internet.

Other gainers are likely to be the retailers, once a secure way of paying for goods over the Internet is developed. An example given is 'Barclays Square', a virtual electronic shopping mall with sites rented to retailers such as Toys-R-Us and J. Sainsbury. The challenge to distributors and retailers is clearly there.

Instructive for the effects of this technological trigger for change is the authors' final comment: 'As Charles Finnie and David Locke, analysts with Volpe, Welty, the US stock brokerage, put it: "The Internet will not cure cancer, ensure world peace or make you thinner. Yet in the long term it is likely to alter, perhaps obliterate, time-worn models of interaction and transaction among individuals and enterprises." '

Source: Based on Kehoe, L., and Taylor, P., 'The online challenge flowers', *Financial Times*, 14 March 1996, p. 23.

ACTIVITY 2.1

Using as your basis the description in Illustration 2.2, draw a multiple-cause diagram to identify the causes for change, and the relationships between them.

ENVIRONMENTAL TURBULENCE

The discussion above illustrates how important it is for managers to remain alert to changes in their organisation's environments. This includes not only the 'here and now' external and internal environments but, as the Shell case showed, an awareness of social and cultural norms influenced by the temporal environment – that is historical, time-dependent trends. It is too easy, living in an advanced post-industrial society, to forget that, in some cultures, industrial and pre-industrial norms of living may still prevail. Using multiple-cause analysis helps an appreciation of the complex interactions of environmental triggers for change as well as their relationship to organisations' internal environments.

The dynamics of any organisation's environment have also been described in terms of the degree of environmental turbulence. Ansoff and McDonnell (1990) state that a firm's performance is optimised when its aggressiveness and responsiveness match its environment. They propose five levels of environmental turbulence.

Level 1 *Predictable*
A repetitive environment characterised by stability of markets; where the challenges repeat themselves; change is slower than the organisation's ability to respond; the future is expected to be the same as the past.

Level 2 *Forecastable by extrapolation*
Complexity increases but managers can still extrapolate from the past and forecast the future with confidence.

Level 3 *Predictable threats and opportunities*
Complexity increases further when the organisation's ability to respond becomes more problematic; however, the future can still be predicted with some degree of confidence.

Level 4 *Partially predictable opportunities*
Turbulence increases with the addition of global and socio-political changes. The future is only partly predictable.

Level 5 *Unpredictable surprises*
Turbulence increases further with unexpected events and situations occurring more quickly than the organisation can respond.

These levels can be compared to three different kinds of change situations proposed by Stacey (1996), namely: closed change, contained change and open-ended change – a description of which can be found in Illustration 2.3.

Both Ansoff and McDonnell's levels of environmental turbulence and Stacey's closed, contained and open-ended kinds of change situation can also be related to Stacey's (1996, p. 26) concepts of 'Close to certainty' and 'Far from certainty'. Thus, close to certainty describes a situation where organisational members face closed and contained change, or in Ansoff and McDonnell's terms, when the environment resembles levels 1 to 3. As the degree of environmental turbulence moves from level 4 to level 5, or, in Stacey's terms, to a situation of open-ended change, organisations

Illustration 2.3
CLOSED, CONTAINED AND OPEN-ENDED CHANGE

Closed change

When we look back at the history of an organisation, there are some sequences of events that we can clearly recount in a manner commanding the widespread agreement of the members involved. We are able to say what happened, why it happened, and what the consequences are. We are also able to explain in a widely accepted way how such a sequence of events and actions will continue to affect the future course of the business. We will call this a closed change situation.

Such closed change would normally apply to the continuing operation of an existing business. For example, consider a business that supplies pop records and tapes to the teenage market. Managers in that business are able to say with some precision how the number of customers in what market has changed over the past and furthermore how it will change for the next fifteen years or so. Those customers already exist. The managers can establish fairly clear-cut relationships between the number of customers and the number of records and tapes they have bought and will buy.

Contained change

Other sequences of events and actions flowing from the past are less clear-cut. Here we find that we are able to say only what probably happened, why it probably happened, and what its probable consequences were. The impact of such a sequence of events upon the future course of the business has similarly to be qualified by probability statements.

For example, the supplier of records and tapes will find it harder to explain why particular kinds of records and tapes sold better than others. That supplier will find it somewhat difficult to forecast what kinds of tapes and records will sell better in the future; but market research, lifestyle studies and statistical projections will enable reasonably helpful forecasts for at least the short term.

Open-ended change

There are yet other sequences of events and actions arising from the past and continuing to impact on the future where explanations do not command anything like widespread acceptance by those involved.

The company supplying records and tapes may have decided in the past to diversify into video film distribution, by acquiring another company already in that business. That acquisition may then become unprofitable and the managers involved could well subscribe to conflicting explanations of why this is so. Some may claim that the market for video films is too competitive. Others that the diversification was a wrong move because it meant operating in a different market with which they were not familiar. Others may say that it is due to a temporary decline in demand and that the market will pick up in the future. Yet others may ascribe it to poor management of the acquisition, or to a failure to integrate it properly into the business, or to a clash of cultures between the two businesses. What that team of managers does next to deal with low profitability obviously depends upon the explanation of past failure they subscribe to.

Source: Stacey, Ralph D. (1996), *Strategic Management and Organisational Dynamics* (London, Pitman, pp. 23–4).

can be said to be far from certainty. These changing situations have significant implications for the actions of managers as they attempt to choose appropriate strategies to deal with them. These issues will be discussed later in the chapter and will pervade much of what is said throughout the rest of the book.

Activity 2.2 offers the opportunity to carry out a simple environmental assessment of one or more organisations. Activity 2.2 is challenging and you will, almost certainly, say you need further information. However, organisations always exist in situations of imperfect knowledge and managers have to do their best in the circumstances. A start may be made by (simply?), identifying whether the forces for change are strong, moderate or weak. Strebel (1996a) describes a strong change force

---

ACTIVITY 2.2 Environmental turbulence

Think about organisations with which you are familiar – three would be a good number.

Carry out a simple environmental assessment for each organisation. To help this, consider the following:

1. *The PETS factors and the organisations' internal environments.*
2. *Whether past historical developments (either in societal terms or organisational terms) have an influence on the organisations' strategies and operations.*

Using Ansoff and McDonnell's framework, make a judgement about the level of environmental turbulence prevailing for each organisation.

Match these levels to Stacey's types of change situations.

Identify the similarities and differences in the three organisations' environments.

What lessons can you draw about the probability of each organisation responding to future environmental triggers for change?

---

as one causing a substantial decline or a substantial improvement in performance. He identifies a moderate force for change as one causing only a minor impact on performance while a weak one is one whose nature and direction are difficult to discern.

The strength of the forces for change can be related to the degree of turbulence in the environment: the stronger the force the more probable it is that the environment is moving to Ansoff and McDonnell's level 5. What this implies is that the ability to plan and manage change becomes ever more difficult as the forces and levels of turbulence increase. This is related to, but complicated further by, the different types of change which can be experienced by organisations.

THE CHANGING FACES OF CHANGE

Any investigation of the nature of change itself, that is organisational change as a response to environmental triggers for change such as described above and in Chapter 1, is contentious. For instance, Strebel (1996a, p. 5) says, 'Change may be a constant but it is not always the same'. What follows in this section is a discussion of a number of frameworks for categorising change. It starts with a broad generalisation of the concept of change.

Varieties of change

A starting point for considering the nature of change experienced by organisations is Grundy's three 'varieties of change' (Grundy, 1993), as shown in Figure 2.3. As a background to proposing these, Grundy states that many managers perceive change as a homogeneous concept, while others describe change as being primarily the enemy

Figure 2.3

Major types of change

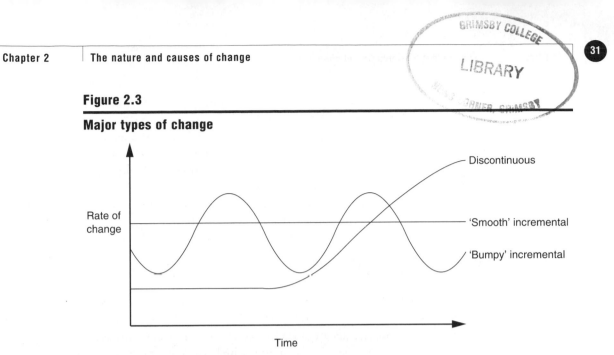

Source: Grundy, T. (1993), *Implementing Strategic Change* (London, Kogan Page, p. 25).

of stability. However, he maintains that it is possible to differentiate a number of characteristic types of change.

The first of the main types of change Grundy defines as 'smooth incremental change'. This is the type of change experienced by organisations which could be said to be operating in environments described by Ansoff and McDonnell as being at turbulence levels 1 and 2. Smooth incremental change is change which evolves slowly in a systematic and predictable way. Grundy maintains that this type of change is mainly reminiscent of the UK situation from the 1950s to early 1970s, but that this situation would be relatively exceptional in the 1990s and the future. It is important to note that, in Figure 2.3, the vertical axis represents *rate* of change, not *amount* of change. Thus, smooth incremental change does involve an amount of change but this happens at a constant rate.

The second variety of change Grundy terms 'bumpy incremental change'. This is characterised by periods of relative tranquillity punctuated by acceleration in the pace of change. He likens the 'bumps' to 'the movement of continental land masses where the "fault" enables periodic readjustment to occur without cataclysmic effect'(p. 24). He says that the triggers for this type of change are likely to include those from both the external and internal environments and which are perceived as 'overload'. An example given is the periodic reorganisations that organisations go through. One way of categorising both types of incremental change is to see them as change which is associated more with the *means* by which organisations achieve their goals, rather than as a change in the goals themselves.

Grundy's third variety of change is 'discontinuous change', which he defines as, 'change which is marked by rapid shifts in either strategy, structure or culture, or in all three' (p. 26). An example given is that of the privatisation of previously publicly owned utilities, for instance electricity generation and distribution. Another example is what Strebel (1996b) calls a 'divergent breakpoint', that is, change which results from the discovery of a new business opportunity and he instances the first Apple computer, the arrival of the Macintosh and, most recently, the new chips and software. The opportunities offered by the development of the Internet are most likely to lead to forms of discontinuous change in many organisations. However, not all instances of discontinuous change are linked to technological innovations. Health scares rendering some food products unsaleable can have cataclysmic effects throughout an industry. Thus, discontinuous change can be likened to change in response to the higher levels of environmental turbulence detailed by Ansoff and McDonnell.

Organisational convergence and upheaval

A framework for describing change which is similar to Grundy's is the one put forward by Tushman, Newman and Romanelli (1988). On the basis of an examination of numerous organisational studies and case histories, these writers propose a model of organisational life which consists of 'periods of incremental change, or convergence, punctuated by discontinuous changes' (p. 707).

They suggest there are two types of converging change: fine-tuning and incremental adaptations. Both these types of change have the common aim of maintaining the fit between organisational strategy, structure and processes. However, whereas fine-tuning is aimed at doing better what is already done well, incremental adaptation involves small changes in response to minor shifts in the environment – what the authors popularly call the 'ten-percent change'.

Both fine-tuning and incremental adjustments to environmental shifts allow organisations to perform more effectively and optimise the consistencies between strategy, structure, people and processes. Yet, Tushman *et al.* show how, as organisations grow, become more successful and develop internal forces for stability, these same forces eventually produce resistance when, for whatever reason, an organisation's strategy must change. Thus at times of major change in an organisation's environment, incremental adjustment will not bring about the major changes in strategy, structure, people and processes which might be required. At times such as these, Tushman et al. maintain that most organisations will be required to undergo discontinuous or frame-breaking change. Thus, in any organisation's life-cycle, periods of relative tranquillity will be punctuated with (probably shorter) periods of frame-breaking change.

Illustration 2.4 summarises the definition of frame-breaking change advanced by Tushman *et al.*

An example of frame-breaking change can be found in the privatisation of British Rail, in particular the splitting of the management of the rail infrastructure (the track, stations, timetabling, signalling etc.) from the running of the trains. At the time of writing, the prospectus for the flotation on the stock market of Railtrack, the organisation which manages the infrastructure, has just been issued. This is not the first frame-breaking change which has happened to British Rail since its nationalisation in 1962.

Illustration 2.4
ON FRAME-BREAKING CHANGE

The need for discontinuous change springs from one or a combination of the following:

- *Industry discontinuities* – sharp changes in the legal, political or technological conditions which shift the basis of competition. These could include: deregulation, substitute product technologies, substitute product technologies, substitute process technologies, the emergence of industry standards or dominant designs, major economic changes (e.g. oil crises), legal shifts (e.g. patent protection, trade/regulator barriers).
- *Product-life-cycle shifts* – changes in strategy from the emergence of a product to its establishment in the market, the effects of international competition.
- *Internal company dynamics* – the implications of size for new management design, new management style as inventor-entrepreneurs give way to the need for more steady state management, revised corporate portfolio strategy which can sharply alter the role and resources assigned to business units or functional areas.

The scope of frame-breaking change includes discontinuous change throughout the organisation. Frame-breaking change is usually implemented rapidly. Frame-breaking changes are revolutionary changes of the system as opposed to incremental changes in the system. Frame-breaking change usually involves the following features:

- *Reformed mission and core values* – new definition of company mission.
- *Altered power and status* – reflecting shifts in the bases of competition and resource allocation.
- *Reorganisation* – new strategy requires a modification in structure, systems and procedures, change of organisation form.
- *Revised interaction patterns* – new procedures, work flows, communication networks, decision-making patterns.
- *New executives* – usually from outside the organisation.

Frame-breaking change is revolutionary in that the shifts reshape the entire nature of the organisation. It requires discontinuous shifts in strategy, structure, people and processes concurrently. Reasons for the rapid, simultaneous implementation of frame-breaking change include:

- *Synergy* – the need for all pieces of the organisation to pull together.
- *Pockets of resistance* – have a chance to grow and develop when frame-breaking change is implemented slowly.
- *Pent-up need for change* – when constraints are relaxed, change is in fashion.
- *Riskiness and uncertainty* – the longer the implementation period, the greater the period of uncertainty and instability.

Source: Based on Tushman, M. L., Newman, W. H., and Romanelli, E. (1988), 'Convergence and Upheaval: Managing the Unsteady Pace of Organizational Evolution', in Tushman, M. L., and Moore, W. L. (eds.) (1988) *Readings in the Management of Innovation*, New York, Ballinger Publishing Company, pp. 712–13.

In 1984, British Rail was restructured from a monolithic entity into three passenger product sectors – (1) Inter-City (long-distance passenger services), (2) London and South East (London commuter services), (3) provincial services (the necessary, but basically unremunerative services). This left freight and parcel services as a separate business. For the first time since nationalisation, the organisation was asked by government to produce a corporate business plan.

A second fundamental reorganisation took place in 1992 entitled, 'Organising for Quality'. This included transferring the responsibilities of the six geographically based regions entirely to a business management structure based on the type of rail service provided (Thomas, 1992). This prevailed until 1993 when the government passed another Act which sought to 'provide and encourage the injection of private sector involvement, expertise and discipline into the provision of public services' (Smith, 1993, pp. 12–13). The effects of this Act are now taking place with the transfer of passenger services to private sector management by franchising arrangements. In total, 25 train operating units have been created and are included in the franchise arrangements.

The changes British Rail has gone through since 1993 fit the definition of revolutionary change advanced by Tushman *et al.*, that is changes of the system. They also meet their requirement that frame-breaking change should be rapid, by which they mean implementation in something like an 18–24 month period. It remains to be seen how the different parts of this industry settle down to a convergence pattern of change.

Tushman *et al.* say, 'Our research strongly suggests that the convergence/upheaval pattern occurs within departments . . . at the business-unit level . . . and at the corporate level of analysis' (p. 708). This suggests that frame-breaking change is not restricted to the strategic level of organisations. The distinction between operational and strategic levels in the consideration of types of change has been defined more clearly by two Australian researchers whose work goes a step further than the Tushman *et al.* model.

Fine-tuning to corporate transformation

Grundy (1993) does not claim any particular status for his typology of change; he states specifically that it is not an empirically tested model. The power of the Tushman *et al.* typology is its claim to be based on research and investigation. This is also the case with the typology put forward by Australian academics Dunphy and Stace (1993). What is more, they claim the status of a model when their typology of change, on the one hand, is combined with a typology of styles of change management, on the other. The full Dunphy and Stace model is discussed further in Chapter 6. What is interesting for this discussion of the nature of change is the four descriptions which represent their scale of change. Illustration 2.5 reproduces these descriptions.

A simple correspondence between Grundy's and Dunphy and Stace's categorisations of change is not possible. However, it is reasonable to suggest that Dunphy and Stace's scale types 1 and 2 are typical of Grundy's concept of smooth incremental change, while their scale types 3 and 4 are reminiscent of Grundy's bumpy incremental and discontinuous types of change respectively. The benefit of the Dunphy and Stace model, though, is in the detailed descriptions of each scale type and its testing with the executives, managers and supervisors of 13 Australian organisations from the service sector. Interestingly, organisations operating scale 1 and 2 type changes were in the minority, leading the researchers to conclude that modular and corporate transformations had become the norm rather than the exception.

Of more interest is the correspondence between the typology of Tushman *et al.* and that of Dunphy and Stace. It is fairly clear that Dunphy and Stace found the same two types of change as are grouped by Tushman *et al.* under the concept of converging change. Both sets of researchers use identical names – 'fine-tuning' and 'incremental

Illustration 2.5
DEFINING THE SCALE OF CHANGE

Scale Type 1: Fine tuning

Organizational change which is an ongoing process characterized by fine tuning of the 'fit' or match between the organization's strategy, structure, people, and processes. Such effort is typically manifested at departmental/divisional levels and deals with one or more of the following:

- Refining policies, methods, and procedures.
- Creating specialist units and linking mechanisms to permit increased volume and increased attention to unit quality and cost.
- Developing personnel especially suited to the present strategy (improved training and development; tailoring award systems to match strategic thrusts).
- Fostering individual and group commitment to the company mission and the excellence of one's own department.
- Promoting confidence in the accepted norms, beliefs, and myths.
- Clarifying established roles (with their associated authorities and posers), and the mechanisms for allocating resources.

Scale Type 2: Incremental adjustment

Organizational change which is characterized by incremental adjustments to the changing environment. Such change involves distinct modifications (but not radical change) to corporate business strategies, structures, and management processes, for example:

- Expanding sales territory.
- Shifting the emphasis among products.
- Improved production process technology.
- Articulating a modified statement of mission to employees.

- Adjustments to organizational structures within or across divisional boundaries to achieve better links in product/service delivery.

Scale Type 3: Modular transformation

Organizational change which is characterized by major realignment of one or more departments/divisions. The process of radical change is focused on these subparts rather than on the organization as a whole, for example:

- Major restructuring of particular department/ divisions.
- Changes in key executives and managerial appointments in these areas.
- Work and productivity studies resulting in significantly reduced or increased workforce numbers.
- Reformed departmental/divisional goals.
- Introduction of significantly new process technologies affecting key departments or divisions.

Scale Type 4: Corporate transformation

Organizational change which is corporation-wide, characterized by radical shifts in business strategy, and revolutionary changes throughout the whole organization involving many of the following features:

- Reformed organizational mission and core values.
- Altered power and status affecting the distribution of power in the organization.
- Reorganization – major changes in structures, systems, and procedures across the organization.
- Revised interaction patterns – new procedures, work flows, communication networks, and decision-making patterns across the organization.
- New executives in key managerial positions from outside the organization.

Source: Dunphy, D., and Stace, D. (1993), 'The Strategic Management of Corporate Change', *Human Relations*, Vol. 45, No. 8, pp. 917–18.

adjustment'. Where Dunphy and Stace go beyond Tushman *et al.* is in, apparently, splitting what Tushman *et al.* termed 'frame-breaking' change into two types – 'modular transformation' and 'corporate transformation'. This is a useful development in detailing more clearly the different levels at which frame-breaking change can take place. It still recognises the implications of these types of change for goals and purposes, but identifies the fact that these may have different meanings at the departmental/divisional level than at the corporate/organisational level.

ACTIVITY 2.3

Look again at Dunphy and Stace's scale types of change (see Illustration 2.5). Position an organisation with which you are familiar on the following scale.

Fine-tuning	Incremental adjustment	Modular transformation	Corporate transformation

Tushman et al. (1988) say, 'The most effective firms take advantage of relatively long convergent periods. These periods of incremental change build on and take advantage of organization inertia. Frame-breaking change is quite dysfunctional if the organization is successful and the environment is stable. If, however, the organization is performing poorly and/or if the environment changes substantially, frame-breaking change is the only way to realign the organization with its competitive environment.' (1986, pp. 713–14).

Form a view as to whether the type of change now being experienced by your organisation fits the environment in which it is currently operating and which is likely to prevail in the foreseeable future.

Planned and emergent change

Fine-tuning and incremental change are features of all organisational life and are associated with change as it *emerges*. The idea of emergent change has been linked by Wilson (1992) with the concept of organisations as open systems. Writers such as McAleer (1982), Checkland (1972), von Bertanlanfy (1971) and Kast and Rosenzweig (1970) have produced detailed discussions of the concept of a system which includes organisational systems. Briefly, these discussions include the idea of organisations striving to maintain a state of equilibrium where the forces for change are balanced by the forces for stability. Therefore, organisations viewed as systems will always strive to restore equilibrium whenever they are disturbed. According to this view, the organisational system is constantly sensing its environment in order continuously to adjust to maintain its purpose and optimum state.

It could be speculated that, in an ideal world, organisational sensing of the environment would be so effective as to render frame-breaking change unnecessary. If organisations responded continuously to the need for change, they would have no need for the periodic upheavals which sometimes seem inevitable. In other words, through their assessing continuously the internal, external and temporal environments in which they operate, change should emerge almost 'naturally'.

However, writers such as Tushman *et al.* (1988) and Johnson (1987, 1988) describe a phenomenon whereby managers and other organisational personnel become so comfortable with 'how we work here' and 'what we hold important here' that they also become impervious to warning signs of impending difficulties from the environment. According to Tushman *et al.*, this is the effect of what they call the 'double-edged sword' of converging periods of change. Thus, the habits, patterns of behaviour, finding out the best way to do things and commitment to values which have been built up during periods of converging change can contribute significantly to the success of the organisation. However, the organisational history built up during this period can also be counter-productive in restricting the vigilance needed towards the environment and may become a source of resistance to the need for more radical forms of change.

Johnson (1988, p. 44) refers to the organisational 'paradigm' to describe the core set of beliefs and assumptions held commonly by the managers of an organisation. He says:

> This set of beliefs, which evolves over time, might embrace assumptions about the nature of the organisational environment, the managerial style in the organisation, the nature of its leaders, and the operational routines seen as important to ensure the success of the organisation.

The fact that the paradigm is held relatively commonly, is taken for granted, and is not, therefore, seen as problematical, means that signals from the environment are filtered through it. These signals are only made sense of in terms of what Johnson (1988, p. 44) calls 'the way we do things around here'. Therefore, when signals for change come from the environment, he says,

> [their] relevance is determined, not by the competitive activity, but by the constructs of the paradigm [and] in these circumstances it is likely that, over time, the phenomenon of 'strategic drift' will occur: that is gradually, probably imperceptibly, the strategy of the organisation will become less and less in tune with the environment in which the organisation exists. (Johnson, 1988, p. 44.)

As the process of strategic drift continues, an organisation's strategy, structure and processes gradually move further away from a path which would take account of the triggers for change coming from the environment. It is at these points that more frame-breaking or revolutionary change becomes necessary to re-align the organisations' purposes and operations with environmental imperatives.

From the discussion above, it is clear that the process of strategic drift forces organisations into a more conscious deliberate *planning* of change. However, the distinction between emergent and planned change is not clear-cut. Criticisms of the idea that change can be planned logically and systematically have been made by Wilson (1992). He argues that planned change is a management concept which relies heavily on a single view of the way change ought to be done. This view assumes that the environment is known and, therefore, that a logical process of environmental analysis can be harnessed in the service of planning any change. Wilson says this view emphasises the role of human agency, that is, that chief executives and managers are able to invoke the changes they feel are necessary and that this process is not problematic. His argument is that this view does not take account of the context in which change must take place; for instance, the cultural and political components which influence most, if not all, implementations of any planned change.

Quinn (1980) has also criticised the idea of planned change as something which is deliberately and carefully thought through and then implemented. His research into the decision-making processes of a number of organisations demonstrated that most strategic decisions are made in spite of formal planning systems rather than because of them. As reinforcement of this idea, Stacey (1996, pp. 35–6) summarises the key points made by Quinn as follows:

1. Effective managers do not manage strategically in a piecemeal manner. They have a clear view of what they want to achieve, where they are trying to take the business. The destination is thus intended.

2. But the route to that destination, the strategy itself, is not intended from the start in any comprehensive way. Effective managers know that the environment they have to operate in is uncertain and ambiguous. They therefore sustain flexibility by holding open the method of reaching the goal.

3. The strategy itself then emerges from the interaction between different groupings of people in the organisation, different groupings with different amounts of power, different requirements for and access to information, different time spans and parochial interest. These different pressures are orchestrated by senior managers. The top is always reassessing, integrating and organising.

4. The strategy emerges or evolves in small incremental, opportunistic steps. But such evolution is not piecemeal or haphazard because of the agreed purpose and the role of top management in reassessing what is happening. It is this that provides the logic in the incremental action.

5. The result is an organisation that is feeling its way to a known goal, opportunistically learning as it goes.

Quinn terms this process 'logical incrementalism' in that it is based in a certain logic of thinking but is incremental in its ability to change in the light of new information and the results of ongoing action. Opportunism plays an important part in this process (*see* Illustration 2.6).

Illustration 2.6

PROACTIVELY MANAGING INCREMENTALISM IN THE DEVELOPMENT OF CORPORATE STRATEGIES

Quinn (1979) makes the following statement to illustrate how executives proactively manage incrementalism in the development of corporate strategies.

Typically you start with general concerns, vaguely felt. Next you roll an issue around in your mind till you think you have a conclusion that makes sense for the company. You then go out and sort of post the idea without being too wedded to its details. You then start hearing the arguments pro and con, and some very good refinements of the idea usually emerge. Then you pull the idea in and put some resources together to study it so it can be put forward as more of a formal presentation. You wait for 'stimuli occurrences' or 'crises', and launch pieces of the idea to help in these situations. But they lead toward your ultimate aim. You know where you want to get. You'd like to get there in six months. But it may take three years, or you may not get there. And when you do get there, you don't know whether it was originally your own idea – or somebody else had reached the same conclusion before you and just got you on board for it. You never know. The president would follow the same basic process, but he could drive it much faster than an executive lower in the organization

Source: Quinn, J. B. (1979), 'Xerox Corporation (B)', copyrighted case, Amos Tuck School of Business Administration, Dartmouth College, Hanover, NH.

PREDICTABLE CHANGE

In some respects, change could be viewed as neither wholly emergent nor planned. As cycles of growth and activity are an essential part of living, so the concept of an organisational life-cycle (Greiner, 1972; Kimberley and Miles, 1980) has been used to describe the stages through which organisations go as they grow and develop. Figure 2.4 illustrates these in terms of the size and maturity of organisations.

Greiner maintains that, as organisations grow in size and mature, their activities go through five phases, each of which is associated with a different growth period in an organisation's life. In addition, as each growth period moves into the next, the organisation goes through a shorter-lived crisis period. These are, respectively, the evolution and revolution stages shown in Figure 2.4. Illustration 2.7 is a brief description of a typical life-cycle pattern which is complemented by Clarke's (1994) useful categorisation of the characteristics and crisis points associated with each phase of growth (*see* Table 2.1).

Figure 2.4

The organisational life-cycle

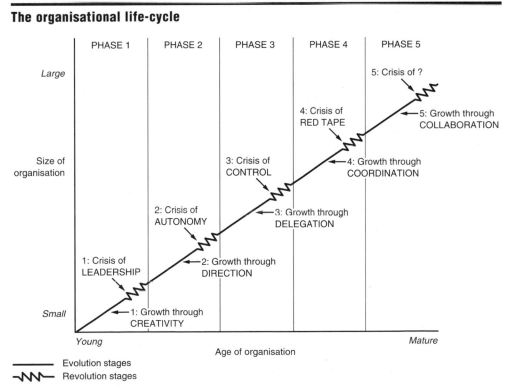

Illustration 2.7
A TYPICAL LIFE-CYCLE PATTERN

1. The entrepreneurial stage

In this first (often entrepreneurial) stage, the first task to be achieved is to provide a service or manufacture product. Survival is the key strategy. Organisational culture is fashioned by the founders of the organisation. It may be a brand-new organisation or a new subsidiary or part of an established, larger organisation. Success brings growth and the need to recruit more staff. Staff need managing, and the question of future organisational strategy becomes more complex. The alternatives are to limit growth and remain small (but risk being unable to sustain competition) or to grow and recruit professional managers.

2. The collective stage

The organisation begins to take 'shape'. Departments and functions begin to be defined and the division of labour is the dominant theme. The professional managers recruited tend to be strong leaders who share the same vision as the founders. Further growth brings the need for management control and delegation. The organisation has begun to establish its position; internal tasks are allocated and who has responsibility and autonomy to carry them out become pre-eminent.

3. The formalisation stage

Systems of communication and control become more formal. There is a need to differentiate between the tasks of management – to make strategic decisions and to implement policy – and those of lower-level managers, who are expected to carry out and oversee operational decisions. Bureaucratisation occurs as systems of co-ordination and control emerge, including salary structures, reward and incentive schemes, levels in the hierarchy, reporting relationships and formalised areas of discretion and autonomy for lower-level managers. The organisation continues to grow, but burdened by the process of bureaucratisation and the need for the structure to be 'freed up' becomes pressing.

4. The elaboration stage

This is the stage of strategic change. The organisation may have reached a plateau in its growth curve and may even show the first stages of decline in performance. Managers used to handling bureaucratic structures and processes usually have to learn new skills to achieve change, such as team work, self-assessment and problem confrontation. This stage may also include the rapid turnover and replacement of senior managers.

Source: Based on Greiner, L. (1972), 'Evolution and revolution as organizations grow', *Harvard Business Review*, July–August.

ACTIVITY 2.4

Consider an organisation you know well.

Using the descriptions in Illustration 2.7 and Table 2.1, position the organisation on the Greiner graph in Figure 2.4.

Table 2.1
Characteristics of Greiner's phases of growth

	Phase 1 Creativity	Phase 2 Direction	Phase 3 Delegation	Phase 4 Co-ordination	Phase 5 Collaboration
Structure	• Informal	• Functional • Centralised • Hierarchical • Top-down	• Decentralised • Bottom-up	• Staff functions • Strategic business units (SBUs) • Decentralised • Units merged into product groups	• Matrix-type structure
Systems	• Immediate response to customer feedback	• Standards • Cost centres • Budget • Salary systems	• Profit centres • Bonuses • Management by exception	• Formal planning procedures • Investment centres • Tight expenditure controls	• Simplified and integrated information systems
Styles/people	• Individualistic • Creative • Entrepreneurial • Ownership	• Strong directive	• Full delegation of autonomy	• Watchdog	• Team-oriented • Interpersonal skills at a premium • Innovative • Educational bias
Strengths	• Fun • Market response	• Efficient	• High management motivation	• More efficient allocation of corporate and local resources	• Greater spontaneity • Flexible and behavioural approach
Crisis point	• Crisis of leadership	• Crisis of autonomy	• Crisis of control	• Crisis of red tape	?
Weaknesses	• Founder often temperamentally unsuited to managing • Boss overload	• Unsuited to diversity • Cumbersome • Hierarchical • Doesn't grow people	• Top managers lose control as freedom breeds parochial attitudes	• Bureaucratic divisions between line/staff, headquarters/field, etc.	• Psychological saturation

Source: Clarke, L. (1994), *The Essence of Change* (Hemel Hempstead, Prentice-Hall, p. 12).

The Greiner model is useful for identifying an organisation's situation, thus providing warning of the next crisis point it may have to face. It therefore helps in the planning of necessary change. It also assists managers and other organisational personnel to realise that change is, to some extent, inevitable; organisations must of necessity change as they grow and mature. It therefore helps legitimise the need for change and may be useful in discussions to bring about a reduction in resistance to change. However, while it may be possible to predict the next crisis point (through application of the concept of the organisational life-cycle), more needs to be done to develop ways of bringing about the necessary changes from one stage to another. It therefore becomes necessary to have some models and techniques for diagnosing the type of change situation prevailing at any one time in order to determine what kind of change approach to take.

DIAGNOSING CHANGE SITUATIONS

Those who pretend that the same kind of change medicine can be applied no matter what the context are either naive or charlatans. (Strebel, 1996a, p. 5.)

Strebel begins an article entitled 'Choosing the Right Path' with these words. He goes on to say, 'Thus, change leaders cannot afford the risk of blindly applying a standard change recipe and hoping it will work. Successful change takes place on a path that is appropriate to the right situation' (p. 5). Pettigrew and Whipp (1993, p. 108), reporting on their study of a range of UK companies across four industry sectors, said, 'One of the central characteristics of the firms under study, therefore, is that the management of strategic and operational change for competitive success is an uncertain and emergent process.'

Being able to diagnose change situations is, therefore, important if organisations are going to have any chance of responding to and managing change successfully. However, diagnosing any organisational situation is not an exact science. There are, though, some tools and techniques which can help. For instance, the Greiner model of the organisational life-cycle is useful for drawing attention to periods when organisational change is likely to be needed. In addition, there are a number of techniques for strategic planning (e.g. stakeholder, SWOT and PETS analyses), the application of which can lead to consciously planned change. In particular, an analysis of an organisation's strengths and weaknesses and the opportunities and threats (SWOT) presented by changes in its environments can increase awareness of the need for continuous incremental type change and, hopefully, avoid the process of strategic drift discussed above. Using multiple-cause diagrams assists a greater understanding of the interactions between the many different and often simultaneous causes of change.

There are, however, a number of other methods which can be used for anticipating when change is imminent and for deciding an appropriate approach to use for its management and implementation.

Looking for breakpoints

The discussion above has focused on the requirement to scan the organisational environment for signals which could trigger change within organisations. To help with this, Strebel (1996b) has suggested a model of *industry* behaviour. This model is similar to that of Greiner in the concept of a cycle of behaviour. However, while Greiner links his model mainly to changes in the structure and management of organisations, Strebel links his model more to an organisation's competitive environment (*see* Figure 2.5). He uses the concept of the 'evolutionary cycle of competitive behaviour' to introduce the idea of 'breakpoints', that is those times when organisations must change their strategies in response to changes in competitors' behaviour.

Figure 2.5

Evolutionary cycle of competitive behaviour

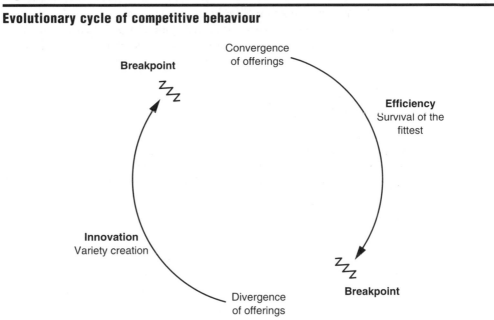

Source: Strebel, P. (1996b), 'Breakpoint: how to stay in the game', *Mastering Management*, Part 17, *Financial Times*.

The cycle of competitive behaviour involves two main phases. One is the innovation phase when someone discovers a new business opportunity, whatever its source. This triggers a breakpoint to introduce a phase in the evolutionary cycle which causes a *divergence* in competitors' behaviour as they attempt to exploit the new opportunity with innovative new offerings. Strebel (1996b) says this phase corresponds to variety creation in the evolutionary cycle and gives examples of the first Apple computer, the arrival of the Macintosh and, most recently, the new chips and software, all of which triggered breakpoints. He goes on to say:

> Divergent competitive behaviour aimed at enhancing the value of offerings continues until it becomes impossible to differentiate offerings because value innovation has run its course and imitation of the competitors' best features has taken over. As the offerings converge and the returns to value innovation decline, someone sees the advantage of trying to reduce delivered cost. Competitors converge on total quality management, continual improvement, and re-engineering or restructuring of the business system in an attempt to cut costs and maintain market share. (p. 13.)

This brings about the other of the two phases – that of *convergence*. During this phase, the least efficient leave the scene and only the fittest survive. This is a phase of cost-cutting and consolidation until the returns from cost reduction decline, and people see the advantage of looking for a new business opportunity – bringing a new breakpoint with the cycle starting all over again. In summary Strebel (1996b, p. 5) says:

> The competitive cycle suggests that there are two basic types of breakpoint:
> - Divergent Breakpoints associated with sharply increasing variety in the competitive offerings, resulting in more value for the customer.
> - Convergent Breakpoints associated with sharp improvements in the systems and processes used to deliver the offerings, resulting in lower delivered cost.

It should be noted that although the competitive cycle repeats itself, the industry continues to evolve and Strebel presents this in diagram form with respect to the computer industry (*see* Figure 2.6).

Figure 2.6

Breakpoint evolution of personal computer industry

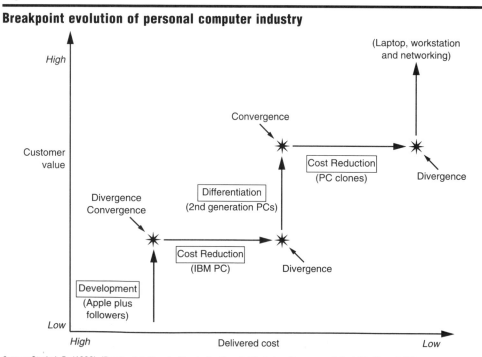

Source: Strebel, P. (1996), 'Breakpoint: How to Stay in the Game', *Mastering Management*, Part 17, *Financial Times*.

The vertical axis in Figure 2.6 represents the innovation–variety creation phase of the cycle of competitive behaviour; the horizontal axis represents the efficiency–survival phase. The vertical arrows denote periods of innovation (following divergence breakpoint) while the horizontal arrows denote periods of efficiency seeking and cost cutting (following convergence breakpoint). Strebel stresses that the diagram is not to scale. However, he says that, over time, industries move up the diagonal with increasing customer value and lower delivered cost. Clearly, some industries (e.g. those based on commodities) offer less opportunity for innovation and customer-value creation. Others (e.g. clothing and fashion) offer fewer opportunities for cost reduction. They evolve mainly through innovation in the direction of customer value.

Strebel's model is very useful in explaining the external environment in which organisations operate, in particular the economic and technological aspects. What is as useful is his advice on how to detect patterns in the environment that indicate a breakpoint might be imminent. Illustration 2.8 details this advice.

It is clear there are a number of issues associated with the identification of breakpoints. First, organisations need to have both formal and informal systems

---

Illustration 2.8

LOOKING FOR BREAKPOINTS, WITH LEADING INDICATORS

The timing of breakpoints is impossible to predict because they might be triggered by many different factors and because they require both a latent market and a supplier with the right business system. However, with an understanding of an industry's evolution it is possible to look for patterns indicating that a breakpoint may be imminent. Specifically, the competitive cycle can be used to look for leading indicators of a potential breakpoint.

The tendency of the competitive cycle to oscillate between divergence (variety creation) on the one hand and convergence (survival of the fittest) provides the framework.

Convergence is usually easier to anticipate, because it is built on an offering that already exists. Typical indicators are listed below. When several of these are in place, all that is needed is a player, or event, to trigger the breakpoint.

- Competitors: Convergence is visible in increasingly similar products, service and image.
- Customers: The differentiation between offerings looks increasingly artificial to customers and the segmentation in the market starts breaking down.

- Distributors: The bargaining power in the industry often shifts downstream to distributors who play competitors off against each other.
- Suppliers: They cannot provide a source of competitive advantage because everyone knows how to use their inputs.

Divergence is more difficult to anticipate because it is based on a new offering that does not yet exist. However, if the following are in place, the industry is ready for a new offering that breaks with the past.

- Customers: An increasingly saturated market is accompanied by declining growth rates and restless customers.
- New Entrants: Restless customers are attracting new entrants.
- Competitors: Declining returns may force them to experiment with new offerings or look elsewhere for profits.
- Suppliers: New resources and, especially, new technology are frequently the source of a divergent breakpoint.
- Distributors: They lag behind because they have to adapt to the new offering.

Source: Strebel, P. (1996), 'Breakpoint: how to stay in the game', *Mastering Management*, Part 17, *Financial Times*, p. 14.

attuned to searching for indicators from the environment. The formal systems will probably include those involved with: environmental scanning, benchmarking and data collection and interpretation. In addition, the way in which organisations are structured must help, rather than hinder, these activities.

As important are the more informal aspects of organisations, such as open attitudes on the part of managers and personnel, a degree of co-operation rather than destructive competition between divisions and departments, and a culture supportive of innovation and change. Part Two of the book discusses these factors and others in more detail. Before moving on to this, the final section of this chapter describes another way of assessing both the impact and the magnitude of impending change as an essential tool in determining the most appropriate methodology for carrying out the change management process. However, rather than diagnosing change by scanning the organisation's competitive environment (as Strebel recommends), this approach characterises organisational problems (and therefore the need for change) in terms of their complexity, variability, people involvement, and how much consensus there is on what constitutes the problem and what might bring a solution.

Hard (difficult) and soft (messy) problems

The discussion above shows how situations forcing change vary in complexity and seriousness. Thus, a minor upset in some part of an organisation's environment (most likely to be the internal environment) can bring about small-scale, incremental change. Other disturbances (more likely to come from the external environment) will have a much more wide-ranging impact on an organisation's strategy, structure and processes.

In the preceding section, reference was made to Strebel's advice on identifying industry breakpoints. Sometimes, however, the signals arriving on managers' desks are not as clearly categorised as Strebel implies, nor can they always be separated easily into those concerned with competitors, customers, suppliers and distributors. These signals are frequently confused and diffuse and it is not easy to see clearly just what type of situation prevails – the only thing managers perceive are 'problems'. These problems may vary in complexity and seriousness, ranging from minor upsets to major catastrophes, from temporary hitches to gnawing 'tangles'. McCalman and Paton (1992) use the terms 'hard' and 'soft' to describe, respectively, these two types of problems. Alternatively, the Open University (1985) uses the terms 'difficulties' and 'messes', the latter term based on Ackoff's (1993) article entitled 'The art and science of mess management'.

Illustration 2.9 demonstrates some differences between difficulties and messes.

Illustration 2.9 shows how difficulties are simply more limited sorts of problems while messes are larger and much more taxing for those who want some kind of change to 'solve' the problem. However, messes are not just bigger problems, they are *qualitatively* different from difficulties.

In distinguishing between these two types of problem, the Open University authors use the concepts of 'hard complexity' as characteristic of difficulties and 'soft

Illustration 2.9

DIFFICULTIES AND MESSES

Difficulties are bounded in that they:

- Tend to be smaller scale.
- Are less serious in their implications.
- Can be considered in relative isolation from their organisational context.
- Have clear priorities as to what might need to be done.
- Generally have quantifiable objectives and performance indicators.
- Have a systems/technical orientation.
- Generally involve relatively few people.
- Have facts which are known and which can contribute to the solution.
- Have agreement by the people involved on what constitutes the problem.
- Tend to have solutions of which the type at least is known.
- Have known time scales.
- Are 'bounded' in that they can be considered separately from the wider organisational context and have minimal interactions with the environment.

Messes are unbounded in that they:

- Tend to be larger scale.
- Have serious and worrying implications for all concerned.
- Are an interrelated complex of problems which cannot be separated from their context.
- Have many people of different persuasions and attitudes involved in the problem.
- Have subjective and at best semi-quantifiable objectives.
- Have an absence of knowledge of factors and uncertainty as to what need be known.
- Have little agreement on what constitutes the problem let alone what might be possible solutions.
- Have usually been around for some time and will not be solved quickly, if at all; bringing about an improvement may be all that can be hoped for.
- Have fuzzy time scales.
- Are 'unbounded' in that they spread throughout the organisation and, sometimes, beyond.

complexity' as characteristic of messes. In beginning an explanation of these they say:

> Complexity is not just a matter of there being many different factors and interactions to bear in mind, of uncertainty concerning some of them, of a multitude of combinations and permutations of possible decisions and events to allow for, evaluate and select. It is not only a computational matter – such as operational researchers deal with. Complexity is also generated by the very different constructions that can be placed on those factors, decisions and events. (Open University, 1985, p. 18.)

The consequence of these different interpretations of complexity is to describe hard complexity as characteristic of those problems which lend themselves to quantification and an optimal solution – an example is working out the best timetables for workers on production lines to achieve the most output. Soft complexity, on the other hand, is indicative of situations where the description of events is ambiguous and there is a 'tantalising multiplicity of different interpretations and reconstructions' (Open University, 1985, p. 18) which can be put upon a problem, let alone its possible solution.

The introduction of new working practices is an example of a messy problem involving soft complexity. For instance, not everyone will agree there is a problem and a need for new working practices. Some will interpret this action as a wish to reduce numbers of staff. Others may see it as an attempt to split up possibly troublesome groups. Yet others may even view this optimistically in terms of getting extra experience and, perhaps, new responsibilities. Management is likely to think it a 'good thing' while any trade union will want to know what is in it for the other employees. What is more, if the changes have implications for pay and status, the possible 'losers' will see the world very differently from the possible 'winners'.

ACTIVITY 2.5

1   *Note three difficulties you have faced at work or in similar situations elsewhere.*

2   *Note two (if possible three) messes you have ever faced or been involved in.*

3   *Using Illustration 2.9, list the ways in which the difficulties differ from the messes. What might this tell you about ways of dealing with them?*

The change spectrum

Asking a number of questions about a change situation may help to identify whether it is likely to involve hard or soft complexity and whether it can, therefore, be seen to be more of a difficulty or more of a mess. Using the terms 'hard' and 'soft' to distinguish these two types of problem, McCalman and Paton (1992) have devised what they call the 'TROPICS' test to help locate a change situation on a continuum from hard to soft. Illustration 2.10 presents the TROPICS factors as dimensions on which a change situation can be positioned, according to whether it is further towards the hard or soft end of each factor.

The TROPICS test, as with any analysis of problems according to the lists in Illustration 2.9 and Illustration 2.10, can only be a guide to the nature of the problem. What is important is to have undertaken exercises such as these in order to understand more clearly the type of change situation faced, in order to guide the design, planning and implementation of any change. This is because problem-solving and managing subsequent change is not simply an intellectual problem. As situations move away from being difficulties and towards what has been termed a mess, they encompass not only issues which can be addressed through the application of intellect, but also issues which have emotional and social dimensions which require different kinds of approaches for their solution. Simplistically, these approaches can be categorised as hard and soft and there are a number of models of change which, in broad terms, attach to these different approaches. These are considered further and in much more detail in Part Three of the book when the issues of 'doing' change are addressed.

Illustration 2.10
THE TROPICS FACTORS

Hard		Soft
Time scales clearly defined/ short to medium term		Time scales ill-defined/ medium to long term
Resources needed for the change clearly identified		Resources needed for the change uncertain
Objectives clearly stated and could be quantified		Change objectives subjective and ambiguous
Perceptions of the problem and its possible solution shared by all		No consensus on what constitutes the problem/ conflicts of interest
Interest in the problem is limited and defined		Interest in the problem is widespread and ill-defined
Control is maintained by the managing group		Control is shared with people outside the managing group
Source of the problem originates from within the organisation		The source of the problem originates from outside the organisation

ACTIVITY 2.6

Take each example you thought of in answer to Activity 2.5 and apply the TROPICS test to it. To do this, put a cross on each line according to whether your example is nearer to one end or the other of the factor. When you have done this for all factors for each example, make a judgement as to whether your example is, overall, a hard or soft problem/ change situation.

Did the TROPICS test confirm or refute your judgement of what is a difficulty and what is a mess in terms of your answer to Activity 2.5?

DISCUSSION QUESTIONS AND ACTIVITIES

1   Discuss the proposition that: 'All change can be categorised as either incremental or radical'. Use examples from your own experience to support points made.

2   To what extent do you think change situations can be chacterised as either hard or soft?

3   Give examples to support or refute Quinn's (1979) contention that change occurs through a process of 'logical incrementalism'.

REFERENCES

Ackoff, R. L. (1993), 'The art and science of mess management', in Mabey, C., and Mayon-White, B. (eds.), *Managing Change*, London, P.C.P.

Ansoff, I. H., and McDonnell, E. J. (1990), *Implanting Strategic Management*, Englewood Cliffs, NJ, Prentice-Hall.

Checkland, P. B. (1972), 'Towards a systems based methodology for real world problem solving', *Journal of Systems Engineering*, Vol. 3, No. 2.

Clarke, L. (1994), *The Essence of Change*, Hemel Hempstead, Prentice-Hall.

Corzine, R., and Adams, P. (1996), 'Shell may face fresh pressure over Nigerian oil discovery', *Financial Times*, 8 March, P. 1.

Dawson, P. (1994), *Organizational Change. A Processual Approach*, London, P.C.P.

Dunphy, D., and Stace, D. (1993), 'The Strategic Management of Corporate Change', *Human Relations*, Vol. 46, No. 8, pp. 905–20.

Greiner, L. (1972), 'Evolution and revolution as organizations grow', *Harvard Business Review*, July–August.

Grundy, T. (1993), *Managing Strategic Change*, London, Kogan Page, pp. 24–6.

Johnson, G. (1987), *Strategic Change and the Management Process*, Oxford, Blackwell.

Johnson, G. (1988), 'Processes of Managing Strategic Change', Management Research News, Vol. 11, No. 4/5, pp. 43–6. This article can also be found in, Mabey, C., and Mayon-White, B. (eds.), *Managing Change* (2nd edn.), London, P.C.P.

Kast, F. E., and Rosenzweig, J. E. (1970), *Organization and Management: A Systems Approach*, New York, McGraw-Hill.

Kehoe, L., and Taylor, p. (1996), 'The online challenge flavers', *Financial Times*, 14 March, p. 23.

Kimberley, J. R., and Miles, R. H. (1980), *The Organizational Life-cycle*, San Francisco, Jossey-Bass.

McAleer, W. E. (1982), 'Systems: A concept for business and management', *Journal of Applied Systems Analysis*, Vol. 9, pp. 99–129.

McCalman, J., and Paton, R. A. (1992), *Change Management. A Guide to Effective Implementation*, London, P.C.P.

Open University (1985), 'Managing and Messy Problems', in Block 1: Problems in Organizations, Course T244 *Managing in Organizations*, Milton Keynes, Open University Press.

Pettigrew, A., and Whipp, R. (1993), *Managing Change for Competitive Success*, Oxford, Blackwell.

Quinn, J. B. (1979), 'Xerox Corporation (B)', copyrighted case, *Amos Tuck School of Business Administration*, Dartmouth College, Hanover, NH.

Quinn, J. B. (1980), 'Managing strategic change', *Sloan Management Review*, Summer, pp. 3–20.

Smith, D. (1993), *The History of British Rail*, Department of Transport, London, Cloister Press, pp. 12–13.

Stacey, R. (1996), *Strategic Management and Organisational Dynamics*, London, Pitman.

Strebel, P. (1996a), 'Choosing the right path', *Mastering Management*, Part 14, *Financial Times*.

Strebel, P. (1996b), 'Breakpoint: How to Stay in the Game', *Mastering Management*, Part 17, *Financial Times*.

Thomas, C. (1992), *A History of the Rail Network*, London, British Railways Board, pp. 4–5.

Tushman, M. L., Newman, W. H., and Romanelli, E. (1988), 'Convergence and upheaval: managing the unsteady pace of organizational evolution', in Tushman, M. L., and Moore, W. L. (eds.) *Readings in the Management of Innovation*, New York, Ballinger Publishing Company.

von Bertanlanfy, L. (1971), *General Systems Theory*, Harmondsworth, Penguin.

Wilson, D. C. (1992), *A Strategy of Change*, New York, Routledge.

Part Two

ORGANISATIONS FOR CHANGE

Introduction to Part Two

Everything exists in the context of a wider environment. This is true for entities such as organisations. The idea of organisations as systems operating in a wider environment was developed in Part One of the book, where there was some discussion of the environmental triggers for change and their potential for influencing organisational policy and practices. However, organisations are not simply the hapless recipients of the winds of change blowing from this external environment. They, in turn, form an environment – the internal environment – for the activities which take place within them. Thus, the strategy an organisation pursues and the way in which it is structured will be significant for its capacity to respond to and initiate change.

Strategy and structure can be thought of as the more formal, overt aspects of an organisation's functioning. As important, however, are the more informal, covert aspects of organisational life such as organisational culture (set in the context of its national culture), organisational politics and issues of power, co-operation and conflict, as well as the way the organisation is led.

Part Two of the book extends the discussion in Part One, to investigate the internal life of the organisation in terms of its relations with the external environment and the opportunities and constraints for change. The four chapters in Part Two reflect this focus and, with the discussion from Part One, prepare the ground for the more practically oriented material on the designing and implementing of change to be presented in Part Three.

Chapter 3 is oriented to the more formal structural aspects of organisational life while Chapters 4 and 5 concentrate on the more informal contexts of organisational culture and politics and their significance for the success or otherwise of any change process. The final chapter of the Part, Chapter 6, discusses the role of leadership in the change process as a lead into Part Three of the book, which is oriented towards the more practical issues of designing and implementing change.

CHAPTER 3

Organisational structure and change

This chapter discusses the characteristics of different types of organisational structures and provides details of the advantages and disadvantages of each in relation to organisational performance and the ability of organisations to introduce and implement change. More recent examples of network and 'virtual' organisational forms are examined as having the potential to respond more quickly to changes in organisations' internal and external environments. Factors such as an organisation's strategy, its size and the technology used are examined as to the degree of influence they may have on choice of structure. There is recognition that there is still ample 'room' for managers to exercise personal choice in these matters.

Objectives

To:

- define what is meant by organisational structure and the organisational forms through which it manifests itself;

- discuss the relationship between an organisation's strategy and its structure;

- evaluate the contingency relationships between organisational structure, size, technology and the external environment;

- assess the extent to which different types of organisational structure and form can cope with and adapt to a variety of change processes.

THE MEANING OF ORGANISATION STRUCTURE

The introduction to this Part of the book states that everything exists in a wider environment. This is true for entities such as organisations, as discussed in Part One of the book. However, organisations as systems are, in particular, *social* systems. They are social because, in most organisations, to get work done requires the grouping of individuals and the activities they do into departments or divisions. Thus, in order to achieve its goals and objectives, an organisation needs to have some way of dividing work up so that it can be allocated to members of the organisation for its execution. In other words, the work and the people who will manage and do it must be structured if chaos is not to ensue. The allocation of responsibilities, the grouping of functions, co-ordination and control of these, are all basic elements of what is called an organisation's structure which is in essence the social structuring of people and processes. Wilson and Rosenfeld (1990, p. 215) offer the following definition of organisation structure:

> The established pattern of relationships between the component parts of an organization, outlining both communication, control and authority patterns. Structure distinguishes the parts of an organization and delineates the relationship between them.

Bartol and Martin (1994, p. 283) include the additional element of 'designed by management' in their definition of structure, which is:

> The formal pattern of interactions and coordination designed by management to link the tasks of individuals and groups in achieving organizational goals.

ACTIVITY 3.1

What other elements do Bartol and Martin give in their definition of organisation structure which do not appear in Wilson and Rosenfeld's definition?

These two definitions taken together give a sense of the objectives which any structure must serve (meeting the goals of the organisation) as well as the process through which these objectives can be met (the effective and efficient ordering of activities and delineation of the relationships between them). Note, however, the emphasis in Bartol and Martin's definition on individuals *and* groups. In addition, the word 'formal' in Bartol and Martin's definition draws attention to the fact that organisational structures are typically created by management for specific purposes. From one perspective, therefore, an organisation's structure could be regarded as the official definition of the way that particular organisation functions. However, organisational life is never as neat as this. Organisations also have what has become known as 'informal' structures which are not designed by management but are the outcome of friendship and interest groupings as well as those which serve political purposes, sometimes not related to the organisation's goals. These issues are not ignored in this chapter but arise mainly in relation to the topics associated with the other chapters in this Part of the book.

THE DIMENSIONS OF STRUCTURE

Organisation structure can vary along a number of dimensions. An early, but influential, piece of research by Pugh, Hickson, Hinings and Turner (1969) identified the following six primary dimensions of organisation structure:

- *Specialisation* – the number of different specialist roles in an organisation and their distribution.
- *Standardisation* – the number of regularly occurring procedures which are supported by bureaucratic procedures of invariable rules and processes.
- *Formalisation* – the number of written rules, procedures, instructions and communications.
- *Centralisation* – where authority lies in the hierarchy to make decisions that have an impact for the whole organisation.
- *Configuration* – the width and the height of the role structure, i.e. the 'shape' of the organisation, how many layers there are and the number of people who, typically, report to any one person.
- *Traditionalism* – how many procedures are 'understood' rather than having to be written down, how commonly accepted is the notion of 'the way things are done around this organisation'.

As a result of the research done to confirm these dimensions, Pugh *et al.* established four underlying dimensions which they described as:

- *Structuring of activities* – the extent to which there is formal regulation of employee behaviour through the processes of specialisation, standardisation and formalisation.
- *Concentration of authority* – the extent to which decision-making is centralised at the top of the organisation or at some other headquarters.
- *Line control of workflow* – the extent to which control of the work is exercised directly by line management rather than through more impersonal procedures.
- *Support component* – the relative size of the administrative and other non-workflow personnel performing activities auxiliary to the main workflow.

In another large study, Child (1988), found general confirmation of the dimensions established by Pugh *et al.*, and made some additions of his own. These were:

- the way sections, departments, divisions and other units are grouped together;
- systems for communication, the integration of effort and participation; and
- systems for motivating employees, for instance, performance appraisal and reward.

It is clear from the above that structure, applied to organisations, is a multi-dimensional concept and the assumption is that organisations can be structured in many different ways according to where they might be placed on any of the dimensions mentioned. Thus, in theory, there could be a limitless number of different combinations of these variables. However, most people would agree that some categorising of organisation structures is possible. What is more, there is some evidence to show that some types of structures are more appropriate to some types of organisational situations than others. This is discussed later in the chapter. First, it is necessary to understand the broad range of structures that are possible.

MODELS OF STRUCTURE

Bureaucratic structure

One of the best known forms or organisation structure is the bureaucratic form. Morgan (1989) states that the term bureaucracy was coined in the eighteenth century by the French economist Vincent de Gournay. However, it was the German sociologist, Max Weber, in the early twentieth century, who defined and expanded its meaning and indeed maintained that it was the only effective way to organise work. An account of Henderson and Parsons' (1947) translation of Weber's writing on 'Legitimate Authority and Bureaucracy' can be found in Pugh (1990). This identifies three ideas which are central to the concept of bureaucracy. These are:

- the idea of rational legal authority;
- the idea of 'office';
- the idea of 'impersonal order'.

There are a number of fundamental elements to these ideas. These are:

- a continuous organisation of official functions bound by rules;
- a specified sphere of competence, i.e. differentiation of function;
- the organisation of offices (i.e. positions) follows the principle of hierarchy;
- the separation of members of the administrative staff from ownership of production or administration;
- no appropriation of his/her official position by the incumbent;
- administrative acts, decisions and rules are formulated and recorded in writing, even in cases where oral discussion is the rule or is even mandatory.

Illustration 3.1 summarises the characteristics of the pure form of bureaucratic structure.

The endurance of the bureaucratic form of organisation structure is evident in many organisations. Indeed, Simon (1960) argues that hierarchy is the natural order of things. For example, he points to biological systems which are composed of sub-systems such as the digestive and circulatory sub-systems which in turn are composed of sub-sub-systems of tissues and the tissues are composed of cells. Weber was convinced of the case for the prevalence and endurance of the bureaucratic form. For instance, he says (Pugh, 1990, p. 12):

Illustration 3.1

BUREAUCRACY

Weber specified several characteristics of his ideal organization structure. The four major ones are the following:

- *Specialisation and division of labour.* Work is finely divided between well defined and highly specialised jobs or roles.
- *Hierarchical arrangement of positions.* Roles are hierarchically arranged with a single chain of command from the top of the organisation to the bottom.
- *A system of impersonal rules.* The incumbents of roles (or positions) carry out their duties impersonally in accordance with clearly defined rules.
- *Impersonal relationships.* Co-ordination of activities relies heavily on the use of rules, procedures and written records, and on the decision of the lowest common superior to the people concerned.

   Other characteristics of a bureaucracy identified by Weber are: the selection of officials solely on the basis of technical qualifications; appointment not election; remuneration by fixed salaries with a right to pensions; only under certain conditions can the employing authority terminate an employment; the employee can leave at any time; a system of promotion according to seniority or achievement or both.

Source: Based on Weber, M. (1947), *The Theory of Social and Economic Organisation*, Free Press, translated and edited by Henderson, A. M., and Parsons, T. in Pugh, D. (1990), *Organization Theory Selected Readings*, Penguin. (German original published in 1924.)

It would be sheer illusion to think for a moment that continuous administrative work can be carried out in any field except by the means of officials working in offices. . . . For bureaucratic administration is, other things being equal, always, from a formal, technical point of view, the most rational type. For the needs of mass administration today, it is completely indispensable.

Illustration 3.2 is a brief description of a construction company called the Beautiful Buildings Company (known as the BB Company. The organisation chart illustrates its current bureaucratic structure. The BB Company will be used in later parts of the chapter to illustrate other types of organisational structures, when it will be seen that Weber's commitment to the bureaucratic form is not shared by everyone.

   Clearly, structuring on bureaucratic principles according to Weber implies high specialisation, standardisation, formalisation and centralisation (*see* the reference to Pugh *et al.* above). However, a knowledge of the principles on which Weber proposed the bureaucratic form does not help in determining the number of levels for any particular organisation or how many people should report to any one manager. In other words it does not help in determining how 'tall' or 'flat' the structure should be and how 'wide' or 'narrow' the span of control should be at each level of the hierarchy.

Illustration 3.2
THE BEAUTIFUL BUILDINGS COMPANY . . .

The Beautiful Buildings Company (known as the BB Company) is a construction company involved in the design and building of a variety of different types of building.

For instance, it prides itself on having won contracts to build a new civic hall in one of the world's leading cities. It is known for its imaginative designs and the construction of a range of factory and other industrial type buildings. Just over 12 months ago, it took over a smaller building company specialising in home building for middle to higher income families. It would like to develop further into the area of commercial office buildings.

During the past 20 years, the company has grown from operating solely in the UK to securing contracts in Australia and North America, and has footholds in a number of mainland European countries.

The BB Company is headed by Gillian Lambeth, the daughter of the previous owner. There are a number of directors reporting to Gillian who are each in charge of one of the company's main functions. Marcos Davidson, the marketing director, has been the person most involved in promoting the company's activities outside the UK.

Currently the company is structured on typical bureaucratic lines as shown in the simplified chart opposite.

ACTIVITY 3.2

If you are currently working in an organisation, draw an organisation chart for it. Otherwise, draw one for an organisation with which you are familiar.

After you have produced your own chart, try to obtain any official chart or description of the organisation.

Compare your version with the official version.

How much of a match is there between either of these versions and the BB Company's bureaucratic structure?

How do you think managers (or whoever designed the structure) decided upon the number of levels in the organisation, or the number of people reporting to each manager? Was the basis for the groupings of activities similar to that of the BB Company? If not, on what basis are jobs grouped?

How 'large' is each job in terms of the range of tasks which it involves?

How much autonomy do people in general have? Is most of the decision-making done by top management?

Tall and flat bureaucracies

Figures 3.1 to 3.3 illustrate the difference between tall and flat structures. Figure 3.2 is of interest in demonstrating how widening the span of control (the number of people reporting to any one superior) reduces the number of levels in the structure, while retaining all the staff. Figure 3.3, on the other hand, shows how flattening the structure through doubling the span of control can 'save' 780 managers, that is 57 per cent of the number of management positions while retaining the number of lower level positions. Knowing this, however, does not reveal how many levels an organisation should have (how vertically differentiated it should be) or what the span of control (horizontal differentiation) should be at each level.

Figure 3.1

Flat and tall hierarchical structures

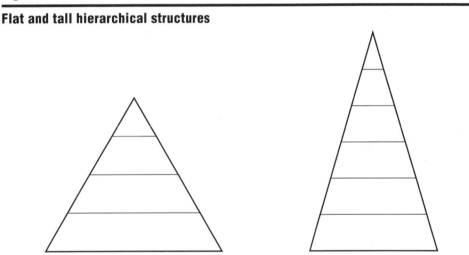

Source: Mullins, L. J. (1996), *Management and Organisational Behaviour*, 4th edn. (London, Pitman Publishing, p. 349).

One rule of thumb is, that the more similar are the jobs to be done by individuals at any one level (the standardisation of jobs), the more people a manager can co-ordinate and control. Managing many people doing very different kinds of jobs occupies a manager's attention far more than when all are doing the same. Butler (1991) says that as task ambiguity increases (the extent to which the task is ill-defined) there is an increase in the number of problems which a manager has to solve, and these add to managerial overload. Another rule of thumb is that, the more decentralised is the decision-making and, therefore, the fewer decisions which have to be made by the manager (and it is difficult to tell this from simply looking at an organisation chart), the broader the span of control. Where most decisions have to be made by managers, then the larger the number being managed (the greater the span of control) the more overloaded is the manager. Mullins (1996) mentions other factors which affect the span of control such as the physical location or geographical spread

Figure 3.2

Flattening the structure but retaining the people

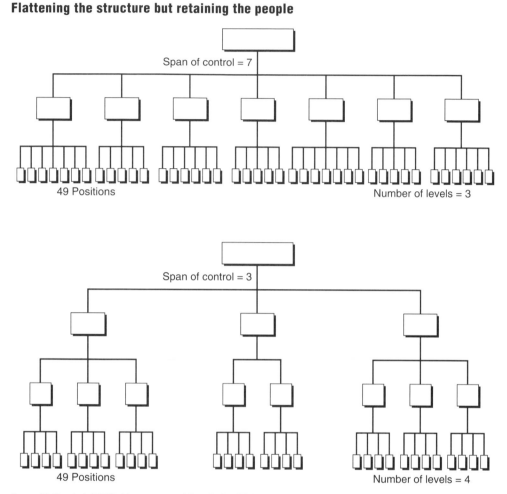

Span of control = 7

49 Positions

Number of levels = 3

Span of control = 3

49 Positions

Number of levels = 4

Source: Mullins, L. J. (1996), *Management and Organisational Behaviour*, 4th edn. (London, Pitman Publishing, p. 348).

of subordinates, the abilities of subordinate staff and the ability and personal qualities of the manager concerned.

With regard to the number of levels in the structure of the organisation (often referred to as the 'scalar chain' or 'chain of command'), Drucker (1989) suggests that these should be as few as possible. Too many levels bring difficulties in understanding of objectives and communicating both up and down the hierarchy. The current desire in many organisations for flatter structures follows this principle. However, a more precise method of calculating the number of levels for an organisation has been devised by Jaques (1990). He claimed to have identified time-span boundaries which can be drawn around an individual's role.

Figure 3.2

Flattening the structure to 'save' people

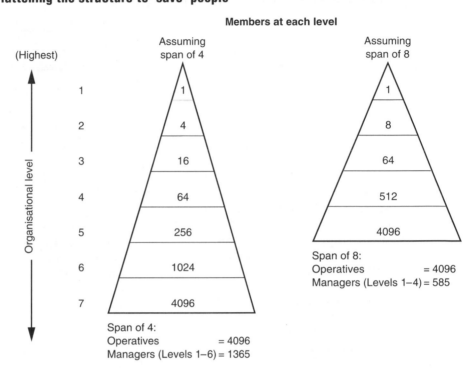

Source: Robbins, S. P. (1996), *Organizational Behavior*, 7th edn. (Englewood Cliffs, NJ, Prentice-Hall, p. 556).

Jaques used the term 'the time-span of discretion' to refer to the target completion time of the most complex tasks which make up any job role. He makes clear that this target completion time is not always made explicit, but is inevitably always there – otherwise the carrying out of the task could not be planned. For example, someone labouring on one of the BB Company's building sites will see (or others will see) the results of his or her work in a very short time from carrying it out. For instance, the results of mixing concrete (a typical task for a building labourer), well or otherwise, will show within a few hours, and certainly within days. On the other hand, the results of the work that Gillian Lambeth, head of the BB Company, does – such as devising strategy for the next five years or formulating policy regarding moves into additional areas – will not show up as successful or otherwise for many years. Thus, Gillian Lambeth might have a time-span of discretion of five years or more while the labourer will have a time-span of discretion of no more than the time it takes to check whether the concrete mix is right or not.

Illustration 3.3 shows how different time-spans are mapped to different levels (stratum in Jaques' terms) in the organisational hierarchy. Of note is the geometric progression of the time-span differences compared to the arithmetic progression of

Illustration 3.3

ELLIOT JAQUES AND THE TIME-SPAN OF DISCRETION

This regularity – and it has so far appeared constantly in over 100 studies – points to the existence of a structure underlying bureaucratic organisation, a sub-structure in depth, composed of managerial strata with consistent boundaries measured in time-span as illustrated.

The data suggest that this apparently general depth-structure of bureaucratic stratification is universally applicable, and that it gives a formula for the design of bureaucratic organisation. The formula is easily applied. Measure the level of work in time-span of any role, managerial or not, and that time-span will give the stratum in which that role should be placed. For example, if the time-span is 18 months, that makes it a Str-3 role; or 9 months, a Str-2 role.

If the role is a managerial role, not only can the stratum of the role be ascertained, but also how many strata of organisation there should requisitely be, including shop- or office-floor Str-1 roles if any. Measure the level of work in time-span of the top role of the bureaucratic hierarchy – say, chief executive of the hierarchy, or departmental head of a department within the hierarchy – and that time-span will give the stratum in which the role will fall, and therefore the number of organisational strata required below that

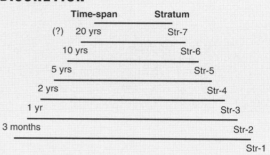

Time-span	Stratum
(?) 20 yrs	Str-7
10 yrs	Str-6
5 yrs	Str-5
2 yrs	Str-4
1 yr	Str-3
3 months	Str-2
	Str-1

(*Note*: Later work by Jaques and Clement (1994) give an additional stratum level 8, of 50 years time-span.)

role. For example, if the role has a time-span of 3 years, it makes the bureaucracy a Str-4 institution, and calls for four levels of work organisation including the top role and the shop- or office-floor if the work roles go down to that level. If the bottom work role, however, is above the 3-month time-span – say, for example, 6 months, as may be the case in some types of professional institution – then the institution will require only three levels of work organization, namely, Str-4, an intermediate Str-3, and the bottom professional Str-2.

Source: Jaques, E. (1990), 'The stratified depth-structure of bureaucracy', in Pugh, D. S., *Organization Theory* (Harmondsworth, Penguin, pp. 23–4).

Note: The chapter by Jaques from which this is taken and which is reproduced in Pugh (1990) comes from Jaques, E. (1976), *A General Theory of Bureaucracy* (Oxford, Heinemann).

the bureaucratic levels, a pattern which Jaques says became observable after very many investigations of his theory. He claims this progression has its basis in the operation of a fundamental psychological process. If this is the case, it suggests a certain 'naturalness' in the way the time-span theory operates. Jaques' theory is, however, of more than academic interest. He claims it can be used in a practical sense to design the number of levels for any organisation. The latter part of Illustration 3.3 gives the details of how this can be done.

The way in which an organisation is configured, that is, the 'shape' of the organisation in terms of its height and width, is one consideration for those who are charged with designing its structure. However, different organisations choose different ways of defining 'specialisation' of tasks. Thus, the division of tasks horizontally across the organisation can be done in a number of different ways.

Horizontal differentiation – the departmentalisation of work

The decision on which way to departmentalise frequently relies on the characteristics of the work to be done, the size of the organisation, the physical location(s) of its activities and the need to maintain a balance between high-level strategic decision-making and lower-level operational imperatives. Some people argue for departmentalisation by function, others argue for departmentalisation by product, or customer or geographical location. Each method of structuring has its advantages and disadvantages.

Departmentalisation by function

This is one of the most frequently found ways of structuring, particularly in the stages of an organisation's development when the early entrepreneurial phase is giving way to a more settled phase of sustained growth guided by able and directive leaders, the phase Greiner (1972) calls the 'Growth through direction' phase (see Figure 2.4 in Chapter 2).

Some frequently found functions are: finance, production (whether goods or services), marketing/sales, personnel/human resource management. Some types of organisations such as hospitals will have medical services, housekeeping and ancillary services as well as finance and perhaps research and development. Depending on the culture of the hospital, customer care might be important. Retailers will have buying and selling departments, customer care and finance. Any of these types of organisation could also have personnel or human resource management departments which might include training and health and safety. The organisation chart of the BB Company in Illustration 3.2 is a simplified example of a functional structure – only the operations department is developed below level 3.

Associated with departmentalisation by function is the degree of specialisation of departments. The example of the operations function of the BB Company shows it splitting up into separate projects, each managed by a different Project Manager. Each project includes sections dealing with work scheduling, site management, and plant and materials procurement. All the different specialist building crafts (joinery, bricklaying, roofing, electrical works, heating/plumbing, etc.) are found at the lower levels of the hierarchy.

A functional structure serves organisations well as they move from what Greiner (1972) termed the 'growth by creativity' stage in a company's development to the 'growth by direction' stage (see Figure 2.6 in Chapter 2). However, as they grow and diversify in customer and product markets, they pass through what Greiner calls a 'crisis of autonomy'. This is characterised by demands for greater autonomy on the part of lower-level managers who frequently possess greater knowledge about markets and operations than do top management. Situations likely to arise are those in which each different class of product experiences a different level of turbulence in its environment. This may, therefore, signal that the time has come to departmentalise by product rather than by function.

> **Illustration 3.4**
> # ADVANTAGES AND DISADVANTAGES OF FUNCTIONAL STRUCTURES
>
> **Advantages**
> Departmentalisation by function has advantages in its logical mirroring of the basic functions of business. Each function has its high-level representative to guard its interests. Tight control is possible at the top. It encourages the development of specialist skills and expertise and provides a career structure within the function. Training can be organised relatively easily along specialist lines. In organisations where technical skill gives competitive advantage, the functional structure can enhance this.
>
> **Disadvantages**
> The advantages of a functional structure to small and medium-sized organisations become disadvantages as organisations grow and diversify products or services, or locate in geographically distant places. There can be delays as one function waits for another to complete its work and co-ordination of activities across functions can be difficult. Functionalism sometimes encourages narrowness of viewpoint and works against the development of innovation which requires co-operation from a number of sources. Functional structures limit the opportunity for the development of general managers.

Departmentalisation by product or service

It is not difficult to imagine the problems that the BB Company might have given a functional structure. Its current and hoped-for activities cross at least four product areas (public buildings, industrial buildings, houses/homes, office and other commercial-type accommodation). Each of these product areas is governed by different sets of customer expectations, research and design problems and building regulations. Each is prey to different political, economic, technological and socio-cultural influences.

Departmentalising by product might then be a sensible move for the BB Company. Figure 3.4 shows a product-based structural grouping for the BB Company.

Figure 3.4

The BB Company – departmentalisation by product

> ## Illustration 3.5
> ## ADVANTAGES AND DISADVANTAGES OF DEPARTMENTALISATION BY PRODUCT
>
> **Advantages**
>
> Departmentalisation by product or service has advantages of maximising the use of employees' skills and specialised knowledge. Staff are able to specialise more than with a strict functional structure. For instance, building designers may specialise in factory design or design for homes. Sales people in particular can concentrate on developing expertise in just one range of products. Product differentiation facilitates the use of specialised capital (money and equipment). Product divisions can be made cost centres, and maybe profit centres, in their own right thus making them responsible for budgets and sales. Differentiation by product makes it easier to concentrate on different classes of customer, particularly when different products coincide with different customer groupings. Where a product division has its own set of business functions, these can be co-ordinated towards the product's markets. Finally, this type of structure offers good opportunities for the training of general managers.
>
> **Disadvantages**
>
> There can be overlap of functions from one product division to another, that is, duplication of central service and other staff activities. Overall administration costs tend to be higher than in pure functional structures. Where business functions are not wholly devolved, product-based divisions are 'top sliced' to provide resources for more centralised functions. This can be felt by product line managers as overburdensome overheads which detract from their overall profits. Top management may have more difficulty in controlling what happens at the product divisional level. Co-ordinating policy and practice across product areas can be complex.

For the BB Company, the division of work into groupings based on its four main categories of building projects enables staff with expertise in a particular area to share it with others working on the same products. The people working in each department have collective responsibility for the business processes and cycles of activity for that department's products. Departmentalisation by product or service becomes more effective as an organisation grows and begins to diversify its activities into a number of differentiated product/service areas. As might be expected, there are disadvantages as well as advantages in structuring on a product/service basis as Illustration 3.5 shows.

It is obvious from looking at the BB Company's product-based structure that, once a pure functional structure has been rejected, functionalism still has a place. This will be either in centralised functions before product departmentalisation takes place, or within product/service divisions. Whatever the structure base, functionalism has its place.

Departmentalisation by location

The description of the BB Company indicates that its operations span more than one country. The company might, therefore, be advised to structure on the basis of its being located in different geographical places (*see* Figure 3.5).

Figure 3.5

The BB Company structured on a geographical basis

Departmentalisation by location is common where organisations operate over a wide geographical area, whether this involves a number of different countries, areas within the same country or very widespread sites. It is attractive to large organisations whose activities are physically dispersed. Thus, managers may be put in charge of geographical regions, each of which is further differentiated on a functional or product/service basis. Although not shown in Figure 3.5, further differentiation of product or function could occur at the next level down. On the other hand, some territorial differentiation might occur within other structure types. For example, in hotels, housekeeping staff may be allocated to particular floors and bar staff to particular bars. Some government organisations (e.g. the postal service), which operate on a national basis, structure themselves geographically. This enables them to offer a similar service across the nation but, where necessary, modify this service to suit more localised geographical requirements. Illustration 3.6 identifies the advantages for this form of structure but also its disadvantages.

An overall advantage of differentiation by any means other than purely by function is that it offers the opportunity for variations in structure to occur in different parts of the organisation. For instance, a geographically based structure can be differentiated on the basis of product, or indeed customer, at other levels. Similarly, a product-based structure could incorporate aspects of differentiation by geography and/or customer.

A summary of the discussion in this chapter to date is that, despite Weber's arguments for the strict functionally based, bureaucratic form, there are many complex and different ways of structuring organisations, each of which has its advantages and disadvantages. However, the examples of the BB Company have all shown a similar adherence to the principles of hierarchy and a single chain of

Illustration 3.6

ADVANTAGES AND DISADVANTAGES OF DEPARTMENTALISATION BY GEOGRAPHIC AREA OR TERRITORY

Advantages

Departmentalisation by geographic area/territory offers the advantage of being close to conditions in a division's locality and can clearly offer the opportunity to co-ordinate activities in a region. The employment of locally based staff means that travelling time is reduced. Local staff are more likely to know the conditions prevailing in a region. The establishment of manufacturing or service operations in the region reduces transportation costs. In some cases, labour costs may be lower in one region than another and it may, therefore, be advantageous for organisations to set up a division in that region. Structures based on geography provide good training grounds for general managers.

Disadvantages

The more geographically differentiated the structure, the more the requirement for management and administration. For example, with a head office in Belgium and regional divisions in Hong Kong and San Francisco, it would be difficult to give personnel services wholly from the centre. Each location would need to develop its own personnel functions. This duplication of services can be costly. Control from top management can be a problem, particularly where headquarters is very far from some regions. In some regions, it may be difficult to recruit the skills required. This may be for reasons of culture or that the local population has not had the level of general education deemed sufficient for the purposes of the work they would have to do.

command. This goes against the view of Morgan (1989) who maintains that most bureaucratically structured organisations are being reshaped in response to the changing demands and challenges of the world around them. He says some of these changes are marginal but others are more radical and result in significant transformations in organisational form. This category of new organisational form can be loosely termed a *network* structure of which the matrix or grid organisation is a forerunner.

Matrix organisation

The essence of a matrix structure is that a set of departments or divisions is superimposed, horizontally, across a traditional hierarchically organised structure. Thus the structure is (normally) functionally designed in terms of its vertical axis, but designed on some other principle (product, customer, region) in terms of its horizontal axis. There are, therefore, two chains of command, one vertical and one horizontal, which operate at the same time.

Figure 3.6 shows a hypothetical matrix structure for an advertising agency. In this case, the heads of marketing, finance, personnel, research and development form the vertical lines of reporting while the different customer bases represent the divisions which operate horizontally across the structure.

Figure 3.6

Matrix structure for an advertising agency

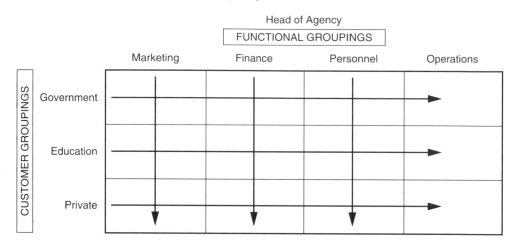

According to Greiner (1972), organisations move to a matrix form of structure through a 'crisis of red tape' brought about as they mature in the 'cooordination' phase of the organisational life-cycle. Thus, staff begin to resist the control systems which centralised managers impose on decentralised product/customer or geographical groupings. He says this is particularly the case as organisations become too large and complex to be managed through formal programmes and bureaucratic paper systems. A move to a matrix structure emphasises interpersonal collaboration in an attempt to overcome the red-tape crisis.

Drawing on Davis and Lawrence's (1977) work, Bartol and Martin (1994) maintain that organisations which ultimately adopt a matrix structure usually go through four identifiable stages. These are:

Stage 1 is a *traditional structure*, usually a functional structure, which follows the unity-of-command principle.

Stage 2 is a *temporary overlay*, in which managerial integrator positions are created to take charge of particular projects (e.g. project managers), oversee product launches (e.g. product managers), or handle some other issue of finite duration that involves co-ordination across functional departments. These managers often lead or work with temporary inter-departmental teams created to address the issue.

Stage 3 is a *permanent overlay* in which the managerial integrators operate on a permanent basis (e.g. a brand manager coordinates issues related to a brand on an ongoing basis), often through permanent interdepartmental teams.

Stage 4 is a *mature matrix*, in which matrix bosses have *equal* power. (Bartol and Martin, 1994, pp. 321–2.)

Matrix structures rely heavily on teamwork for their success, with managers needing high-level behavioural and people-management skills. The focus is on solving

> **Illustration 3.7**
> ## ADVANTAGES AND DISADVANTAGES OF MATRIX STRUCTURES
>
> **Advantages**
> With a matrix organisational design, decisions can be decentralised to the functional and divisional/project-level managers. This facilitates speed of operation and decision-making. There is increased flexibility in being able to form and re-form cross-functional teams according to business priorities. These teams can monitor their own localised business environments and move quickly to adapt to changes in them. Staff belonging to particular functional departments have the opportunity of working with staff from other functional departments, yet maintain their alliance and information-sharing with their own professional grouping. Through allocating functional staff to one or more projects on a permanent or semi-permanent basis, loyalties to the projects are built. Matrix structures allow for flexible use of human resources and the efficient use of support systems.
>
> **Disadvantages**
> Matrix structures are complex and, because they add a layer of project managers, can be administratively expensive. There can be confusion over who is ultimately responsible for staff and project outcomes, particularly if things go wrong. The dual arrangement and need for enhanced communications between the 'arms' of the matrix can increase the potential for conflict, particularly between the functional and project managers. Staff may have to juggle their time between different projects or divisions and project managers may make competing demands on staff who work across more than one team. The emphasis on group decision-making could increase the time to respond to change.

problems through team action. In a mature matrix structure, team members are managed simultaneously by two different managers – one is their functional line manager and the other the team or project leader. This type of organisational arrangement, therefore, requires a culture of co-operation, with supporting training programmes to help staff develop their teamworking and conflict-resolution skills.

Illustration 3.7 summarises the advantages and disadvantages of matrix structures.

ACTIVITY 3.3

Koontz and Weihrich (1990) say that matrix-type organisations occur frequently in construction, aerospace, marketing and management consulting firms in which professionals work together on a project.

Figure 3.6 shows a matrix structure for an advertising agency which is an example of the last of the instances mentioned above. The BB Company, as a building construction company, is an example of the first of Koontz and Weihrich's examples.

Using any general knowledge you may have of the building industry to embellish the description of the BB Company, design a matrix structure for the way the organisation, as a whole, might operate. Then design a matrix structure for a division or department which dealt only with the building of homes.

Compare your results with those of anyone else who can be persuaded to do this. Argue the pros and cons for any differences.

Wilson and Rosenfeld (1991) say it is usually not worth investing in a matrix structure unless the tasks to be performed are complex, unpredictable and highly interdependent. While many organisations continue to operate in stable predictable environments, many others are required to innovate in the face of environmental turbulence. The matrix form of organisation will help in this objective. However, some organisations have gone beyond a matrix structure to devise structures which Morgan (1989) calls 'loosely coupled networks', but which can be (more generally) called 'network organisations' (Snow, Miles and Coleman, 1992).

Network organisations

The process through which organisations go as they reshape themselves from being rigidly structured bureaucracies to what might be termed 'loosely coupled or organic networks' has been set out by Morgan (1989). Figure 3.7 is a pictorial representation of the transition from the rigid bureaucracy to the loosely coupled organic network.

The discussion above has already set out the characteristics of models 1 to 4 in Figure 3.7, that is, the three bureaucratic types and the matrix organisation. Of interest here is what Morgan calls the 'project organisation' and the 'loosely-coupled organic network'.

According to Morgan, the project organisation carries out most of its activities through project teams. Although there are, notionally, still functional departments, they are there only to play a supporting role. The main work of the organisation is done wholly through the work of teams which rely for their success on being 'dynamic, innovative, powerful and exciting' and to which senior management tries to give free rein within what has been defined as the strategic direction of the organisation. Morgan summarises the nature of the project organisation in the following way.

> The organisation is much more like a network of interaction than a bureaucratic structure. The teams are powerful, exciting, and dynamic entities. Co-ordination is informal. There is frequent cross-fertilisation of ideas, and a regular exchange of information, especially between team leaders and the senior management group. Much effort is devoted to creating shared appreciations and understandings of the nature and identity of the organisation and its mission, but always within a context that encourages a learning-oriented approach. The organisation is constantly trying to find and create the new initiatives, ideas, systems, and processes that will contribute to its success. (Morgan, 1989, p. 67.)

The project organisation has overlapping characteristics with what Mintzberg (1983, p. 262) calls 'The Adhocracy'. The adhocracy, as its name suggests, is an *ad hoc* group of people (mainly professionals) who are brought together for a single purpose associated with a particular project. The team may be together for a few months or, in rarer cases, for several years. Once the project is complete or moves into a different stage of its life, the team will disband. An example is that of a group of professionals coming together to make a film. Adhocracies are characterised by having few formal rules and regulations or standardised routines – in terms of the dimensions of structure advanced by Pugh *et al.* (1969), they are low on

Figure 3.7

From bureaucracies to matrix, project and network organisations

Model 1: The Rigid Bureaucracy

Model 2: The Bureaucracy with a
senior 'management' team

Model 3: The Bureaucracy with Project Teams
and Task Forces

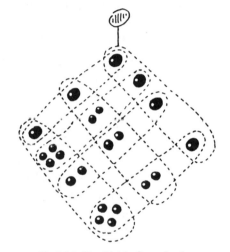

Model 4: The Matrix Organization

Model 5: The Project Organization

Model 6: The Loosely-coupled
Organic Network

Source: Morgan, G. (1989), *Creative Organization Theory. A Resource Book* (London, Sage, p. 66). Copyright 1989 by Sage.
Reprinted by permission of Sage Publications, Inc.

standardisation and formalisation. The shape of the organisation is flat, but with horizontal differentiation generally high because adhocracies are staffed mainly by professionals each with his/her own specialism.

The project organisation usually employs its own staff. The adhocracy may also do this but may additionally have staff who, for the time the adhocracy exists, work on a contract basis. This contrasts with Morgan's (1989) description of the loosely coupled organic network. In terms of a continuum of organisational forms, this type of network organisation might be said to be at the end furthest from the rigid bureaucracy. The loosely coupled organic network describes a form of structure which, rather than employing large numbers of people directly, operates in a subcontracting mode. The small number of permanent staff set the strategic direction and provide the necessary operational support to sustain the network. However, while project teams and adhocracies have limited lives, the loosely coupled network can be a permanent structure. Figure 3.8 depicts three types of network.

Internal networks

According to Snow *et al.* (1992, p. 11), the internal network 'typically arises to capture entrepreneurial and market benefits without having the company engage in much outsourcing'. Hinterhuber and Levin (1994), on the other hand, depict internal networks as collections of profit centres or semi-independent strategic business units.

Internal networks are typical of situations where an organisation owns most or all of the assets associated with its business. However, it has usually created 'businesses within the business' which, although still owned by the organisation as a whole, operate independently in terms of the discipline of the market. The argument is that, if they are subject to market forces, they will constantly seek innovations that improve performance. What is interesting is that these quasi-independent units are encouraged to sell their output to buyers outside the organisation to which they belong.

A typical example would be the training and development unit which, on the one hand, 'sells' its services to its parent organisation and, on the other hand, seeks to sell its services to other organisations. The internal network is not dissimilar to Morgan's description of a project organisation.

Vertical networks

A second network type is the vertical network (Hinterhuber and Levin, 1994). This is typical of the situation where the assets are owned by several firms, but are dedicated to a particular business. This is similar to what Snow *et al.* call a 'stable' network which consists of 'A set of vendors . . . nestled around a large "core" firm, either providing inputs to the firm or distributing its outputs'. (Snow *et al.*, 1992, p. 13). Thus, the core organisation spreads asset ownership and risk across a number of other independent organisations and, additionally, gains the benefits of dependability of supply and/or distribution. The distributors can be franchisees. Toyota in Japan could be perceived as the core firm within a stable network of organisations. Clegg (1990), referring to Cusamano (1985), notes that Toyota has some 220 primary subcontractors of which 80 per cent had plants within the production complex

Figure 3.8

Common types of network

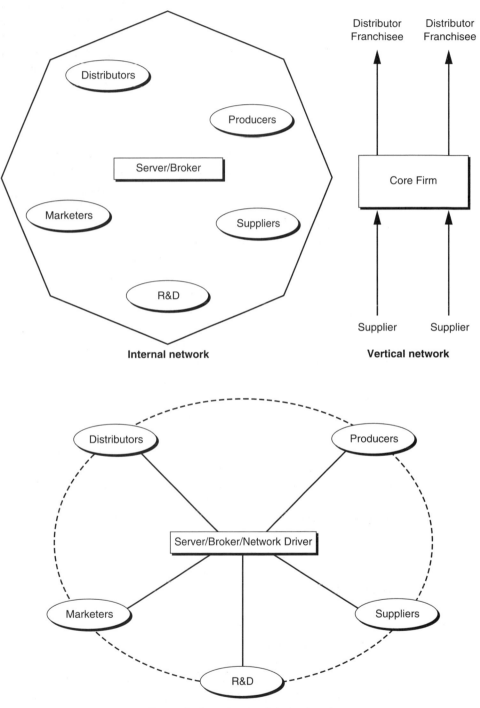

Internal network

Vertical network

Dynamic, loosely completed network

surrounding Toyota in Toyota City. Handy's (1989, p. 110) description of what he terms the 'federal organisation' is reminiscent of the Toyota example. He says:

> [Federalism] allows individuals to work in organisation villages with the advantages of big city facilities. Organisational cities no longer work unless they are broken down into villages. In their big city mode they cannot cope with the variety needed in their products, their processes, and their people. On the other hand, the villages on their own have not the resources nor the imagination to grow. Some villages, of course, will be content to survive happy in their niche, but global markets need global products and large confederations to make them or do them.

Dynamic, loosely coupled networks

For Snow *et al.* (1992), the dynamic network organisation is the one which has 'pushed the network form to the apparent limit of its capabilities' (p. 14). This form operates with a lead firm (sometimes called the 'server', 'broker' or 'network driver') which identifies and assembles assets which are owned by other companies. The lead firm may, itself, provide a core skill such as manufacturing or design. However, in some cases the lead firm may merely act as broker. The dynamic network is probably the form which is nearest to Morgan's loosely coupled organic network.

Illustration 3.8 describes 'TFW Images', a communications and image design organisation where the lead firm provides the core skill of design and 'brokers' other activities such as photography and illustration, printing, translations into other languages, and marketing.

If TFW Images also chose to outsource the design and writing process and the invoicing of clients and collection of payments, it would be as far along the network continuum as is apparently possible.

However, whether dynamic networks operate in a partial or pure broker capacity, they are unlikely to function effectively without good and effective communications between their 'parts'. This is what is likely to distinguish dynamic or loosely-coupled organic networks from the more 'in-house' internal and stable networks. For instance, TFW Images could not operate without fast and effective information technology links to the other organisations with which it associates. The power of the computer allied to telecommunication links enables TFW Images' design team to send its output anywhere in the world to be modified or added to by other writers and illustrators, to be marketed appropriately and, where appropriate, printed or manufactured to the specification for the finished product. Except for its relatively permanent status, the company might be likened to what some are now calling the 'virtual organisation', particularly given its current situation of joining together in partnership with Omni-Graphics.

The virtual organisation

The concept of the virtual organisation can be allied to that of the network organisation. The virtual organisation (Davidow and Malone, 1992, referred to in Luthans, 1995) comes from the idea of 'virtual memory' rather than 'virtual reality' – virtual memory being a way of making a computer's memory capacity appear greater

Illustration 3.8
TFW IMAGES

TFW Images was formed in 1989 by two ex-employees of IBM who became the Managing Director and Creative Director of the company. They were very soon joined by a Sales Director with experience from a range of companies, mainly manufacturing. The main business of TFW Images is communications in its widest sense. Examples of its activities are: designing corporate brochures which might include annual reports as well as advertising material, designing and organising conferences and all the material that goes with them, and creating company logos and other symbols of corporate identity.

TFW Images' main client was, and still is, IBM. In fact, the rise of the company coincided with the large-scale changes which IBM went through as it refocused its efforts away from the mainframe computer market towards that of the personal computer market. As technology began to replace people, TFW Images was able to take advantage of the willingness of companies like IBM to outsource some of their design requirements.

From a high point of employing, directly, 17 people (two of whom were in Paris), TFW Images now has seven direct employees. Of the original three directors, one remains, the Creative Director, although he does not currently carry a particular title.

In a volatile market – there are other competitors and the fortunes of IBM are less certain nowadays – one reason for the company's success is its ability to maintain a flexible structure which can be tailored to the demands of the market. Essentially, TFW Images is an organisation which 'brokers' services from other organisations to bring its products to the market. Thus, rather than employing printers, photographers, illustrators, market researchers and additional writers and designers directly, it closely associates with other companies and independent consultants who offer these services. The use of sophisticated computer systems facilitates the transfer of the part-finished products from one part of the network to another, wherever it might be in the world.

Most recently, TFW Images has joined in partnership with Omni-Graphics, a well-established design company operating mainly in the publishing and arts spheres of activity. Examples of Omni-Graphics' activities are: the design of calendars, brochures for and layout of art galleries, and the design of news magazines.

Given the equality of skills and size of the two organisations, the benefits of the partnership will come from their complementary activities (TFW Images is business oriented while Omni-Graphics is arts oriented) and the financial advantages which will flow from this. The management of the two partner organisations will remain separate and both will keep their own names. Thus, to any client, nothing will have changed. Yet, conceptually and financially, a new overarching organisation has been 'virtually' created.

Source: Author.

than it is. Simply put, 'the virtual organisation is a temporary network of companies that come together quickly to exploit fast-changing opportunities. Different from traditional mergers and acquisitions, the partners in the virtual organisation share costs, skills, and access to international markets. Each partner contributes to the virtual organisation what it is best at' (Luthans, 1995, p. 487). Illustration 3.9 summarises the key attributes of the virtual organisation.

It seems clear from Illustration 3.9 that network (particularly dynamic network) and virtual organisations are suited to organisational environments which are themselves dynamic. The emphasis in these forms of organisation is on horizontal rather than vertical structuring and the concept of partnership rather than command and control. However, organisations structured on these principles have implications

---

Illustration 3.9
KEY ATTRIBUTES OF THE VIRTUAL ORGANISATION

- *Technology.* Informational networks will help far-flung companies and entrepreneurs link up and work together from start to finish. The partnerships will be based on electronic contracts to keep the lawyers away and speed the linkups.
- *Opportunism.* Partnerships will be less permanent, less formal, and more opportunistic. Companies will band together to meet all specific market opportunities and, more often than not, fall apart once the need evaporates.
- *No borders.* This new organisational model redefines the traditional boundaries of the company. More co-operation among competitors, suppliers, and customers makes it harder to determine where one company ends and another begins.
- *Trust.* These relationships make companies far more reliant on each other and require far more trust than ever before. They'll share a sense of 'co-destiny', meaning that the fate of each partner is dependent on the other.
- *Excellence.* Because each partner brings its 'core competencies' to the effort, it may be possible to create a 'best-of-everything' organisation. Every function and process could be world-class – something that no single company could achieve.

Source: 'The Virtual Corporation', *Business Week*, 8 February 1993, pp. 98–102.

---

for employment and the reward expectations of employees, whether full-time, part-time, contract or in other kinds of relationships with the organisation. Network and virtual organisations are only able to offer stable secure employment to a few, from whom they expect commitment and loyalty. The idea of the ultra-flexible firm is attractive for the owners and core staff, but can bring a sense of being used to those who are employed on a short-term contract basis, particularly if these people are employed in temporary, perhaps part-time, less skilled, lower paid jobs. Lack of commitment may not be restricted to the lower paid. More highly paid consultants and contractors will give service as long as it suits them, but may desert as soon as something more attractive comes along.

Luthans (1995) uses the term 'horizontal organisations' to cover the more recent matrix and network type of organisational design. He maintains that, in these organisations, teams are used to manage everything, with team performance, rather than individual performance, being rewarded. Yet, teamworking does not always come naturally to people; they frequently require training for this form of working. The emphasis on empowerment and more democratic ways of working, which comes with these 'modern organisation designs' (Luthans, 1995, p. 458), does not happen without planned human resource development. What is more, the move away from classical ways of organising may not suit every organisational situation. The main issue for organisations is not whether one form of structure is any *better* than another. It is whether the structure currently adopted is one which is able to facilitate the achievement of the organisation's purpose and respond to the need for organisational change in the particular environmental circumstances prevailing for particular organisations.

CHOOSING AN ORGANISATIONAL STRUCTURE

Choosing how to structure is not straightforward for any management. The way an organisation is structured is closely linked to many factors as Figure 3.9 shows.

As shown in Figure 3.9, one of the most important links is the relationship between organisational strategy and organisational structure – as an organisation changes its strategy to respond to political, economic, technological or socio-cultural changes in its external environment, so should its structure change to maintain the strategy–structure relationship. However, apart from technological advances from outside the organisation, which may force changes in production methods or in the way that services are delivered, the organisation's own use of technology, particularly information technology, will affect the way in which it is structured. The discussion above shows also how organisational structure is likely to change as organisational size increases.

What is less tangible is the role that organisational culture and politics have on decisions to structure one way rather than another. That is why, in Figure 3.9, these two factors are shown as mediating variables rather than as direct influences. There is nothing set, however, in the way all these variables should be regarded. Figure 3.9 is offered as a helpful descriptive device for summarising the factors which influence organisational forms rather than as a tried and tested model of how they work in practice. Even so, there is a body of literature which is of help in deciding which organisational structure is most appropriate to which set of circumstances. Before moving to this, it is salutary to stop and think why 'good' or appropriate organisational structure is so important to the efficient and effective operation of organisations.

Figure 3.9

The determinants of organisational structure

The consequences of deficient organisational structures

An example of the consequences, for the organisational functioning of a deficient organisational structure, is a list produced by Child (1988) (*see* Illustration 3.10). What is interesting about this list is that some of the main 'dysfunctions' listed (e.g. 'Motivation and morale may be depressed') could be regarded as having little to do with structure. Yet, as the other points make clear, structural deficiencies could very well be major contributing causes.

A well-structured organisation (i.e. one which is functioning effectively and efficiently) can be compared to a healthy human being. For instance, a healthy human being will have a fully functioning brain which controls what the body does; the nervous system carries messages from the brain to all parts of the body. The body, in turn, has a skeletal structure which, if damaged to will severely hamper its movements and the ability to respond to the brain's messages. Without the skeleton the body will collapse. Blood is needed to feed the brain and other parts of the body. Muscles help strengthen the skeleton and the whole body in order to help it operate more efficiently. Thus, all components are required to ensure a fully operating, effective organism. However, the skeletal structure is that part of the person which supports the rest. It is not sufficient to ensure effective functioning of the person, but it is a necessary pre-condition upon which the other parts depend.

In such a way does an organisation work. The analogy here is that the brain is the organisation's strategy, the skeleton the structure, the blood supply the financial resources, the nervous system and the muscles, the people and the technology and information systems. So, however intelligent the *strategic* 'brain', and developed the nervous system and the muscles (the people, technology and information systems) without an appropriate structure – the 'skeleton' – to provide the basic support, the organisation will, at the least wobble, and possibly collapse. Conversely, without a strategy (a brain) to direct it, the structure (the skeleton) will become misaligned to its purpose. The first contingency factor to be considered is, therefore, the relationship between strategy and structure.

The strategy–structure 'fit'

As always when considering concepts associated with the behaviour of people, there is rarely one accepted and clear definition. According to Burnes (1996) this is also true of any attempt to define strategy and strategic management. It is not the purpose here to rehearse all the arguments for one definition against another. For the purpose of this discussion, the definition given by Johnson and Scholes (1993, p. 10) will suffice for a start. They say:

> Strategy is the *direction* and *scope* of an organisation over the *long term*: ideally, which matches its *resources* to its changing *environment*, and in particular its *markets*, *customers* or *clients* so as to meet *stakeholder* expectations.

Illustration 3.10
CONSEQUENCES OF STRUCTURAL DEFICIENCIES

There are a number of problems which so often mark the struggling organisation and which even at the best of times are dangers that have to be looked for. Child suggests the following list which he says structural deficiencies will exacerbate.

1. *Motivation and morale may be depressed because*:
   (a) Decisions appear to be inconsistent and arbitrary in the absence of standardised rules.
   (b) People perceive that they have little responsibility, opportunity for achievement and recognition of their worth because there is insufficient delegation of decision-making. This may be connected with narrow spans of control.
   (c) There is a lack of clarity as to what is expected of people and how their performance is assessed. This could be due to inadequate job definition.
   (d) People are subject to competing pressures from different parts of the organisation due to absence of clearly defined priorities, decision rules or work programmes.
   (e) People are overloaded because their support systems are not adequate. Supervisors, for instance, have to leave the job to chase up materials, parts and tools as there is no adequate system for communicating forthcoming requirements to stores and tool room.

2. *Decision-making may be delayed and lacking in quality because*:
   (a) Necessary information is not transmitted on time to the appropriate people. This may be due to an over-extended hierarchy.
   (b) Decision-makers are too segmented into separate units and there is inadequate provision to co-ordinate them.
   (c) Decision-makers are overloaded due to insufficient delegation on their part.
   (d) There are no adequate procedures for evaluating the results of similar decisions made in the past.

3. *There may be conflict and a lack of co-ordination because*:
   (a) There are conflicting goals which have not been structured into a single set of objectives and priorities. People are acting at cross-purposes. They may, for example, be put under pressure to follow departmental priorities at the expense of product or project goals.
   (b) People are working out of step with each other because they are not brought together into teams or because mechanisms for liaison have not been laid down.
   (c) The people who are actually carrying out operational work and who are in touch with changing contingencies are not permitted to participate in the planning of the work. There is therefore a breakdown between planning and operations.

4. *An organisation may not respond innovatively to changing circumstances because*:
   (a) It has not established specialised jobs concerned with forecasting and scanning the environment.
   (b) There is a failure to ensure that innovation and planning of change are mainstream activities backed up by top management through appropriate procedures to provide them with adequate priority, programming and resources.
   (c) There is inadequate co-ordination between the part of an organisation identifying changing market needs and the research area working on possible technological solutions.

5. *Costs may be rising rapidly, particularly in the administrative area, because*:
   (a) The organisation has a long hierarchy with a high ratio of 'chiefs' to 'Indians'.
   (b) There is an excess of procedure and paperwork distracting people's attention away from productive work and requiring additional staff personnel to administer.
   (c) Some or all of the other organisation problems are present.

Source: Reprinted with permission from: Child, J. (1988), *Organizations: A guide to problems and practice*, 2nd edn. Copyright 1988 Paul Chapman Publishing Ltd., London.

The term stakeholder is taken to represent anyone who has an interest in the organisation which is affected by the policies and practices of that organisation. This includes not only shareholders, suppliers, financiers and customers – that is, interested parties outside the organisation – but also employees.

To accompany this definition, Johnson and Scholes list seven characteristics which they say are associated with the words 'strategy' and 'strategic decisions'. Essentially this list elaborates the notion that strategy and strategic decisions encompass all the organisation's activities; that they are concerned with the organisation's internal and external environments; that they are influenced by the values and beliefs of those who have power in the organisation; and that they affect the long-term direction of the organisation.

Mintzberg, Quinn and James (1988), in asking the question, 'Is strategy a process or the outcome of a process?' draw attention to the issue of whether strategy should be regarded as being amenable to rational planning or whether it is the emergent result of a social and political process. Mintzberg's (1994) own view is that effective strategies are a mixture of both deliberate and emergent strategies. It is clear that, sometimes, strategy can be thought about and planned prior to the process of its implementation. The organisational changes that follow will be incremental or more radical, depending on the nature of the process of implementing the strategy. Such changes most frequently involve changes in the organisation's structure, because it is the structure that must provide the framework within which the strategic process must operate to achieve the organisation's objectives. According to Robbins (1993) structure should follow strategy, a statement which confirms Miles and Snow's (1984a, p. 10) statement that

> it is becoming increasingly evident that a simple though profound core concept is at the heart of many organisation and management research findings as well as many of the proposed remedies for industrial and organisational renewal. The concept is that of *fit* among an organisation's strategy, structure, and management processes.

The implications of this are that different types of strategy can be identified and consideration given to the most appropriate structure for each type. A number of scholars and researchers have discussed this proposition. The first to be considered is Chandler (1962).

Chandler's strategy–structure thesis

Chandler's strategy–structure thesis has been summarised by Miles and Snow (1984b). This summary shows that Chandler developed his thesis from an extensive study of nearly one hundred large United States companies, whose history he traced from around the mid-1800s. What Chandler found was that owner-managed companies were predominant during the 1800s. These organisations usually started simply with a single product line and a structure where the owner-manager took all of the major decisions as well as attempting to monitor the activities of the employees. Miles and Snow refer to this type of organisation as having an 'agency' structure, given that key subordinates would act as agents of the owner-manager to ensure his/her wishes. The term agent was used to imply that these subordinates did not occupy specialised functional roles as might be found in today's organisations.

As companies grew, they became more complex and were then more likely to employ professional managers who began the process of dividing the organisation into different functional areas. The appearance of the functional organisation (around the turn of the century) enabled some growth to occur, particularly through acquiring suppliers, to ensure guaranteed inputs, and through market penetration. The strategy of these organisations was to supply a limited number of standardised products, with the aim of supplying a national rather than a purely regional market. The structure of these functional organisations provided the means of standardised production on a high-volume basis to a limited number of markets. This structure proved cost effective and delivered profits accordingly. The disadvantages of this type of structure were first that it did not allow ease of movement into new products and markets, and second, it produced specialists rather than generalists, with few managers able to look at the overall picture of the company activities and its prospects. In Miles and Snow's (1984b, p. 40) words, 'each succeeding product or market innovation became increasingly difficult to administer within the confines of the specialised functional structure. It was against this backdrop – the desire to diversify thwarted by administrative complexity – that the search for another organisational form began'.

This new form turned out to be the divisional structure, which, according to Chandler, appeared simultaneously in four pioneering firms during the 1920s and 1930s: General Motors, Du Pont, Standard Oil of New Jersey, and Sears, Roebuck. The divisional structure could take the form of departmentalisation by product or region. However, whatever the basis of this move to horizontal differentiation, each division was most likely to become its own cost and profit centre, which was seen as essential if control was to be maintained and growth encouraged. What is more, each division would be able to develop its own strategy in line with its products, markets and (if organised into geographical divisions) its cultural environment. These different strategies might well produce their own types of structure.

According to Miles and Snow (1984b), during the 1960s and 1970s two competing strategies were pushing companies into a new form of structure. These strategies were first, the pressure for functionally structured organisations to improve their capacity for product development – which sometimes resulted in project groupings being added to the basic structure. The second strategy was the pressure for organisations structured into product-differentiated divisions to take advantage of cost savings by centralising some functions such as manufacturing which would, for instance, allow economies of scale. These two apparently competing strategies came together in the form of the organisation which has been discussed above as the matrix form. Table 3.1 illustrates the evolution of these organisational forms, together with their associated mechanisms and means of control. It includes the dynamic network structure already described and which, at the time of writing (1984) and in the later paper by Snow *et al.* (1992), was held to be the structure for the year 2000 onwards.

Table 3.1
Evolution of organisation forms

	Product/market strategy	*Organisation structure*	*Core activating and control mechanisms*
1800	Single product or service. Local/regional markets.	Agency	Personal direction and control.
1850	Limited, standardised product or service line. Regional/national markets.	Functional	Central plan and budgets.
1900	Diversified, changing product or service line. National/international markets.	Divisional	Corporate policies and division profit centres.
1950	Standard and innovative products or services. Stable and changing markets.	Matrix	Temporary teams and lateral allocation devices such as internal markets, joint planning systems etc.
2000	Product or service design. Global, changing markets.	Dynamic network	Broker-assembled temporary structures with shared information systems as basis for trust and co-ordination.

Source: Based on Miles, R. E., and Snow, C. C. (1984a), 'Fit, failure and the hall of fame', *California Management Review*, Vol. 26, No. 3, pp. 10–28.

Levels of strategy

Burnes (1996) distinguishes between corporate level strategy and business level strategy. At the corporate level, he says, strategy deals with the 'game plan' for managing diversified enterprises. He suggests strategy at this level concerns itself with the following questions:

● What is the mission of the organisation?
● How should the business portfolio be managed?
● Which existing businesses should be disposed of and which new ones acquired?
● What priority and role should be given to each of the businesses in the current portfolio? (p. 154.)

He quotes Thompson and Strickland (1983) as saying that the central strategic concerns at the business level are:

● How should the firm position itself to compete in distinct, identifiable and strategically relevant markets?
● Which types of products should it offer to which groups of customers?
● How should the firm structure and manage the internal aspects of the business in support of its chosen competitive approach? (p. 154.)

The set of questions for the corporate level seem to assume a large divisionalised organisation while the questions for the business level could well refer to any size of business. It is these questions which are most closely linked to the organisation's structure. According to Porter (1980) there are three basic business-level strategies. These are:

- Cost leadership, which aims to maintain lower costs than those of competitors, while maintaining quality of product. High-volume sales are required for this strategy to succeed, as well as the associated economies of scale supporting the low-cost focus.
- Product differentiation, which aims to achieve industry-wide recognition of products and services which are different from those of direct competitors through quality or design or, perhaps, the type of customer service associated with them. Sometimes, customers are prepared to accept higher prices if there is perceived added value.
- Specialisation by focus, when organisations concentrate on a limited number of markets, products and geographical areas in which to compete. This could well approximate what is known as niche marketing.

There is a certain association between Porter's three strategy types and the first three of Chandler's different product-market strategies as illustrated in Table 3.1. However, in contrast to Porter's assertion that it is not possible to pursue, successfully, more than one strategy at a time, Chandler's typology suggests that, in the matrix form of organisation, this is possible.

Miles and Snow's strategic types

Miles and Snow (1984b) have developed a categorisation of business strategies which can also be likened to Chandler's typology, as Miles and Snow themselves discuss. Illustration 3.11 describes Miles and Snow's three basic types of strategic behaviour, together with a fourth strategy which is really not a strategy at all in that organisations described as 'reactors' might be said to have no clear strategy of their own.

Miles and Snow liken their strategy types to Chandler's historical discussion of strategy and structure, saying that today's organisations are the products of their ancestors. For instance, they associate *Defenders* with the organisations which were typical of the period before the 1920s, that is, those with limited product/service lines, functional structures and centralised planning and control systems focused on cost efficiency.

Prospectors are likened to the divisionalised organisations of the 1920s and 1930s which proliferated in the 1950s. They seek to develop diversified products and structure themselves into product groups organised into decentralised operating divisions. *Analysers* are said to have the characteristics of the most recent of Chandler's organisation forms. Thus, small Analysers 'are alert to diversification opportunities but tend to limit their expansion activities to those that can be handled by the present production technology and organisation structure (typically functional)' (Miles and Snow, 1984b, p. 41). Of large Analysers, Miles and Snow (*ibid.*) say:

Illustration 3.11

MILES AND SNOW'S TYPOLOGY OF STRATEGIC BEHAVIOUR

On the basis of their research and observations of many hundreds of companies in a wide range of industries, Miles and Snow claim to have identified four types of strategic behaviour with associated organisational characteristics. The types are as follows:

- *Defenders* have narrow and relatively stable product-market domains. As a result of this, they seldom need to make major adjustments in their technology, structure or methods of operation. They focus on improving the efficiency of their existing operations. Defenders' characteristics include a limited product line; single, capital-intensive technology; a functional structure; and skills in production efficiency, process engineering and cost control.

- *Prospectors* continually search for product and market opportunities and regularly experiment with potential responses to emerging environmental trends. They are often the creators of change and uncertainty to which their competitors must respond. Because of this, they are usually not completely efficient. Prospectors' characteristics include a diverse product line; multiple technologies; a product or geographically divisionalised structure;

and skills in product research and development, market research and development engineering.

- *Analysers* operate in two types of product-market domains – one relatively stable, the other changing. In their stable areas, these organisations operate routinely and efficiently through use of formalised structures and processes. In their more innovative areas, key managers watch their competitors closely for new ideas, and then they rapidly adopt those that appear to be the most promising. Analysers' characteristics include a limited basic product line; search for a small number of related product and/or market opportunities; cost-efficient technology for stable products and project technologies for new products; mixed (frequently matrix) structure; and skills in production efficiency, process engineering and marketing.

- *Reactors* are those organisations in which strategy–environment inconsistency exists, or in which strategy, structure, and process are poorly aligned. There is some evidence that, in highly regulated industries, Reactors perform less well than the other three types.

Source: Based on Miles, R. E., and Snow, C. C. (1984b), 'Designing strategic human resource systems', *Organisational Dynamics*, Vol. 13, Part 8, pp. 37–8.

Larger Analysers create semiautonomous divisions to handle major diversification efforts but tend to do so only when those products and markets are viewed as relatively stable and manageable. Typically, large Analyzers use matrix structures to handle market and product innovations until these can be incorporated into the established production system.

Mintzberg's forces and forms

A more recent paper by Mintzberg (1991) offers the concepts 'forces' and 'forms' which can be loosely translated as strategy and structure, although Mintzberg, himself, uses these latter terms sparingly. However, his descriptions of the forces which drive organisations to adopt particular forms are similar to the strategies which Chandler, and Miles and Snow, identify. Figure 3.10 illustrates the seven forces, each of which is associated with a particular form.

The seven forces which drive the organisation can be described briefly as follows:

- The force for *direction*, which can be likened to having a 'strategic vision'. This gives a sense of where the organisation must go as an integrated entity.

- The force for *efficiency*, which balances the costs and benefits – the lower the ratio of costs to benefits the higher the efficiency. The force for efficiency tends to

encourage standardisation and formalisation, focusing on rationalisat
restructuring for economy.

- The force for *proficiency*, that is for carrying out tasks with high level
knowledge and skills.
- The force for *concentration*, which means the opportunity for particular units to
concentrate their efforts on serving particular markets. This is necessary in
organisations that are diversified in structure.
- The force for *innovation*, which encourages the search for new products or services
or for different ways of delivering them. The force for innovation encourages
adaptation and learning.
- The forces for *co operation* and *competition* are the forces which Mintzberg calls
'catalytic'. Co-operation describes the pulling together of ideology, that is, the
culture of norms, beliefs and values that 'knit a disparate set of people into a

Figure 3.10

A system of forces and forms in organisations

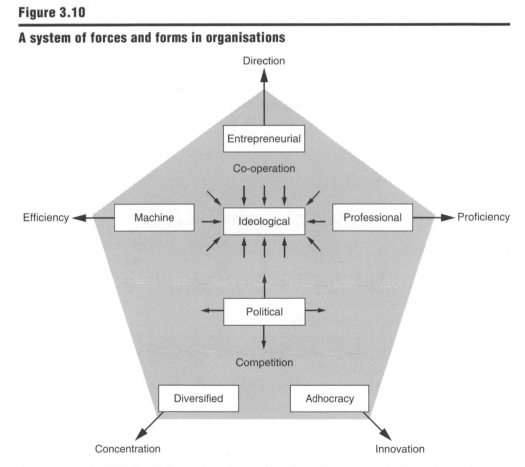

Source: Mintzberg, H. (1991), 'The effective organization forces and forms', *Sloan Management Review*, Winter 1991, Vol. 32, Part 2, p. 55.

...ious, cooperative entity' (Mintzberg, 1991, p. 55). Competition describes ...ng apart of politics in the sense of politics as the non-legitimate, technically ...oned organisational behaviour.

...es the term 'configuration' to describe the situation when any one of ...rives an organisation to its corresponding form – as evidenced by the ...xed areas in Figure 3.10 and which are described in Illustration 3.12.

According to Mintzberg, the *entrepreneurial* form tends to dominate when the forces for direction are paramount. This tends to be in start-up and turn-around situations and in small, owner-managed organisations. The *machine* form tends to appear when the forces for efficiency become paramount, for instance, in situations of mass production and mass service organisations. Mintzberg gives examples of hospitals, accounting practices and engineering offices to illustrate the *professional* form of organisation which results from the force for proficiency. The drive here is for perfecting existing skills and knowledge rather than inventing new ones. This is different from the force for innovation which pushes organisations into an *adhocracy* form, which is characterised by independent project teams with fluid structures. Finally, the *diversified* form arises as a result of the force for an organisation to concentrate on more than one distinct product or market. Each division will have a different structure and enjoy considerable autonomy from the small central headquarters.

Mintzberg calls the fit between the forces and forms that organisations take 'configuration'. To quote: 'My basic point about configuration is simple: when the form fits, the organisation may be well advised to wear it, at least for a time' (Mintzberg, 1991, p. 58). This argument supports those of Chandler and Miles and

---

Illustration 3.12
MINTZBERG'S ORGANISATIONAL FORMS

- *Entrepreneurial form* – tends to be low in formalisation and standardisation, but high in centralisation with authority located in a single person.
- *Machine form* – high formalisation and standardisation, centralised authority vested in rules and regulations, functional departments.
- *Professional form* – high in complexity and formalisation, but low in centralisation; allows the employment of trained specialist staff for the core work of the organisation.
- *The adhocracy form* – very low in standardisation and formalisation, little hierarchy, much use of project teams which may well be temporary.
- *Diversified form* – a combination of functions and products, with products dominating; they can be of matrix form or organised as divisions on the basis of products/markets.

These five forms are based on descriptions given by Mintzberg in his 1979 and 1983 books. In his 1991 paper, on which much of this section is based, he added the *ideological* and *political* forms, giving as examples the Israeli kibbutz and a conflictual regulatory agency respectively. However, he says these two forms are not common and restricts his discussion to the five forms described above.

Snow that organisational structure should align itself with organisational strategy. The implications of this are that, as an organisation's strategy changes, so must its structure if tensions, contradictions and, eventually, crises are not to ensue. However, strategy is not the only factor upon which structure is contingent.

Other contingency factors

Size

One of the outcomes of the large research projects carried out by Pugh and his associates (1969), which have already been mentioned above, was that size of organisation (measured by numbers employed) is positively correlated with overall role-specialisation and formalisation (measured by the amount of paperwork procedures and usage). However, as Pugh (1973) points out, there are organisations whose size suggests particular structural configurations, but which confound the predictions. Even so, he suggests that the degree of constraint on organisational form imposed by variables such as size and technology is substantial, possibly accounting for some 50 per cent of the variability.

The work of Pugh and his associates does not have much to say about the relationship between organisational size, structure *and* economic performance. However, Child (1988) did carry out a study of the effects of size on organisational performance. His findings were that, for large organisations, the more bureaucratically structured they were, the better they performed. Smaller organisations performed better if they were less bureaucratically structured. The significant size appeared to be around 2000 employees. Thus, in organisations below this size, performance is assumed to be better in those which have little formal structure whereas in organisations with more than 2000 employees the association between more bureaucracy and superior performance was greater.

Both Pugh's and Child's research was done some time ago and might be assumed to precede the prevalence of the more 'modern' types of structure such as the matrix or the network. Thus the use of number of employees as a measure of size might not be as useful a measure for organisations with either of these types of structure. In highly divisionalised organisations, the size of the divisions is more likely to influence structure than is the size of the organisation as a whole. In network structures, it is perhaps not size in its relation to structure which is significant in determining performance, but the type of relationship existing between core and other parts of the network and between permanent and temporary or contract staff.

The discussion above of different types of structure certainly suggests that the trends identified in Illustration 3.13 are believable.

> **Illustration 3.13**
> ## SUMMARY OF TRENDS IDENTIFIED BY STUDIES OF EFFECTS OF SIZE ON STRUCTURE
>
> 1. As organisations grow, they are likely to add more departments and levels, making their structures increasingly complex. With functional structures such growth creates pressure for a change to some type of divisional structure.
> 2. Growing organisations tend to take on an increasing number of staff positions in order to help top management cope with the expanding size. This tendency levels off when a critical mass of staff has been achieved, but it helps lead to the following trend.
> 3. Additional rules and regulations seem to accompany organisational growth. While such guidelines can be useful in achieving vertical co-ordination, the unchecked proliferation of additional rules and regulations may lead to excessive formalisation and lower efficiency.
> 4. As organisations grow larger, they tend to become more decentralised. This is probably due in part to the additional rules and regulations that set guidelines for decision-making at lower levels.
>
> *Source*: Bartol, K. M., and Martin, D. C. (1994), *Management* Maidenhead, McGraw-Hill, p. 328).

Technology

Two major studies are usually referred to in any discussion of the relationship of technology to organisational structure. These are, first, the work of Woodward (1965) and second the work of Perrow (1967).

Woodward studied 100 manufacturing firms in the south-east of England to investigate the relationship between organisational performance and elements of organisational structure such as unity of command and span of control. The companies were divided into three categories according to their methods of production, that is, the type of technology used. These were: unit or small batch production; large batch and mass production; and process production.

Woodward found that there was a definite relationship between the types of technology used and aspects of organisational structure – in particular, the number of levels of management authority and the span of control of first line supervisors. In addition, she concluded that the effectiveness of organisations was related to the 'fit' between technology and structure. In her words, 'not only was the system of production an important variable in the determination of organisational structure, but also that one particular form of organisation was most appropriate to each system of production'. (p. 69). For instance, firms falling within the large batch/mass production category were more likely to be successful if they had adopted a more mechanistic type of structure (e.g. similar to Mintzberg's machine form). Firms falling into either of the other two categories were more likely to be successful if they adopted a more organic structure (e.g. more flexible, decentralised with low standardisation and formalisation).

A criticism of Woodward's study is that it was done using only manufacturing organisations and, therefore, defined technology in a particular kind of way. The work of Perrow (1967), therefore, defined technology in a more general way which was more concerned with knowledge technology (that is, with both the ends and the means of achieving an output) than production technology. He suggested that technology could be viewed as a combination of two variables. The first of these he called 'task variability' and the second 'problem analyzability'. Thus, a task which is highly routine would be low in task variability and vice versa, in other words variability refers to the number of exceptional or unpredictable cases which have to be dealt with. Problem analysability refers to the extent to which problems are clearly defined and can be solved by using recognised routines and procedures, in other words, whether a task is clearly defined or whether it is ambiguous in terms of the task itself and how it might be completed. Where task completion requires innovative thinking, it is likely to be low on problem analysability.

Perrow used these two dimensions to construct a two-by-two matrix which provided a continuum of technology ranging from the routine to the non-routine as shown in Figure 3.11. The cells in the matrix represent four types of technology: routine, engineering, craft and non-routine.

In line with Woodward, Perrow argued that each type of technology would produce the best organisational performance if linked to an appropriate structure. Consequently, technologies such as are described in cell 1 are most likely to fit well with mechanistic structures. Cell 2 technologies require mechanistic structures but with aspects of organic organisational forms. It is proposed that cell 4 technologies link most closely to much 'looser' organic structures (perhaps of the matrix, project or network type) while cell 3 technologies require mainly organic structures with aspects of mechanistic bureaucracies.

Butler (1991, p. 100) says that, 'In complex organisations technologies cannot be operated by individuals acting singly', which leads to his discussion of Thompson's

Figure 3.11

Perrow's technology classification

	Few exceptions	Many exceptions
Problems can be analysed	**Routine** Mechanised production of standard products, e.g. mass produced cars. 1	**Engineering** Made-to-order products, e.g. houses, fashionable restaurant meals. 2
Problems cannot be analysed	**Craft** Deal with relatively difficult problems but with limited set of exceptions, e.g. repair tasks. 3	**Non-routine** The most difficult of problems, e.g. aerospace operations, psychiatric care. 4

Source: Based on summaries by Robbins (1993) and Mullins (1996).

Illustration 3.14

TECHNOLOGICAL INTERDEPENDENCE

Pooled interdependence

This is the lowest degree of interdependence, which occurs when units operate independently but their individual efforts are still significant for the overall success of the organisation. There is no flow of products or services between the different units, but they are all dependent on a central headquarters for resources and are responsible to it for outputs. Thompson calls this form of interdependence a *mediating technology*. An example would be a bank which mediates resources between lenders and borrowers.

Sequential interdependence

This involves a higher degree of interdependence between units in that one unit must complete its work before another takes over. Sequential interdependence is typified by the traditional assembly line type of production. Thompson called this type of technological interdependence *long-linked technology*.

Reciprocal interdependence

This is the most complex situation, with the highest degree of interdependence amongt units. For example, one unit's inputs to another are reciprocated by that unit's outputs becoming inputs to the first unit. This is further complicated where a network of units operate in this way. Examples might be the work of a hospital in looking after patients, or a university in educating students. Thompson called this form of technological interdependence *intensive technology*.

(1967) identification of an additional dimension of technology: interdependence. According to Butler, interdependence applies to the way that work activities flow from one unit, group or department to another. Thompson suggests three types of technological interdependence: pooled, sequential and reciprocal (*see* Illustration 3.14).

It is not difficult to speculate on the different organisational structures which would support one form of technological interdependence rather than another. Butler (1991) uses the concept of decision-making capacity to differentiate between those situations where the capacity for decision-making would need to be large and others where it would need to be small. Situations where mediating technology prevailed would be examples of the former and those of intensive technology examples of the latter. Long-linked technology would require something in between. Thus, intensive technologies are likely to require more horizontal linkages throughout the organisation, with mediating and long-linked technologies requiring more vertical integration.

From the above discussion, in particular of the work of Woodward, Perrow and Thompson, it appears that there is a link between organisation structure and technology, and the hypothesis that organisational structure is contingent upon type of technology predominating in organisations is upheld. Robbins (1993) summarises the evidence for this. He divides the evidence up in terms of its relationship to different aspects of structure. Thus, he finds that technologies involving more routine work are moderately associated with structures that are highly differentiated both horizontally and vertically and vice versa. As regards formalisation of processes and procedures, the more routine the technology the more formalised the structure. However, although routine technologies might be related to centralisation of decision-making, where highly developed formalised rules and regulations exist, decision-making might be devolved but in line with the requirements of the formalised documentation.

While Robbins' summary is useful, it tends to assume a single technology for a single organisation. Although this might be true, there are many cases where large organisations in particular have multiple technologies. Butler (1991, p. 110) asks the question: 'From an organisational design viewpoint what basis is there for deciding about the hierarchical priority to be given to particular units?' Drawing on Thompson's (1967) findings, he suggests that intensive technologies, as the most costly to operate, should first of all be identified and units organised around these. The implication is that these units would be structured into more organic forms than those based on mediating and long-linked technologies. However, where there are a number of units using intensive technologies, these, in turn, would need to be linked together through some form of sequential or pooled interdependence. Thus, for the multi-divisional organisation, there may be a variety of technologies and associated structures in the divisions, with each division linked to the central hub of the organisation through pooled interdependence. The consequences for management are complex but it is clear that, along with size, technology must take its place as one of the determinants of organisational structure. In addition, the fact that organisations operate in environments external to them means that these also will influence the form they take.

The external environment

The discussion in the previous section relating technology to structure has taken as uncontentious the distinction between technology as part of an organisation's operations, and technology as part of an organisation's environment which impacts upon the organisation together with other environmental elements. This section seeks to remedy that by discussing the way the external organisational environment can affect an organisation's structure.

The nature and components of any organisation's external environment have already been discussed in the previous chapters. The use of the PETS mnemonic drew attention to the political, economic, technological and socio-cultural components of the external environment. Ansoff and McDonnell's (1990) categorisation of levels of environmental turbulence was used to warn about the need for organisations to maintain a state of appropriate responsiveness to changes from one level to another (see Chapter 2). A conclusion from these discussions is that an organisation's structure will be affected by its external environment because of environmental uncertainty.

One of the best-known studies on the effects of the environment on organisational structure is that of Burns and Stalker (1961). In studying some twenty British industrial organisations, these researchers concluded that organisations had different structures depending on whether they operated in more stable environments which changed little over time or in more dynamic, changeable environments which were unpredictable in their instability. They claim to have identified two main types of structure – mechanistic structures which they maintain were more suited to the more stable unchanging environments and organic structures which were more suited to the unpredictable, more dynamic environments. Illustrations 3.15 and 3.16 describe these two structural types.

Illustration 3.15

MECHANISTIC STRUCTURES

A mechanistic management system is appropriate to stable conditions. It is characterized by:

(a) the specialized differentiation of functional tasks into which the problems and tasks facing the concern as a whole are broken down;

(b) the abstract nature of each individual task, which is pursued with techniques and purposes more or less distinct from those of the concern as a whole, i.e. the functionaries tend to pursue the technical improvement of means, rather than the accomplishment of the ends of the concern;

(c) the reconciliation, for each level in the hierarchy, of these distinct performances by the immediate superiors, who are also, in turn, responsible for seeing that each is relevant in his own special part of the main tasks.

(d) the precise definition of rights and obligations and technical methods attached to each functional role;

(e) the translation of rights and obligations and methods into the responsibilities of a functional position;

(f) hierarchic structure of control, authority and communication;

(g) a reinforcement of the hierarchic structure by the location of knowledge of actualities exclusively at the top of the hierarchy, where the final reconciliation of distinct tasks and assessment of relevance is made.

(h) a tendency for interaction between members of the concern to be vertical, i.e. between superior and subordinate;

(i) a tendency for operations and working behaviour to be governed by the instructions and decisions issued by superiors;

(j) insistence on loyalty to the concern and obedience to superiors as a condition of membership;

(k) a greater importance and prestige attaching to internal (local) than to general (cosmopolitan) knowledge, experience, and skill.

Source: Burns, T., and Stalker, G. M. (1961), 'Mechanistic and organic systems', in *The Management of Innovation* (London, Tavistock Publications, p. 120).

Lawrence and Lorsch (1967) went further than Burns and Stalker in suggesting that different departments within organisations face different environments and that, in successful organisations, each department would structure itself in line with its specific sub-environment. Thus in organisations operating in fairly stable environments, there would be less need for departments to be differentiated one from another. However, to ensure success, those organisations operating in highly uncertain environments would need to differentiate those departments most exposed to the environment (e.g. research and development) from those which were less exposed (e.g. production). In addition, where differentiation of departments was required, an organisation would need to ensure appropriate integrating mechanisms between departments to avoid the negative effects of different structures and operating procedures for different departments.

To test their hypotheses, Lawrence and Lorsch made a study of six organisations operating in the more turbulent environment of the plastics industry, two organisations operating in the moderately dynamic environment of the food industry, and two organisations operating in the stable environment of the container industry. Their findings confirmed their hypotheses. Those organisations operating in the most uncertain environments were most successful when highly departmentally differentiated. The most successful organisation operating in the stable environment of the container industry was the least differentiated in structure. The most successful organisation in the food industry was midway between the others in terms of differentiation. In addition, the successful organisations in all the industries were the ones which had a high degree of integration between departments.

Illustration 3.16

ORGANIC STRUCTURES

The organic form is appropriate to changing conditions, which give rise constantly to fresh problems and unforeseen requirements for action which cannot be broken down or distributed automatically arising from the functional roles defined within a hierarchic structure. It is characterized by:

(a) the contributive nature of special knowledge and experience to the common task of the concern;

(b) the 'realistic' nature of the individual task, which is seen as set by the total situation of the concern;

(c) the adjustment and continual re-definition of individual tasks through interaction with others;

(d) the shedding of 'responsibility' as a limited field of rights, obligations and methods. (Problems may not be posted upwards, downwards or sideways as being someone else's responsibility);

(e) the spread of commitment to the concern beyond any technical definition;

(f) a network structure of control, authority, and communication. The sanctions which apply to the individual's conduct in his working role derive more from presumed community of interest with the rest of the working organization in the survival and growth of the firm, and less from a contractual relationship between himself and a non-personal corporation, represented for him by an immediate superior;

(g) omniscience no longer imputed to the head of the concern; knowledge about the technical or commercial nature of the task may be located anywhere in the network; this location becoming an *ad hoc* centre of control authority and communication;

(h) a lateral rather than a vertical direction of communication through the organization, communication between people of different rank, also, resembling consultation rather than command;

(i) a content of communication which consists of information and advice rather than instructions and decisions;

(j) commitment to the concern's tasks and to the 'technological ethos' of material progress and expansion is more highly valued than loyalty and obedience;

(k) importance and prestige attach to affiliations and expertise valid in the industrial and technical and commercial milieux external to the firm.

Source: Burns, T., and Stalker, G. M. (1961), 'Mechanistic and organic systems', in *The Management of Innovation* (London, Tavistock Publications, p. 120).

Robbins (1993) concludes from this research that:

(a) organisations face multiple specific environments, each of which has a different degree of uncertainty;

(b) to be successful, organisations' departments or sub-units must meet the demands of their sub environments in terms of an environment–structure fit;

(c) the more differentiated an organisation, the greater the need to bridge the departmental divide through the setting up of appropriate integrating mechanisms.

Robbins suggests that environments can be characterised in terms of three key dimensions. The first is the *capacity* of the environment which refers to the degree to which it can support growth. The second is the degree of *stability* in the environment; stable environments are low in volatility whereas unstable environments are characterised by a high degree of unpredictable change. The third is environmental *complexity*, that is the degree of homogeneity or heterogeneity among environmental elements.

Given this three dimensional definition of environment, Robbins concludes that the scarcer the capacity, and the greater the degree of instability and complexity, the more organic a structure should be; the more abundant, stable, and simple the environment, the more mechanistic a structure should be.

ORGANISATIONAL STRUCTURE AND CHANGE

The discussion in this chapter has led to the conclusion that there are many influences on the way an organisation might structure for successful performance and to cope with change. What is apparent is that there is no one best way to design organisational structures nor any particular form which will guarantee successful performance. Depending on factors such as strategy, size, technology used and the degree of predictability of the environment, an organisation could well be successful and respond to the need for change whether it was structured along strict bureaucratic, mechanistic lines or as one of the newer network forms.

Care must be taken, however, not to assume that these contingency relationships are straightforward and that, provided the 'formula' is learned and applied, success will result. Robbins (1993, p. 528), drawing on the work of Child (1972) and Pugh (1973), states that: 'Strategy, size, technology and environment – even when combined – can at best explain only fifty percent of the variability in structure.' In addition, the idea that there is a one-way causal relationship between an organisation's environment and its structure is open to question. Organisations not only are influenced by their environments, but may, in turn, be able, themselves, to influence certain parts of their environments. For instance, the political environment can be influenced through lobbying, customers in the economic environment influenced through advertising and people's expectations of employment influenced by the way groups of organisations design jobs. The existence of monopoly conditions clearly helps organisations modify their environments. In times of high unemployment, the introduction of technology which significantly changes working practices will be easier.

If organisations are able, to some extent, to manipulate their environments to suit their strategies and structures, this will enable them to preserve existing structures and operational arrangements. The pressure to do this is evident from Mullins' (1996, p. 385) statement that: 'developing organisations cannot, without difficulty, change their formal structure at too frequent an interval. There must be a significant change in contingency factors before an organisation will respond.' This implies a considerable time-lag between situational change and changes in structure. Therefore, even if changes in strategy, size, technology and environmental factors do build forces for changes in organisational structure, there are other factors which may accelerate or, more likely, impede this process.

One of these factors is associated with the concept of 'strategic choice' (Child, 1972) and draws attention to the power of senior managers to choose which criteria they will use in assessing what organisational changes should take place. Managers who may lose power and/or position are unlikely to choose those alternatives which, from a logical-rational point of view, maximise the organisation's interest. Robbins (1993) summarises this view of structure as the 'power-control' explanation of organisational structure, that is, 'An organisation's structure is the result of a power struggle by internal constituencies who are seeking to further their interests' (Robbins, 1993, p. 528). Thus, given the discretion available to management, rather than changes in organisational structure being logically planned and implemented, what results will be a structure which 'emerges' to satisfy, not only the imperatives of the internal and external environments, but the personalities and power needs of dominant stakeholders.

Organisational politics and the issue of power balance are not the only factors influencing structural change in organisations. Nor does the mere process of changing an organisation's structure necessarily bring about permanent change in management strategy, style of operating and other employees' attitudes and behaviours. The pervasiveness of organisational and national cultures can be strong enough to work against change. Thus the mechanisms for managing any kind of organisational change must take account of what French and Bell (1990) call the informal, 'covert' aspects of organisational life such as people's values and feelings, the informal, as opposed to formal, groupings and the norms of behaviours which become part of any organisation but which are rarely 'spelt out'. Johnson (1990) puts emphasis on the role of symbols, rituals, stories and myths as being important parts of an organisation's culture. He says that organisational change cannot be brought about simply by changing strategy and structure. The organisational culture has a significant, and maybe dominant, role to play if anything more than incremental change is to happen.

Organisational structure can be likened to the skeleton of the organisation supporting the implementation of strategic decision-making and operational processes. This chapter has focused on issues associated with the strategy, size, technology, environment and structure 'fit'. Structural change is seen to be influenced by changes in these situational factors. A number of different organisational forms have been described and their appropriateness to different situations in which organisations find themselves, discussed. Of particular interest, in environments which push for organisational change, are the newer project and network forms of organisation. However, focusing on the formal aspects of organisational life can furnish only part of the explanation of why and how organisations choose to change and, if they do so, what form that change might take.

The next two chapters, therefore, extend this discussion further by addressing the more informal, 'covert' aspects of organisational life; that is, the prevailing values, attitudes and beliefs about what should be done and how – the culture which is part of, and surrounds, organisations – and the politics which are equally important in any examination of organisations and change.

DISCUSSION QUESTIONS AND ACTIVITIES

1 How realistic is Jaques' method for determining numbers of organisational levels – in terms of an organisation you know well?

2 In spite of the talk about network and virtual organisations, most organisations conform to more traditional structure types. Discuss.

3 Compare and contrast three types of organisational structures in terms of their capacity to cope with different change processes. Illustrate points made with examples from your own experience.

REFERENCES

Ansoff, I. H., and McDonnell, E. J. (1990), *Implanting Strategic Management*, Englewood Cliffs, NJ, Prentice-Hall.

Bartol, K. M., and Martin, D. C. (1994), *Management* (2nd edn.), Maidenhead, McGraw-Hill International.

Burnes, B. (1996), *Managing Change. A Strategic Approach to Organisational Dynamics*, London, Pitman.

Burns, T., and Stalker, G. M. (1961), *The Management of Innovation*, London, Tavistock.

Business Week (1993), 'The Virtual Corporation', *Business Week*, 8 February, pp. 98–102.

Butler, R. (1991), *Designing Organizations: a Decision Making Perspective*, London, Routledge.

Chandler, A. D., Jun. (1962), *Strategy and Structure: Chapters in the History of the Industrial Enterprise*, Cambridge, MA, MIT Press.

Child, J. (1972), 'Organization structure, environment and performance: the role of strategic choice', *Sociology*, January, pp. 1–22.

Child, J. (1988), *Organizations: A Guide to Problems and Practice* (2nd edn.), London, Paul Chapman.

Clegg, S. R. (1990), *Modern Organizations: Organisation Studies in the Postmodern World*, London, Sage.

Cusamano, M. (1985), *The Japanese Automobile Industry: Technology and Management at Nissan and Toyota*, Cambridge, MA., Harvard Industry Press.

Davidow, W. H., and Malone, M. S. (1992), *The Virtual Corporation*, New York, Harper Business.

Davis, S. M., and Lawrence, P. R. (1977), *Matrix*, Reading, MA, Addison-Wesley.

Drucker, P. F. (1989), *The Practice of Management*, Oxford, Heinemann Professional.

French, W. L., and Bell, C. H., Jun. (1990), *Organization Development. Behavioral Science Interventions for Organization Improvement* (4th edn.), Englewood Cliffs, NJ, Prentice-Hall.

Greiner, L. (1972), 'Evolution and revolution as organizations grow', *Harvard Business Review*, July–August.

Handy, C. B. (1989), *The Age of Unreason*, London, Business Books.

Hinterhuber, H. H., and Levin, B. M. (1994), 'Strategic networks – the organization of the future', *Long Range Planning*, Vol. 27, No. 3, pp. 43–53.

Jaques, E. (1990), 'The stratified depth-structure of bureaucracy', Chapter 2 in Pugh, D. S. (ed.), *Organization Theory*, London, Penguin.

Jaques, E., and Clement, S. D. (1994), *Executive Leadership*, Oxford, Blackwell.

Johnson, G. (1990), 'Managing strategic action; the role of symbolic action', *British Journal of Management*, Vol. 1, pp. 183–200.

Johnson, G., and Scholes, K. (1993), *Exploring Corporate Strategy. Texts and Cases*, (3rd edn.), Hemel Hempstead, Prentice-Hall.

Koontz, H., and Weihrich, H. (eds.) (1990), *Essentials of Management*, New York, McGraw-Hill, pp. 155–72.

Lawrence, P. R., and Lorsch, J. W. (1967), *Organization and Environment: Managing Differentiation and Integration*, Boston, Harvard Business School.

Luthans, F. (1995), *Organizational Behavior* (7th edn.), New York, McGraw-Hill.

Miles, R. E., and Snow, C.C. (1984a), 'Fit, failure and the hall of fame', *California Management Review*, Vol. 26, No. 3, pp. 10–28.

Miles, R. E., and Snow, C. C. (1984b), 'Designing strategic human resource systems', *Organisational Dynamics*, Vol. 13, Part 8, pp. 36–52.

Mintzberg, H. (1979), *The Structuring of Organizations*, Englewood Cliffs, NJ, Prentice-Hall.

Mintzberg, H. (1983), *Structure in Fives: Designing Effective Organizations*, Englewood Cliffs, NJ, Prentice-Hall.

Mintzberg, H. (1991), 'The effective organization forces and forms', *Sloan Management Review*, Winter, Vol. 32, Part 2, pp. 54–67.

Mintzberg, H. (1994), 'Rethinking Strategic Planning. Part I: Pitfalls and fallacies', *Long Range Planning*, Vol. 27, No. 3, pp. 12–21.

Mintzberg, H., Quinn, J. B., and James, R. M. (1988), *The Strategy Process: Concepts, Contexts and Cases*, London, Prentice-Hall.

Morgan, G. (1989), *Creative Organization Theory. A Resource Book*, London, Sage.

Mullins, L. (1996), *Management and Organisational Behaviour* (4th edn.), London, Pitman.

Perrow, C. (1967), *Organizational Analysis: A Sociological View*, London, Tavistock.

Porter, M. (1980), *Competitive Strategy*, New York, Free Press.

Pugh, D. S. (1973), 'The measurement of organisation structures: does context determine form?', *Organisational Dynamics*, Spring, 1973, pp. 19–34. Also in Pugh, D. S. (ed.) (1990), *Organization Theory. Selected Readings*, London, Penguin.

Pugh, D. (1990), *Organization Theory. Selected Readings*, London, Penguin.

Pugh, D. S., Hickson, D. J., Hinings, C. R., and Turner, C. (1969), 'Dimensions of organization structure', *Administrative Science Quarterly*, Vol. 17, pp. 163–76.

Robbins, S. P. (1993), *Organizational Behavior*, Englewood Cliffs, NJ, Prentice-Hall.

Simon, H. A. (1960), *The New Science of Management Decision*, New York, Harper.

Snow, C. C., Miles, R. E., and Coleman, H. J., Jun. (1992) 'Managing 21st century network organizations', *Organizational Dynamics*, Winter, pp. 5–19.

Thompson, A. A., Jun., and Strickland, A. J. (1983), *Strategy Formulation and Implementation*, Irvine, IL, Business Publications Inc.

Thompson, J. D. (1967), *Organizations in Action*, New York, McGraw-Hill.

Weber, M. (1947), *The Theory of Social and Economic Organisation*, Free Press, translated and edited by Henderson, A. M., and Parsons, T., in Pugh, D. S. (1990), *Organization Theory. Selected Readings*, London, Penguin. (German original published in 1924.)

Wilson, D. C., and Rosenfeld, R. H. (1990), *Managing Organizations, Text, Readings and Cases*, Maidenhead, McGraw-Hill.

Wilson, D. C., and Rosenfeld, R. H. (1991), *Managing Organizations, Text, Readings and Cases: Instructors Resource Book*, Maidenhead, McGraw-Hill.

Woodward, J. (1965), *Industrial Organization: Theory and Practice*, London, Oxford University Press.

CHAPTER 4

Cultures for change

This chapter begins the process of addressing the informal aspects of organisational functioning with an exploration of the concept of culture as it influences organisational life and organisational change processes. The meaning of culture at both the organisational and national levels is discussed, and different models and typologies are compared. The concept of the cultural web is used as a means of describing organisational culture. The sources of culture and the relationship between culture, strategy, structure and the environment are identified as the background to discussing the role of culture in the process of change.

Objectives

To:

- recognise the importance of the informal organisation and its role in relation to organisations and change;

- explain the meaning of culture as a significant element of the informal organisation;

- compare and contrast different cultural models and typologies;

- identify the sources from which an organisation derives its culture;

- explain the significance of culture for organisational change processes.

THE INFORMAL ORGANISATION

It is clear from the discussion in the previous chapters that organisations are composed of formal elements such as structure, strategy and technology. In addition, there is, apparently, little that is contentious in describing their size, whether this is measured by number of employees or by one or more financial indicators. The goals of an organisation and its financial resources might also be regarded as fairly understood and explicit elements of organisational life. As explained previously, these aspects of organisational functioning can be termed the formal organisation. Thus, the determination of an organisation's goals, its strategy and structure, the technology it will use and its need for financial resources can, legitimately, be associated with logical thinking and rational methods of decision-making. In addition, because these more formal organisational features can be reasonably understood by most people, they are, in the main, susceptible to the process of *planned* change (*see* Chapter 2).

However, as the comments at the end of Chapter 2 showed, organisational life is not nearly as neat and tidy as this implies. This has been well expressed by French and Bell (1990) in their use of the concept of the informal organisation and the metaphor of the 'organisational iceberg'. Figure 4.1 illustrates this idea pictorially.

The iceberg metaphor can be used to depict two contrasting aspects of organisational life. The first is that part of the iceberg which is visible above the water and which is composed of the more easy to see formal aspects of an organisation. The

Figure 4.1

The organisational iceberg

second is the hidden part of the iceberg which is composed of the more covert aspects of organisational life. These include, for instance, the values, beliefs and attitudes held by management and other employees, the emergent informal groupings which occur in every organisation, the norms of behaviour which direct how things are done but which are rarely talked about, and the politics of organisational life which are mainly hidden but which, for all that, are a powerful driver of decisions and actions.

It is significant that the metaphor of an iceberg not only points to the overt and covert aspects of organisations, but draws attention to the proposition that the informal systems, as well as being hidden are the greater part of the organisational iceberg. However, as with an iceberg, they may not become apparent until one collides with them unwittingly. Thus the difficulties in detecting the extent and characteristics of the hidden part of the iceberg are analogous to the difficulties encountered in examining and understanding the more informal, hidden aspects of organisational behaviour. Indeed, French and Bell (1990, p. 18) go so far as to say, 'Traditionally, this hidden domain either is not examined at all or is only partially examined'. The truth of this comment is debatable. However, whether it is wholly true or not, the acceptance that the informal organisation exists and can act powerfully to influence organisational activity is reason enough to examine how it impinges upon the extent to which organisations can deal with change.

The concepts of culture, politics and power have come to embrace much of what is included in the hidden part of the organisation. What is more, they play an important role in helping or hindering the process of change, as Morgan (1989) confirms in his statement: 'The culture and politics of many organisations constrain the degree of change and transformation in which they can successfully engage, even though such change may be highly desirable for meeting the challenges and demands of the wider environment.' Therefore, regardless of how well change might be planned in terms of the more formal organisational characteristics, it is the hidden informal aspects of organisational life which will act to help or hinder it. The discussion which follows, in this chapter and the next, explores the nature and influence of culture and politics in terms of their significance for organisations in times of change.

THE MEANING OF CULTURE

Many definitions of culture can be found in the literature and Kroeber and Kluckhohn (1952, p. 181) claim to have examined well over a hundred. It seems reasonable, therefore, to give their summary definition which is:

> Culture consists in patterned ways of thinking, feeling and reacting, acquired and transmitted mainly by symbols, constituting the distinctive achievements of human groups, including their embodiment in artifacts; the essential core of culture consists of traditional (i.e. historically derived and selected) ideas and especially their attached values.

Another, often quoted definition is that of Hofstede (1981, p. 24) which is:

> Culture is the collective programming of the human mind that distinguishes the members of one human group from those of another. Culture in this sense is a system of collectively held values.

Both these definitions refer to culture on the 'grand scale'. In the first case, the definition refers to characteristics in terms of which different *societies* differ one from another. In the second case, Hofstede uses his definition to delineate one *national* culture from another. For instance, his reference to 'human groups' is taken to mean groupings based on nationality.

These definitions can be compared to those which are used more specifically to describe organisational cultures. The following three are chosen from a list given by Brown (1995) in his book entitled *Organisational Culture*. They span the years from 1952 to the present.

> The culture of the factory is its customary and traditional way of thinking and of doing things, which is shared to a greater or lesser degree by all its members, and which new members must learn, and at least partially accept, in order to be accepted into service in the firm. Culture in this sense covers a wide range of behaviour: the methods of production; job skills and technical knowledge; attitudes towards discipline and punishment; the customs and habits of managerial behaviour; the objectives of the concern; its way of doing business; the methods of payment; the values placed on different types of work; beliefs in democratic living and joint consultation; and the less conscious conventions and taboos. (Jaques, 1952, p. 251.)

> A set of understandings or meanings shared by a group of people. The meanings are largely tacit among members, are clearly relevant to the particular group, and are distinctive to the group. Meanings are passed on to new group members. (Louis, 1980.)

> Culture is 'how things are done around here'. It is what is typical of the organization, the habits, the prevailing attitudes, the grown-up pattern of accepted and expected behaviour. (Drennan, 1992, p. 3.)

An examination of all these definitions illustrates a degree of overlap. Thus, in general, people are seen as being from different cultures if their ways of life as a group (whether societal or organisational) differ significantly, one from another.

Collectively, these definitions imply that culture is an objective entity which can be identified and which delineates one human grouping from another. It is clear that culture has cognitive (to do with thinking), affective (to do with feeling) and behavioural characteristics. However, this tends to give the impression that different cultures are easily identified and, on the whole, this is not so. Schein (1992, p. 6) sums this up by referring to organisational culture as:

> the deeper level of basic assumptions and beliefs that are shared by members of an organisation, that operate unconsciously and define in a basic 'taken for granted' fashion an organisation's view of its self and its environment.

The fact that these elements of culture operate 'tacitly' as Louis says, or 'unconsciously' as Schein says, reinforces the metaphor of the hidden part of the iceberg. This is not to say, however, that writers have avoided explanations of the way one type of culture differs from another and the way these are formed and maintained.

MODELS OF ORGANISATIONAL CULTURE

A number of writers have sought to elaborate further on the brief definitions of culture such those given above. For instance, Brown (1995, p. 8) lists the following:

- artifacts
- language in the form of jokes, metaphors, stories, myths and legends
- behaviour patterns in the form of rites, rituals, ceremonies and celebrations
- norms of behaviour
- heroes
- symbols and symbolic action
- beliefs, values and attitudes
- ethical codes
- basic assumptions
- history

A comparison of this list with that of Robbins (1993) (*see* Illustration 4.1) illustrates well the two parts of the organisational iceberg in that Brown emphasises more strongly the more informal aspects of organisational life while Robbins includes some of the more formal elements. In addition, Robbins offers the possibility of devising a more practical way of describing an organisation's culture, as Activity 4.1 shows.

Models of organisational culture such as those of Brown and Robbins rely on the simple identification of a list of cultural characteristics. Other writers, however, go somewhat further than this in suggesting that different cultural characteristics are linked to one another through a hierarchy of 'levels' of culture. An example is shown

---

Illustration 4.1
THE CHARACTERISTICS OF ORGANISATIONAL CULTURE

1. *Member identity*: The degree to which employees identify with the organisation as a whole rather than with their type of job or field of professional expertise.
2. *Group emphasis*: The degree to which work activities are organised around groups rather than individuals.
3. *People focus*: The degree to which management decisions take into consideration the effect of outcomes on people within the organisation.
4. *Unit integration*: The degree to which units within the organisation are encouraged to operate in a coordinated or interdependent manner.
5. *Control*: The degree to which rules, regulations, and direct supervision are used to oversee and control employee behaviour.
6. *Risk tolerance*: The degree to which employees are encouraged to be aggressive, innovative, and risk-seeking.
7. *Reward criteria*: The degree to which rewards such as salary increases and promotions are allocated according to employee performance rather than seniority, favouritism, or other nonperformance factors.
8. *Conflict tolerance*: The degree to which employees are encouraged to air conflicts and criticisms openly.
9. *Means–ends orientation*: The degree to which management focuses on results or outcomes rather than on the techniques and processes used to achieve those outcomes.
10. *Open-system focus*: The degree to which the organisation monitors and responds to changes in the external environment.

Source: Robbins, S. P. (1993), *Organizational Behavior* (Englewood Cliffs, NJ, Prentice-Hall International, p. 602).

ACTIVITY 4.1   Appraising your own organisation

The scales below relate to the organisational culture characteristics listed in Illustration 4.1. Put a cross on each scale according to how you rate your own organisation (or one with which you are familiar). If possible, ask colleagues in different parts of the organisation to your own to carry out this rating process.

1 **Member identity**
   Job .... Organisation

2 **Group emphasis**
   Individual .... Group

3 **People focus**
   Task .... People

4 **Unit integration**
   Independent .... Interdependent

5 **Control**
   Tight .... Loose

6 **Risk tolerance**
   Low .... High

7 **Reward criteria**
   Other .... Performance

8 **Conflict tolerance**
   Low .... High

9 **Means–ends orientation**
   Means .... Ends

10 **Open-system focus**
   Internal .... External

Compare your own view of your organisation's culture with that of your colleagues. Where there are any differences, consider why their views might be different from your own.

---

in Figure 4.2 which depicts the model devised by Hofstede *et al.* (1990). This suggests that culture manifests itself at the deepest level through people's values and at the shallowest level in terms of the things which symbolise those values.

Other 'levels' models are those of Schein (1992) and Dyer (1985). Schein suggests three levels which are from the shallowest to the deepest: the *artifacts* level (the visible organisational structures and processes such as language, environment, rituals, ceremonies, myths and stories); the *espoused values* level (the organisation's strategies, goals, philosophies); and the *basic underlying assumptions* level (the unconscious, taken-for-granted beliefs, perceptions, thoughts and feelings which are the ultimate source of

Figure 4.2

Different levels of culture

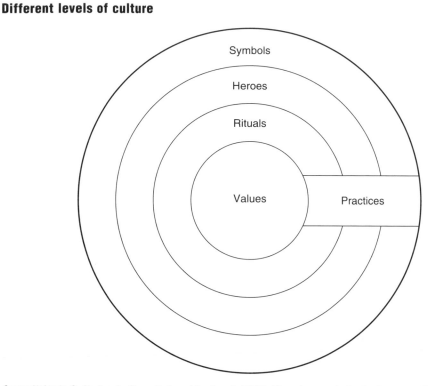

Source: Hofstede, G., Neuijen, B., Ohayv, D. D., and Sanders, G. (1990), 'Measuring organizational cultures: a qualitative and quantitative study across twenty cases', *Administrative Science Quarterly*, Vol. 35, p. 291.

values and actions). Thus, the rituals, heroes and symbols level of Hofstede *et al.* equates with Schein's artifacts level. However, Hofstede's values level is, apparently, split into two levels by Schein who distinguishes between the beliefs, values and attitudes associated with the espoused values level and the deeper level of basic assumptions. As far as Dyer's (1985) model goes, the only difference from that of Schein is that Dyer proposes four levels – *artifacts, perspectives, values* and *tacit assumptions.*

While the levels models have much in common with Brown's list of the elements of organisational culture, at first sight it seems that the 10 characteristics of organisational culture identified by Robbins have little to do with them yet, as mentioned above, Robbins' list appears much more amenable to being *used* to describe an organisation's culture in practical terms. However, it is possible to use the levels model to get some understanding of an organisation's culture. In this case, the process requires interpretation of signs and symbols, as well as language used, to assess the prevailing values and underlying assumptions about how the organisation should operate. Illustration 4.2 shows how a combination of Schein's and Dyer's models might be applied to the Beautiful Buildings Company whose structure is described in Chapter 3.

> **Illustration 4.2**
> ## LEVELS OF CULTURE IN THE BB COMPANY
>
> 1. *Artifacts*: The annual report of the company includes policies concerned with employees as well as customers and shareholders. Building sites have well kept, clean facilities for the workers. Gillian Lambeth is frequently referred to by her first name.
> 2. *Perspective*: It is acceptable for the trades union representatives to know what volume of work might be expected in the future, but the directors are not expected to talk about details of the proposed expansion until it becomes a well-established fact.
> 3. *Values*: Although there is a clear distinction between directors/managers and site workers, pay and conditions for workers should be fair and their views taken into account on matters pertaining to them. However, gaining contracts and satisfying customers is a priority.
> 4. *Basic/tacit assumptions*: All people should be treated with dignity whatever their level and function.

Objectivist and interpretive views of culture

Attempts to build models of organisational culture, such as those represented by Robbins' list and the levels models, throw up the issue of how to bring meaning to the concept of culture itself. In pursuit of this, Brown (1995) and Alvesson (1993) draw attention to the distinction between two classifications of culture. The first, of which Robbins' list and the levels models might be considered examples, treats culture as a critical variable which forms a partial explanation for differences in organisational operations. This can be termed the objectivist or functional view of culture (Alvesson, 1993) or, alternatively, culture defined as a set of behavioural and/or cognitive characteristics (Brown, 1995). This view places culture alongside structure, technology and the environment (for instance) as one of the variables which influence organisational life and performance.

There is, however, a second view of culture which interprets the meaning of culture as a metaphor for the concept of organisation itself. Thus, Pacanowsky and O'Donnell-Trujillo (1982, p. 126) say, 'Organizational culture is not just another piece of the puzzle. From our point of view, a culture is not something an organization has; a culture is something an organization is.' This is echoed by Morgan (1986) who uses the metaphor 'organisations as cultures' as one of a range of metaphors which present different images of organisation. Morgan's definition of culture gives some sense of this. He says:

> Shared meaning, shared understanding, and shared sense making are all different ways of describing culture. In talking about culture we are really talking about a process of reality construction that allows people to see and understand particular events, actions, objects, utterances, or situations in distinctive ways. These patterns of understanding also provide a basis for making one's own behaviour sensible and meaningful.' (Morgan, 1986, p. 128.)

Morgan maintains that, in doing the above, members of organisations are, in fact, creating the organisation itself. In essence this means that organisations are *socially* constructed realities, and that, rather than being defined by their structures, rules and regulations, they are constructed as much in the heads and minds of their members. This implies looking at the routine aspects of everyday life as well as at the more obvious and more public signs, symbols and ceremonies which are more frequently associated with organisational leaders. It also implies an examination of how culture is created and sustained, which relates far more to the deepest-level culture illustrated above. This further implies an exploration of the links between national culture at a more macro level and organisational sub-cultures at a more micro level. These links are discussed in more detail later in the chapter.

A model of organisational culture which appears to bring together the idea of culture as congruent with everything that happens in an organisation is Johnson and Scholes' (1997) 'cultural web' as described in Illustration 4.3.

Illustration 4.3
THE CULTURAL WEB

Johnson and Scholes explain the different elements of the cultural web as follows:

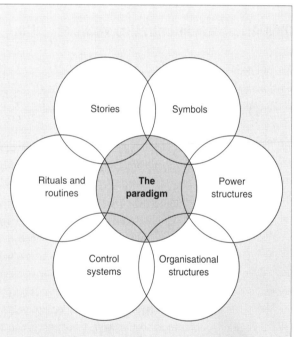

- The *routine* ways that members of the organisation behave towards each other, and that link different parts of the organisation, comprise 'the way we do things around here', which at their best lubricate the working of the organisation and may provide a distinctive and beneficial organisational competency. However, they can also represent a taken-for-grantedness about how things should happen which is extremely difficult to change and highly protective of core assumptions in the paradigm.

- The *rituals* of organisational life, such as training programmes, promotion and assessment, point to what is important in the organisation, reinforce 'the way we do things around here' and signal what is important and valued.

- The *stories* told by members of the organisation to each other, to outsiders, to new recruits and so on, embed the present in its organisational history and flag up important events and personalities, as well as mavericks who 'deviate from the norm'.

- The more *symbolic aspects* of organisations, such as logos, offices, cars and titles, or the type of language and terminology commonly used, become a shorthand representation of the nature of the organisation.

- The *control systems*, measurements and reward systems emphasise what it is important to monitor in the organisation and to focus attention and activity on.

- *Power structures* are also likely to be associated with the key constructs of the paradigm. The most powerful managerial groupings in the organisation are likely to be the ones most associated with core assumptions and beliefs about what is important.

- The formal *organisational structure*, or the more informal ways in which the organisations work, are likely to reflect power structures and, again, to delineate important relationships and emphasise what is important in the organisation.

Source: Based on Johnson, G., and Scholes, K. (1997), *Exploring Corporate Strategy Texts and Cases* (Hemel Hempstead, Prentice-Hall International, pp. 69–74).

It can be seen from Illustration 4.3 that the cultural web is all-encompassing in the organisational elements which it includes. Johnson (1990) and Johnson and Scholes (1997) draw attention to the influence of prevailing organisational paradigms (i.e. the beliefs and assumptions of the people making up the organisation) in any attempt to bring about strategic change. The link between the beliefs and assumptions making up the paradigm and other aspects of organisational functioning is exemplified in the statement by Johnson and Scholes (1993, p. 61) that: 'It would be a mistake to conceive of the paradigm as merely a set of beliefs and assumptions removed from organisational action. They lie within a cultural web which bonds them to the day-to-day action of organisational life.'

Johnson and Scholes probably do not go as far as Morgan in equating culture fully with organisation, but neither do they completely objectify culture as separate from other aspects of organisational life. In addition the subtitle of Johnson's (1990) article, 'The role of symbolic action', illustrates the emphasis put upon the rituals or routines, stories or myths, and symbols elements of the cultural web in any attempt to bring about change resulting in a shift in the organisational paradigm. For Johnson (1996), changing organisational structures, control systems and even power structures will not necessarily bring about a paradigm shift. He argues that, for this to happen, a much greater effort must be put into bringing about changes in the other elements of the cultural web.

ACTIVITY 4.2   Creating a cultural web for your organisation

*Illustration 4.4 shows the cultural web for an organisation involved in buying paper in bulk and then cutting and preparing it for sale to large scale paper users.**

Using this as a guide, construct a cultural web for an organisation you know well (or if it is large, one particular division or department).

If you wished to institute change at the strategic level, how would you go about changing the rituals or routines, stories and symbols elements of your cultural web?

*Additional examples of the use of the cultural web can be found in Johnson and Scholes (1997, pp. 70 and 460–1).

Johnson and Scholes' cultural web has been applied mainly to organisational cultures. In contrast, Morgan's proposal that organisations *are* cultures discusses (among other things) differences in national cultures, including the way these have formed through historical processes. The notion of culture as a metaphor for organisation also encompasses the concept of sub-cultures. This is reinforced by Alvesson (1993) who recommends combining perspectives at three levels. These are:

- the organisation as a culture (unitary and unique);
- the organisation as a meeting place for great cultures (which includes national ethnic and class cultures);
- local perspectives on organisational sub-cultures.

Illustration 4.4

A CULTURAL WEB OF PAPER UNLIMITED, A LARGE UK-BASED PAPER DISTRIBUTOR

Stories
- Son of the founder (recently deceased) and his influence on the company policies and practices – a people-oriented company
- Frequent need to expand paper stacking space as example of continuing success

Symbols
- New building and warehouses
- Swimming pool and leisure facilites for employees and families
- IIP award
- Quality award
- Award for excellence in the use of IT

Paradigm
Dedicated to the philosophy laid down by the recently deceased original owner's son, who ran the company for over 40 years. This implies being:
- A people-oriented organisation also dedicated to high task performance
- Provider of long-term employment
- Aware of success while also aware of the need to continuously analyse the environment to detect new markets
- Committed to incremental rather than radical changes

Rituals and routines
- Walk-about management – always available to employees
- Management can be interrupted
- Lots of talking
- Yearly employee/family outing

Power structures
- Long serving managers and workforce
- Can 'work your way up'
- Positions based on expertise in the business rather than on qualifications
- Paternalistic style of management
- Emphasis on continuity
- Relaxed attitudes
- Co-operation at head office, competition between the branches where selling occurs

Controls
- IT controls most operations
- Error measurement
- Help given to improve

Organisation structure
- Hierarchical at head office – bureaucracy with a human face
- Team working in the branches with team-based rewards
- Profit-related pay
- Responsibilities clearly defined

From this point of view, in order to analyse organisational culture, it is necessary to understand the mixture of cultural manifestations at all three levels.

Someone who has attempted to do this is Hall (1995), who includes all these manifestations of culture in her detailed framework designed to analyse culture in terms of three constituent dimensions (artifacts, behaviours and core values – the ABC of culture) in relation to national, industrial, organisational and organisational sub-cultural levels (*see* the left-hand side of the diagram in Figure 4.3).

Figure 4.3

What is culture? Forty-eight cultural concepts

CULTURE DIMENSIONS	Individual	Department	Daughter Company	Company	Industry	Nation	Individual–Individual	Individual–Company	Individual–Nation	Company–Company	Company–Nation	Nation–Nation	Intra-National	Intra-MNC Company	Intra-(one) Company	Industry–Company	Other
	1	2	3	4	5	6	7	8	9	10	11	12	13	14	15	16	Other
C. CORE VALUES	1C	2C	3C	4C	5C	6C	7C	8C	9C	10C	11C	12C	13C	14C	15C	16C	
B. BEHAVIOURS	1B	2B	3B	4B	5B	6B	7B	8B	9B	10B	11B	12B	13B	14B	15B	16B	
A. ARTIFACTS	1A	2A	3A	4A	5A	6A	7A	8A	9A	10A	11A	12A	13A	14A	15A	16A	

'CULTURE' ➤ CULTURAL SEGMENTS, OF GROUPS, AND INTERACTIONS BETWEEN GROUPS
'SEC' SEGMENTS — 'RELATIONS' SEGMENTS

Source: Hall, W. (1995), *Managing Cultures. Making Strategic Relationships Work* (Chichester, Wiley, p. 259). Reprinted by permission of John Wiley and Sons Ltd.

In addition, Hall has identified cross-cultural relationships within and between levels (*see* the right-hand side of the diagram in Figure 4.3). The results of her research, however, apply only to four segments of the model – segments 7B, 10B, 12B and 14B – all of which concern behaviour. (These four segments are highlighted in the diagram.) However, crossing the three ABC levels with the six sector and 10 relationship levels gives a possible 48 ways of analysing culture. The complexity of this is daunting, which is probably the reason that Hall has only yet managed to investigate the segments shown. Even so, Hall's model is a clear example of an attempt to 'objectify', and so measure, culture. The result is to identify a number of different types of culture. These are discussed further below.

ORGANISATIONAL CULTURE TYPOLOGIES

Exploring definitions and the dimensions of culture leads to some understanding of *what* culture means. However, something more is required to identify *how* one organisation's culture differs from another. Some models make this easier to do than others. Those which treat culture as one objective organisational element among many are probably easier to use in this sense than those which maintain the 'organisations as culture' metaphor.

However, while all models are susceptible to being used to identify differences between one culture and another, not all give rise to means for identifying specific types of culture. What is more, some typologies of culture appear not to be derived from any theoretical model. They relate more to one or more other elements of organisational functioning. The first of these is a well-known typology of organisational culture closely related to structural form.

The structural view of culture

Structural views of culture inevitably draw on descriptions of different structural forms for their expression. One of the leading proponents of this view is Handy (1993) who draws on Harrison's (1972) studies in this respect. Handy refers to organisational culture as atmosphere, ways of doing things, levels of energy and levels of individual freedom – or collectively, the 'sets of values and norms and beliefs – reflected in different structures and systems' (p. 180). On the basis of Harrison's studies, he suggests four organisational culture types. Illustration 4.5 describes these.

Handy does not claim high levels of rigour for the descriptions given in Illustration 4.5, saying that a culture cannot be defined precisely. However, these descriptions could be used to determine a particular organisation's way of doing things. Pheysey (1993) builds on Handy's and Harrison's typologies to propose a categorisation of role, power, support and achievement cultures. The definitions of role and power cultures are those used by Handy, with support and achievement cultures having similar characteristics to Handy's task and person cultures. However Pheysey goes beyond Handy in linking her four types of culture not only to organisational structure (i.e. the design of organisations) but also to control systems, employee motivation, leadership styles and organisation development.

It is not difficult to see how Miles and Snow's (1984) typologies of strategic behaviour and Mintzberg's (1983) organisational forms discussed in Chapter 3 (*see* Illustrations 3.11 and 3.12) might be linked to Handy's and Pheysey's cultural typologies.

Organisational culture, structure, strategy and the environment

Handy's and Pheysey's typologies of organisational culture are firmly associated with organisational structures. By contrast, Scholz (1987) proposes types of culture which are associated with three dimensions, of which structure is only one. The first of these is the evolution-induced dimension which is related to the strategic orientation of the organisation. Five corporate culture types are identified as follows:

1. *Stable*, with a time orientation towards the past and an aversion to risk.
2. *Reactive*, with a time orientation towards the present and an acceptance of 'minimum' risk.
3. *Anticipating*, also oriented towards the present but more accepting of 'familiar' risks.
4. *Exploring*, with a time-orientation towards the present and the future and an acceptance of increasing risk.
5. *Creative*, looking forward to the future and accepting risk as normal.

Illustration 4.5
A STRUCTURAL VIEW OF ORGANISATIONAL CULTURE

The power culture

Power cultures are those in which a single person or group tends to dominate. Handy refers to this culture as a *web* in the sense that the spider in the middle controls what happens throughout the organisation. Decision-making is centralised. This type of culture is seen as, essentially, political in that decisions are taken on the basis of influence rather than through a logical rational process. Power is held by the centre by virtue of personal charisma or the control of resources. Family businesses, small entrepreneurial companies and occasionally trade unions are likely to have this type of culture. The strength of this type of culture depends on the strength of the centre and the willingness of other organisational members to defer to this power source. Handy likens this culture to the Greek god Zeus who ruled by whim and impulse, by thunderbolt and shower of gold from Mount Olympus.

The role culture

Handy likens role cultures to a *Greek temple*. The patron god here is Apollo, the god of reason, the argument being that role cultures work by logic and rationality. The pillars of the temple are strong in their own right and activity is controlled more by rules and regulations than by personal directive from the top. The pediment of the temple is seen as co-ordinating activity rather than overtly controlling it. Emphasis is on defined roles and occupants are expected to fulfil these but not overstep them. Role cultures flourish in stable situations and a sellers' market.

The task culture

The task culture is represented by a *net*. The dominant concept in a task culture is project work associated with matrix type structures. Handy pushes the Greek god association somewhat here in suggesting Athena whose emphasis was on getting the job done. The task culture, therefore, is not particularly concerned with personal power or hierarchy, but with marshalling the required resources to complete work efficiently and effectively. Decision-making is devolved to the project groups to enhance flexibility of working method and speed the outcomes. The task culture is said to flourish where creativity and innovation are desirable, particularly in organisations concerned with such activities as research and development, marketing, advertising and new ventures.

The person culture

According to Handy, this culture is an unusual one. It exists only to service the needs of the participating members. It does not have an overarching objective such as is found in more conventionally structured organisations. Examples of person cultures are barristers' chambers, doctors' centres, hippy communes, and small consultancy firms. Person cultures have minimal structures and can be likened to a cluster or galaxy of individual stars. Handy proposes Dionysus as its patron deity who is the god of the self-oriented individual.

Source: Based on Handy, C. (1993), *Understanding Organisations* (London, Penguin, pp. 183–91).

ACTIVITY 4.3   The strategy/structure–culture link

Look back at the discussion, in Chapter 3, of Miles and Snow's typologies of strategic behaviour and Mintzberg's organisational forms and come to a conclusion as to how well or poorly they fit with the types of culture proposed by Handy and Pheysey.

ACTIVITY 4.4

Compare and contrast Scholz's evolution-induced dimension with Miles and Snow's identification of the evolution of organisational forms in Table 3.1 in Chapter 3. How far can you 'map' each of Scholz's evolution-induced types of culture to each of Miles and Snow's corporate strategies and forms?

The second of Scholz's dimensions of culture is the internal-induced dimension which identifies three culture types (production, bureaucratic and professional) derived from organisational structure characteristics. This contrasts with his third dimension of culture which is the external-induced dimension. This links types of culture to the external environment (the marketplace) and depends, for its description, on Deal and Kennedy's (1982) four culture types of the tough-guy macho culture, the work-hard/play-hard culture, the bet-your-company culture and the process culture (*see* Illustration 4.6 for a more detailed description).

Deal and Kennedy's typology was constructed in the early 1980s. While the cultural types may still be relevant and can be found in today's organisations, it is arguable whether the examples of each type, which Deal and Kennedy give, still hold today. For instance, banks (as examples of process cultures) have evolved more into sales-type organisations but do not, perhaps, yet fit the work-hard/play-hard culture suggested for sales-oriented companies. Many government agencies in the UK have become 'privatised' in the way they operate and are moving away from the process-oriented culture of old. It is also clear that organisations do not always fit neatly into one typology or another. This inevitably, gives rise to difficulties in describing a particular organisation's culture and in choosing which framework of typologies to use. In addition, Alvesson (1993), through his identification of different levels of organisation, implies that the wider society and sub-cultures within the organisation also need to be addressed.

Hall's (1995) model of culture has already been discussed in this context. Therefore, the final example of culture typologies is that of Hall.

The compass model of culture

Hall's model of culture and its associated culture typologies have been developed through an apparent interest in cultural differences in 'partnerships' by which she means inter-company relationships which may be in the form of alliances, mergers, acquisitions or some other form. She concentrates on the B of the ABC cultural dimensions – that is the behaviours and actions dimension (refer back to Figure 4.3). From her research, she claims to have identified two components of behaviour or cultural styles of behaviour.

The first of these is *assertiveness*, which is the degree to which a company's behaviours are seen by others as being forceful or directive. She says:

> Companies which behave in high assertive ways are seen to be decisive, quick and firm. There
> is little hesitation in their action. If they introduce a new product or enter a new market they

Illustration 4.6
THE DEAL AND KENNEDY TYPOLOGY

From their examination of hundreds of companies Deal and Kennedy (1982) claim to have identified four generic cultures:

The tough-guy, macho culture

These organisations are peopled with individuals who regularly take high risks and receive rapid feedback on the outcomes of their actions. Examples cited are police departments, surgeons, publishing, sports and the entertainment industry. In tough-guy, macho cultures, the stakes are high and there is a focus on speed rather than endurance. Staff in these cultures tend to be young and financial rewards come early, but failure is punished severely through 'the sack'. Burn-out is likely before middle age is reached. Internal competition and conflict are normal, and this means tantrums are tolerated and everyone tries to score points off each other. However, while tough-guy cultures can be highly successful in high-risk, quick-return environments they are less suited to making long-term investments. Being unable to benefit from co-operative activity, these organisations tend to have a high turnover of staff, and thus often fail to develop a strong and cohesive culture.

The work-hard/play-hard culture

This culture exists in organisations where there is low risk but quick feedback on actions – the world of sales organisations which incorporate hard work and fun. Examples are Avon, Mary Kay cosmetics and encyclopaedia companies as well as companies like McDonald's. Persistence, keeping at it and working to recognised procedures are typical of work-hard/play-hard cultures. In these cultures, the risks are small because no individual sale will severely damage the salesperson. In addition production systems are built to withstand temporary hitches or deviations from normal. However, being selling oriented, all employees gain quick feedback on their performance. Heroes in these organisations are the super salespeople who turn in volume sales. Contests, conventions and other means of encouraging intense selling are used. Yet the culture emphasises the team because it is the team which makes the difference, not the achievements of single individuals. However, although work/play cultures can achieve sales volumes, this can be at the expense of quality – they frequently forget that success may be 'one shot' only.

Bet-your-company culture

These cultures are typical of organisations where the risks are high and the feedback on actions and decisions takes a long time. Bet-your-company organisations are those which invest millions or billions in projects which take years to come to fruition. Examples include large aircraft manufacturers such as Boeing, oil companies like Mobil and large-systems businesses. In contrast to tough-guy cultures, people working in bet-your-company cultures bet the company rather than themselves. Consequently, there is a sense of deliberateness which manifests itself in ritualised business meetings. All decisions are carefully weighed and based on careful research. Decision-making tends to be top-down, reflecting the hierarchical nature of the organisation. The survivors in these organisations respect authority and technical competence and have the stamina to endure long-term ambiguity with limited feedback. They will act co-operatively, and have proved themselves over a number of years – immaturity is not tolerated in this culture. Bet-your-company cultures lead to high-quality inventions and major scientific breakthroughs, but their slow response times make them vulnerable to short-term economic fluctuations in the economy. However, it is said that these companies may be those which the economy most needs.

The process culture

This culture is typical of organisations where there is low risk and slow feedback on actions and decisions. Examples are banks, insurance companies, public and government organisations and other heavily regulated industries. Working with little feedback, employees have no sense of their own effectiveness or otherwise.

Consequently, they tend to concentrate on the means by which things are done rather than what should be done. Values tend to focus on technical perfection, working out the risks and getting the process right. Protecting one's back is what most employees will do, so the people who prosper are those who are orderly and punctual and who attend to detail. The ability to weather political storms and changes becomes a desirable trait. In process cultures, there is considerable emphasis on job titles and status and the signs which symbolise them, such as style of office furniture. Position power is desired. Staying with the organisation is revered by the institution of long-service awards. Process cultures are effective when dealing with a stable and predictable environment, but find it difficult to react quickly to changing circumstances. On a positive note, they offer a counterpoint to the other three cultures described above.

do so with full force. . . . Low assertive companies behave in more slow and steady ways. They are careful to consider what they do before they take firm action. They introduce a new product or enter a new market step by step, keeping their options open. Unlike the one-track mind of the high assertive company, the low assertive company has a 'multi-track mind'. (Hall, 1995, p. 52.)

The second behavioural component of culture is *responsiveness*, which is the degree to which a company's behaviours are seen by others as being emotionally expressed. Thus:

Companies which behave in high responsive ways are seen to be employee friendly, relaxed or spontaneous. These companies give the impression that they compete on feelings more than on facts. In industry gatherings, high responsive companies tend to be very 'likable'. They seem more open than other companies. Low responsive companies behave in more reserved or closed ways. They are not so much liked as 'respected'. They tend to be more rigid, their employees serious. Low responsive companies compete more on facts than on feelings. (Hall, 1995, pp. 54–5).

Illustration 4.7 lists the behaviours which indicate high and low assertiveness and responsiveness. An example of a moderately assertive but more highly responsive organisation is given in Illustration 4.8.

Hall maintains that the four different combinations of the two behavioural components she has identified result in four different cultural styles. Figure 4.4 illustrates why this model is called the compass model in that each of the four styles is labelled as one of the four points of the compass.

Hall claims that the compass model with its four culture styles can be used to analyse culture, not only with a single organisation, but also with respect to individual–individual, company–company, nation–nation, and intra-MNC (multi-national corporation) company relationships and she reports research to support this

---

Illustration 4.7
ASSERTIVE AND RESPONSIVE BEHAVIOURS

Behaviours which indicate high and (low) assertveness are:

- individualistic
- demanding rather than obliging
- taking control
- pushy
- authoritative
- charging ahead
- challenging
- hardworking
- quick moving
- (low) cautious (indecisive)

Behaviours which indicate high and (low) responsiveness are:

- sensitive
- loyal
- compromising
- trusting
- team players
- value harmony
- unpredictable
- (low) quantitative rather than qualitative
- (low) factual rather than emotional
- (low) precise rather than inexact
- (low) task rather than people oriented
- (low) consistent (methodological)

Source: Hall, W. (1995), *Managing Cultures Making Strategic Relationships Work* (Chichester, Wiley, pp. 54–5).

Illustration 4.8

RS COMPONENTS – A MODERATELY ASSERTIVE, BUT MORE HIGHLY RESPONSIVE ORGANISATION

RS Components is a Corby-based company which supplies, from a mail order catalogue, a range of components varying from capacitors, bearings, bushes and seals to the cleaning agents, fastenings and power tools to trade organisations, other organisations and members of the public. However, as one of the product buyers says, 'The company sells just one thing, and that is service to the customer'.

Visiting the company, one is struck by the quiet efficiency with which orders are taken by around one hundred staff, working in specially designed open plan environments. Orders are taken at the rate of some 20 000 a day and a customer service standard of answering any telephone call within 5 seconds is maintained. In the order-taking areas, overhead displays give continuous information on the number of orders taken that day, the number of customers waiting and the number of staff available and waiting to take calls.

Within 15 minutes of an order being taken, it is received in the huge warehouse where product-collecting containers travel on rail-type tracks around the shelves holding the products to take the quickest route past 'pickers' who fill them to satisfy the order before continuing to the packing and despatch areas. The company guarantees delivery the day after the order is taken or the same day if required. The complete operation, from a customer requesting a product to its despatch, is computer controlled. At any time, computer displays give up-to-the-second information about any part of the process.

RS Components is not, however, just a distributor of products which are required in a hurry. It also offers technical advice and support on the range of products it sells, thus increasing the probability of achieving nearly 100 per cent satisfied customers.

Through its large, on-the-road, sales staff and other market-intelligence gathering activities, it is successful in keeping up with projected market demands. Yet, it does not act hastily in offering a full service for the latest emerging products. If a new product appears to fit the company's selling policy, buyers will proceed cautiously in holding small stocks of the item until the demand can be more clearly discerned. As the demand becomes more established, the item will be stocked in quantities appropriate to meet customers' needs and the 'boast' to be able to supply the day after order.

Given the high level of computerisation which also allows almost every employee to be monitored, it might be thought that care for employees comes some distance after attention to the task. It is clear, however, to anyone spending time in the company, that care for employees is important. Every employee is identified by name, either by a name 'tag' attached to his or her computer (if one of the staff taking orders) or attached to their work station (if in the 'pick and pack' warehouse). With a fairly large workforce, this enables everyone, whether known to each other or not, to address others by their name. The majority of staff work in teams which, although led by a team leader, are to a large extent self managing. Wages are slightly above the average for the type of work, and pleasant restaurant facilities are available. The site which the company occupies includes garden areas where staff can sit or walk in the break times. A series of different start and finish times are available to suit the demands of the business, but which also provide flexible working hours to suit the different needs of different employees.

claim. In addition, it would appear that the choice of the 'compass' analogy seems to be derived from the identification of different national cultures and the positioning of these in terms of the points of a compass. As illustration of this, Figure 4.5 plots seven different countries on the assertiveness-responsiveness cultural style dimensions.

It should be noted that, in Figure 4.5, the further to the edge of the plot, the more extreme the cultural style. For instance, West Germany has a very high assertive, very low responsive cultural style, while Italy is more moderately placed on both of the cultural style dimensions. France is almost in the middle of the responsiveness

Figure 4.4

The compass model: characteristics of each style

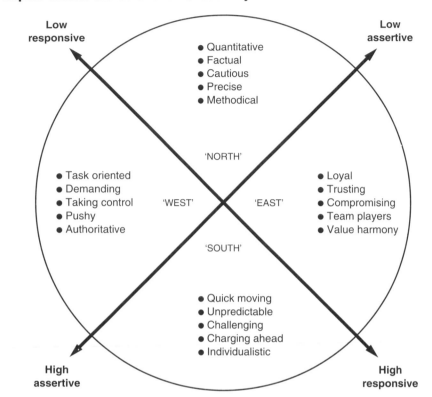

Source: Hall, W. (1995), *Managing Cultures. Making Strategic Relationships Work* (Chichester, Wiley, p. 58). Reprinted by permission of John Wiley and Sons Ltd.

dimension, but higher on the assertiveness scale. These results were based on a total of 211 responses from executives with experience of living and working in the seven countries represented. However, it should be noted that the executives were not, necessarily, of the nationalities on which they gave their views. These views were mainly those of executives who had, through their own work across national boundaries, experience of managers from the countries in the sample. It is not clear, therefore, how much the executives who were questioned were working from stereotypes of the managers on whom they were giving their views. In addition, the research used a sample of executives from two industries only – the automobile industry and the high technology industry.

Given these reservations, Hall's typology is detailed and comprehensive. It attempts to link Alvesson's (1993) three levels of culture and more. In addition, it hints at one of the influences on organisational culture through its focus on differences between national cultures.

Figure 4.5

Cultural plots of nations

US = United States of America	WG = West Germany	NL = Netherlands
JA = Japan	IT = Italy	FR = France
GB = Great Britain		

Source: Hall, W. (1995), *Managing Cultures. Making Strategic Relationships Work* (Chichester, Wiley, p. 95). Reprinted by permission of John Wiley and Sons Ltd.

THE SOURCES OF ORGANISATIONAL CULTURE

Hofstede (1981, p. 27) maintains that: 'The subculture of an organization reflects national culture, professional subculture, and the organization's own history.' Regarding the last of these, Robbins (1992) puts emphasis on the philosophy of the organisation's founder and, as time passes, on how the top management define acceptable behaviour. The importance of leadership as a source of organisational culture is discussed by Brown (1995), who cites examples of Henry Ford at the Ford Motor Company, Ken Olsen at Digital Equipment Corporation and Gerard and Anton Philips at Philips. Sir John Harvey-Jones is well known for his influence at ICI and is an example of a leader continuing, through his writings, to influence the business scene with his views beyond his retirement. The cultural web of Paper Unlimited (*see* Illustration 4.4) is almost wholly derived from the way the company founder's son and long-time managing director established an organisational philosophy while setting up the organisation's structure, operating systems and procedures, criteria for recruitment and promotion and the style of management to be observed. Through his own behaviour, he was an example of how he wanted the company managed and run.

The influence of history is not, however, limited to the influence of particular people of importance to an organisation. A broader influence is referred to by Hofstede (1981, p. 27) who says: 'The rules of behavior in industrial workshops in the nineteenth century were modelled after those in armies and monasteries. The structure and functioning of organizations are determined not merely by rationality, or, if they are, by rationality that varies according to the cultural environment.' Goodman's (1995) discussion of the different ages of wealth creation described in Chapter 1 are evidence of the way historical processes influence all aspects of organisational functioning including an organisation's culture. Even so, these processes and their timing are not the same for every society. They will be modified to some extent by the national culture in which they take place. However, the extent to which differences in national cultures permeate organisational life is debatable.

The influence of national culture

A survey of the literature on the cultural similarities and differences between nations identifies a long-standing debate known popularly as the convergence–divergence debate. In summary, those who support the convergence view argue that the forces of industrialisation (for instance, *see* Kerr, Dunlop, Harbison and Myers, 1960) and the use of similar technologies (*see* Woodward, 1965; Castells, 1989) as well as increasing size (*see* Chandler, 1962; Pugh and Hickson, 1976; Hickson and MacMillan, 1981) will push organisations, whatever their location, towards particular configurations with respect to strategy, structure and management. In addition, the growth of international organisations and those who trade abroad increases the need for 'international managers' who bring common management practices to all parts of their organisations wherever they are in the world. In support of this view, Ohmae (1991) puts forward the concept of the 'global organisation' which has no national allegiance, only an international common purpose. Furthermore, Ohmae argues for 'getting rid of the headquarters mentality', implying the possibility that an organisation's national cultural base will have no influence on the culture of the organisation itself.

In contrast to this view is the notion that differences in countries' languages, religions, social organisation, laws, politics, education systems, and values and attitudes (Hofstede, 1980, Tayeb, 1989 and Wilson, 1992) will, of necessity, mean that one nation's culture will diverge significantly from another's. According to Wilson (1992), there are no definitive studies to support one view or another. However, there is sufficient evidence of national cultural differences for the influence of national culture on organisational culture to be taken seriously.

The diversity of national cultures

There is an expanding body of research that claims to have identified how cultures vary. A frequently referenced framework is that of Kluckhohn and Strodtbeck (1961) who claim there are six basic dimensions which describe the cultural orientation of societies. These are:

1. People's qualities as individuals in terms of whether people are seen as basically good or basically bad: societies that consider people good tend to trust people while those that consider people bad tend to start from a premise of mistrust and suspicion.
2. People's relationship to their world: some societies believe they can dominate their environment while others believe the environment and themselves to be inseparable and therefore, they must live in harmony with it.
3. People's personal relationships in terms of individualism or collectivism: some societies encourage individualism and the notion of being self-supporting, and achievement is based on individual worth, while others are more group oriented, where people define themselves as members of clans or communities (which might be the work organisation) and consider the group's welfare to be more important than the individual.
4. An orientation to either doing or being: societies which are doing and action oriented stress accomplishments which are measurable by standards believed to be external to the individual; societies oriented to being are more passive, believing that work should be enjoyed, and live more for the moment.
5. People's orientation to time: some societies are past oriented, believing that current plans and actions should fit with the customs and traditions of the past while future-oriented societies justify innovation and change in terms of future pay-offs, believing radical change to be desirable as well as acceptable.
6. People's use of space: societies differ on such matters as offices in relation to status, the designation of public space compared to private space, the separation of managers from subordinates.

Both Adler (1997) and Robbins (1996) draw on this framework in their discussions of societal and national cultures. In her book, Adler gives many examples of differences between societies and nations on these cultural dimensions. Regarding the good–evil dimension or trust–mistrust dimension, the way one group of people regard another will differ according to whether they set off with the assumption that people are trustworthy or that all people will cheat if given the opportunity. This translates, for instance, into whether things are kept locked up or not, whether information is freely available, and how one group's actions are interpreted by another. Adler contrasts the North Americans with the Chinese and Navaho in terms of the former's belief that they can dominate nature and the latter's belief that they must live in harmony with nature.

She describes Americans' strong individualistic tendencies as evidenced in their language such as, 'trounced the opposition', and their recruitment and promotion practices based on criteria relating to individual knowledge and skills. This contrasts with more group-oriented societies such as Japan, China, Indonesia and Malaysia who put more stress on assignments, responsibilities and reporting relationships in collective terms. People in these societies are more likely to gain employment through personal contacts who can vouch for their trustworthiness and ability to work with others. Finding jobs for family and friends is not seen as unusual or nepotism as it might be in more individualistic societies. Adler makes an interesting comparison between do-ers and be-ers in their typically different reactions to a salary rise. The do-ers react to higher pay rates by working more hours because they can earn more. The be-ers react to higher pay rates by working fewer hours, arguing that they can earn the same money in less time, so leaving more time for enjoying life. Offering overtime bonuses may work in 'doing' societies but will not work in 'being' societies.

Adler points out that different time orientations can impact significantly on people's attitudes to time-keeping and punctuality. Different time orientations also bring differences in the length of time someone might be given to show his or her worth in a job. If employees are recruited with the expectation of staying many years with an organisation they will not have to show achievement in the short time expected in societies which recruit in the knowledge that the person may move on before very long. Finally, Adler uses the examples of North Americans and Japanese to contrast different societies' attitudes to the use of space. The former prefer closed offices and meetings behind closed doors while the latter prefer open plan working areas which include managers as well as subordinates. Other interesting differences can be seen in how close one desk is to another and whether an office can be entered without ceremony or whether people must wait outside for permission to enter.

Figure 4.6 is based on Robbins' summary of the Kluckhohn–Strodtbeck framework with a profile for the United States plotted on it. It is obvious, from a reading of these descriptions that variations will occur within societies as well as between societies. However, evidence from another well-known piece of research (Hofstede, 1980)

Figure 4.6

Variations in Kluckhohn and Strodtbeck's cultural dimensions

Dimensions	Variations		
Nature of people	Good	Mixed	Bad
Relationship to the environment	Domination	Harmony	Subjugation
Focus of responsibility	Individualistic	Group	Hierarchical
Activity orientation	Being	Controlling	Doing
Time orientation	Past	Present	Future
Conception of space	Private	Mixed	Public

Source: Based on Robbins, S. P. (1996), *Organizational Behavior, Concepts, Controversies, Applications* (Englewood Cliffs, NJ, Prentice-Hall International, p. 56).

appears to support the concept of geographically identifiable, culturally differentiated regions which are based on national boundaries. The research referred to was carried out in IBM and involved the analysis of questionnaires from some 116 000 employees in 50 different countries. This analysis resulted in the identification of four dimensions which were found to differentiate national cultural groups. Illustration 4.9 describes these.

Illustration 4.9
HOFSTEDE'S DIMENSIONS OF NATIONAL CULTURE

Power distance

Power distance refers to how a society deals with the fact that people are unequal, for instance, in physical and intellectual abilities. Some societies let these inequalities grow over time into inequalities in power and wealth. Other societies try to play down inequalities in power and wealth. In organisations, the level of power distance is related to the degree of centralisation of authority and the degree of autocratic leadership. In high power distance societies, inequalities of power and wealth are accepted not only by the leaders, but also by those at the bottom of the power hierarchy, with corresponding large differences in status and salaries. In high power distance societies the people without power accept the situation just as much as those with the power, thus satisfying a psychological need for dependence on the part of those without the power. In low power distance societies, inequalities among people will tend to be minimised, with subordinates expecting to be consulted by superiors over decisions which affect them and treated more as equals of those with the power.

Individualism/collectivism

Individualism/collectivism refers to relationships between an individual and his or her fellow individuals. In an individualistic society, the ties between individuals are very loose. Everybody is expected to look after his or her own self-interest and perhaps that of their immediate family. Individuals in these societies have a large amount of freedom of action. Contracts between employers and employees are based on mutual advantage. Recruitment and promotion are said to depend on objective criteria such as knowledge and skills. In collectivist societies the ties between individuals are very tight. The concept of the extended family is important and can extend to work groups and organisations. Everybody is supposed to look after the interests of their in-group, which will protect them when they are in trouble. Contracts between employers and employees tend to be cast in moral terms and

recruitment and promotion may be based on criteria related to the group's needs as well as the individual's.

Masculinity/femininity

Masculinity/femininity refers to the degree to which social gender roles are clearly distinct. In high-masculinity societies, the social division between the sexes is maximised, with traditional masculine social values permeating the society. These values include the importance of showing off, of making money and of 'big is beautiful'. In more feminine societies, the dominant values – for both men and women – are those more traditionally associated with the feminine role of nurturing and caring, putting relationships before money, minding the quality of life and 'small is beautiful'. In feminine societies, managers in organisations use intuition as much as logical thinking for problem-solving. Conflicts are resolved by compromise and negotiation. In contrast to the masculine value of living to work, the feminine value is working to live.

Uncertainty avoidance

Uncertainty avoidance refers to how a society deals with the fact that time runs only one way – from the past to the future – and that the future is unknown and, therefore, uncertain. Some societies accept this uncertainty and do not get upset about it; others seek to reduce the uncertainty as much as possible. People in weak uncertainty avoidance societies tend to accept each day as it comes and are comfortable with a higher degree of risk-taking. They are relatively tolerant of others with different views to their own. Societies demonstrating strong uncertainty-avoidance characteristics socialise their people into trying to beat the future. Because the future is unpredictable, people in these societies are likely to be more anxious, emotional and aggressive. They fear ambiguous situations and unfamiliar risks. Precision and punctuality are important with a seeking for security.

Source: Based on Hofstede, G. (1980), *Culture's Consequences* (Beverly Hills, CA, Sage).

Figures 4.7, 4.8 and 4.9 show the position of each country on the four dimensions. All the figures are based on Hofstede's 1983 publication.

Country and region names are depicted as follows:

ARA	Arab countries (Egypt, Lebanon, Libya, Kuwait, Iraq, Saudi-Arabia, UAE)	ITA	Italy
		JAM	Jamaica
		JPN	Japan
		KOR	South Korea
ARG	Argentina	MAL	Malaysia
AUL	Australia	MEX	Mexico
AUT	Austria	NET	The Netherlands
BEL	Belgium	NOR	Norway
BRA	Brazil	NZL	New Zealand
CAN	Canada	PAK	Pakistan
CHL	Chile	PAN	Panama
COL	Columbia	PER	Peru
COS	Costa Rica	PHI	Philippines
DEN	Denmark	POR	Portugal
EAF	East Africa (Kenya, Ethiopia, Zambia)	SAF	South Africa
		SAL	Salvador
EQA	Equador	SIN	Singapore
FIN	Finland	SPA	Spain
FRA	France	SWE	Sweden
GBR	Great Britain	SWI	Switzerland
GER	Germany	TAI	Taiwan
GRE	Greece	THA	Thailand
GUA	Guatemala	TUR	Turkey
HOK	Hong Kong	URU	Uraguay
IDO	Indonesia	USA	United States
IND	India	VEN	Venezuela
IRA	Iran	WAF	West Africa (Nigeria, Guana, Sierra Leone)
IRE	Ireland		
ISR	Israel	YUG	Yugoslavia

An examination of Figure 4.7 shows that, among the countries of Europe, France (FRA), Belgium (BEL), Great Britain (GRB) and The Netherlands (NRT) are all individualistic in focus; this is apparently the trend as countries become more affluent. Yet, France and Belgium differ from Great Britain, and more so from The Netherlands, in their tolerance of inequalities among their populations, as indicated by their position on the power distance dimension. Asian countries such as Hong Kong (HOK), Malaysia (MAL) and Singapore (SIN) typify countries which are collectivist (group oriented) yet still believe that some degree of inequality is normal in their societies.

Figure 4.7

The position of the 50 countries on the power distance and individualism scales

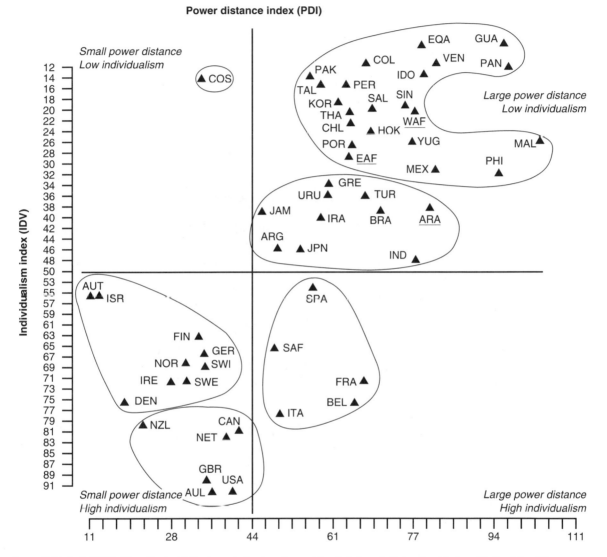

Source: Hofstede, G. (1983), 'The cultural relativity of organizational practices and theories', *Journal of International Business Studies*, Fall, p. 82.

The different positions of all these countries on the dimensions of masculinity–femininity and uncertainty avoidance in Figure 4.8 (each one falls into a different quadrant) show how differentiating one country's culture from another is not simple.

Figure 4.9 illustrates the interaction of the power-distance and uncertainty avoidance dimensions. Hofstede (1994) notes that a country's culture, according to these dimensions, affects the way people organise themselves in their work. To quote:

Figure 4.8

The position of the 50 countries on the masculinity and uncertainty avoidance scales

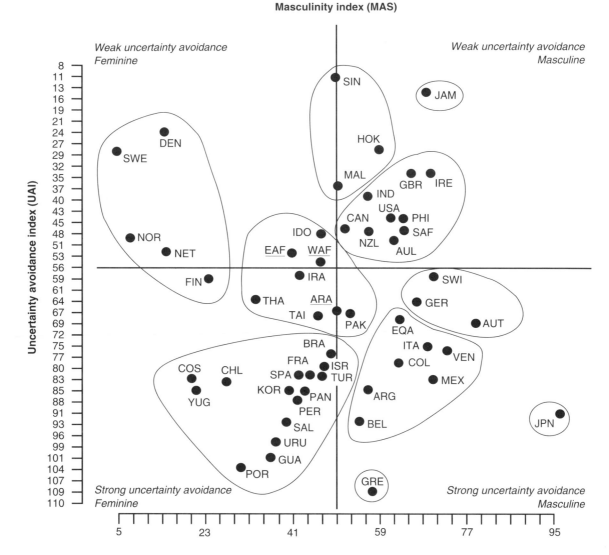

The two dimensions cover the two crucial questions which have to be answered in any effort at organizing. Power Distance deals with who will decide what; Uncertainty Avoidance with establishing predictability of outcomes, with the need for structures and rules ... other things being equal, in countries with smaller Power Distances, the leaders as well as those led will function best with a wider spread of decision power than in countries with larger PDs; in countries with stronger Uncertainty Avoidance, all will need more structure and rules than in countries with weaker UA (p. 7).

Figure 4.9

The position of the 50 countries on the power distance and uncertainty avoidance

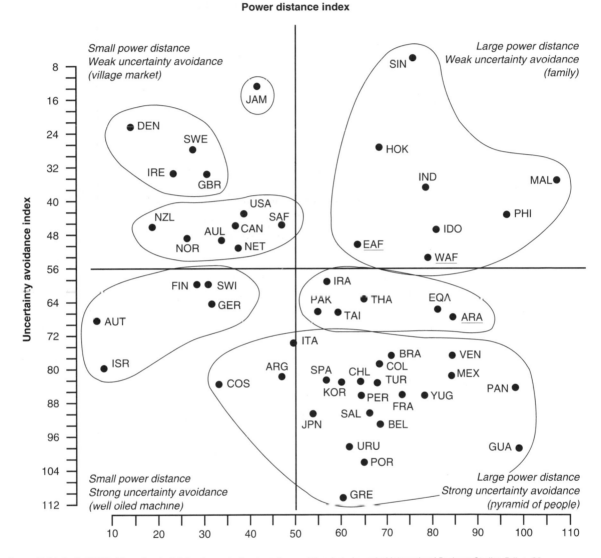

Source: Hofstede, G. (1983), 'The cultural relativity of organizational practices and theories', *Journal of International Business Studies*, Fall, p. 86.

Hofstede (1994) refers to empirical evidence of a relationship between a country's position on the Power Distance/Uncertainty Avoidance matrix and models of organisations implicit in the minds of people from those countries regarding the way organisations operate. Figure 4.10 depicts this idea graphically.

Figure 4.10

Implicit models of organisation

Adapted from Hofstede, G. (1994), 'Management scientists are human', *Management Science*, Vol. 40, No. 1, January.

Hofstede used the metaphors of a village market, a well-oiled machine, a pyramid and a family to describe different approaches to organising. Thus, people from countries with a 'village market' culture do not appear to have the same need for hierarchy and certainty as those from a pyramid type culture. These contrast with people from cultures reminiscent of 'well-oiled machines' – such as Germany – where hierarchy is not particularly required because there are established procedures and rules to which everyone works. People who live in countries located in the 'family' quadrant – such as India, West Africa and Malaysia – are said to have an implicit model of organisation which resembles a family in which the owner-manager is the omnipotent (grand-) father.

It is clear that, if, as Hofstede maintains, these differences between cultural groupings exist and any convergence across them will be very slow, then there is a good chance that they will influence organisational cultures in correspondingly different ways. It should not be forgotten, however, that Hofstede's research was carried out some time ago and mainly within a single multi-national organisation. The clustering of countries into the four models depicted in Figure 4.10 is a simplification of the complexity of distinguishing one country's culture from another, let alone differences within countries.

There is, however, support for Hofstede's views on national cultural differences from the research carried out by Laurent (1983). In contrast to Hofstede's research which sampled the views of employees at all levels of a single organisation, Laurent's research focused on the views of upper and middle level managers in a large number of different organisations, spread across nine European countries and the United States. Laurent's hypothesis was that the national origin of managers significantly affects their views of what proper management should be. Consequently, the focus was, perhaps, slightly narrower than that of Hofstede, but had the advantage of sampling across several different organisations.

Illustration 4.10
LAURENT'S DIMENSIONS OF NATIONAL CULTURE

Organisations as political systems

This dimension deals with the political role played by managers in society, their perception of power motivation within the organisation, and the degree to which organisational structures are clearly defined in the minds of the individuals involved. Managers from countries scoring high on this dimension are more likely to see organisations as political systems, but with only a vague idea of structure, as compared with those scoring low on the dimension.

Organisations as role-formalisation systems

This dimension focuses on the relative importance of defining and specifying the functions and roles of organisational members. This includes the necessity or otherwise for detailed job descriptions and precisely defined management roles. Managers from countries scoring high on this dimension emphasise the values of clarity and efficiency. Managers with lower scores are less concerned with specifying the precise boundaries of people's jobs.

Organisations as authority systems

This dimension includes the concept of organisations as hierarchical structures designed to specify authority relationships. Managers from countries scoring high on this dimension view authority as more the property of the individual. Those scoring low view authority more as an attribute of the role or function. High scorers were much more likely to agree with one of the statements of this dimension that 'Today there seems to be an authority crisis in organisations', than those who scored low.

Organisations as hierarchical-relationship systems

This dimension includes questions relating to the type of hierarchical relationships considered desirable between managers and subordinates. It also includes reference to organisational conflict in that the dream of eliminating conflict from organisations is associated with the belief that a manager should definitely know more than his or her subordinates and that organisations should not be upset by such practices as bypassing or having to report to two bosses.

Source: Based on Laurent, A. (1983), 'The cultural diversity of Western conceptions of management', *International Studies of Management and Organisation*, Vol. XIII, No. 1–2, pp. 75–96.

From his survey of 817 managers across the 10 countries, Laurent identified four dimensions which he labelled: organisations as political systems, organisations as authority systems, organisations as role-formalisation systems, and organisations as hierarchical-relationship systems. Illustration 4.10 explains these dimensions which Laurent says: 'represent attempts to capture a structure of collective managerial ideologies that meaningfully differentiate national cultures' (Laurent, 1983, p. 78).

Table 4.1 summarises the relative position of the European countries on each of Laurent's dimensions.

Table 4.1 shows that the French and Italian managers score high or reasonably high on all Laurent's dimensions. This mirrors, to some extent, the findings of Hofstede regarding his power distance dimension which could, conceptually, be likened to all of Laurent's dimensions. The other countries' scores on all but the dimension of organisations as role-formalisation systems are also in line with their scores on Hofstede's power distance dimension. Laurent's dimension of organisations as role-formalisation systems is conceptually close to Hofstede's uncertainty avoidance dimension. The position of Germany on both these dimensions is congruent with this interpretation. However, the positions of Denmark and Great Britain on these dimensions give an opposite result.

Table 4.1
Summary of Laurent's findings

Dimension	Denmark	UK	The Netherlands	Germany	Sweden	USA	Switzerland	France	Italy	Belgium
Organisations as:										
Political systems	26	32	36	36	42	43	51	62	66	missing
Authority systems	46	48	49	34	46	30	32	65	61	61
Role-formalisation systems	80	80	67	85	57	66	85	81	84	81
Hierarchical-relationship systems	37	36	33	47	25	28	43	50	66	50

Source: Summarised from: Laurent, A. (1983), 'The cultural diversity of Western conceptions of management', *International Studies of Management and Organisation*, Vol. XIII, Nos. 1–2, pp. 75–96.

Laurent does not, apparently, have a dimension which is close in concept to Hofstede's individualism dimension. However, an inspection of Figure 4.7 shows that the dimensions of individualism and power distance may not be very distinct. Only France (FRA), Belgium (BEL) and Costa Rica (COS) are positioned clearly away from the main groupings, which show scores on the individualism dimension to be almost congruent with scores on the power distance dimension. This is supported by Pugh's (1993) argument that Hofstede's individualism dimension is positively correlated with Hall's (1976) concepts of high-context and low-context cultures (*see* Illustration 4.11).

In spite of the reservations stated previously, what is clear, from Illustration 4.11, is that Laurent found differences between national cultures which were not too dissimilar to those found by Hofstede.

Both Hofstede's and Laurent's findings can be criticised in terms of their methods – in their reliance on questionnaires and the identification of a few dimensions. This criticism can, however, be balanced by other studies (e.g. d'Iribarne, 1989; Maurice, Sorge and Warner, 1980) which have found differences between national cultures, but which were based on in-depth, comprehensive examinations of a limited number of organisations or organisational units. Yet a third method was used by Calori and De Woot (1994) when they used non-directive interviews with 51 human resource directors in 40 large international companies with headquarters or major operating units in Europe.

Illustration 4.11
HIGH-CONTEXT AND LOW-CONTEXT CULTURES

Hall (1976) maintains that we interpret and create communications in a context of social and situational cues and that this interpretation is influenced by our cultural experience. Thus cultures vary in how much or how little they will depend on the context when communicating and developing relationships. This idea finds its expression in the distinction between high-context and low-context cultures as follows:

High-context cultures

In high-context cultures, the environment, situation, and non-verbal behaviour are essential in interpreting and creating communications. The spoken word carries only part of the meaning – other clues such as methods of greeting, physical settings and more importantly non-verbal signals and inferences act to 'fill out' the spoken word. According to Mead (1994), high-context cultures have the following characteristics:

- Long-lasting relationships between individuals with deep personal involvement with each other.
- Economical, fast and efficient communication achievable because of shared codes.
- Loyalty to and from superiors and subordinates.
- Spoken rather than written agreements, with the assumption that written agreements can be changed according to changing circumstances.
- Tight distinctions between insiders and outsiders, the latter being defined mainly as not belonging to the family.

- Cultural patterns which are ingrained and slow to change.

Low-context cultures

In low-context cultures the context of communication is less important for interpreting and creating communication – the meaning of a communication being carried mainly in the spoken word. A direct 'blunt' communication style is commonly used. Because it is the words which carry most of the meaning, they are used more extensively than in low-context cultures. Mead (1994) lists the following characteristics of low-context cultures.

- Relatively short-duration relationships between individuals; deep personal involvement not greatly valued.
- Messages must be made explicit because there is less dependence on the context or non-verbal signals for understanding.
- Authority is diffused throughout the bureaucratic system and personal responsibility is difficult to pin down.
- Agreements tend to be written not spoken; contracts are legal and binding; written legal systems are used to resolve disputes.
- Family and outsiders are less closely distinguished, making it easier for foreigners to integrate themselves into a culture different from their own.
- Cultural patterns are faster to change.

On the basis of the results of these interviews, Calori and De Woot claim to have found country clusters which suggest a typology of management systems (*see* Figure 4.11). Illustration 4.12 summarises Calori and De Woot's conclusions on the characteristics typical of the first two levels of segmentation, that is the Anglo Saxon, Latin, and Northern Europe (using the German model as an example) groupings.

Calori and De Woot suggest a simplified view of management philosophies, structures and practices in Europe, as shown in Figure 4.12.

Figure 4.11

Typology of management systems in Europe

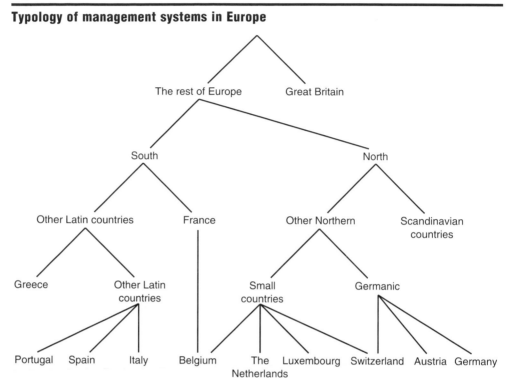

Source: Calori, R., and De Woot, P. (1994), *A European Management Model Beyond Diversity* (Hemel Hempstead, Prentice-Hall, p. 20).

Figure 4.12

The stretching forces in European management

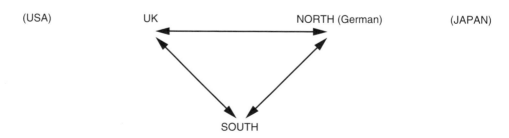

Source: Calori, R., and De Woot, P. (1994), *A European Management Model Beyond Diversity* (Hemel Hempstead, Prentice-Hall, p. 28).

Illustration 4.12
DIFFERENCES BETWEEN GREAT BRITAIN, SOUTHERN EUROPE (INCLUDING FRANCE) AND NORTHERN EUROPE (TYPIFIED BY GERMANY)

The United Kingdom, an exception in Europe

Management in the UK has more in common with the United States of America than the rest of Europe. It has:

- A short-term orientation (more than continental Europe).
- A shareholder orientation (whereas the rest of Europe has more of a stakeholder orientation).
- An orientation towards trading and finance (the importance of the stock market is more developed than in continental Europe).
- A higher turnover of managers.
- A greater liberalism towards foreigners (e.g. the Japanese).
- More freedom for top management *vis-à-vis* the workers and government.
- More direct and pragmatic relationships between people.
- More variable remuneration.

However, different from the United States of America, it has:

- Adversarial relationships with labour.
- The tradition of the manager as a 'gifted amateur' (as opposed to the professionalism of US managers).
- The influence of class differences in the firm.

The Latin way of doing business

Southern Europe (including France) differs from the rest of Europe in that it has:

- More state intervention.

- More protectionism.
- More hierarchy in the firm.
- More intuitive management.
- More family business (especially in Italy).
- More reliance on an élite (especially in France).

The German model

Characteristic of Germany, Austria and, to some extent, Switzerland as well as the Benelux countries, the German model is based on three cultural and structural characteristics.

- Strong links between banks and industry.
- A balance between a sense of national collectivity and the Länder (regional) system.
- A system of training and development of managers. It has the following five components:
- The system of co-determination with workers' representatives present on the board.
- The loyalty of managers (and employees in general) who spend their career in a single firm, which then gives priority to in-house training.
- The collective orientation of the workforce, which includes dedication to the company, team spirit and a sense of discipline.
- The long-term orientation which appears in planning, in the seriousness and stability of supplier–client relationships and in the priority of industrial goals over short-term financial objectives.
- The reliability and stability of shareholders, influenced by a strong involvement of banks in industry.

Source: Based on Calori, R., and De Woot, P. (1994), *A European Management Model Beyond Diversity* (Hemel Hempstead, Prentice-Hall, pp. 22–9).

ACTIVITY 4.5

Compare and contrast Calori and De Woot's country groupings and country characteristics with their positions on Hofstede's and Laurent's cultural dimensions and on Hall's compass model of cultural differences.

National culture and organisational culture

The result of carrying out Activity 4.5 illustrates the complexity of attempting to build tight categories into which different national cultures can be put. It would be difficult to argue, however, that these differences do not occur. In addition, the evidence points to the influence of national culture on organisational culture as it, in turn, influences organisational life in general. For instance, a study by Furnham and Gunter (1993) provides examples of organisations in countries (e.g. Australia, Israel and Denmark), the scores of which on Hofstede's power distance culture dimension were low, but which had common organisational structures. Their structures incorporated low centralisation of decision-making and flatter pyramids of control, reminiscent of Handy's task organisational culture (Handy 1993). These organisations' structures contrasted with those in countries such as the Philippines, Mexico and India, which score highly on Hofstede's power distance dimension of culture. These latter organisations were typified by strict hierarchical structures and centralised decision-making, reminiscent of Handy's role organisational culture.

ACTIVITY 4.6

Look back at Figure 4.10 which positions four implicit models of organisation on Hofstede's power distance and uncertainty avoidance dimensions.

Consider Deal and Kennedy's four culture types described in Illustration 4.6 and decide how far each can be related to one or more of Hofstede's organisational models.

It is not difficult to link Deal and Kennedy's 'Bet-your-company' culture with countries which score similarly to Germany on Laurent's dimensions of culture (*see* Table 4.1). In fact, because Laurent focused his questions on managers and their perceptions of organisational life, it is not surprising that there is a large overlap between his dimensions of national culture and others' dimensions of organisational culture. Both Hofstede (1994) and Adler (1991) draw attention to the way organisational theory (e.g. as it relates to motivation, decision-making, leadership, etc.) is culturally determined. Because most management and organisational theory derives from the work of scholars based in Western academic institutions, caution is advised about applying it, indiscriminately, to organisations in other parts of the world. For instance, organisational cultures which imply an adherence to participative styles of leadership and decision-making, and which are part of Western national cultures, may not be welcomed in societies which see consultation on the part of leaders as a weakness and where workers would be embarrassed if consulted by their managers. Chambers (1996), in an article entitled, 'Russia's different problems', points out a number of elements in Western guides to management which are of little practical use to Russian managers. For instance, the concepts of 'just-in-time' and 'lean production' make little sense in a situation of uncertainties of supply of both raw materials and components. In an environment of minimal structures for data collection and market intelligence and no framework of commercial law, Western sales and marketing strategies are of little use.

Organisations in Russia are a product of a previous non-commercial culture and the infrastructure of business still reflects this.

It must not be forgotten, however, that, even though influenced to a smaller or larger extent by national culture, organisational cultures can change, although change is not easy. Conversely, some organisational cultures are more conducive than others to supporting organisational change.

ORGANISATIONAL CULTURE AND CHANGE

Wilson and Rosenfeld (1990, p. 237) say: 'The pervasive nature of organisational culture cannot be stressed too much. It is likely to affect virtually all aspects of organisational life.' According to Schwartz and Davis (1981, p. 35), 'culture is capable of blunting or significantly altering the intended impact of even well-thought-out changes in an organisation'. This is a popular view of culture and its implications for instigating any kind of change are clear. However, as the discussion above shows, organisational culture comes in many forms and, therefore, can be more or less supportive of change.

There are a number of different views on the relationship between culture and change. Figure 4.13 depicts various elements of organisational culture as they might influence organisational change.

Figure 4.13

Organisational culture and change

Cultures in defence against, or supportive of, change

Figure 4.13 depicts the way some elements of organisational culture might support change but, on the other hand, how they might work against it – in other words how they might put up a defense against change. One element of organisational design which is particularly relevant to the ease with which change comes about is that of an organisation's structure. Some of the typologies of organisational culture (e.g. Handy, Harrison, and Pheysey) discussed earlier in the chapter are related closely to types of organisation structure. Indeed, in these cases, culture and structure seem almost to be interchangeable. A similar case can be made for the mechanistic and organic organisational structures identified by Burns and Stalker (1961) and which were discussed in Chapter 3. Burns and Stalker's research is a good example of the merger of the concepts of structure and culture, as is seen in their argument that organic types of organisation are much more likely to be able to respond to the need for change than are mechanistic ones. However, it could be going too far to say that Burns and Stalker would have regarded mechanistic-type organisations to be *defensive* against change, because all organisations change, to some extent, incrementally, all the time. The use of the term 'defensive against change' is not, therefore, intended to imply, necessarily, that mechanistic and role-type organisational cultures will not support change. They are, however, unlikely to support, without serious trauma, the frame-breaking (*see* Tushman *et al.*, 1988), transformational (*see* Dunphy and Stace, 1993) or revolutionary types of change (*see* Johnson, 1987) discussed in Chapter 2. This is likely to be the case because of their structural characteristics, but might also be because of the attitudes, beliefs and values held by the people who work in them.

Kanter (1983) gives detailed descriptions of two extremes of organisational culture which not only are different in structural characteristics but also differ in the underlying attitudes and beliefs of the people working in them. The first she calls a 'segmentalist' culture and the other an 'integrative' culture. Illustration 4.13 summarises the characteristics of these two cultures.

In addition to the summary of a segmentalist culture given in Illustration 4.13, Kanter (1983, p. 101) offers the following 'Rules for stifling innovation' as further elucidation of this concept.

1. Regard any new idea from below with suspicion – because it's new, and because it's from below.
2. Insist that people who need your approval to act first go through several other levels of management to get their signatures.
3. Ask departments or individuals to challenge and criticize each other's proposals. (That saves you the task of deciding; you just pick the survivor.)
4. Express your criticisms freely, and withhold your praise. (That keeps people on their toes.) Let them know they can be fired at any time.
5. Treat identification of problems as signs of failure, to discourage people from letting you know when something in their area isn't working.
6. Control everything carefully. Make sure people count anything that can be counted, frequently.

Illustration 4.13

SEGMENTALIST AND INTEGRATIVE CULTURES

Segmentalist cultures

- Compartmentalise actions, events and problems.
- See problems as narrowly as possible.
- Have segmented structures with large numbers of departments walled off from one another.
- Assume problems can be solved by carving them up into pieces which are then assigned to specialists who work in isolation.
- Divide resources up among the many departments.
- Avoid experimentation.
- Avoid conflict and confrontation.
- Have weak co-ordinating mechanisms.
- Stress precedent and procedures.

Integrative cultures

- Are willing to move beyond received wisdom.
- Combine ideas from unconnected sources.
- See problems as wholes, related to larger wholes.
- Challenge established practices.
- Operate at the edge of competencies.
- Measure themselves by looking to visions of the future rather than by referring to the standards of the past.
- Create mechanisms for exchange of information and new ideas.
- Recognise and even encourage differences, but then be prepared to co-operate.
- Are outward looking.
- Look for novel solutions to problems.

Source: Based on the discussion in Kanter, R. M. (1983), *The Change Masters* (London, Routledge, Chapter 1).

---

7. Make decisions to reorganise or change policies in secret, and spring them on people unexpectedly. (That also keeps people on their toes.)

8. Make sure that requests for information are fully justified, and make sure that it is not given out to managers freely. (You don't want data to fall into the wrong hands.)

9. Assign to lower-level managers, in the name of delegation and participation, responsibility for figuring out how to cut back, lay off, move people around, or otherwise implement threatening decisions you have made. And get them to do it quickly.

10. And above all, never forget that you, the higher-ups, already know everything important about this business.

The Open University course 'Managing in Organizations' (1985) discusses Argyris and Schon's (1978) identification of what appear to be the 'unwritten rules' governing some organisational relationships which mirror Kanter's rules for stifling change. These are:

1. Keep your views of sensitive issues private; enforce the taboo against their public discussion.

2. Do not surface and test differences in views of organisational problems.

3. Avoid seeing the whole picture; allow maps of the problem to remain scattered, vague and ambiguous.

4. Protect yourself unilaterally – by avoiding both direct interpersonal confrontation and public discussion of sensitive issues which might expose you to blame.

5. Protect others unilaterally – by avoiding the testing of assumptions where that testing might evoke negative feelings, and by keeping others from exposure to blame.

6. Control the situation and the task – by making up your own mind about the problem and acting on your view, by keeping your view private, and by avoiding the public inquiry which might refute your view.

The Open University material (pp. 47–9) contrasts this set of rules, which they say typifies what they call a 'defensive climate', with the following rules which they say are more typical of a 'supportive' climate.

1. Surface sensitive issues, and encourage others to do so.
2. Ensure differences of view are publicly tested and that statements are made in ways that can be tested.
3. Bring together dispersed information and clarify vague and ambiguous data.
4. Do not avoid interpersonal confrontation even if it involves negative feelings.
5. Make protection of oneself and others a joint task oriented towards growth.
6. Control the task jointly.

It is clear from both Kanter and Argyris and Schon's writings that a segmentalist or defensive culture will mitigate against organisational change. Of additional interest, is that many of the items in all the lists of rules frequently become the 'symbols' and 'symbolic acts' which Johnson (1990) says are so important to the maintenance or changing of organisational paradigms. They form the basis on which organisational learning and therefore organisational change may or may not take place.

Organisational learning and types of change

Argyris (1964) was one of the first people to point out the difference between two kinds of learning. The first, called *single-loop learning*, is indicative of a situation where an objective or goal is defined and an individual works out the most favoured way of reaching the goal. In single-loop learning, while many different possibilities for achieving personal or organisational goals might be considered, the goal itself is not questioned. Single-loop learning is also referred to as individual learning, that is, learning which an individual achieves but which seldom passes throughout the organisation in any coherent way.

This type of learning is contrasted by Argyris with *double-loop learning* where questions are asked, not only about the *means* by which goals can be achieved, but about the *ends*, that is, the goals themselves. Johnson (1990) refers to this type of learning as *organisational re-learning* which he says is a 'process in which that which is taken for granted and which is the basis of strategic direction – the paradigm – is re-formulated'. (p. 189). Given that the organisational paradigm contains all the elements of Johnson and Scholes' (1993) cultural web, this implies change throughout the organisation in all aspects of its behaviour.

Individual or single-loop learning is most likely to be the dominant type of learning to take place within a segmentalist or defensive culture. The characteristics of this type of culture mitigate, significantly, against the sharing of information and openness which is required for organisational learning to take place. Therefore, while it could be said to be sufficient for the types of change which Dunphy and Stace (1993) define as 'fine-tuning' and 'incremental adjustment', it will be blind to the need for the kind of radical thinking required to bring about change in the organisation's direction, that is, strategic change. In addition, the inability of an organisation to operate double-loop learning contributes to the process of 'strategic drift' (Johnson 1987), which was discussed in Chapter 2, a process which can lead to change being forced upon an organisation.

Strong and weak cultures

'Organisational cultures differ markedly in terms of their relative strengths' (Brown, 1995, p. 74). Whether defensive or supportive, intuitively, the existence of a strong culture implies a commonly understood perspective on how organisational life should happen, with most organisational members subscribing to it. Conversely, a weak culture implies no dominant pervasive culture but an organisation made up of many different cultures, some of which will be in conflict with each other. Payne (1990) has suggested that the strength of an organisation's culture can be measured by, first, the degree to which it is shared by all members and, second, by the intensity with which organisational members believe in it. The greater the intensity of an organisation's culture, the greater the degree to which it pervades all levels at which culture manifests itself, that is, in influencing not only people's attitudes, but also their values, basic assumptions and beliefs.

The strength or weakness of organisational cultures is important in that it performs a number of functions for the organisation. A popular view is that it is the glue which holds the organisation together. Brown (1995) suggests the following functions at the organisational level.

Conflict resolution

As organisations can be characterised as grounds for disagreement and conflict, culture can be a force for integration and consensus. Knowing 'how things are done around here' can help avoid conflict.

Co-ordination and control

If a strong organisational culture helps avoid conflict, it will, conversely, facilitate the processes of co-ordination and control. Strongly held values and beliefs will ensure that all concerned will pull together in the same direction.

Reduction of uncertainty

For new recruits to an organisation, the more quickly they 'learn' the norms of behaviour, the more confident they will become in their assumptions about how others will behave and the way in which organisational processes are carried out. This has the advantage of reducing the complexity of the organisational world, neutralising uncertainties so that any actions taken are in tune with organisational rationalities as seen by the majority of organisational members.

Motivation

While extrinsic rewards such as pay, bonuses and promotions can motivate employees to perform well, a culture which can offer employees a means of identification with their work, which can foster loyalty and assist their belief that they are valued, will add to their motivation and presumably the overall organisational performance.

Competitive advantage

A strong culture is said to improve organisational performance. Peters and Waterman (1982) and Kanter (1983) are just three well-known writers and consultants who claim to have found recipes for cultures which are presumed to link to performance. Their arguments are that the more closely an organisation sticks to their particular recipe, the greater the probability that it will be a high performer. It is debatable, however, whether a strong culture, even of the supportive kind, necessarily links to increased competitive advantage. For instance, Kotter and Heskett's (1992) research during the period 1977–88, identified 10 large and well-known organisations (including Sears, Procter & Gamble and Goodyear), all of which had exceptionally strong cultures, but all of which had weak performances.

In some organisations, the existence of a weak dominant culture with multiple sub-cultures may be an advantage. Strong, all-pervasive cultures, can be a disadvantage when they become so controlling that there is little potential for the nonconformity which brings innovation and the capacity to adapt to change.

CHANGING ORGANISATIONAL CULTURE TO BRING ABOUT ORGANISATIONAL CHANGE

The discussion in this chapter shows that it is difficult to deny the importance of culture as a dominant influence on the whole of organisational life. From this it could be deduced that, in order to bring about any kind of significant organisational change, the organisation's culture must be managed accordingly. This view is subscribed to by scholars such as Johnson and Scholes (1993) in their depiction of the cultural web. It is also evident in the arguments which recommend organisations to take on the characteristics of a supportive (integrative) culture (*see* Kanter, 1983) linked to an organic structure (Burns and Stalker, 1961) or those which will bring excellence in performance (*see* Peters and Waterman, 1982). From these points of view, permanent organisational change will only be brought about by first changing people's attitudes and values – in other words changing the culture at the deeper levels of its meaning as illustrated in Figure 4.2 above.

However, changing an organisation's culture is not easy, as Schwartz and Davis (1981) point out from their observations of change at companies they researched. In relation to one of these – AT&T, which, in the late 1970s, undertook a large-scale corporate and organisational reorientation – Schwartz and Davis (1981, p. 31) say:

> Despite the major changes in structure, in human resources, and in support systems, there is a general consensus both inside and outside AT&T that its greatest task in making its strategy succeed will be its ability to transform the AT&T culture. *It will probably be a decade before direct judgements should be made as to its success.* [Italics added.]

Yet another example they quote is the case where the president of an engineering company resigned after six years of trying to change the company's culture from being production oriented to being market oriented. At this point he reckoned he had managed to dent but not change the culture.

Given this background, some means of measuring organisational culture and its relationship to organisational change appears desirable.

Assessing cultural risk

Activity 4.1 is one way of measuring organisational culture and this method can obviously be applied to any list of culture characteristics. For instance, Furnham and Gunter (1993) suggest this in relation to Schein's (1985) list of dimensions of corporate culture – a list not dissimilar to that of Robbins – and in addition give a list of various quantitative measures of culture. However, measuring organisational culture, of itself, is only a means to an end. The end is to determine how culture should be managed as part of the process of organisational change.

It was, therefore, in pursuit of this end that Schwartz and Davis devised a means of measuring culture in terms of descriptions of the way management tasks are typically handled in companywide, boss–subordinate, peer and interdepartment relationships so as to assess the degree of cultural compatibility with any proposed strategic change. Figure 4.14 is an example of Schwartz and Davis's corporate culture matrix which they designed to carry out the first part of this process. It has been completed for the UK-based division of a company in the computer services industry.

Once you have carried out Activity 4.7, you can use the results of this analysis to assess the compatibility of the culture of this organisation to any proposed changes in the organisation's approach to its strategy, structure and operations. The framework for this comparative assessment is shown in Figure 4.15 as a matrix which allows elements of the proposed strategy changes to be plotted against their importance to that strategy and the degree to which they are compatible with the culture. From this matrix, it can be seen that the nearer the elements of any proposed strategic change

ACTIVITY 4.7

For any organisation you know well, use the basic matrix in Figure 4.14 to do the following:

1 *Insert, in each cell of the main body of the matrix, words and/or phrases which encapsulate the different relationships (listed horizontally) according to the management of the tasks (listed vertically).*

2 *In the final column on the right, summarise the corporate culture for each task.*

3 *In the final row, summarise the corporate culture for each of the relationships.*

What do the summaries tell you about this organisation's overall culture?

Figure 4.14 Corporate culture matrix

| Tasks | Relationships | | | | Summary of culture in relation to tasks |
	Companywide	Boss–subordinate	Peer	Inter-department	
Innovating	Innovation if part of the mission.	Bosses open to suggestions.	Team work.	Team work.	Encourage creativity and innovation.
Decision-making	Has to fit in with strategy.	Input from subordinates encouraged – boss has final word.	Collective decisions.	Work together to produce an integrated package.	Collaborative decision-making but boss has the final word; corporate strategy rules.
Communicating	Easy, use of E-mail and phone.	Friendly.	Face-to-face and open.	Easy, use of E-mail and phone.	Easy, informal and friendly communications.
Organising	Market focus.	Democratic.	Professional relationships.	Collaborative.	Organised on the basis of skills and professional relationships.
Monitoring	Shareholder-led organisation.	Meet short-term profit targets and deadlines.	Project management.	Project management.	Need to meet short-term profit goals.
Appraising and rewarding	Encourage performers.	Hard work = good rewards.	Results important.	Results important.	Meritocracy.
Summary of culture in relation to relationships	Allow freedom to managers as long as they operate within the strategy and meet profit targets; output oriented.	Friendly, rely on each other for success.	Highly skilled professionals who help each other out.	Work together to support sales.	Overall performance and profit matter in a culture which welcomes dynamic and performance-related individuals.

Source: Matrix adapted from Schwartz, H., and Davis, S. M. (1981), 'Matching corporate strategy and business strategy', *Organizational Dynamics*, Summer, p. 36; example from the author's own experience.

are to the top right-hand corner, the lower the chance that they will be accepted, given the prevailing culture. For instance, if a change to a matrix structure is of the utmost importance to a proposed strategic change, yet the culture is one which is reminiscent of Handy's (1993) 'role-oriented' culture or of Hall's (1995) 'north' culture, the need for a matrix structure would be positioned in the top right cell of the matrix in Figure 4.15. Other elements of the proposed change might still be low in level of culture compatibility but of low importance in the overall change strategy. They would, therefore, be positioned towards the lower right-hand part of the matrix.

Figure 4.15

Assessing cultural risk

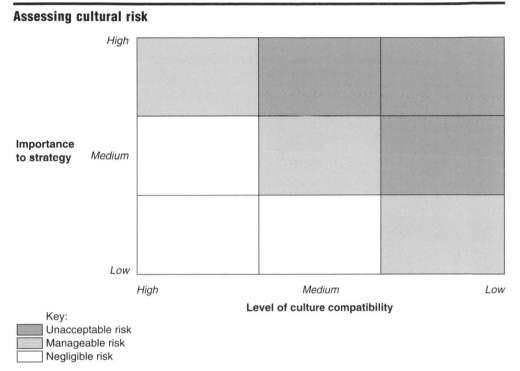

Source: Based on Schwartz, H., and Davis, S. M. (1981), 'Matching corporate strategy and business strategy', *Organizational Dynamics*, Summer, p. 41.

The relevance of culture change to organisational change

Assessing cultural risk helps management pinpoint where they are likely to meet resistance to change because of incompatibility between strategy and culture. This further allows them to make choices regarding whether to: (a) ignore the culture; (b) manage around the culture; (c) try to change the culture to fit the strategy; or (d) change the strategy to fit the culture, perhaps by reducing performance expectations.

Ignoring the culture

Ignoring the culture is not recommended unless the organisation has sufficient resources to draw on to weather the subsequent storm and the possibility of an initial downturn in business.

Managing around the culture

The second option – managing around the culture – is a real possibility given that there are, in most cases, more ways than one of achieving desired goals. Figure 4.16 reproduces Schwartz and Davis's (1981) example of how to manage around an

Figure 4.16 How to manage around company culture

	Strategy	'Right' approach	Cultural barriers	Alternative approaches
Company A	Diversify product and market.	Divisionalise.	Centralised power. One-man rule. Functional focus. Hierarchical structure.	Use business teams. Use explicit strategic planning. Change business measures.
Company B	Focus marketing on most profitable segments.	Fine-tune reward system. Adjust management-information system.	Diffused power. Highly individualised operations.	Dedicate full-time personnel to each key market.
Company C	Extend technology to new markets.	Set up matrix organisation.	Multiple power centres. Functional focus.	Use programme coordinators. Set up planning committees. Get top management more involved.
Company D	Withdraw gradually from declining market and maximise cash throw-offs.	Focus organisation specifically. Fine-tune rewards. Ensure top management visibility.	New-business driven. Innovators rewarded. State-of-the-art operation.	Sell out.

Source: Schwartz, H., and Davis, S. M. (1981), 'Matching corporate strategy and business strategy', *Organizational Dynamics*, Summer, p. 44.

organisation's culture. This outlines four typical strategies that companies might pursue and, what Schwartz and Davis call the 'right' organisational approaches to implement them. The final two columns set out the cultural barriers to these 'right' approaches and the alternative approaches that could, therefore, be used.

Changing the culture

The third option, changing the culture to fit the desired strategic changes, is also a possibility but, as much of the literature cautions, this can be an extremely difficult and lengthy process, particularly if the culture is a strong one (Scholz, 1987; Furnham and Gunter, 1993). Furthermore, there are strong arguments (e.g. Hope and Hendry, 1995) against cultural change as a concept for organisations of the 1990s given what Hope and Hendry (p. 62) describe as the move away from the large-scale hierarchies characteristic of the multinationals of the 1970s and 1980s, towards much leaner and more focused units. According to Hope and Hendry, this move has been accompanied by an increase in the employment of what Drucker (1992) calls 'professional knowledge workers' but also by an erosion of security of employment and predictable career paths, with consequent difficulties of employee control. Two problems are said to arise from this. The first is that the 'knowledge workers' who are likely to flourish in these new types of organisation are least likely to be open to cultural manipulation.

Second, any new managerial practice must allow for a degree of cynicism in the context of the downsizing which has removed several layers of middle management and therefore removed the opportunity for steady advancement once assumed as almost everyone's right. As a consequence of all this, 'employees in general may be less receptive to evangelical calls for shared cultural values' (Hope and Hendry, 1995, p. 62).

This view is supported by Beer, Eisenstat and Spector (1993) who argue that trying to change attitudes and values directly is futile; the way to bring about organisational change is first to change behaviour. The behavioural change will bring about the desired changes in attitudes and values. Thus, Beer *et al.* argue for changing the organisational context (people's roles, responsibilities and the relationships between them) first, which will then result in changed behaviour and associated attitudes. This view of change rests on the assumption that changing organisational structures, systems and role relationships, which comprise, in the main, the formal aspects of organisational life, will bring about desired cultural changes incorporating organisational members' attitudes and beliefs. Many models of planned change subscribe to this view and the 'Six steps to effective change' propounded by Beer *et al.* are an example of this (*see* Illustration 4.14).

Both Beer *et al.* and Hope and Hendry can be said to have their views supported by Hofstede (1981, p. 26) who quotes Bem (1970, p. 60) as saying, 'One of the most effective ways of changing mental programmes of individuals is changing behavior first'. He continues, 'That value change has to precede behavior change is a naive (idealistic) assumption that neglects the contribution of the *situation* to actual behaviour'.

The literature does not help in deciding whether cultural change is a real possibility or whether managers requiring organisational change should work around the culture. Some methods of bringing about culture change depend upon education and persuasion, or, in some cases, coercion, to help bring about changes in attitudes (Anthony, 1994). Others rely more on changing recruitment, selection, promotion, reward and redundancy policies to alter the composition of the workforce and so retain those who have the desired beliefs, values and attitudes associated with the

---

Illustration 4.14
SIX STEPS TO EFFECTIVE CHANGE PROPOUNDED BY BEER *ET AL.*

1. Mobilise commitment to change through joint diagnosis of business problems.

2. Develop a shared vision of how to organise and manage for competitiveness.

3. Foster consensus for the new vision, competence to enact it, and cohesion to move it along.

4. Spread revitalisation to all departments without pushing it from the top.

5. Institutionalise revitalisation through formal policies, systems and structures.

6. Monitor and adjust strategies in response to problems in the revitalisation process.

Source: Beer, M., Eisenstat, R. A., and Spector, B. (1993), 'Why change programs don't produce change', in Mabey, C., and Mayon-White, B. (eds.), *Managing Change* (London, P.C.P.).

desired culture (Dobson, 1988). It seems that a combination of approaches would be most effective unless the organisational changes proposed can, themselves, be changed to be more compatible with the existing culture.

Changing the strategy to match the culture

Schwartz and Davis (1981) give the merging of two organisations as an example of changing the strategy to be more compatible with the existing cultures. This choice for an organisation is similar to that of managing around the culture and further emphasises the possibilities inherent in the idea that organisations are able to choose the means by which they achieve their ends. In addition, those who view culture as a metaphor for organisations (Morgan, 1986) would find it difficult to preach wholesale cultural change. Some accommodation between changing the culture and adapting the strategy is more likely to be accepted.

Overall, compromise between these different approaches to managing organisational culture within a context of organisational change is counselled. Using a process which combines education and persuasion (to bring about attitude and value change) with changes in structures and systems (to bring about changes in behaviour) will help modify organisational culture as it is linked to organisational change on a broader scale. However, Pettigrew (1990) offers a timely reminder that cultural and strategic change is associated with organisational politics as well as with the core beliefs of the top decision-makers. The next two chapters address these issues.

DISCUSSION QUESTIONS AND ACTIVITIES

1 Depending on what you know about cultures in countries other than your own, plot your own and two or three other countries on the dimensions illustrated in Illustration 4.9. Consider any similarities and differences between the plots and attempt to explain why these might be the case.

2 Position an organisation you know well on the matrix in Figure 4.9. Explain your decision.

3 Discuss the proposition that: 'organisational cultures should always "fit" with organisational strategy'. Therefore, any strategic change must always be accompanied by appropriate culture change.

REFERENCES

Adler, N. J. (1991), *International Dimensions of Organizational Behavior* (2nd edn.), Belmont, CA, Wadsworth Publishing Company.

Adler, N. J. (1996), *International Dimensions of Organizational Behavior* (3rd edn.), Cincinnati, OH, South Western College Publishing, ITP.

Alvesson, M. (1993), *Cultural Perspectives on Organizations*, Cambridge, Cambridge University Press.

Anthony, P. (1994), *Managing Culture*, Buckingham, Open University Press.

Argyris, C. (1964), *Integrating the Individual and the Organization*, New York, Wiley.

Argyris, C., and Schon, D. A. (1978), *Organizational Learning: A Theory of Action Perspective*, Reading, MA, Addison-Wesley.

Beer, M., Eisenstat, R. A., and Spector, B. (1993), 'Why change programs don't produce change', in Mabey, C., and Mayon-White, B. (eds.), *Managing Change*, London, P.C.P., pp. 99–107.

Bem, D. J. (1970), *Beliefs, Attitudes and Human Affairs*, Belmont, CA, Brooks/Cole.

Brown, A. (1995), *Organisational Culture*, London, Pitman.

Burns, T., and Stalker, G. M. (1961), *The Management of Innovation*, London, Tavistock.

Calori, R., and De Woot, P. (1994), *A European Management Model Beyond Diversity*, Hemel Hempstead, Prentice-Hall.

Castells, M. (1989), 'High technology and the new international division of labour', *Labour and Society*, Vol. 14, Special Issue, pp. 7–20.

Chambers, D. (1996), 'Russia's different problems', *Financial Times*, 23 February, pp. 9–10.

Chandler, A. D., Jun. (1962), *Strategy and Structure: Chapters in the History of the Industrial Enterprise*, Cambridge, MA, MIT Press.

Deal, T. E., and Kennedy, A. A. (1982), *Corporate Cultures: the Rites and Rituals of Corporate Life*, Reading, MA, Addison-Wesley.

d'Iribarne, P. (1989), *La Logique de l'Honneur: Gestion des Entreprises et Traditions Nationales*, Paris, Seuil.

Dobson, P. (1988), 'Changing culture', *Employment Gazette*, December, pp. 647–50.

Drennan, D. (1992), *Transforming Company Culture*, London, McGraw-Hill.

Drucker, P. (1992), 'The new society of organisations', *Harvard Business Review*, September–October, pp. 95–104.

Dunphy, D., and Stace, D. (1993), 'The strategic management of corporate change', *Human Relations*, Vol. 46, No. 8, pp. 905–20.

Dyer, W. (1985), 'The cycle of cultural evolution in organizations', in Kilmann, R. H., Saxton, M. J. and Serpa, R., *Gaining Control of the Corporate Culture*, San Francisco, Jossey-Bass.

French, W. L., and Bell, C. H., Jun. (1990), *Organization Development. Behavioral Science Interventions for Organization Improvement* (4th edn.), Englewood Cliffs, NJ, Prentice-Hall.

Furnham, A., and Gunter, B. (1993), 'Corporate culture: diagnosis and change', in Cooper, C. L. (ed.) *International Review of Industrial and Organisational Psychology*, Chichester, Wiley.

Goodman, M. (1995), *Creative Management*, Hemel Hempstead, Prentice-Hall.

Hall, E. T. (1981), *Beyond Culture*, London, Anchor Books, Doubleday.

Hall, W. (1995), *Managing Cultures. Making Strategic Relationships Work*, Chichester, Wiley.

Handy, C. (1993), *Understanding Organizations*, London, Penguin.

Harrison, R. (1972), 'How to describe your organization', *Harvard Business Review*, September–October.

Hickson, D. J., and MacMillan, C. J. (1981), *Organization and Nation: The Aston Programme IV*, Aldershot, Gower.

Hofstede, G. (1980), *Culture's Consequences: International Differences in Work-related Values*, London and Beverly Hills, Sage.

Hofstede, G. (1981), 'Culture and organisations', *International Studies of Management and Organizations*, Vol. X, No. 4, pp. 15–41.

Hofstede, G. (1983), 'The cultural relativity of organizational practices and theories', *Journal of International Business Studies*, Fall, pp. 75–89.

Hofstede, G. (1994), 'Management scientists are human', *Management Science*, Vol. 40, No. 1, January.

Hofstede, G., Neuijen, B., Ohayv, D., and Sanders, G. (1990), 'Measuring organizational cultures: a qualitative and quantitative study across twenty cases', *Administrative Science Quarterly*, Vol. 35, pp. 286–316.

Hope, V., and Hendry, J. (1995), 'Corporate cultural change – is it relevant for the organisations of the 1990s?', *Human Resource Management Journal*, Vol. 5, No. 4, Summer, pp. 61–73.

Jackson, T. (ed.) (1995), *Cross-Cultural Management*, Oxford, Butterworth-Heinemann.

Jaques, E. (1952), *The Changing Culture of a Factory*, New York, Dryden Press.

Johnson, G. (1987), *Strategic Change and the Management Process*, Oxford, Blackwell.

Johnson, G. (1990), 'Managing strategic action: the role of symbolic action', British Journal of Management, Vol. 1, pp. 183–200.

Johnson, G. (1996), Lecture to Diploma in Management Studies students at Nene College of Higher Education, Northampton.

Johnson, G., and Scholes, K. (1993), *Exploring Corporate Strategy. Texts and Cases*, Hemel Hempstead, Prentice-Hall International.

Johnson, G., and Scholes, K. (1997), *Exploring Corporate Strategy, Texts and Cases*, Hemel Hempstead, Prentice-Hall International.

Kanter, R. M. (1983), *The Change Masters*, London, Routledge.

Kerr, C., Dunlop, J. T., Harbison, F. H., and Myers, C. A. (1960), *Industrialism and Industrial Man*, London, Heinemann.

Kluckhohn, F., and Strodtbeck, F. L. (1961), *Variations in Value Orientations*, Evanston, IL, Row, Peterson.

Kotter, J. P., and Heskett, J. L. (1992), *Corporate Culture and Performance*, New York, The Free Press.

Kroeber, A. L. and Kluckhohn, F. (1952), *Culture: A Critical Review of Concepts and Definitions*, New York, Vintage Books.

Laurent, A. (1983), 'The cultural diversity of Western conceptions of management', *International Studies of Management and Organisation*, Vol. XIII, Nos. 1–2, pp. 75–96.

Louis, M. R. (1980), 'Organizations as culture-bearing milieux', in Pondy, L. R. *et al.* (eds.), *Organizational Symbolism*, Greenwich, CT, JAI.

Maurice, M., Sorge, A., and Warner, M. (1980), 'Societal differences in organising manufacturing units', *Organization Studies*, 1, pp. 63–91.

Mead, R. (1994), *International Management. Cross Cultural Dimensions*, Oxford, Blackwell.

Miles, R. E. and Snow, C. C. (1984), 'Designing strategic human resource systems', *Organisational Dynamics*, Vol. 13, Part 8, pp. 36–52.

Mintzberg, H. (1983), *Structure in Fives: Designing Effective Organizations*, Englewood Cliffs, NJ, Prentice-Hall.

Morgan, G. (1986), *Images of Organization*, London, Sage.

Morgan, G. (1989), *Creative Organization Theory, A Resource Book*, London, Sage.

Ohmae, K. (1991), 'Getting rid of headquarters mentality, in *The Borderless World, Power and Strategy in the Interlinked Economy*, London, Fontana, pp. 101–24.

Open University (1985), Block III, 'Organizations', Course T244, *Managing in Organizations*, Milton Keynes, Open University.

Pacanowsky, M. E., and O'Donnell-Trujillo, N. (1982), 'Communication and organizational culture', *The Western Journal of Speech Communication*, Vol. 46, Spring, pp. 115–30.

Payne, R. L. (1990), 'The concepts of culture and climate', Working Paper 202, Manchester Business School.

Peters, T. J., and Waterman, R. H. (1982), *In Search of Excellence*, New York, Harper & Row.

Pettigrew, A. M. (1990), 'Is corporate culture manageable?', in Wilson, D. C., and Rosenfeld, R. H., *Managing Organizations, Text, Readings and Cases*, Maidenhead, McGraw-Hill.

Pheysey, D. C. (1993), *Organizational Cultures Types and Transformations*, London, Routledge.

Pugh, D. S. (1993), 'The convergence of international organizational behaviour', in Weinshell (ed.), *Culture and Management*, Berlin, De Gruyk.

Pugh, D. S., and Hickson, D. J. (1976), *Organizational Structure in its Context: The Aston Programme 1*, Aldershot, Gower.

Robbins, S. P. (1992), *Essentials of Organizational Behavior*, Englewood Cliffs, NJ, Prentice-Hall.

Robbins, S. P. (1993), *Organizational Behavior, Concepts, Controversies Applications* (6th edn.), Englewood Cliffs, NJ, Prentice-Hall International.

Robbins, S. P. (1996), *Organizational Behavior, Concepts, Controversies Applications* (7th edn.), Englewood Cliffs, NJ, Prentice-Hall International.

Schein, E. H. (1985), *Organizational Culture and Leadership*, San Francisco, CA, Jossey-Bass.

Schein, E. H. (1992), *Organizational Culture and Leadership*, San Francisco, CA, Jossey-Bass.

Scholz, C. (1987), 'Corporate culture and strategy – the problem of strategic fit', *Long Range Planning*, Vol. 20, No. 4, pp. 78–87.

Schwartz, H., and Davis, S. M. (1981), 'Matching corporate strategy and business strategy', *Organizational Dynamics*, Summer, pp. 30–48.

Tayeb, M. (1989), *Organizations and National Culture: a Comparative Analysis*, London, Sage.

Tushman, M. L., Newman, W. H., and Romanelli, E. (1988), 'Convergence and upheaval: managing the unsteady pace of organizational evolution', in Tushman, M. L., and Moore, W. L. (eds.), *Readings in the Management of Innovation*, New York, Ballinger Publishing Company.

Wilson, D. C. (1992), *A Strategy of Change, Concepts and Controversies in the Management of Change*, London, Routledge.

Wilson, D. C., and Rosenfeld, R. H. (1990), *Managing Organizations*, Text, Readings and Cases, Maidenhead, McGraw-Hill.

Woodward, J. (1965), *Industrial Organization: Theory and Practice*, London, Oxford University Press.

CHAPTER 5

The politics of change

Issues of power, co-operation and conflict are part of the politics of organisational life. Their importance is recognised in this chapter through a discussion of the sources of power and the way political action, as an expression of power, can be used in the management of change. This discussion is extended to include issues of powerlessness, with particular attention being paid to the position of women and members of minority groupings. A debate about the role of conflict concludes that not all conflict is dysfunctional to organisational performance and the ability of organisations to change.

Objectives

To:

- explain the meaning of 'organisational politics';
- distinguish between different sources of power and ways of using power to influence people and events;
- define and discuss the link between power, politics and conflict;
- identify different types of conflict as a means of suggesting possible actions for conflict resolution;
- discuss the relationship between power, conflict and change and ways of managing these.

ORGANISATIONAL POLITICS

Observation of small children left to their own devices shows a natural curiosity evidenced by a propensity to explore, experiment, form friendships with some children and not others and, quite frequently, thwart the intentions of their parents and other adults. These childlike characteristics do not disappear as children become adult and members of different organisations. In fact, learning how to thwart parents is probably good training for learning how to thwart the more formal aspects of organisational life such as rules and regulated procedures. Stacey (1996, p. 387) calls this type of activity 'self-organisation', that is, the self-forming patterns and processes which 'shadow' the formal organisation and which are endemic in all organisations. These patterns and processes are essentially political processes which imply the exercise of power and the management of conflict. As such, they are of intrinsic interest in any discussion of organisational change.

The previous chapter discussed the culture of organisations as part of the informal or hidden part of organisational life; that is, part of the hidden section of the organisational iceberg. One conclusion about the nature of organisational culture is: it may be that it is so all-pervasive that it is not so much hidden as not noticed until some kind of change occurs. The same might be said about the political processes which appear to be an essential part of an organisation's functioning. Yet, the concepts of politics, power and conflict frequently appear in the role of the more undesirable aspects of organisational life. For instance, Robbins (1996, p. 462), drawing on the writings of Kanter (1979), says: 'Power has been described as the last dirty word. . . . People who have it deny it, people who want it try not to appear to be seeking it, and those who are good at getting it are secretive about how they got it.' Most managers would like to manage conflict out of organisations.

Politics, which Robbins (1996, p. 477) calls 'power in action', happens whenever people get together in groups and where an individual or group seeks to influence the thoughts, attitudes or behaviours of another individual or group. Acting politically is also a part of negotiation, as a means to resolving conflict. It can be the cause of conflict in that an individual or group seeks to affect, negatively, another individual or group. Thus, conflict may be the result of the use of power to affect others adversely. However, as Hardy (1994) points out, power can be used to overcome conflict but can also be used to avert it. Therefore, as will be seen later in this discussion, conflict in organisations is not all bad.

A number of definitions of organisational politics can be drawn on at this point. The first, which emphasises the shadowy (Stacey, 1996) aspects of organisational life, that is, the informal hidden processes, is offered by Robbins (1996, p. 477) who says:

> For our purposes, we shall define *political behaviour* in organizations as those activities that are not required as part of one's formal role in the organization, but that influence, or attempt to influence, the distribution of advantages and disadvantages within the organisation.

Hardy (1994, p. 220) defines politics as the use of power, whereas Morgan (1986), rather than defining organisational politics as an aspect of organisational life, draws

> **Illustration 5.1**
> # ORGANISATIONS AND MODES OF POLITICAL RULE
>
> - *Autocracy*: absolute government where power is held by an individual or small group and supported by control of critical resources, property or ownership rights, tradition, charisma, and other claims to personal privilege.
>
> - *Bureaucracy*: rule exercised through use of the written word, which provides the basis for a rational-legal type of authority, or 'rule of law'.
>
> - *Technocracy*: rule exercised through use of knowledge, expert power, and the ability to solve relevant problems.
>
> - *Codetermination*: the form of rule where opposing parties combine in the joint management of mutual interests, as in coalition government or corporatism, each party drawing on a specific power base.
>
> - *Representative democracy*: rule exercised through the election of officers mandated to act on behalf of the electorate, and who hold office for a specified time period or so long as they command the support of the electorate, as in parliamentary government and forms of worker control and shareholder control in industry.
>
> - *Direct democracy*: the system where everyone has an equal right to rule and is involved in all decision making, as in many communal organizations such as cooperatives and kibbutzim. This political principle encourages self-organization as a key mode of organizing.
>
> *Source*: Morgan, G. (1986), *Images of Organizations* (London, Sage, p. 145).

a close parallel between organisations and political systems. As a consequence of this, he says that different types of organisations can be characterised as displaying different types of political rule. Illustration 5.1 describes the varieties of political rule which Morgan claims can be found in organisations.

In his discussion of different types of political rule, Morgan draws attention to how the suffix *cracy*, which appears in these terms, is derived from *kratia* which is a Greek term meaning power or rule. Thus the word autocracy implies the rule of one person, that is, the use of dictatorial power; the term bureaucracy is associated with people who sit at *bureaux* or desks making and administering rules; a technocracy is associated with the power of those with technical knowledge and skills; and democracy draws on the meaning of the prefix *demos* or populace, so that in democratic forms of organisation, power rests with the people as a whole or through their representatives.

Given these expressions of organisational politics, it is not difficult to conclude that politics are a part of everyday organisational life. That this is so becomes evident, most clearly, in the small and large conflicts which arise in all organisations and in the outcomes of the exercise of power. In order to understand, more thoroughly, the relationship between the political aspects of organisations and their ability to cope with change, some attention should be paid to power and conflict as component parts of organisational politics.

POWER IN ORGANISATIONS

The characteristics of power

A number of definitions of power may be quoted at this point.

> Power influences who gets what, when and how. (Morgan, 1986, p. 158.)

> Power is the potential or actual ability to influence others in a desired direction. An individual, group, or other social unit has power if it controls information, knowledge, or resources desired by another individual, group, or social unit. (Gordon, 1993, p. 392.)

> Power is defined as the potential ability to influence behaviour, to change the course of events, to overcome resistance, and to get people to do things that they would otherwise not do. (Pfeffer, 1993, pp. 204–5.)

> Power refers to a capacity that A has to influence the behaviour of B, so that B does something he or she would not otherwise do. (Robbins, 1996, p. 462.)

All these definitions have one thing in common – having power means being able to influence someone else's behaviour. Pfeffer's and Robbins' definitions bring in the added dimension of influencing that behaviour in a direction which the person or group would not, otherwise, have chosen. Robbins (1996, p. 462), in relation to his own definition, says it implies: '(1) a *potential* that need not be actualised to be effective, (2) a *dependency* relationship, and (3) the assumption that B has some *discretion* over his or her own behaviour.' Power, therefore, is a function of relationships. It is not something a person 'has' regardless of what other people are thinking or doing; it only becomes valid when one person has something that the other values. For instance, a bank's ability to lend money to businesses gives it power over those businesses only if they are in need of finance and cannot obtain it anywhere else on the same terms.

Power also derives from differences between people and groups. Some people have more knowledge, expertise or resources than others and, if these are scarce and desired, that person or group will have greater amounts of power than others. Robbins (1996, p. 469) refers to this as the 'elasticity of power', a term taken from economics. In the field of Higher Education, staff with good research records are more highly valued than those without. Therefore, the power of staff to seek employment in many places is directly related to their publication records. The power of a Head of Department is inversely related to the strength of his or her staff's publication records.

Not all people in an organisational situation would agree on who has power, of whatever type, and who has not. Power exists, to a large extent, only in the eye of the beholder. It is not necessarily the resources or knowledge controlled that give someone power, but the belief by others that he or she has that power of control. Many employees have not progressed in their organisations because they misjudged those who had the power to help them and those who did not. Others may potentially have power of one kind or another but perceive themselves to be powerless and thus miss the opportunity to exercise it on their own behalf. Handy (1993, p. 125) refers to the 'relativity of power' to describe the situation where one person or group perceives another to have power while a second person or group believes otherwise. As he says (*ibid.*): 'The group that overawes one person with its prestige and renown looks ludicrous to another. . . . Bribes will sway some but repulse others.'

Handy also notes that power is rarely one-sided. Hitting back or saying no is an option open to those who are seemingly powerless. The dominance of one person over another depends on the power balance – how much one can put into the equation against the power of the other. One type of power can often be traded for another, for instance, money for image, as in the case of a company giving money to a university to fund a professorial chair which is intended to improve that company's image in the eyes of the community.

In summary, power is about the *potential* to influence as well as the *actuality* of influence and it is a function of relationships and differences between people, people's beliefs about it, and how much one person has it in relation to another.

The relationship between power and influence

Many writers separate *what* power is from the *means* by which it is used. Handy (1993) distinguishes the concept of power from that of influence as evidence of this. Illustration 5.2 summarises Handy's descriptions.

Illustration 5.2
POWER AND INFLUENCE

Power as a source of influence
The possible sources of individual power which give one the ability to influence others are:

- *Physical power*: the power of superior force.
- *Resource power*: the possession of valued resources; the control of rewards.
- *Position power*: legitimate power; comes as a result of the role or position held in the organisation.
- *Expert power*: vested in someone because of their acknowledged expertise.
- *Personal power*: charisma, popularity; resides in the person and in their personality.
- *Negative power*: Illegitimate power; the ability to disrupt or stop things happening.

Methods of influence
Different types of power are used in different kinds of ways. Particular methods of influence attach themselves (more or less) to particular types of power. Some methods of influence draw on two or more sources of power.

- *Force*: derived from having physical power; physical bullying, hold-ups, loss of temper.
- *Rules and procedures*: derived from having position power, backed by resource power; devising rules and procedures to result in particular outcomes.
- *Exchange*: derived from having resource power; bargaining, negotiating, bribing.
- *Persuasion*: derives from having personal power; use of logic, the power of argument, evidence of facts.
- *Ecology*: derives from different power sources; manipulating the physical and psychological environment to achieve certain purposes.
- *Magnetism*: derives from personal and sometimes expert power; inspiring trust, respect; using charm, infectious enthusiasm.

Source: Based on Handy, C. (1993), *Understanding Organizations* (London, Penguin, pp. 126–41).

Illustration 5.3
MORGAN'S SOURCES OF POWER IN ORGANISATIONS

1. Formal authority.
2. Control of scarce resources.
3. Use of organisational structure, rules, and regulations.
4. Control of decision processes.
5. Control of knowledge and information.
6. Control of boundaries.
7. Ability to cope with uncertainty.
8. Control of technology.
9. Interpersonal alliances, networks, and control of 'informal organisation'.
10. Control of counterorganisations.
11. Symbolism and the management of meaning.
12. Gender and the management of gender relations.
13. Structural factors that define the stage of action.
14. The power one already has.

Source: Morgan, G. (1986), *Images of Organizations* (London, Sage, p. 159).

Handy's classification of power and influence is useful, but life is not always as clear cut as he suggests. For instance, a particular method of influence could be used in conjunction with several sources of power. In addition, the distinction between power and influence may, to some extent, be artificial, one shades into another. Morgan (1986), in his chapter entitled, 'Organizations as political systems', does not differentiate between power and influence but discusses a list of 14 sources of power (*see* Illustration 5.3).

Paton (1994) discusses many of the sources of power found in Morgan's list but, usefully, divides them into what he calls 'visible' and 'invisible' sources of power. Many of these categorisations overlap with Hardy's (1994) identification of four 'dimensions' of power – decision-making power, non-decision-making power, symbolic power and the power of the system. Yet another example of a discussion of different types of power is that of Gordon (1993), but she also uses the concept of negotiation as a way of distinguishing the *process* through which desired outcomes are achieved. However, regardless of whose account is read, a number of common themes occur. The first of these is a recognition that power comes with position and the ability to control resources.

Position power and the control of resources

Almost all writers list position power or formal authority as an obvious source of power in organisations. Weber (1947), in his studies of organisations, drew attention to three types of authority. The first derives from *tradition*, that is, authority legitimised by custom and practice and a belief in the right of certain individuals to rule others. The second is *charismatic authority* which is legitimised through the leader's particular qualities being valued and an inspiration to others. The third type of authority is what Weber called *'rational-legal authority'*. It is this type of authority which characterises the power held by people because of their position in some formal or understood hierarchy which has some independent standing with regard to the rules and procedures sustaining it. Position power bestows certain rights on those who have it, for instance, the right to order others to do things or to refuse other people's requests.

Handy (1993) links position power with resource power by arguing that, if some control over resources does not come with the position, the source of this power will be invalid. This implies the backing of the organisation for the decisions of the individual concerned. In most modern organisations, some resource power accrues automatically to particular positions by virtue of the rational-legal basis on which the organisation is structured.

Resource power

Resource power comes with the power to distribute valued rewards or to withhold or withdraw something which someone else values. Illustration 5.4 describes two different, but related, strategies associated with the ability to withdraw or bestow valued rewards. These are 'push' and 'pull' strategies.

Illustration 5.4
INFLUENCING OTHERS THROUGH PUSH AND PULL STRATEGIES

'Push' strategies

Push strategies attempt to influence people by imposing or threatening to impose 'costs' on the people or group concerned if they do not do what is required. This may be done either by *withdrawing* something that the 'target' of your influence values, for example your co-operation and support, or by threatening a *sanction* if your 'target' does not comply, for example disciplinary action, a poor appraisal, removal of a bonus or perk or often it may be public criticism or shaming. The ability to impose such costs will depend largely on a person's *position* and the *resources* that she or he controls.

'Pull' or 'reward' strategies

If push strategies are the stick, then 'pull' or 'reward' strategies are the carrot. They are 'the stuff' of theories of motivation that emphasise material, social and other extrinsic rewards. . . . Rewards are often used to influence people by a process of *exchange*: 'I will give you so and so if you will do this for me.' Pull strategies may follow from any of the power bases; resources, for example extra pay or extra staff may be offered; expertise or information may be traded; increased status may be conferred, or access to valuable contacts given. Less obvious, but perhaps more common, there are friendship and favour, approval, and inclusion in a group.

Source: Open University (1991), Book 8, 'Power, leadership and empowerment', Course B789, *Managing Voluntary and Non-profit Making Enterprises* (Milton Keynes, Open University, pp. 17–18).

ACTIVITY 5.1

Describe some occasions when you have tried to use either a 'push' strategy or a 'pull' strategy to achieve an outcome you desired – perhaps to influence how other people acted.

Were the strategies successful? If so, why do you think they worked?

If any of the strategies were not successful, why do you think this was so?

Invisible power

Control over resources such as determining other people's budgets or rate of promotion are examples of what Paton (1994) calls *visible assets* of the power holder. However, both Handy (1993) and Paton draw attention to what they term *invisible assets*. These are first, the power to control information, which is also referred to in Morgan's list of sources of power. Handy (1993, p. 129) says:

> A flow of information often belongs as of right to a 'position' in the organisation. If it does not already belong it can often be originated as a necessary input to that position. This can be horizontal information, i.e. information, often of a technical nature, from the same level of the organisation; vertical information, from above or from below but potentially trapped in the particular 'position' and to be dispersed with the agreement of the occupant. Information, above all else in life, seems to display the essential features of synergy. The whole is so often much more meaningful than the parts. An informational jig-saw, even though all the pieces are separately available, is nothing until put together. A 'position' can be, or can be made to be, simply by function of its position, a junction-box for information.

Morgan (1986, p. 167) echoes this by saying:

> These (people) are often known as 'gatekeepers' who open and close channels of communication and filtering, summarising, analysing, and thus shaping knowledge in accordance with a view of the world that favours their interests.

The ability to slow down or accelerate the flow of information gives power to many people who probably do not occupy 'high' positions, but who simply act as messengers or copiers of information from one part of the organisation to another. It is interesting that the advent of electronic mail and other means of electronic communication have become 'protected' by the use of personal passwords which control who gets what information and when. Illustration 5.5 is an example of invisible power which became visible only in one of its uses.

A second type of invisible asset (Handy, 1993) is that of right of access, which is similar to what Morgan refers to as having access to interpersonal alliances, networks, and the 'informal organisation'. Certain positions in organisations give the right of entry to a variety of networks. While many of these are formal, there exist many informal networks and groupings to which entry comes more easily because of a person's position. Morgan (1986, p. 173) says:

Illustration 5.5

LISTENING IN AT THE BEAUTIFUL BUILDINGS COMPANY

Just recently, the BB Company has secured contracts for three large-scale office buildings which are to be located in Manchester, Melbourne and New York. As a consequence of the need to maintain quick and reliable communications across the company, whose head office is currently in Milton Keynes, Gillian Lambeth, the managing director, and her co-directors have decided to install a technologically based information system to facilitate communications using systems such as electronic mail.

A few weeks after staff had been trained to use the E-mail system, Marcos Davidson, the Marketing Director, sent messages to his project manager in New York asking for information on another company's building which was similar to the one BB Company was erecting in Manchester.

Imagine his surprise when a message came back within an hour from Gillian Lambeth asking to be informed of the results of his enquiry. He thought that, with the use of his personal (secret) password, no-one else but himself, and whoever else he designated, had access to his messages. What he did not know, until then, was that Gillian had asked the system installers to place her in a position where she could 'listen in' to any messages sent by anyone to anyone else on the system.

Marcos decided, there and then, to take care, in the future, about the type of messages he sent and to use other communication channels for information he did not yet want Gillian to know about. On the other hand, he thought it might be a good idea if he had the same 'rights' over his staff that his managing director had over him!

> The skilled organisational politician systematically builds and cultivates such informal alliances and networks, incorporating whenever possible the help and influence of all those with an important stake in the domain in which he or she is operating.

An invisible asset mentioned by both Paton (1994) and Handy (1993) is the right to organise, which tends to be part of position power. Here again, this is not unlike Morgan's (1986) statement that a source of power is being able to use the organisation's structure, rules and regulations to suit one's own purposes. The right to organise is linked to methods of influence associated with ecology. An example is the power to say who occupies which organisational spaces or to waive certain rules according to convenience. Morgan and Paton both argue that organisational and work group structure can be used as a political instrument. Reorganisation always means a redistribution of power. Therefore, the power to restructure an organisation or part of it can be regarded as visible power. However, hidden agendas to use this process to accomplish other aims (e.g. reducing someone's access to certain information; changing someone else's committee memberships) are good examples of the use of invisible power.

Non-decision-making power

Position power almost always includes the right to make particular decisions. This is one of Hardy's (1994) dimensions of power – decision-making power. This power is frequently visible and unquestioned because of the power of the position. However, both Hardy and Paton (1994) show how issues which are not, strictly speaking, directly concerned with the decision itself, can, even so, be presented in such a way as to influence the outcome (*see* Illustration 5.6).

Illustration 5.6
CONTROLLING THE DECISION AGENDA

The marketing manager of an insurance company was on the brink of launching a large product development campaign. At the next management meeting, it had been decided to discuss poor profit performance in the previous two quarters. At issue was whether to deploy resources to expand sales or to cutting costs by increasing automation (via electronic data processing). He knew that if this issue were to be raised at the meeting, he would be outvoted by a small minority of peers who leaned toward investing the funds in automation. However, he was convinced that automation didn't sell insurance! Therefore, he needed to find an issue that would rearrange the coalition structure currently against him. He realized that the key issue that he would prefer to have discussed was market share

and not profits, so he did three things. First, he sent a report to all the management committee members that showed how losses in market share could be regained by his proposal. Second, he sent to all members of the management committee a memo asking them to consider ways in which his proposed product development program could be carried out effectively and at a lower cost. Third, he persuaded the chief executive to place his project proposal first on the agenda. When the meeting started, the issue was not whether the product launch should take place or not, but what funds would be required to launch the product; the automation proposal was postponed, because some marginal members of the automation coalition had become committed to the market share issue.

Source: Paton, R. (1994), 'Power in organizations', in Arson, R., and Paton, R., *Organizations, Cases, Issues, Concepts* (London, P.C.P., p. 194).

Wilson (1992, p. 54) refers to the type of power described in Illustration 5.6 as 'covert' power, saying: 'Here power is exercised through "non-decision making" rather than by means of influence attempts on readily identifiable (and commonly known) decision topics'. Invisible or covert power associated with decision-making takes many forms. For instance, as shown in Illustration 5.6, it may take the form of the power to 'set' the agenda under which something will be discussed, or limiting who may or may not take part in the discussion, or defining the scope of the discussion. Hardy (1994) discusses the notion of 'safe' agendas where some issues do not even get discussed. Thus, some topics and people are deliberately excluded from the decision-making process. Exclusion from this process can also come about because participants do not have the knowledge or expertise to express a view or take part in any meaningful debate. The role of the 'expert' appears in many guises.

Expert or knowledge power

Paton (1994, p. 191) says: 'Organisations use specialist knowledge to cope with task and environmental uncertainty. This means that on certain issues they must rely on and accept the judgement of those who possess that knowledge.' Those who have specialist knowledge or expertise which is in scarce supply have resource power of a particular kind. Paton (1994, p. 191) gives an example of this:

> The middle-ranking research chemist who calmly says 'it just can't be done' can stop the marketing director of a chemical firm dead in his or her tracks. If the director is unwise enough to press the point he or she simply invites a lecture on, say, some finer points of polymer chemistry, whereupon – whether he or she pretends to understand and agree, or instead admits to not understanding and refuses to agree – the point is irretrievably lost.

However, as Handy (1993, p. 130) says: 'expert power is hedged about by one major qualification; it can only be given by those over whom it will be exercised'. Therefore, unless someone's claim to expertise is recognised, it will not become a power source for that person.

Morgan (1986, p. 171) says: 'From the beginning of history technology has served as an instrument of power, enhancing the ability of humans to manipulate, control, and impose themselves on their environment.' Knowledge of how to design and operate information technology systems is a special form of expert power. So many organisational functions and processes are dependent on information technology. Therefore, those who can solve the frequently recurring operating problems have power, often above their status. Many of these people are classed only as technicians, yet they have the power to reduce, instantly, the frustrations of others who are reduced to sitting impotently in front of a computer, or prolong those frustrations through operating their own informal queuing system of those in need of help.

An interesting aspect of expert power (Handy, 1993) is that it is relative. To accumulate expert power, the expertise does not have to be very much greater than that of other people. A small amount of extra expertise can bring large amounts of power. However, as Handy points out, this power can easily be lost if someone comes along who has even a small degree of further expertise. As he says (p. 131): 'In the country of the blind the one-eyed man is king – until he with two eyes comes along'.

Symbolic power

In an article in the *Guardian* (26 July 1996) on the selling of copied computer software programmes alongside religious amulets, John Ryle says:

> An amulet is an ally, a reminder of an exemplary life, but its deepest meaning is decipherable only by priests and scholars. Likewise with software: the programs promise power and knowledge, but can be fully exploited only by cognoscenti (especially if the manufacturers, anticipating piracy, have protected them from encryption devices).

He goes on to say that the pleasure found in CD-Roms does not necessarily relate to their use. This pleasure, and feeling of power-knowledge relates more to the 'mystical potency (ascribed) to the software inscribed – invisibly – on its surface.'

Implicit in this story is the concept of expert or knowledge power. However, the CD-Rom is also spoken of as an icon or symbol of pure information which, although invisible, is perceived as incorruptible. Such is the power of symbols, in this case a physical symbol representing something more profound. Hardy (1994) draws attention to this aspect of symbols – that they stand for something other than themselves. The power which comes from the ability to manipulate symbols comes, therefore, from their capacity to signal to others the meaning, not of the symbol itself, but of what they stand for. This is implicit in Morgan's (1986) reference to symbolism as the management of meaning.

Symbolic power is, therefore, the power to manipulate and use symbols to create organisational environments and the beliefs and understandings of others to suit one's own purposes. Hardy includes the use of language, rituals and myths as examples of symbolic power. The use of phrases such as: 'All pulling in the same direction', 'We are a happy team', 'Flatten the opposition' or 'argumentative (as opposed to conciliatory)' all give their own specific, covert messages about expected behaviour. The use of phrases such as, 'We are a happy team', negates the necessity to say, 'Conflict and disagreement are not tolerated in this organisation'. Rituals involving who sits where at meetings and how people greet each other are indications of who holds power in relation to whom. Leaving the chair at the head of the table free for the most senior person or addressing someone as 'Boss' symbolises one person's power in relation to another's. If a high-status person deliberately chooses to position her or himself next to a particular person, this could very well symbolise the chosen person's 'favourable' standing with regard to the other.

Morgan (1986) uses the term 'theatre' to describe the physical settings, appearances and styles of behaviour which can add to someone's power. He says (p. 177) of those who seek to add to their power in this way: 'many deserve organisational Oscars for their performances'. Examples of the use of theatre are the size and furnishing of offices, the seating of visitors and the (unspoken) rules of dress. Morgan says (p. 27):

> Style also counts. It's amazing how you can symbolise power by being a couple of minutes late for that all-important meeting where everyone depends on your presence, or how visibility in certain situations can enhance your status.

He gives an example of how some people visiting the American President in the White House turn up early so as to be seen by as many people as possible while waiting for their appointment, thus dramatising their supposed importance.

As discussed in the previous chapter, Johnson and Scholes (1993) include symbols, rituals and routines, and stories as elements of their cultural web. They present these as representative of the dominant culture of an organisation, thus providing clear evidence that symbols of power are inevitably intertwined with an organisation's culture and are, frequently, an outward expression of it. In summary, therefore, any analysis of power in organisations must take account of not only the types of power which are exercised over the content of decisions, but also the types of power that influence attitudes and behaviour, frequently in ways that those influenced are hardly aware of. Activity 5.2 presents some questions, the answers to which can be used to increase understanding of how symbolic power is used in a particular organisation.

ACTIVITY 5.2

The following questions are designed to help identify the routines and rituals and other symbols prevalent in an organisation and who uses them for their own purposes.

Think of your own organisation or one you are familiar with.

1   *Which routines and rituals are most emphasised? Who enforces these?*

2   *What kind of language do the organisation's leaders use to motivate employees and*

gain their loyalty? What does this tell you about which topics could be debated and which not? Which people appear to be able to 'go against the grain' – and why do you think this is acceptable for them but not others?

3 *Who, in the organisation, has the most impressive 'trappings' of office (office, furnishings, car, expense account, etc.)? What kind of power do they symbolise?*

4 *Give examples of two different people who use the skills of 'gamesmanship' to get their own way: (a) one who does so through aggressive means; and (b) one who does so through operating craftily and with an apparently low profile. Consider just what it is they are manipulating in these processes.*

THE POLITICS OF POWERLESSNESS

If there is one thing that symbols of power are intended to do, it is to make others, who do not control these symbols, feel their own lack of power. On the other hand, many people are relatively powerless because of the way particular organisational factors affect them. In addition, some groups of people, for instance women and those from some ethnic minority groupings, appear powerless in relation to, on the one hand men and, on the other hand, the majority groupings. Physically disabled people may be excluded from positions of status and decision-making because of prejudice or simply a lack of physical access to the places where the exercise of power takes place.

Women's lack of power

A number of writers (Morgan, 1986; Gordon, 1993; Handy, 1993; Kanter, 1979) have discussed the position of women in relation to their perceived powerlessness compared to men. For instance, Morgan (1986) argues that formal organisations typically mirror what, in the West, has been (and, to a large extent, still is) a patriarchal society. Thus, those jobs which involve strategic decision-making and the control of finances, as well as those which relate to machines and technology, are generally done by men. Jobs which involve caring, supporting others (e.g. secretaries), helping others (e.g. receptionists) tend to be done mainly by women.

Wilson (1995) has compiled a comprehensive summary of statistics showing that women, on average, earn less than men, that they occupy a much greater proportion of jobs at the lower levels of organisations relative to their overall numbers, and that they make up the vast majority of part-time workers (frequently doing more than one part-time job), thus having little employment protection, sickness benefits and, if they become unemployed, unemployment benefit. The Department of Employment publication (1996) *Labour Market and Skills Trends 1996/97* shows that in 1994 81 per cent of all part-time employees were female and 46 per cent of all female employees were part-time compared to 10 per cent of males. In addition, it reports that jobs held by women are disproportionately (compared to men) concentrated in a narrow range of industries and occupations, for instance, in clerical and secretarial occupations and in public administration, education and health. Of concern must be the expected decline in the need for clerical and secretarial services.

Unfortunately, the situation regarding any increase in the proportion of women occupying higher-level jobs is not encouraging. The report referred to above says (p. 30):

> There is still female under-representation in the higher level occupations. It has been suggested that the current practice of de-layering has actually lessened female representation at the top levels by reducing the middle layers of management.

This statement follows on from the *Labour Market and Skills Report 1994/95* which says (p. 37):

> Even highly qualified women graduate engineers and scientists can face barriers in deploying and developing their professional skills. . . . There was evidence of continuing barriers to the career progression of women scientists and engineers, including outmoded attitudes about the role of women, the absence of proper child care facilities and inflexible structures for work and careers.

The metaphor of the 'glass ceiling' has become well known in discussions of the lack of any significant number of women in middle to top management jobs. Wilson (1995, p. 153) features a cartoon by Amanda Martin which says: 'Girls, DO NOT shatter the glass ceiling – it hurts.' It goes on to give advice about the elaborate precautions that need to be taken in order to dismantle this kind of ceiling. Illustration 5.7 demonstrates the extent of discrimination against women academics in their attempts to become readers and professors.

Illustration 5.7

CHIPPING AWAY AT THE GLASS CEILING

The 26 July 1996 edition of *The Times Higher*, a newspaper mainly for people working in the higher education sector, reports data taken from *Beyond the Glass Ceiling*, a book by Sian Griffiths. The data illustrate the very low numbers of women academics promoted to the position of professor. Of 63 institutions of higher education surveyed, in only three were more than 15 per cent of professors female. Fifty of the institutions had fewer than 10 per cent female professors. Yet, as is pointed out, women occupy half the places on most university courses. Overall, the statistics reported include:

- Only 7.3 per cent of professors were women, although women made up 30 per cent of academics.
- New universities topped the league table for women professors.
- One university – UMIST – had no women professors.

- In engineering and technology the proportion of women professors dropped to 1 per cent.
- None of the professors in either agriculture or veterinary science was a woman.

The article also features two Oxford University women academics, who, in spite of international renown for their work, had only just been made professors. Each of them had worked at the university for some 20 years. One of the women, Gillian Morriss-Kay notes that, on the issue of promotion, 'the university had deliberately excluded "promotion" from its code of equal opportunities, on the grounds that it was an unnecessary complication'. Even with a much larger number of promotions in 1996 than usual, the proportion of women professors rose only to 8.1 per cent out of an eligible pool of 15 per cent.

Source: Based on *The Times Higher*, 26 July, 1996, pp. 16–17.

A week prior to the publication of the article referred to in Illustration 5.7, the same publication (*The Times Higher*, 19 July 1996) reported the advancement of Fay Gale, Vice-Chancellor of one of Australia's most prestigious universities, to head the Australian Vice-Chancellors Committee. At the time of writing she is only the third female to have held this position in almost 150 years of its existence. Evidently, Professor Gale had long been a critic of the way the academic community is overwhelmingly male dominated. She is quoted as saying (p. 11): 'Australia does have positive discrimination in higher education – only it is men who enjoy the benefits.'

There are a number of explanations of why women occupy jobs characterised by low skills and low pay and, if they have achieved professional status, still do not rise in any significant numbers to the higher levels in their profession or the higher levels of management and thus, gain at least position power. One is that, because of the need to absent themselves for childbearing, women are not committed to their work and employer. However, although it is clear that this belief about women prevails in the minds of many recruiters and senior managers, the evidence shows this to be a myth (Wilson, 1995). Women who commit themselves to a job and career do so in no way differently to men. A more complex reason which is put forward by a number of writers (e.g. Kanter, 1979; Morgan, 1986) is that the prevailing structures and power balances in organisations, which are predominantly based on a male model of what organisation and management is about, conspire indirectly to reduce the power sources of women. For instance, Morgan (1986) shows how theories of organisational behaviour promote those characteristics (e.g. notions of logical rational thinking, aggressiveness to overcome the competition, exploitativeness to gain career progression, and independence of action rather than group facilitation) which are considered, traditionally, to be those possessed by men. Women who wish to progress in this type of world must either suppress any traits associated with caring and nurturing or be labelled 'soft', 'not leader material', 'insufficiently independent' or simply 'not up to it' – whatever 'it' might be.

The source of power which comes last in Morgan's (1986) list in Illustration 5.3, 'The power one already has' is relevant to the lack of power of many groups, including women. Morgan says (p. 184): 'Power is a route to power, and one can often use power to acquire more.' Clearly, if men as the more powerful gender group already have power, they will be unwilling to relinquish it and can use it to gain even more. Morgan calls this the 'honey-pot' characteristic of power. Thus (p. 184):

> The presence of power attracts and sustains people who wish to feed off that power, and actually serves to increase the power holder's power. In the hope of gaining favour, people may begin to lend the power holder uninvited support or buy into his or her way of thinking so that he or she can see that they are on the same side. When the time comes for the power holder to recognise this interest with active support, people then actually become indebted to the power holder, with all kinds of IOUs coming into play. Power, like honey, is a perpetual source of sustenance and attraction among the worker bees.

The implications of this for women seeking power are twofold. First, if they are relatively powerless already, they have a reduced capacity to engender more power – others will not see them as a honey-pot. Second, trying to be noticed by a power holder (who is regarded as a honey-pot) requires some familiarity with the culture surrounding that person. Given that the power holder is likely to be a man, this is frequently developed through the stories men tell each other (sometimes 'not fit for' women's ears), socialising (drinking) together and conversations in toilets and wash rooms. The form of dress which might be favoured has to be interpreted by women and, if misinterpreted, can bring accusations of either being too 'mannish' or too 'frivolously female'. Of course, this situation can operate in reverse, in those sectors which are staffed and managed predominantly by women.

It is easy to over-stress the role of gender-related values that bias organisational life in favour of one sex or another. What may underlie many prejudices of one group of people towards another is the fact that there are sufficient differences for these to be noticeable and, unfortunately, differences are frequently taken to mean 'not as good'.

ACTIVITY 5.3

Think of someone whom you consider does their job very well, but has been passed over for promotion. Assuming there is no reason why this person could not do the higher-level job (given time and training if necessary), why do you think they have not progressed?

In your analysis, draw on the concepts of power discussed above and any explanations related to the possible lack of power of the person concerned.

Powerlessness because of cultural differences

The previous chapter discussed how national cultural differences can influence many aspects of organisational life. Care must be taken, therefore, not to assume that practices in one culture can be transferred, without question, to another. For instance, it would be unwise to assume that factors which motivate some groups of people will, similarly, motivate others; a leadership style which works well in organisations where a Westernised culture prevails may not be popular in countries where the power distance between levels in an organisation is much greater.

The implications of these cultural differences for a discussion of power and powerlessness hinge on the very issue of difference. For instance, as the previous chapter showed, there are definite differences in the behaviour of people from different cultures but, more importantly – because they are so difficult to change – in the values and attitudes which they bring to the workplace. Therefore, people from cultures scoring high on Hofstede's (1981) high power distance cultural dimension will *expect* managers to make all major decisions (and even some minor ones). However, in Western cultures which characteristically score low on the power distance cultural dimension, these expectations can frequently be interpreted as a lack of ambition and unwillingness to take responsibility for actions. This, in turn, does not train these people to gain power sources such as 'control of decision processes' and 'formal authority', two of the sources of power given by Morgan (1986). Morgan also cites 'ability to cope with uncertainty' as another source of power. This relates directly to another of Hofstede's cultural dimensions – uncertainty avoidance. Consequently, if a minority group's cultural upbringing is one where ambiguity must be controlled, they will not be prepared to demonstrate attitudes and behaviour which will gain them power in this direction.

A final example is the difference in orientation towards others that is found between different cultural groupings. The perspective of power in Western society is based mainly on the power of the individual, yet in many other societies (particularly in East Asian countries) people are expected to show loyalty to their group. It is the performance of the group that matters. Power is linked to the power of the group. Yuet-Ha (1996) points this out in her discussion of the differences between Western and East Asian work-related values and their relationship to work-related competencies. Her findings suggest that, for people from an East Asian culture, it is relatively easy to implement team working and shared responsibility and support. However, it is relatively difficult to implement such things as: open communication, participation, decisiveness, empowerment, delegation of authority and responsibility, taking responsibility in leadership, and sharing information. Given that most of these competencies are favoured ones in Western societies, people from ethnic minority groups which favour other competencies are unlikely to progress, when working in British, American and some European countries, unless they can change others' perceptions of their differences. As Morgan points out with another of his sources of power, their lack of power in the first place makes this difficult to achieve.

Positions of powerlessness

The discussion above demonstrates the relationship between powerful and powerless groups which mirrors the areas selected for legislation as attempts have been made to provide more equality of opportunity in an organisational world where power has, traditionally, gravitated to white men. Legislation has certainly helped to eliminate the more overt prejudices which have prevented women and people from ethnic minority groups from enjoying the benefits given to others, even if certain organisational and covert processes still contrive to reduce their access to power sources and forms of influence. However, there are other groups of people who do not have the benefit of legislation – because no particular prejudice is shown against them – yet still find themselves relatively powerless. These groups are not, as might be expected, those working at the lowest levels of the organisation. They are powerless because of the particular positions they occupy. It is nearly 20 years since Kanter (1979) singled out, among others, first-line supervisors and staff professionals as examples of people lacking power.

According to Kanter, power comes from access to resources, information and support to get a task done; as well as the co-operation of others in doing what is necessary. She maintains that both of these capacities derive not from leadership style and skill but from a person's location in the formal and informal systems of the organisation. This includes both the way the job is defined and the types of connections to other important people in the organisation. Three 'lines' of organisational power are defined: (1) lines of supply; (2) lines of information; (3) lines of support. These have been discussed above as being basically related to resource and position power. Of additional relevance here is the power which comes from *connections* with other parts of the organisational system. Kanter identifies this as deriving from two sources – job activities and political alliances. She says (pp. 65–6):

1. Power is most easily accumulated when one has a job that is designed and located to allow *discretion* (nonroutinised action permitting flexible, adaptive, and creative contributions), *recognition* (visibility and notice), and *relevance* (being central to pressing organisational problems).

2. Power also comes when one has relatively close contact with *sponsors* (high level people who confer approval, prestige, or backing), *peer networks* (circles of acquaintanceship that provide reputation and information, the grapevine often being faster than formal communication channels), and *subordinates* (who can be developed to relieve managers of some of the burdens and to represent the manager's point of view).

When people are in situations where they have strong lines of supply, information and support, their job allows them discretion and their work is recognised as being relevant to the organisation's purposes, they can more easily let go of control downwards and, thereby, develop their staff more effectively. In contrast to this situation, Kanter (1979, p. 67) says:

The powerless live in a different world. Lacking the supplies, information, or support to make things happen easily, they may turn instead to the ultimate weapon of those who lack productive power – oppressive power: holding others back and punishing with whatever threats they can muster.

This latter situation is quite frequently that of the first-line supervisor. Illustration 5.8 is a multiple-cause diagram which demonstrates the combined effects of different facets of powerlessness on the attitudes and behaviour of first-line supervisors and people in similar positions.

Kanter also discusses the position of staff professionals, that is, those people who act as 'advisers behind the scenes'. These are people who must 'sell' their knowledge and expertise and bargain for resources, but who, quite often, do not have power to bargain with – they have few favours to offer in exchange. Experience of many organisations shows that people working in human resource or personnel departments are frequently in this situation. They frequently have little line experience and, therefore, are not involved in the mainstream organisational power networks. Being specialists, their ability to cross functions or undertake general management positions is restricted. They are, therefore, likely to get 'stuck' in a limited career structure. Having little power themselves, they cannot pass it on to others. In addition, they are prey to having their work contracted to agencies or consultants outside the organisation. The effect of this relative powerlessness is that they tend to become 'turf-minded', protecting their patches, drawing strict boundaries between themselves and

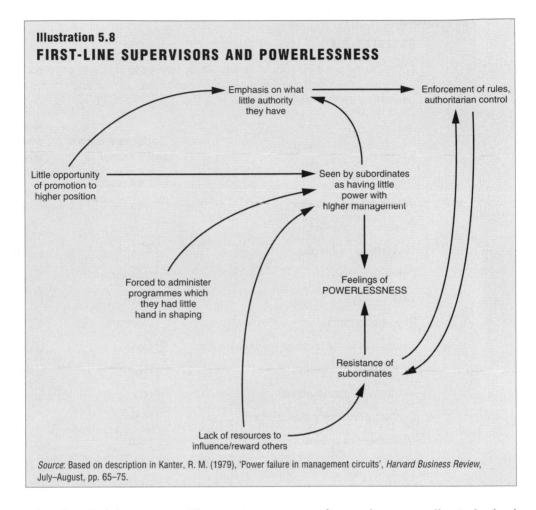

Illustration 5.8
FIRST-LINE SUPERVISORS AND POWERLESSNESS

Source: Based on description in Kanter, R. M. (1979), 'Power failure in management circuits', *Harvard Business Review*, July–August, pp. 65–75.

other functional managers. These various aspects of powerlessness, collectively, lead to a certain conservativeness which is resistant to change. Activity 5.4 (p. 166) asks you to assess a job in terms of its capacity to generate power for its occupant.

THE LINK BETWEEN POLITICS, POWER AND CONFLICT

In the first section of this chapter, politics was described as the use of power. However, as Robbins (1996) points out, political behaviour, although defined as those activities undertaken to influence others, is particularly relevant to those activities which are not part of someone's formal organisational role. In an ideal organisational world, there would probably be no need to behave other than in accordance with one's formal role. However, because the organisational world is made up of human beings, each of whom has his or her own set of values, interests and beliefs, there are bound to be differences of opinion as to the very many issues which pervade everyday organisational life, let alone those that prevail in conditions

ACTIVITY 5.4

Listed below are a number of factors which contribute to power or powerlessness. For your own job, or one you know well, take each factor in turn and tick the middle or last column as appropriate.

Factor	Generates power when factor is:	Generates powerlessness when factor is:
Rules in the job	☐ Few	☐ Many
Predecessors in the job	☐ Few	☐ Many
Established routines	☐ Few	☐ Many
Centralised resources	☐ Few	☐ Many
Communications	☐ Extensive	☐ Limited
Task variety	☐ High	☐ Low
Physical location	☐ Central	☐ Distant
Relation of tasks to current problem areas	☐ Central	☐ Peripheral
Competitive pressures	☐ High	☐ Low
Net-forming opportunities	☐ High	☐ Low
Contact with senior management	☐ High	☐ Low
Advancement prospects of subordinates	☐ High	☐ Low
Authority/discretion in decision-making	☐ High	☐ Low
Meaningful goals/tasks	☐ High	☐ Low
Participation in programmes, meetings, conferences	☐ High	☐ Low

Consider the overall picture obtained of the job. How powerful might the person occupying it be?

Source: Based on factors suggested by Kanter, R. M. (1979), 'Power failure in management circuits', *Harvard Business Review*, July–August, pp. 65–75; and Gordon, J. R. (1993), *A Diagnostic Approach to Organizational Behavior*, Allyn and Bacon, p. 425.

of change. Even in organisations which apparently have a strong dominant culture, the experience of that culture will vary for individuals and groups who carry with them their own subcultures. What is more, a dominant culture will not solve one of the perennial issues in all organisations – the existence of scarce resources, which are never sufficient for everyone to have all they want.

As the previous section discussed, the control of resources is an important source of power in organisations and, as resources (of whatever kind) are almost always scarcer than most people would like, additional resource power is frequently being sought.

This, in its turn, results in individuals and groups seeking to gather more power to themselves. In other words, they will compete for power. The issue then becomes one of whether this type of competition is helpful to the achievement of organisational performance or whether it becomes dysfunctional. Handy (1993, p. 298) appears in no doubt about this when he says: 'Competition for power nearly always turns to conflict', with the implication that, while competition is not necessarily undesirable, conflict is. However, whereas Handy's discussion of conflict implies some disapproval, Morgan (1989, p. 196) takes a more pragmatic view and goes so far as to say: 'Conflict is a familiar feature of life in an organisational society'. His argument rests on the assumption that, because organisations are designed as systems which, at the same time, promote competition as well as co-operation, one of their outputs will, inevitably, be conflict.

This view emphasises the plural nature of interests, conflicts and sources of power and has become known as the 'pluralist' frame of reference (Morgan, 1986, p. 185). This stands in contrast to the 'unitary' frame of reference which emphasises the philosophy that organisations have goals to which all organisational members subscribe, with all working towards their attainment. Whereas managers holding a pluralist view of the way organisations should operate stress the idea of a coalition of divergent interests which will sometimes result in conflict, managers subscribing to a unitary philosophy consider conflict as an aberration from the normal state of affairs which recognises only formal authority as the legitimate source of power. Thus, from a unitary frame of reference, managers are considered as the only people with the 'right to manage' while others are expected to subordinate their own personal interests to the good of the organisation. From this point of view, the only type of power recognised is formal position power. Expert power might be recognised but, in the main, only as a facet of position power.

Robbins (1990, p. 414) prefers the term 'traditional' to describe this view that assumes that all conflicts are bad. He says: 'The traditional approach treats conflict synonymously with such terms as *violence*, *destruction*, *and irrationality*. Consonant with this perspective, one of management's major responsibilities is to try to ensure that conflicts don't arise and, if they do, to act quickly to resolve them.' The ideas of Taylor (1911) and his principles of scientific management are examples of a unitary approach to managing. The idea, still current in many places, that all industrial action by workers is wrong stems from this view. The difficulty in accepting a unitary view of organisational life, as the human relations theorists showed (e.g. Mayo, 1933; Barnard, 1938; McGregor, 1960) is that it leaves no room for dealing with the multiplicity of interests which are now accepted as part of a democratic way of doing things; hence the formulation of the concept of 'pluralism'. Illustration 5.9 summarises these two different views.

A consideration of the unitary frame of reference, as portrayed in Illustration 5.9, shows that organisational politics, in the well-ordered world of the unitarist, should not exist. However, this view sits uncomfortably not only with the notion of a pluralist society, but also with the comments reported in Chapter 2 about the seemingly increasingly chaotic circumstances which are being predicted for organisations now

Illustration 5.9

THE UNITARY AND PLURALIST VIEWS OF INTERESTS, CONFLICT AND POWER

	The unitary view	The pluralist view
Interests	Places emphasis upon the achievement of common objectives. The organisation is viewed as being united under the umbrella of common goals, and striving towards their achievement in the manner of a well integrated team.	Places emphasis upon the diversity of individual and group interests. The organisation is regarded as a loose coalition which has but a remote interest in the formal goals of the organisation.
Conflict	Regards conflict as a rare and transient phenomenon which can be removed through appropriate managerial action. Where it does arise it is usually attributed to the activities of deviants and troublemakers.	Regards conflict as an inherent and ineradicable characteristic of organisational affairs and stresses its potentially positive and functional aspects.
Power	Largely ignores the role of power in organisational life. Concepts such as authority, leadership and control tend to be preferred means of describing the managerial prerogative of guiding the organisation towards the achievement of common interests.	Regards power as a variable crucial to the understanding of the activities of an organisation. Power is the medium through which conflicts of interest are alleviated and resolved. The organisation is viewed as a plurality of power holders drawing their power from a plurality of sources.

Source: Burrell, G., and Morgan, G. (1979), *Sociological Paradigms and Organisational Analysis* (London, Heinemann Educational Books Ltd, p. 204).

and in the future. In such times political behaviour is to be expected, with its associated tendency to generate both competition and co-operation (of which conflict is a part). To ignore the role of conflict as a positive force as well as a negative force in the context of organisations and change is to ignore the realities of human living. Therefore, a more detailed understanding of the nature and sources of conflict and how to manage in situations of conflict is important for anyone involved in organisational change.

CONFLICT IN ORGANISATIONS

The previous section established a link between power, politics and conflict. However, the concept of conflict, itself, is by no means uncontentious. What one person calls conflict, another might call 'hard bargaining'. A number of definitions of conflict can be found in the organisational behaviour literature. Examples of these are:

> We can define conflict . . . as a process that begins when one party perceives that another party has negatively affected, or is about to negatively affect, something that the first party cares about. (Robbins, 1996, p. 505.)

> For our purpose we can see conflict as: behaviour intended to obstruct the achievement of some other person's goals. (Mullins, 1996, p. 723.)

> Conflict is the result of incongruent or incompatible potential influence relationships between and within individuals, groups or organisations. (Gordon, 1993, p. 448.)

Conflict can be a disagreement, the presence of tension, or some other difficulty between two or more parties. . . . Conflict is often related to interference or opposition between the parties involved. The parties in conflict usually see each other as frustrating or about to frustrate, their needs or goals. (Tosi, Rizzo and Carroll, 1994, p. 436.)

These definitions, collectively, include the following aspects of conflict. First, it must be perceived by the parties to it, otherwise it does not exist. Second, one party to the conflict must be perceived as about to do, or actually be doing, something which the other party (or parties) do not want – in other words there must be opposition. Third, some kind of interaction must take place. In addition, almost all accounts of conflict agree that it can take place at a number of levels: between individuals, between groups or between organisations. Gordon (1993) also points out that an individual may experience conflict within themselves; that is, they may experience internal conflict. This might be because of the incompatibility of goals set for them or a confusion over the roles they are asked to play. Conflict, however, is not a unidimensional concept. It comes in different guises according to its degree of seriousness and capacity to disrupt or, in some cases, improve a difficult situation.

The nature of conflict

Organisational conflict can be thought of as occurring in 'layers' (Open University course, *Managing in Organizations*, 1985) as shown in Illustration 5.10.

The identification of 'layers' of conflict is useful in demonstrating that not all conflict is of the 'do or die' variety; it depends on what has caused the conflict. Handy (1993) argues that all conflicts start from two types of difference. These are first, differing goals and ideologies, which relate most nearly to the level of differences in values. The second cause is differences about territory, which relate most closely to the level of differences of interest. Other writers (e.g. Pfeffer, 1981; Robbins, 1990; Tosi *et al.*, 1994; Mullins, 1996), between them, offer the following list of sources of organisational conflict.

Interdependence

Different organisational groupings depend upon each other to a smaller or larger extent. Sometimes the dependence relationship is mutual. For instance, the marketing department is dependent on the production department to produce the goods said to be desired by the customer. Production is dependent on sales and marketing for gaining customers who want the products and thus keep the production workers in jobs. At other times, the dependence is more one-way. The direction of dependence is related to power balances between groupings. Robbins (1990) draws attention to the fact that nearly all line-staff relations are based on one-way task dependence.

Organisational structures

Conflict is likely because of the power imbalances which prevail in hierarchical structures. This sort of conflict, of course, overlaps with the concept of dependence. However, horizontal differentiation brings its own problems. Both Robbins (1990) and

Illustration 5.10
THE 'LAYERS' IN ORGANISATIONAL CONFLICT

Misunderstandings

These are 'Getting the wrong end of the stick' – genuine misconceptions about what was said or done.

Differences of values

These are the other end of the scale, as it were, to misunderstandings. Conflicting values lead to the most serious disagreements. The values involved may be based on ethical considerations such as whether to take bribes (e.g. sales commissions) or not; the level at which safety should be set; whether to deal with regimes which condone particular ways of behaving (e.g. imprisoning those who disagree with them) which would not be acceptable in the home country. Differences of values may also involve disagreements about the purpose of the organisation, that is, the ends for which it exists. Thus differences of values are almost always about ends or goals or objectives.

Differences of viewpoint

Different parties may share the same values but have differences of view on how particular goals or purposes should be attained. Thus differences of viewpoint are disagreements on the *means* by which particular ends should be achieved. For example, two

parties may agree on the goal to increase profitability but disagree on *how* to do this. One may argue for increasing price, the other may argue for keeping price stable and cutting costs.

Differences of interest

Status, resources, advancement and so on are all desirable 'goods' that most people want and, if they have them, they want to keep hold of them. The distribution of these goods is not a once and for all process; it is constantly being adjusted through budget-setting, organisational restructuring, strategic planning and so on. Therefore, competition between individuals and, particularly, departments is ever present.

Interpersonal differences

These are what most people would refer to as 'personality clashes'. For whatever reason, some people find it difficult to get on with one another. This might be because of differences of temperament, style or ways of behaving. Care should be taken, however, not to mistake other types of differences for personality clashes. Accounting for conflict under this heading is often used as an excuse for not facing up to differences which might be occurring for other reasons.

Source: Based on Open University Units 9–10 'Conflict' (1985), in *Managing in Organizations* (course T244) (Milton Keynes, Open University, p. 57).

Tosi *et al.* (1994) refer to research by Lawrence and Lorsch (1969) which demonstrated how research, sales and production departments all had different orientations towards formality of structure, interpersonal relationships and time scales. They both argue that increased differentiation between departments, with each becoming more specialised in its activities, will lead to increased potential for conflict between them. Tosi *et al.* describe the value differences between mechanistic and organic organisational forms.

Rules and regulations

Robbins (1990), in particular, mentions the role of rules and regulations in reducing conflict by minimising ambiguity. For Mullins (1996) this impacts on the clarity of definition of the roles people are expected to play. Robbins maintains that where there is high formalisation (i.e. standardised ways for people and units to interact with each other) there are fewer opportunities for disputes about who does what and when. Conversely, where there is low formalisation, the degree of ambiguity is such that the potential for jurisdictional disputes increases. Robbins maintains that conflict is more likely to be less subversive in highly formalised situations. In situations where the rules are vague, the opportunities to jockey for resources and other power bases increases. What is more, these activities can take place as easily through covert as through overt means. In contrast to this, Tosi *et al.* warn that rules and procedures do not necessarily guarantee an absence of conflict. In situations of over-regulation, people can become frustrated by their lack of autonomy and a perceived lack of trust of them by their superiors.

Limited resources

One of the sources of power in organisations is access to resources and the ability to bestow desired rewards on others. In good times, when resources are plentiful, the potential for conflict through competing for resources is reduced. In conditions of reducing profits or revenues or when redundancies are occurring, the potential for conflict over reduced resources rises. In addition, in economically hard times, gaining resources and extra rewards for subordinates is much more difficult, with the attendant potential for increased dissatisfaction among the workforce.

Cultural differences

The previous chapter identified a number of ways in which people from different nationalities and societies differ. Therefore, conflict can arise through misunderstandings or through inappropriate behaviour on the part of those with one set of cultural characteristics towards those with other characteristics. In addition, it would not be surprising to find cross-cultural differences in relation to resolution of conflicts. For instance, people who come from a collectivist culture, such as Japan, are more likely to avoid outright confrontation than people who come from more individualistic cultures such as the United States. People from cultures scoring high on Hofstede's (1981) power distance dimension are more likely to appeal to a higher authority and use bureaucratic rules and regulations to resolve conflict than people from cultures which score low on the power distance dimension.

Environmental change

Mullins (1996) lists this as one of his sources of conflict. He mentions shifts in demand, increased competition, government intervention, new technology and changing social values as possible causes of conflict. At the time of writing, the United Kingdom government is threatening to withdraw subsidy from the further and adult education sector for the training of sports coaches. This has resulted in articles and letters in newspapers as well as items on news programmes. If the subsidy is withdrawn, it is likely to affect the number of people enrolling on these courses and, therefore, the employment of the tutors concerned.

The identification of different sources of conflict is helpful in understanding more about organisational conflict but is not as straightforward as it looks. The relationship of sources of conflict to the layers of conflict identified above is complex. Many situations involve more than one layer of conflict. For instance, almost all types of conflict will include elements of misunderstanding, and differences of values are often entwined with interpersonal differences. In addition, differences of viewpoint are closely linked to differences of interest. For example, the means which are thought appropriate to gain particular goals (for instance the formulation of rules and procedures) are intimately related to issues about control, status, resources and so on. The Open University material referred to in Illustration 5.10 makes a useful comment on the relationship between interests and views, as follows:

> Interests are not only shaped by our views, they are also masked by them. The pursuit of personal or departmental advantage is a largely covert affair. Interests are modest to the point of prudishness; they do not walk naked through the corridors of organizations but go heavily clothed, preferably in a fashionable attire woven from the latest ideas about the best way to achieve organizational goals. (1985, p. 59.)

This quotation shows how conflict is not necessarily expressed in loud arguments or fights. It also shows how political behaviour is frequently the outcome of differences resulting in conflict. However, conflict resolution does not necessarily imply political behaviour as defined by Robbins at the beginning of the chapter – that is, activities outside the formal organisational role requirements – as some of the strategies for resolving conflict show.

Approaches to conflict

Strategies for managing conflict will vary according to the frame of reference of an organisation's management. The orientation of managers subscribing to a unitary philosophy of organisation will be to suppress conflict whenever possible. Conflict is likely to be seen as the work of agitators and the dominant strategy will, therefore, be one of denigrating those thought to be the cause or dismissing them from the organisation. The paradox, however, is that, in a democratic society, this strategy will either cause further, more extreme conflict behaviour or drive the expression of conflict underground. The suppression of conflict within a unitary frame of reference will be successful so long as those without power fear the consequences of conflict (e.g. lock-outs, dismissal, unemployment) sufficiently to avoid it. However, as soon as acceptable alternatives to the prevailing situation are available (e.g. alternative employment, successful industrial action), then conflict will again manifest itself, thus reinforcing the view that organisations cannot, in general, be managed as unitary wholes. Recognition of their pluralist characteristics is required if conflict is to be managed successfully.

Most writers on the subject of organisational conflict offer advice on how to manage conflict. Schelling (1960) suggests that parties to a conflict can act in three different ways. The first is to compete, in which case one party wins and the other loses. The second is to co-operate, in which case both parties win. The third is mixture of these two where the parties both compete and co-operate, with both winning something but not all they had hoped. A more comprehensive model of conflict resolution behaviours is Thomas's (1976) conflict-handling styles (*see* Figure 5.1).

Figure 5.1

A model of conflict-handling styles

Source: Adapted from Thomas, K. W. (1976), 'Conflict and conflict management', in Dunnette, M. D. (ed.), *Handbook of Industrial and Organizational Psychology* (Chicago, Rand McNally, p. 900).

Reference to Figure 5.1 shows that Thomas identifies five styles for handling conflict: competing; collaborating; avoiding; accommodating; compromising. Each style is positioned on two axes representing two different concerns. The vertical axis represents a concern to satisfy one's own needs. The horizontal axis represents a concern to satisfy the other party's needs. Illustration 5.11 identifies the situations when it would be most appropriate to use each conflict-handling style.

Each conflict-handling style has an outcome in terms of its capacity to tackle the content of the conflict and the relationship with the other party as follows:

1. *Competing*. This creates a win/lose situation, therefore, the conflict will be resolved to suit one of the parties only. The win/lose situation can lead to negative feelings on the part of the loser and damage the relationship.
2. *Collaborating*. This creates a win/win outcome, where both parties gain. It frequently brings a high quality solution through the results of the inputs of both parties. Win/win outcomes result in both sides being reasonably satisfied. They require openness and trust and a flexibility of approach.
3. *Compromising*. The needs of both parties are partially satisfied. It requires a trading of resources. Openness and trust may not be as great as for collaboration but compromise might set up a relationship which, in the future, could move to collaboration.
4. *Avoiding*. This does not tackle the problem. It creates a no-win situation. It does, however, allow a cooling-off period and allows the parties to (perhaps) gather more

Illustration 5.11

SITUATIONS IN WHICH TO USE THE FIVE CONFLICT-HANDLING STYLES

Competing

1. When quick, decisive action is vital – e.g. emergencies.
2. On important issues where unpopular actions need implementing – e.g. cost cutting, enforcing unpopular rules, discipline.
3. On issues vital to company welfare when you know you're right.
4. Against people who take advantage of non-competitive behaviour.

Collaborating

1. To find an integrative solution when both sets of concerns are too important to be compromised.
2. When your objective is to learn.
3. To merge insights from people with different perspectives.
4. To gain commitment by incorporating concerns into a consensus.
5. To work through feelings which have interfered with a relationship.

Compromising

1. When goals are important, but not worth the effort or potential disruption of more assertive modes.
2. When opponents with equal power are committed to mutually exclusive goals.
3. To achieve temporary settlements to complex issues.
4. To arrive at expedient solutions to complex issues.
5. As a backup when collaboration or competition is unsuccessful.

Avoiding

1. When an issue is trivial, or more important issues are pressing.
2. When you perceive no chance of satisfying your concerns.
3. When potential disruption outweighs the benefits of resolution.
4. To let people cool down and regain perspective.
5. When gathering information supersedes immediate decision.
6. When others can resolve the conflict more effectively.
7. When issues seem tangential or symptomatic of other issues.

Accommodating

1. When you find you are wrong – to allow a better position to be heard, to learn, and to show your reasonableness.
2. When issues are more important to others than to yourself – to satisfy others and maintain cooperation.
3. To build social credits for later issues.
4. To minimise loss when you are outmatched and losing.
5. When harmony and stability are especially important.
6. To allow subordinates to develop by learning from mistakes.

Source: Thomas, K. W. (1977), 'Toward multi-dimensional values in teaching: the example of conflict behaviors', *Academy of Management Review*, Vol. 12, p. 487.

information to begin negotiations afresh or decide there is no conflict after all. It can give rise to frustration on one side if they think the issue is important while the other side do not.

5. *Accommodating*. This can create a lose/win situation, but retains a good relationship between the parties. It involves recognising when the other party might have a better solution than oneself. It is used when relationships are more important than the problem. It builds goodwill.

Most people will have a preferred conflict-handling style, depending on their personality, culture, socialisation and organisational experiences. However, effective management of conflict requires the use of any of these styles, depending on the circumstances.

ACTIVITY 5.5

Think of a conflict from your own organisational experience.

Analyse it to identify which one or more of the levels of conflict described in Illustration 5.11 apply to it.

If it has already been resolved, which of Thomas's approach(es) to conflict were used? If it is still happening, which of Thomas's approaches do you think is most appropriate to its resolution?

Sometimes, however, as Morgan (1986) has pointed out, conflict is of a different kind altogether. Rather than having a philosophy of pluralism, some organisations are 'radicalised' to the extent that divisions between managers and other employees are almost irreconcilable. Thus, the radical frame of reference which characterises these organisations derives from a view of society as comprising antagonistic class interests which will only be reconciled when the differences between the owners of production and the workers have disappeared. Based on a Marxist perspective, this view does not usually, in the West, prevail to the extent that behaviour in conflict situations goes so far as to cause the downfall of organisations and the social structures which support them. While occasionally, as a result of industrial action on the part of workers and management, organisations may close down, in the long run the power of the owners tends to prevail.

ACTIVITY 5.6

Read the following story.

Raheel and Veronica both worked at the same level in the sales department of Keen Machine, a large motorcycle agency which held the sole rights to sell one of the leading brands of motorcycle. They each managed a team of sales people. Each team was responsible for a different geographical area. Although the teams operated independently of each other, they shared the services of two administrators who dealt with orders, invoicing, etc. The administrators also carried out typing and other administrative work for Raheel and Veronica. This work was done by whoever was available at a particular time.

Every year, all the sales people had to undergo performance appraisals which were performed by their manager (either Raheel or Veronica). However, it seemed that the administrators had somehow been 'missed out' from this process. The sales director decided therefore that they also should be appraised and, to be fair to both, by the same person (either Raheel or Veronica).

Raheel's sales team had faced some difficulties on their 'patch' recently and Raheel was having to work hard to recoup their previous good performance. The sales director, not wanting to distract Raheel from this task, asked Veronica to carry out the administrative staff appraisals.

Up to this time, Raheel had always had a good relationship with both administrators and had no complaint about their work for him. However, recently, he began to notice that, if both he and Veronica gave work to the administrators at the same time, Veronica's work seemed to get done first

---

ACTIVITY 5.2 continued

– this was in spite of the fact that he had always thought he had a better relationship with them than Veronica. He complained to the administrators, who both declared they did not show any 'favouritism' to either himself or Veronica. He was still not satisfied but could think of no reason why their behaviour towards him should have changed.

Question

Attempt to explain this situation using concepts and ideas related to issues of power and conflict.

POWER AND CONFLICT IN TIMES OF CHANGE

The discussion above shows that power, politics and conflict are indisputable aspects of social and organisational life. They are, therefore, of crucial importance to the issue of organisations and change. On the issue of power, French and Bell (1990, p. 280) take a positive view, saying: 'The phenomenon of power is ubiquitous. Without influence (power) there would be no cooperation and no society.' Others (e.g. Robbins, 1996) speak of the 'functional' role of conflict. Yet, as some of the discussion above shows, power and conflict, turned into politics, can be used to negative effect. The issue for managers of organisational change, therefore, is to use power and conflict in positive ways to enhance the change process and reduce unnecessary resistance. However, this is, as they say, easier said than done.

The two faces of power

The idea that power has two faces was put forward by McClelland (1970) to explain the positive and negative aspects of power. In their discussion of McClelland's theories, French and Bell (1990, p. 280) say: 'the negative face of power is characterised by a primitive, unsocialised need to have dominance over submissive others'. Positive power derives from a more socialised need to initiate, influence and lead. Therefore, positive power recognises other people's needs to achieve their own goals as well as those of management and the organisation. Negative power is about domination and control of others; positive power seeks to empower, not only the self, but also others.

The terms 'constructive and destructive' can also be used in relation to different types of conflict and are clearly linked to the concepts of positive and negative power. The use of negative power almost inevitably results in destructive conflict, with the attendant breakdown in communications and unwillingness to contemplate any view but one's own. Discontent such as this tends to multiply in conditions of uncertainty which are an inherent part of situations of change. It is in such situations that power balances are upset and disagreements which might, normally, have been settled by compromise, escalate into destructive win-lose situations. Organisations facing conditions of change are, in many respects, at their most vulnerable to the political actions of those who stand to gain from the change as well as those who stand to lose.

The problems of change

It could be argued that some types of change are less problematic than others and, clearly, radical, frame-breaking change is more likely to bring the greatest conditions of uncertainty and fear of what the future may bring. Even so, small-scale, incremental change can upset the balance of power through small, but significant, redistributions of resources or changes in structure which make some people's skills or experience more desirable than those of others. However, regardless of the *content* of any change, most writers would agree that it is the *process* through which the organisation must go to get from one state to another, that brings the most problems. Nadler (1988) suggests three major problems associated with this transition process. The first of these is the problem of resistance to change; the second the problem of organisational control and the third is the problem of power. Figure 5.2 builds on these ideas to illustrate some interconnections between power, conflict, change and political action.

Figure 5.2 shows some possible implications for peoples's attitudes and behaviour during periods of organisational change. Thus, the transition process from the current organisational state to the desired one, rather than being merely a series of mechanistically designed steps, is fraught with possibilities of conflict and political action.

Figure 5.2 illustrates the role of power and conflict during periods of organisational change. 'Behind' each of the elements are many of the concepts discussed in relation to power, conflict and their expressions in political action. For instance, some types of change will challenge some people's values and beliefs, and so induce an internal

Figure 5.2

The problems of change

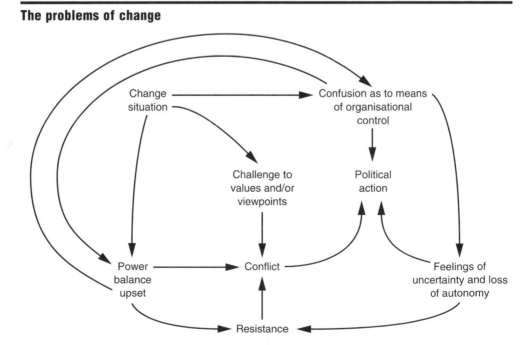

state of conflict which, in turn, means they are likely to resist the change. In addition, because values and beliefs are involved, this resistance will have a moral imperative attached to it. Confusion about the means of organisational control – that is, who and what is being monitored and how – is closely associated with disturbances in the power balance which will most frequently be linked to position and resource power. During times of confusion such as this, opportunities present themselves for taking political action using invisible sources of power. In this context, conflict, viewed as a problem, is likely to be resolved, if at all, by the use of win-lose strategies.

The role of symbolic action in the management of strategic change is discussed by Johnson (1990) and this will be considered further in the next chapter. Of interest here is the fact that during periods of relative stability in organisations, the role of symbols, such as stories and myths, rituals and routines and the more physical manifestations of status and power, play a major part in sustaining that stability. Consequently, in periods of organisational change, these same symbols (and their relationship with symbolic power) can be used in the process of resisting change. What is more, this argument holds whether the change is incremental or concerned with a shift in the organisational paradigm which was discussed in Chapter 4 as the cultural web. In addition, resistance, as a general term, to other than marginal changes incurs what was described in Chapter 2 as 'strategic drift' (Johnson, 1987, Johnson and Scholes, 1997). Thus the process of strategic drift, if allowed to continue without check, leads to confusion as to organisational goals and the means of achieving them. This in turn lays down the conditions for conflict and political action.

The problems of change sometimes appear overwhelming. However, as McClelland said, there is a positive face to power as well as a negative one. There is, equally, a positive face to conflict and political action in the context of organisational change.

The positive use of conflict and power

Robbins (1996) and the Open University (1985) use the terms functional or dysfunctional, and constructive or destructive conflict respectively. Indeed, with respect to functional conflict, Robbins refers to the interactionist approach to conflict which views it as not only a positive force, but also one that is absolutely necessary for a group to perform effectively. In support of this contention he argues that too low a level of conflict is just as dysfunctional as too high a level. Thus, there is a level of conflict – an optimal level of conflict – which engenders self-criticism and innovation to increase unit performance. Robbins says (1996, p. 533) about this:

> when conflict is at an optimal level, complacency and apathy should be minimised, motivation should be enhanced through the creation of a challenging and questioning environment with a vitality that makes work interesting.

The Open University draws attention to the fact that conflict acts to draw those on the same 'side' together in solidarity, but it can also create solidarity among those who are on different sides. This is because, as each side puts its point of view forward (even though in argument), information is revealed and shared, and awareness of each other's goals and views is enhanced. Therefore, conflicts can result in *integrative* effects, but only if attempts to work through the conflict are non-coercive and use methods of openness and honesty.

Mills and Murgatroyd (1991, p. 159) talk about conflict and consent 'being in tension'. Most members of organisations will not revolt if they perceive that the methods of control used to achieve organisational purposes are based on some shared view of how these methods will be applied. For instance, Hofstede's (1981) concept of power distance as one of the dimensions of culture is useful in explaining why people from some cultures will accept a more authoritarian type of decision-making and control than will people from other cultures. If an organisation's workforce is culturally inclined to risk-taking and the tolerance of uncertainty, it will not be as comfortable with strict rules and regulations as one which, in Hofstede's terms, has high uncertainty avoidance.

Furze and Gale (1996) take an optimistic view of conflict in entitling their chapter on this, 'Making conflict useful'. Illustration 5.12 lists a number of guidelines given by Furze and Gale for dealing with conflict. The comments are not necessarily those of Furze and Gale.

Illustration 5.12
GUIDELINES FOR DEALING WITH CONFLICT

1. *Encourage openness*
   This refers to the need to explore objectives, facts, views and the assumptions that surround the issues. Openness requires statements of who benefits and how. It assumes that conflicts cannot be resolved if issues associated with them remain hidden.

2. *Model appropriate responses*
   The issue here is one of role-modelling. If one party is prepared to make positive responses to contention, rather than being defensive or dismissive, this acts to encourage the other party to do likewise.

3. *Provide summaries and restatements of the position*
   Doing this helps to keep communication going and is a helpful slowing-down of the process when it becomes heated and points that are made are in danger of being ignored and lost.

4. *Bring in people who are not directly involved*
   These outsiders can act as additional fact-providers or take on the more process-oriented role of mediator or arbitrator. A mediator can *facilitate* a negotiated solution while an arbitrator can *dictate* one. Other possibilities are conciliators who act as communicators between the two parties (particularly if they won't communicate directly) and consultants. According to Robbins (1996, p. 526): Instead of putting forward specific solutions, the consultant tries to help the parties learn to understand and work with each other.

5. *Encourage people to take time to think and reassess*
   This means building in time for reflection and space apart. It may mean 'shelving' the problem for a short while but not as a means of avoiding it.

6. *Use the strengths of the group*
   This refers to taking advantage of opportunities to use non-combative members of the group to which the combatants belong. Doing this brings others into the conflict, not to take sides, but to play a positive and creative role.

7. *Focus on shared goals*
   Rather than concentrating from the start on differences, seek instead to identify where agreements exist – even if these are very small and, apparently, insignificant. These form a useful base on which to move outwards to assess just where differences exist. Parties to a conflict are often surprised at the amount of agreement which is there but of which they were unaware.

8. *Use directions and interests to develop areas of new gain*
   Concentrating on other people's ideas can identify areas of potential gains. Then using guideline 2, summarise these in order to move forward.

9. *Try to build objectivity into the process*
   Objectivity can be encouraged by asking those involved to express both the strengths and weaknesses of their position. What must be recognised, however, is that objectivity will always be tempered by people's value systems.

10. *Adopt an enquiring approach to managing*
    This means probing through what appear to be the symptoms of conflict to understand the actual causes. Unless the fundamental cause is identified, the conflict will continue to flare up at regular intervals.

Source: Based on Furze, D., and Gale, C. (1996), *Interpreting Management. Exploring Change and Complexity* (London, Thompson International Press, pp. 312–17).

The guidelines for dealing with conflict (Illustration 5.12) are general ones and, if adhered to, may result in what Thomas (see Figure 5.2) called collaboration, where both parties stood to win. These same guidelines are also useful in the context of organisational change and are even more desirable in view of the increased potential for conflict at these times.

Care must be taken, however, to recognise the inevitability of shifting power balances, yet as Illustration 5.13 shows, the use of power in situations of change can be beneficial.

Illustration 5.13

FLIGHT TO REVIVAL – KENYA AIRWAYS' TURBULENT PATH TO PRIVATISATION

Flight to revival

Joel Kibazo reports on Kenya Airways' turbulent path to privatisation

When Brian Davies became managing director of soon-to-be privatised Kenya Airways, he realised he would have to draw on more than just experience to transform the African loss-making state carrier.

A former general manager at British Airways, Davies, together with Malcolm Naylor, the finance director, and Des Hetherington, who has since left the airline, had been part of Speedwing, the British Airways consultancy that carried out a 1992 study of the airline and recommended plans for its revival.

The consultancy team had found an airline on the verge of collapse. There was little cost control, which had contributed to the growing losses which hit $50m (£33m) in 1992. And senior management posts were awarded on the basis of political affiliation and tribal loyalty, with the result that the management hierarchy not only mirrored that of the Kenyan civil service but could have been a case study of the country's social structure.

The board of the company, chaired by the late Philip Ndegwa, a former governor of the central bank of Kenya, subsequently asked the Speedwing team to take over the running of the company and prepare it for privatisation.

Looking back over the last four years, Davies, who prides himself on having a direct but firm management style, says it has been a turbulent but interesting flight. As expatriates they have had to face the additional problem of a press campaign that labelled them 'white colonialists'.

One of the first things Davies had been warned

about was the local custom of never doing anything on time. Arriving an hour late is not always considered rude.

'I have a personal fetish about time and I was warned that you can't do things on time in Africa.' Having decided on times of meetings, he would lock the doors to the meeting room and start without the late-comers. Initially this led to meetings with only about half the number of senior management staff but, as he says, 'the late-comers were soon embarrassed. It worked.'

Management's new promptness clearly percolated through to operations, where the airline's poor record of flight departures was a central issue. Today, he says with pride, 'around 90 per cent of flights leave on schedule and around 85 per cent within 15 minutes of the set departure time. This made me determined to show that other things could also be tackled'.

Another target was staffing. The new team arrived after some 900 people had already been laid off, easing the burden of the staff reorganisation. Yet given the tribal traditions it still proved to be one of the most sensitive operations. The management asked employees to resign and reapply for their jobs.

The reorganisation was complicated by the company's six-tier management structure. Naylor remembers: 'I could not ask for a file without the message having to be passed down a chain of six people. It was crazy but that is how things had always been done here. You have to understand that in this culture position and seniority are very important.'

However, as the account of change in Illustration 5.13 shows, one result of the use of power by Brian Davies was to the detriment of the people who lost their jobs. On the other hand, because the basis on which people were chosen for the new style company was seen to be open and fair – not based on politics or tribal allegiances – the changes appear to have been accepted and new confidence instilled in the employees. As far as can be gained from this account, the use of power has been put to positive effect.

Following the review, the management was streamlined to three tiers, with each manager given specific tasks and budget responsibilities together with spending targets. Nine managers, said to have owed their positions to political or tribal affiliation, were sacked. But Davies says the review brought a new confidence to the staff. 'Everyone was able to see we had not based this on tribe or politics.'

Over the last four years the staff has fallen by a further 400 to 2,300 through a voluntary redundancy scheme, the first such scheme in a Kenyan state-owned company. Losses were reduced to $30m in 1993 and in 1994 the airline recorded its first profit, $7m, which rose to $17m last year. In 1994, the government assumed responsibility for all the airline's external debt arrears of about $82m and converted $33m owed to it into equity. Profits this year are expected to be ahead of the $22m expected by analysts.

Most of the changes in the first year were carried out against a background of a local press campaign against the new management. As the management came from the UK a commonly held view was that it was simply preparing the carrier for sale to British Airways. The more enterprising reporters published the management's hotel bills. Davies admits that at times he wondered what he had let himself in for. 'But in the end I knew we had a job to do and I wanted to see it through.' He says a Time Manager International (TMI) course early on in his career at British Airways which emphasised putting people first, had been useful.

He moved to introduce some elements of TMI into courses he organised at Kenya Airways. 'If you show you value the employees then they too will treat the customer with the same care and attention.'

While arranging a course he discovered that 75 per cent of his staff had never been on an aircraft. 'This meant that they simply had no idea of what we were about.' A lunch aboard an old Boeing 707 aircraft was quickly arranged.

It would have been difficult to usher in so many changes without friction and Davies does admit to a number of misgivings. 'People misunderstood our open management style. We called each other by our first names and openly argued about a point. Here, they observe niceties and people were offended by our way of discussing things. It was an Anglo Saxon way of doing things.' It took a word from the then chairman to highlight the error of the new team's ways.

Davies also says he underestimated the effects of tribal allegiances. 'We would say we are only interested in the Kenya Airways tribe. But in fact we were ignoring reality. Tribe is a powerful aspect that cannot be ignored. For example, people find it difficult to discipline someone from their own tribe. Things are getting better but we have had to learn to live with that factor.'

Last year, the Kenyan government invited international carriers to take a stake in the airline. In January KLM, the Dutch national carrier, announced it had taken a 26 per cent stake. The management is now engaged in a series of briefings for international and local investors ahead of next week's flotation of 48 per cent of the company's shares, to be quoted on the Nairobi stock exchange. The government will retain a 23 per cent holding while 3 per cent of the shares will be used for an employee share ownership scheme.

Those expecting Davies to bow out of the company he has transformed have been wrong footed. He and Naylor have just accepted a two-year extension to their contracts. 'The last three years have been challenging. The next two years will be ones of fun as we enter the growth stage.'

Source: Kibazo, J. (1996), 'Flight to revival', Financial Times, 22 March, p. 12.

Action on power, conflict and change

The story of Brian Davies and his management of change at Kenya Airways (Illustration 5.13) appears to have followed (though not deliberately as far as is known) the four action steps which Nadler (1988) proposes for shaping the political dynamics of change. These actions are proposed in response to what Nadler perceives as one of the problems of change mentioned earlier in the chapter – the problem of power. The first of these is to *ensure or develop the support of key power groups*. This involves identifying those individuals and groups who have the power either to assist change or to block it. As Nadler says, not all power groups have to be intimately involved in the change. However, some groups will need to be included in the planning of any change to guard against their ultimately blocking it, not because it might affect them adversely, but because they had been ignored.

The second of Nadler's action steps is *using leader behaviour to generate energy in support of the change*. The guidelines for dealing with conflict, listed in Illustration 5.12, could very well be guiding principles here. In addition, Robbins (1996) maintains that sets of leaders working in co-ordination can significantly influence the informal aspects of organisational life. The third action step is *using symbols and language to create energy*. This has been discussed above in reference to the use of symbolic power and, in particular, Johnson's (1990) discussion of the role of symbolic action in managing strategic change. Finally, the fourth action step for shaping the political dynamics of change is the need to *build in stability*. This is the use of power to ensure some things remain the same. These might be physical locations, group members, even hours of work. According to Robbins, providing sources of stability such as these gives 'anchors' for people to hold on to during the turbulence of change. He points out, in addition, the need to let people know what will remain stable and what is likely to change.

ACTIVITY 5.7

Apply Nadler's action steps for shaping the political dynamics of change to the account of Brian Davies management of change at Kenya Airways.

How far do you think Brian Davies' actions mirrored those suggested by Nadler?

The discussion in this chapter set out to show the importance of power and conflict as elements in the politics of change. Managers who, in times of change, can reasonably assess who has what power and the way in which it will be used – with possible consequences for potential and actual conflict – have a good chance of implementing the change they seek. The chapter concludes, therefore, with a description of one way of analysing the potential for action of individuals and groups according to: (a) their power to block change, and (b) their motivation to do so.

The first step in analysing the potential for action in favour of or against change, is to identify who holds sufficient power to assist change or, alternatively, to work against it – that is, to carry out a 'power audit'. This can be done by using a questionnaire such as is shown in Figure 5.3. This is based on the descriptions of the characteristics and sources of power discussed earlier in the chapter.

Figure 5.3 Assessing power

Indicators of power to help or hinder change	Individual Group A*	Individual Group B*	Individual Group C*
Position			
1. Status in hierarchy/formal authority.			
2. Power to change organisational structure, rules, and regulations.			
3. Control of strategic decision processes.			
4. Control of operational decision processes.			
Resources			
5. Control of scarce resources.			
6. Control of budgets.			
7. Control of technology.			
8. Ability to reward or punish staff.			
Personal characteristics			
9. Involvement in interpersonal alliances and networks, with links to the informal organisation.			
10. Able to exert 'charismatic' leadership to get others to follow.			
11. Able to cope with uncertainty.			
Knowledge and expertise			
12. Information specific to the change situation.			
13. Skills specific to the change situation.			
14. Knowledge and expertise unique to situation concerned.			
Symbols			
15. Quality of accommodation.			
16. Use of expenses budget.			
17. Membership of high-level decision-making committees.			
18. Receipt of company 'perks'.			
19. Unchallenged right to deal with those outside the organisation.			
20. Access to the 'ear' of top management.			

* Indicate, against each indicator, the degree of power for each individual or group, according to whether it is high (H), medium (M) or low (L).

The questionnaire in Figure 5.3 should be used for each individual or group which is considered to be significant for the success or otherwise of any change process.

The second step is to compare the power of any individual or group to block change with their desire or motivation to do so. Assessing motivation to block change is not straightforward. It can be gauged, however, by considering whether the changes proposed will alter the degree of power held. As a general rule, if this is likely to be lowered, then resistance to change can be expected and vice versa. Figure 5.4 allows any individual or group to be categorised according to their power to block change and their motivation to do so.

Figure 5.4

The power and motivation to block change

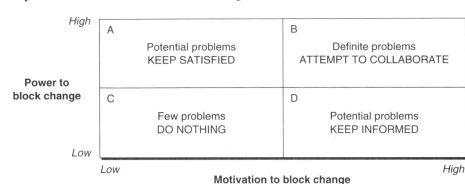

Each cell of the matrix shown in Figure 5.4 represents a different situation and strategy to deal with it. Thus, if an individual or group has little power to block change and, in addition, little motivation to do so (as represented by cell C), no immediate action needs to be taken. However, if there is both power to block change *and* the motivation to do so (cell B) this represents a serious situation in terms of the need to negotiate with those concerned and, if possible, to reach a collaborative agreement.

A potential danger to any change is represented by those who fall into cell A of the matrix – those with a high degree of power but little motivation to do anything about the change. This is because, if the situation itself changes, their interest could be increased and this might then move them into cell B. A strategy towards these people, therefore, should be one of 'keeping them satisfied'. This means maintaining their awareness of how the change might benefit them.

Cell D of the matrix represents a different kind of problem. It might be tempting to ignore these people but, because change situations are dynamic – particularly situations of incremental change – the people categorised into cell D might begin to gain power and thus move into the more contentious group represented by cell B. Consequently, these people should be kept informed of change developments, with some effort being made to persuade them that the change might bring them benefits. However, it must be recognised that these people may be the ones who, in any radical restructuring or change in systems, might lose their jobs. Containment in the short term might, therefore, be the most appropriate strategy.

The axes of the matrix in Figure 5.4 are presented in negative terms in relation to organisational change. It is equally possible to label the axes 'power to facilitate change' and 'motivation to facilitate change'. The categorisation of individuals and groups according to this framework would not necessarily be the converse of that used in Figure 5.4. Therefore, it is worth completing two matrices for a fuller analysis of power, conflict and change.

The capacity for organisations to change, both incrementally and radically, depends on the multiplicity of different interests and values which are part of organisational life.

Power and conflict can be used to further the aims of change, but can also be used to resist them. However, there is some evidence (e.g. Roberts, 1986) that most organisations, both publicly and privately owned, adopt a 'mixed' approach to organisational life generally. Thus, members of organisations will share some common interests and also have some conflicting ones. The traditional concept of the use of power and conflict as 'weapons' represents only a small part of organisational life. An alternative view is that power derives from collective and co-operative action (Roberts, 1986). Care should be taken, however, as the exercise of power and the management of conflict may differ cross-culturally, as is evident from the discussion in Chapter 4.

Finally, the style and function of leadership in the sharing or withholding of power and the management of conflict are crucial for organisational life generally but, particularly, in times of change, and in particular the function of leadership. The next chapter completes Part Two of the book by addressing the role of leadership in organisations and change.

DISCUSSION QUESTIONS AND ACTIVITIES

1 Drawing on the types of power suggested by different writers and researchers, give examples of each based on your organisational experiences.

2 Discuss the idea that power and powerlessness are simply two sides of the same coin.

3 Discuss the proposition: 'In times of change, conflict between individuals and groups is inevitable.'

REFERENCES

Adler, N. J. (1991), *International Dimensions of Organizational Behavior* (2nd edn.), Belmont, CA, Wadsworth.

Barnard, C. I. (1938), *The Functions of the Executive*, Cambridge, MA, Harvard University Press.

Burrell, G., and Morgan, G. (1979), *Sociological Paradigms and Organisational Analysis*, London, Heinemann Educational Books Ltd.

Department of Employment Group Skills and Enterprise Network (1993), *Labour Market and Skill Trends 1994/95*, Crown Copyright, London, Department of Employment.

Department of Employment Group Skills and Enterprise Network (1996), *Labour Market and Skill Trends 1996/97*, Crown Copyright, London, Department of Employment.

French, W. L., and Bell, C. H. (1990), *Organization Development. Behavioral Science Interventions for Organization Improvement*, Englewood Cliffs, NJ, Prentice-Hall International.

Furze, D., and Gale, C. (1996), *Interpreting Management. Exploring Change and Complexity*, London, Thompson International Press.

Gordon, J. R. (1993), *A Diagnostic Approach to Organizational Behavior*, Needham Heights, MA, Allyn and Bacon.

Handy, C. (1993), *Understanding Organizations*, London, Penguin.

Hardy, C. (1994), *Managing Strategic Action. Mobilizing Change*, Concepts, Readings and Cases, London, Sage.

Hofstede, G. (1981), 'Culture and organisations', *International Studies of Management and Organizations*, Vol. X, No. 4, pp. 15–41.

Johnson, G. (1987), *Strategic Change and the Management Process*, Oxford, Blackwell.

Johnson, G. (1990), 'Managing strategic change; the role of symbolic action', *British Journal of Management*, Vol. 1, pp. 183–200.

Johnson, G., and Scholes, K. (1993), *Exploring Corporate Strategy. Text and Cases* (3rd edn.), Hemel Hempstead, Prentice-Hall.

Kanter, R. M. (1979), 'Power failure in management circuits', *Harvard Business Review*, July–August, pp. 65–75.

Kibarzo, J. (1996), 'Flight to revival', *Financial Times*, 22 March, p. 12.

Lawrence, P. R., and Lorsch, J. W. (1969), *Organization and Environment: Managing Differentiation and Integration*, Homewood, IL, R. D. Irwin.

McClelland, D. C. (1970), 'The two faces of power', *Journal of International Affairs*, Vol. 24, No. 1, pp. 29–47.

McGregor, D. (1960), *The Human Side of Enterprise*, New York, McGraw-Hill.

Mayo, E. (1933), *The Human Problems of Industrial Civilization*, New York, Macmillan.

Mills, A. J. and Murgatroyd, S. J. (1991), *Organizational Rules. A Framework for Understanding Organizational Action*, Buckingham, Open University Press.

Mo, Yuet-Ha (1996), 'Orientating values with eastern ways', *People Management*, 25 July, pp. 28–30.

Morgan, G. (1986), *Images of Organizations*, London, Sage.

Mullins, L. J. (1996), *Management and Organisational Behaviour*, London, Pitman.

Nadler, D. A. (1988), 'Concepts for the management of organizational change', in Tushman, M. L. and Moore, W. L. (eds.), *Readings in the Management of Innovation* (7th edn.), New York, Ballinger Publishing Company, pp. 718–32.

Open University (1985), Units 9–10, 'Conflict', Course T244, *Managing in Organizations*, Milton Keynes, Open University.

Open University (1991), Book 8, 'Power, leadership and empowerment', Course B789, *Managing Voluntary and Non-profit Making Enterprises*, Milton Keynes, Open University.

Paton, R. (1994), 'Power in organizations', in Arson, R., and Paton, R., *Organizations, Cases, Issues, Concepts*, London, P.C.P.

Pfeffer, J. (1981), *Power in Organizations*, Marchfield, MA, Pitman.

Pfeffer, J. (1993), 'Understanding power in organizations', in Mabey, C., and Mayon-White, B. (eds.), *Managing Change*, London, P.C.P.

Robbins, S. P. (1990), *Organization Theory, Structure Design and Applications*, Englewood Cliffs, NJ, Prentice-Hall International.

Robbins, S. P. (1993), *Organizational Behaviour* (6th edn.), Englewood Cliffs, NJ, Prentice-Hall International.

Robbins, S. P. (1996), *Organizational Behavior. Concepts, Controversies Applications* (7th edn.), Englewood Cliffs, NJ, Prentice-Hall International.

Roberts, N. C. (1986), 'Organizational power styles: collective and competitive power under varying organizational conditions', *The Journal of Applied Behavioral Science*, Vol. 22, No. 4, pp. 443–58.

Ryle, J. (1996), *The Guardian*, 26 July.

Schelling, T. C. (1960), *The Strategy of Conflict*, Cambridge, MA, Harvard University Press.

Stacey, R. (1996), *Strategic Management and Organisational Dynamics*, London, Pitman.

Taylor, F. W. (1911), *Principles of Scientific Management*, New York, Harper & Row.

Thomas, K. W. (1976), 'Conflict and conflict management', in Dunnette, M. D. (ed.), *Handbook of Industrial and Organizational Psychology*, Chicago, Rand McNally, pp. 889–935.

Thomas, K. W. (1977), 'Toward multi-dimensional values in teaching: the example of conflict behaviors', *Academy of Management Review*, Vol. 12, pp. 484–90.

Tosi, H. L., Rizzo, J. R., and Carroll, S. J. (1994), *Managing Organizational Behavior*, Oxford, Blackwell.

Weber, M. (1947), *The Theory of Social and Economic Organization*, London, Oxford University Press.

Wilson, D. C. (1992), *A Strategy of Change*, London, Routledge.

Wilson, F. M. (1995), *Organizational Behaviour & Gender*, Maidenhead, McGraw-Hill.

Yuet-Ha, M. (1996), 'Orientating values with eastern ways', *People Management*, 25 July, pp. 28–30.

CHAPTER 6

The leadership of change

One of the major debates concerning organisational change relates to the role of those who lead it. This chapter addresses the issue of leading change. It includes a discussion of whether there is one style of leadership best suited to managing change or whether different styles of leadership are required according to different change situations. Issues regarding resistance to change and the identification of strategies for managing it are also recognised.

Objectives

To:

- identify those characteristics which distinguish leadership from management;

- discuss whether there is 'one best way' of leading or whether leadership style and behaviour should vary according to the circumstances;

- explain the possible relationship between organisational life-cycle theories and different leadership styles and behaviours;

- assess the compatibility of different leadership approaches with different types of change situations;

- discuss the issue of resistance to change in terms of its implications for leading the processes of planning and implementing change.

MANAGEMENT AND LEADERSHIP

The issue of leading change links strongly to everything already discussed – both in Part One and in the three preceding chapters which make up the remainder of Part Two of the book. For instance, the management and leadership of organisations is played out through formal organisational structures with their accompanying rules and regulations – as discussed in Chapter 3 – yet the practice of both management and leadership influences, and is influenced by, an organisation's culture, the way power is distributed and the approach taken to conflicts. Thus, management and leadership are both part of the formal and informal aspects of organisational life, as Illustration 6.1 shows.

A distinction can, however, be made which places management rather more firmly in the context of the formal organisation with leadership more naturally associated with the informal aspects of organisations. This chapter is mainly about the role of leadership as part of organisational life and, in particular, its relationship to organisational change. However, it is useful to be clear about the relationship between management and leadership before discussing leadership in more detail.

Management can be thought of as a function which is part of an organisation's formal structure. This is evident in Mullins' (1996, p. 398) statement that he regards management as:

- taking place within a structured organisational setting and with prescribed roles;
- directed towards the attainment of aims and objectives;
- achieved through the efforts of other people; and
- using systems and procedures.

Illustration 6.1
TOUGH TRANSITION FOR HARD-BITTEN BANKER

The drive and passion which James Wolfensohn has brought to his job as World Bank president, coupled with his skills as a lawyer and banker, make the former Australian air force pilot and Olympic fencer a formidable figure. Nine months into the job he needs all these qualities and more if he is to restore drive, purpose, and confidence to an institution which many believe has lost its way.

The Bank's record in Africa – its most formidable challenge – has been mixed at best. Accused of undue secrecy and poor performance by many of its projects, it is seen as cumbersome, bureaucratic and sometimes aloof from other development bodies.

Mr Wolfensohn, 62, a naturalised US citizen, has already made a mark on the Bank, forging closer links with non-governmental organisations as well as the private sector. But it has been a difficult transition for him – from tough-spoken hard-bitten international investment banker, used to getting his way, to a role which requires him to be a diplomat, personnel manager, and catalyst for change in an organisation as large as the Bank, and still so set in its ways.

Source: Holman, M. and Waldmeir, P. (1996), 'World Bank chief's cry from the heart', *Financial Times*, 29 March, p. 4.

He goes on to say

> It is through the process of management that the efforts of members of the organisation are co-ordinated, directed and guided towards the achievement of organisational goals. Management is therefore the cornerstone of organisational effectiveness, and is concerned with arrangements for the carrying out of organisational processes and the execution of work.

This definition draws on the idea that management is a particular function, which is embedded in the organisational structure and which involves a number of different kinds of activities which are, nevertheless, associated with each other. Thus, Fayol (1949) proposed five elements of management – planning, organising, commanding, co-ordinating, and controlling – which can be seen to relate to formal organisational systems.

Other writers and researchers have concentrated more on the *roles* that managers play, that is, what managers do. For instance, Illustration 6.2 describes the 10 roles which Mintzberg (1979) suggested as a result of his study of chief executive officers in both small and large organisations.

Mintzberg (1979) grouped managerial roles into three sets: inter-personal roles (figurehead, leader, liaison); informational roles (monitor, disseminator, spokesman); decisional roles (entrepreneur, disturbance handler, resource allocator, negotiator). An examination of these categories and the roles within them highlights the ambiguity of the relationship between management and leadership. As this framework shows, leadership is just one aspect of a manager's job, a view that is echoed by Handy's (1993) contention that leading (which he takes to include the roles of figurehead, leader and liaison) is mostly concerned with the interpersonal aspects of a manager's activities. Consequently, although a manager must also be a leader, a leader does not always have to be a manager. A useful summary of the differences between leading and managing is given by Kotter (1990), as shown in Illustration 6.3.

Both Mintzberg's and Kotter's distinctions between leadership and management agree with Mullins' (1996) conclusion that management is concerned with activities within the formal structure and goals of the organisation, while leadership focuses more on interpersonal behaviour in a broader context. His statement (p. 247) that 'Leadership does not necessarily take place within the hierarchical structure of the organisation' typifies this view. To support this contention, he refers to Watson's (1983) 7-S organisational framework of: strategy, structure, systems, style, staff, skills and superordinate (or shared) goals. Based on this, Watson maintains that management is more concerned with strategy, structure and systems, while leadership is more concerned with what he calls the 'soft' Ss of: style, staff, skills and shared goals. Leadership then is concerned with establishing shared visions and goals; with interpersonal relationships and communication; and with motivation and getting the best out of people. Basically, leadership is about influencing others in pursuit of the achievement of organisational goals.

However, as Smith (1991) points out, rather than being about absolute influence, leadership is about relative influence, in that 'a leader is someone who has more influence over others than they have over him or her' (p. 207). This introduces the idea of the leader and the *group*, thus implying the importance of *followers*. The discussion

Illustration 6.2
MINTZBERG'S MANAGERIAL ROLES

Figurehead

In the figurehead role, the manager acts as the representative or symbol of the organisation. Examples of this role are attending meetings on behalf of the organisation, giving out long-service awards, or appearing on 'platforms' as a representative of local business.

Leader

The manager, as leader, is concerned with interpersonal relationships, what motivates his or her staff and what needs they might have.

Liaison

The liaison role emphasises the network of contacts with others in and outside the organisation. Liaising with others allows the manager to collect useful information. In the liaison role, a manager might belong to a professional institution.

Monitor

Monitoring the environment to keep informed of competitors' activities, new legislation, changes in the market and so on, are all examples of a manager's monitoring role.

Disseminator

The role of disseminator includes keeping staff and others within the organisation informed. This could be done in a variety of written and spoken forms and may be on a one-to-one basis or through group meetings.

Spokesperson

As spokesperson, the manager gives information to others outside the organisation. He or she speaks on behalf of the organisation, for instance on the organisation's policies and activities.

Entrepreneur

The role of entrepreneur is associated with innovation and change. It includes the design and implementation of different types of change from small scale job redesign to large scale organisational re-structuring depending on the level of the manager concerned.

Disturbance handler

The manager in this role acts to solve problems which arise, often unexpectedly. Thus, managing to intervene in a conflict situation or find a solution to a machine breakdown are examples of this role.

Resource allocator

The majority of managers control some kind of resource (e.g. money, labour, time) which they can use, or allocate, at their discretion. Allocating money according to budgets is one aspect of this role. Other possibilities are the scheduling of subordinates' work and allocating equipment.

Negotiator

All managers have to play the role of negotiator when they debate who will do some things and who will do others. Coming to agreements on the scope of people's jobs and their pay are examples of negotiating.

Source: Based on Mintzberg, H. (1979), *The Nature of Managerial Work* (Englewood Cliffs, NJ, Prentice-Hall).

which follows shows that other factors also influence people's perception of what constitutes 'good leadership'. It will become evident also that there is no universally agreed view as to what this is. There are, however, a number of approaches which offer ways to understanding leadership and its relationship to organisational performance and organisational change.

Illustration 6.3

COMPARING MANAGEMENT AND LEADERSHIP

	Management	Leadership
Creating an agenda	Planning and Budgeting – establishing detailed steps and timetables for achieving needed results, and then allocating the resources necessary to make that happen	Establishing Direction – developing a vision of the future, often the distant future, and strategies for producing the changes needed to achieve that vision
Developing a human network for achieving the agenda	Organizing and Staffing – establishing some structure for accomplishing plan requirements, staffing that structure with individuals, delegating responsibility and authority for carrying out the plan, providing policies and procedures to help guide people, and creating methods or systems to monitor implementation	Aligning People – communicating the direction by words and deeds to all those whose cooperation may be needed so as to influence the creation of teams and coalitions that understand the vision and strategies, and accept their validity
Execution	Controlling and Problem Solving – monitoring results vs. plan in some detail, identifying deviations, and then planning and organizing to solve these problems	Motivating and Inspiring – energizing people to overcome major political, bureaucratic, and resource barriers to change by satisfying very basic, but often unfulfilled, human needs
Outcomes	Produces a degree of predictability and order, and has the potential of consistently producing key results expected by various stakeholders (e.g. for customers, always being on time; for stockholders, being on budget)	Produces change, often to a dramatic degree, and has the potential of producing extremely useful change (e.g. new products that customers want, new approaches to labor relations that help make a firm more competitive)

Reprinted with the permission of The Free Press, a division of Simon & Schuster from *A Force for Change: How Leadership Differs from Management* by John P. Kotter. Copyright © 1990 by John P. Kotter Inc.

APPROACHES TO LEADERSHIP

There are a range of theories which purport to explain what makes a person a good and effective leader. These can be put into two broad categories. The first includes those theories which contend that there is 'one best way' of exercising leadership and, therefore, that there is a particular set of characteristics which 'good' leaders should possess. The second category says the opposite, that there is no one best way, but a range of leadership styles which should be applied differentially according to the situation in which leadership is required.

The 'one best way' to lead

Traits of leadership

The first of the approaches to leadership under this heading is not really a theory of *how* to lead. It is more a theory of what leaders should be like, in other words what traits (e.g. physical and personality characteristics, skills and abilities, and social factors such as interpersonal skills, sociability and socio-economic position) are indicative of a successful leader. However, a survey of the research on this issue shows that there is a degree of confusion as to whether there are certain personality and other characteristics which, when present, 'fit' a person to be a leader. Early research (Stodgill, 1948; Mann, 1959) came to the conclusion that there were few relationships between the traits possessed by leaders and their performance. The notion of 'born to lead' did not hold up under scrutiny. However, more recent studies reveal stronger evidence of an identifiable set of personality and cognitive traits which are said to characterise successful leaders.

The first of these is a meta-analysis (one which surveys and brings together the results of other studies) carried out by Lord, De Vader and Alliger in 1986 which concluded that there could be six traits which distinguish successful leaders from others. These are:

- intelligence
- having an extrovert personality
- dominance
- masculinity
- conservatism
- being better adjusted than non-leaders

A few years later, Kirkpatrick and Locke (1991) also surveyed existing leadership studies and suggested their own list of six leadership traits, which are:

- drive (achievement, ambition, energy, tenacity, initiative)
- leadership motivation (personalised or socialised)
- honesty and integrity
- self-confidence (including emotional stability)
- cognitive ability (the ability to marshal and interpret a wide variety of information)
- knowledge of the business

In 1996, Dulewicz and Herbert (1996) reported on their original research on a sample of 72 managers who, on the basis of several indicators of success, could be identified as either 'high-flyers or low-flyers'. What these two researchers did was to administer two different personality tests to these managers to determine what characteristics differentiated the high-flyers. The results showed that the high-flyers scored higher than the low-flyers on the following:

- risk-taking
- assertiveness and decisiveness
- achievement
- motivation
- competitiveness

They also showed exceptional managerial skills of:

- planning and organising
- managing staff
- motivating others

ACTIVITY 6.1

Read Illustration 6.1 again.

Which of the leadership traits do you think James Wolfensohn possesses?

Do you think the description 'hard-bitten' has positive or negative connotations in this context?

It is interesting to compare and contrast the three lists given above. For instance, the trait of intelligence comes up in the first two studies mentioned and this is given further confirmation in Fiedler's (1989) Cognitive Resource Utilisation Theory (CRUT). This says that, under normal circumstances, a leader's intelligence will add crucially to his or her success as a leader. Consequently, a leader's intelligence is an important resource for any group. However, as Fiedler points out, there are some situations which can prevent leaders using the intelligence they possess – for instance, poor relations with their boss, poor interpersonal relationships and a non-directive style. Therefore, intelligence on its own is not sufficient to guarantee a successful leader. The characteristics of dominance (Lord, De Vader and Alliger, 1986), drive and self-confidence (Kirkpatrick and Locke, 1991) and almost all the characteristics listed by Dulewicz and Herbert (1996, p. 16) are required to support the use of a leader's cognitive capacities. What is particularly relevant about Dulewicz and Herbert's list, in comparison to the other two, is the addition of the characteristic of risk-taking which is probably most relevant in times of organisational change. Two statements from their article make this point.

> Our most successful general managers are also willing to take risks rather than seek comfort in familiar situations; are determined to see things through to completion; set stretching targets for themselves and others; and are highly competitive and poor losers.

> . . . the competencies required of high-flyers will tend to concentrate on the ability to cope with change and uncertainty and the promotion of innovation.

ACTIVITY 6.2

Think of two leaders you know, or have known, well. One should be a person whom you judged to be successful as a leader and the other quite the opposite – that is, unsuccessful.

On the scales below, indicate the extent to which each person possesses that particular trait.

If possible, ask some other colleagues to carry out the same activity.

	Very high	High	Average	Low	Very low
Need to achieve					
Need for power					
Leadership motivation					
Self-confidence					
Honesty and integrity					
Intelligence					
Knowledge of the business					
Assertiveness and decisiveness					
Competitiveness					
Emotional stability					
Extrovert personality					
Willingness to take risks					

From your results, what conclusions can you form as to whether successful leaders possess some traits which others do not? Compare your results with those discussed in the literature and with other people's views.

The results from doing Activity 6.2 are only an indication of the applicability of trait theories of leadership – after all, if you did this on your own, you have a sample of only two leaders! These theories do, however, appear to offer something in relation to the type of person best suited to lead others.

This idea certainly appears to find favour in the many descriptions of supposed leaders of change – what Reich (1991) calls 'the entrepreneurial hero'. This notion that there are some people who are, characteristically, leadership material is supported by implication when Kanter (1991, p. 54) says: 'I discovered the skills of change masters [by which she means those successfully bringing about change] by researching hundreds of managers across more than a half-dozen industries. I put change-master skills in two categories: first, the personal or individual skills and second, the interpersonal ones, how the person manages others.' She goes on to identify what she calls 'kaleidoscope thinking' as well as the ability to communicate visions, and be persistent. Coalition-building and working through teams are aspects of her second category of skills. Other researchers have come to similar conclusions about the nature of leadership. For instance, Westley and Mintzberg (1991) claim to have identified a range of what they term 'salient capacities' of five well-known leaders (Edwin Land, Steven Jobs, Rene Levesque, Lee Iacocca, Jan Carlzon). The capacities of imagination, sagacity and foresight are prominent amongst them. Yet, Reich (1991) warns against the idea of the leader as hero with some set of hero-like characteristics. The concept of successful leadership is seen as more complex than this, as is evident in the title of Reich's article, 'The team as hero'. In support of Reich is the idea that the charismatic individual leader is more relevant to Western thinking than it would be in more 'collective' societies (*see* Chapter 5) such as are found in the Far East.

Even so, there are other scholars who maintain that there is still one best way to lead. However, instead of trying to find a set of characteristics to describe *what* a successful leader is, they concentrate more on *how* a leader ought to *behave* in order to be successful.

Leadership behaviour

Bass (1990) lists no fewer than 29 different systems for classifying leadership behaviour. However, Wright (1996), in commenting on this, maintains that many of the concepts are so similar that four main leadership styles of behaviour can be identified. These are (p. 36):

1. *Concern for task*: the extent to which the leader emphasises high levels of productivity, organises and defines group activities in relation to the group's task objectives and so on. (Also called concern for production, production-centred, task-oriented and task-centred leadership.)
2. *Concern for people*: the extent to which the leader is concerned about his or her subordinates as people – their needs, interests, problems, development, etc. – rather than simply treating them as units of production. (Also called person-centred, person-oriented and employee-centred leadership.)
3. *Directive leadership*: the extent to which the leader makes all the decisions concerning group activities him- or herself and expects subordinates simply to follow instructions. (Also called authoritarian or autocratic leadership.)
4. *Participative leadership*: the extent to which the leader shares decision-making concerning group activities with subordinates. (Also called democratic leadership.)

Given this classification of leadership style, it might be supposed that there are differences in the effects of using one style rather than another. However, Wright's review of a range of studies attempting to link leadership style with high performance and subordinate satisfaction found little evidence of a single style. Consequently, no one style seemed to emerge as the most appropriate in all situations, and where, for instance, a participative leadership style was related to high performance and satisfaction of subordinates, it was not clear whether the leader's style was the causal variable or vice versa. Given this, it is interesting to note that two famous studies of leadership (Stodgill and Coons, 1957; Likert, 1961), known respectively as the Ohio State studies and the University of Michigan studies, separately identified two independent dimensions of leadership which were, in essence, a combination of the four types of behaviour described above. The Ohio researchers named these 'consideration' and 'initiating structure'.

Consideration is the degree to which a leader builds trust and mutual respect with subordinates, shows respect for their ideas and concern for their well-being. This dimension is linked to a participative, human relations approach to leadership. It therefore combines the 'concern for people' and 'participative leadership' styles identified by Wright.

Initiating structure is the degree to which a leader defines and structures his or her own role, and the interactions within the group, towards the attainment of formal goals. It has elements of both the 'directive leadership' and 'concern for tasks' styles described above.

The University of Michigan researchers used the terms employee-centred and production-centred leadership for these dimensions but they were virtually the same in description to those of the Ohio researchers. The main point about these dimensions is that, because they are deemed to be independent of each other, a leader's behaviour can be categorised in four different ways. Thus, leaders can be:

- high on consideration and high on initiating structure
- high on consideration and low on initiating structure
- low on consideration and low on initiating structure
- low on consideration and high on initiating structure

The relationship of these two-dimensional theories to the idea of a 'one-best way' of leading manifests itself most clearly in the way Blake and Mouton (1964) built on these concepts to propose that the most effective leadership style is one which is high on both dimensions. Figure 6.1 gives the positions of five different leadership styles on the latest version of Blake and Mouton's managerial grid – now called the 'leadership grid' (Blake and McCanse, 1991).

The different combinations of concern for people and concern for production set out in Figure 6.1 result in different combinations of leadership characteristics as follows:

The 9,1 Authority-Compliance leader has a high concern for the task and little concern for people, emphasising efficiency and the organisation's needs at the expense of the needs of people. There is a belief that production can only be achieved if people are closely supervised and controlled. According to Blake and McCanse (p. 55): 'A Grid style like 9,1 is unlikely to elicit the cooperation, involvement, or commitment of those who are expected to complete the task.'

The 1,9 Country Club leadership style is based on the assumption that productivity will follow if the needs of people are satisfied. These leaders believe that people cannot be pressured into doing things – they need to be well treated to get them to perform well. According to Blake and McCanse, however, this leadership style, although

Figure 6.1

The leadership Grid®

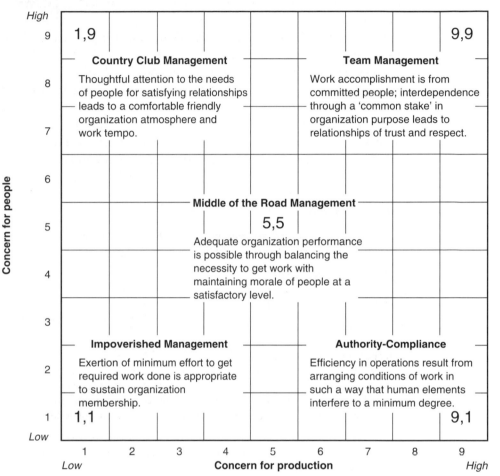

encouraging friendly and pleasant relationships, produces results where productivity suffers. Creativity and innovation are undermined because of the possible conflict which might surface as a result of challenges to existing ways of doing things.

The 1,1 Impoverished Management, or laissez-faire *leadership style* is characterised by minimum concern for both production and the needs of people. The 1,1 leader's desire is to remain as uninvolved as possible with other people, compatible with fulfilling the requirements of the job and sustaining organisation membership. Conflict is deliberately avoided by remaining neutral on most contentious issues.

The 5,5 Middle of the Road leadership style is concerned with moderate rather than high performance. This results from a desire to balance the contradiction between production and people's needs through compromising in the face of conflict. It includes a willingness to yield on some points in order to gain on others. This is a team-oriented style, but because negativity is not tolerated, complacency can set in and the team can lose sight of reality.

The 9,9 style of Team Management incorporates high concern for production with a high concern for people. In contrast to the 5,5 leadership style which assumes an inherent contradiction between production and people, the 9,9 leadership style assumes that concern for both is necessary and that they do not inherently contradict each other. There is an emphasis on working as a team which recognises the interdependence of people with each other, together with the task to be done. Relationships between people are based on mutual trust and respect, and work is assumed to be accomplished only if employees are committed to the task, team and organisation.

ACTIVITY 6.3

Read the following extract from an article about Mrs Isabella Beeton, famous for her book on household management which was written in 1859.

Mrs Beeton: management guru

Mrs Beeton's approach can be summarised in three principles, which would certainly appear in most modern management texts: setting an example and giving clear guidance to staff; controlling the finances; applying the benefits of order and method in all management activities.

An example to staff
(In her own words)

'Early rising is one of the most essential qualities . . . as it is not only the parent of health but of other innumerable advantages. Indeed when a mistress is an early riser, it is almost certain that her house will be orderly and well managed. On the contrary, if she remain in bed till a late hour, then the domestics, who . . . invariably partake somewhat of their mistress's character, will surely become sluggards.'

'Good Temper should be cultivated . . . Every head of a household should strive to be cheerful, and should never fail to show a deep interest in all that appertains to the well-being of those who claim the protection of her roof.'

'The Treatment of Servants is of the highest possible moment . . . If they perceive that the mistress's conduct is regulated by high and correct principles, they will not fail to respect her. If, also, a benevolent desire is shown to promote their comfort, at the same time that a steady performance of their duty is enacted, then their respect will not be unmingled with affection, and they will be still more solicitous to continue to deserve her favour.'

The article continues to quote from Mrs Beeton's book on the need to keep 'a housekeeping account-book . . . punctually and precisely. On the issue of order and method she says, 'Cleanliness, punctuality, order and method are essentials in the character of a good housekeeper'.

Source: Wensley, R. (1996), 'Mrs Beeton: management guru', *Financial Times*, 26 April, p. 15.

Question
Can you place Mrs Beeton on the Leadership Grid of Blake and McCanse? Justify your positioning.

The leadership grid assumes that there is one best style of leadership, that of the 9,9 'Team Management' style – regardless of the situation.

The leadership grid is a simplified way of categorising different aspects of leadership behaviour. There are, however, other categories of leadership behaviour which overlap with these, but which are more detailed in their descriptions; for instance, the 'powers of the person' discussed in an article by Useem (1996) who says that these kinds of behaviours transcend those of particular value to particular situations. These are:

- challenging the process
- searching for opportunities
- experimenting
- inspiring a shared vision
- envisioning a future
- enlisting others
- enabling others to act
- strengthening others
- fostering collaboration
- modelling the way
- setting an example
- celebrating accomplishments
- recognising contributions.

In addition to these, Useem, drawing on a study of 48 firms among the Fortune 500 largest US manufacturers, gives the following behaviours as characterising the most successful chief executive officers:

- being visionary
- showing strong confidence in self and others
- communicating high performance expectations and standards
- personally exemplifying the firm's vision, values and standards
- demonstrating personal sacrifice, determination, persistence and courage.

This is yet another study which implies that there are certain desirable leadership qualities whatever the situation. What is important about this latter list, however, is that these are behaviours which can be likened to those actions said to be characteristic of *transformational* leadership as compared to the less visionary styles of leadership associated with *transactional* leadership (*see* Illustration 6.4) and, therefore, more likely to be effective in times of change.

Illustration 6.4 compares and contrasts transactional and transformational leadership. The essential differences have been neatly summarised by Tichy and Ulrich (1984, p. 60) as follows:

> Where transactional managers make only minor adjustments in the organisation's mission, structure, and human resource management, transformational leaders not only make major changes in these three areas but they also evoke fundamental changes in the basic political and cultural systems of the organisation. The revamping of the political and cultural systems is what most distinguishes the transformational leader from the transactional one.

Illustration 6.4

TRANSACTIONAL AND TRANSFORMATIONAL LEADERS

Transactional leader

- *Contingent reward*: contracts exchange of rewards for effort, promises rewards for good performance, recognises accomplishments.
- *Management by exception (active)*: watches and searches for deviations from rules and standards, takes corrective action.
- *Management by exception (passive)*: intervenes only if standards are not met.
- *Laissez-faire*: abdicates responsibilities, avoids making decisions.

Transformational leader

- *Charisma*: provides vision and sense of mission, instills pride, gains respect and trust.
- *Inspiration*: communicates high expectations, uses symbols to focus efforts, expresses important purposes in simple ways.
- *Intellectual stimulation*: promotes intelligence, rationality, and careful problem solving.
- *Individualized consideration*: gives personal attention, treats each employee individually, coaches, advises.

Source: Bass, B. M. (1990), 'From transactional to transformational leadership: Learning to share the vision', *Organizational Dynamics*, Winter, p. 22.

According to Bass (1990), transactional leaders are those who initiate structure and are considerate to employees – they might, therefore, be considered to be 9,9 leaders. However, transformational leadership goes beyond this as confirmed by Robbins (1996, p. 439) who says: 'Transformational leadership is built *on top of* transactional leadership – it produces levels of subordinate effort and performance that go beyond what would occur with a transactional approach alone'. The relationship between transformational leadership and team and organisational performance is discussed by Tichy and Ulrich through reference to some well-known leaders of American corporations, the conclusion being that transformational leaders are those most likely to 'revitalise organisations . . . transform the organisations and head them down new tracks' (p. 60). Robbins quotes evidence from studies with American, Canadian and German military offices as well as managers at Federal Express to support the superiority of transformational leadership over transactional leadership in terms of being correlated with lower turnover rates, higher productivity and higher employee satisfaction. What is more, the effects of transformational leadership on subordinates is confirmed in Behling and McFillen's (1996) model of charismatic/transformational leadership where the leader's behaviour is said to give rise to inspiration, awe and empowerment in the followers, resulting in exceptionally high effort, exceptionally high commitment and willingness to take risks.

It would appear that transformational leadership behaviours add to the two dimensions of leadership identified in both the Ohio State and Michigan University studies. This view is supported by the results of work by researchers in Finland and Sweden (Ekvall and Arvonen, 1991; Lindell and Rosenqvist, 1992a, 1992b) which shows early evidence of a third dimension related to development-oriented leader behaviour – in other words, behaviour related specifically to leadership in an organisational change context. What is not clear is whether transformational leadership is the most recent leadership behaviour to be recommended whatever the circumstances, or whether it is simply an additional leadership behaviour to be used in situations of radical change. Both Tichy and Ulrich (1984), and Bass seem to argue that transformational leadership is the best way to lead whatever the circumstances. Indeed, Bass (1990, p. 20) goes so far as to say that transactional leadership is, in many instances, 'a prescription for mediocrity', arguing that only transformational leadership can make a difference in an organisation's performance at all levels. By contrast, Ekvall and Arvonen, and Lindell and Rosenqvist seem to suggest that behaviours approaching transformational leadership may be most appropriate in conditions of change.

The question remains, therefore, as to whether one particular way of leading can be appropriate regardless of the stage of development of an organisation, the environment in which it exists, or the people who work in it; or whether different leadership styles and behaviours are required according to the different situations prevailing as organisations' environments change, along with associated changes in strategy and functioning.

Contingency approaches to leadership

From the discussion above, it is clear that trait and simple behavioural theories of leadership have some support. However, as Figure 6.2 shows, there are many things which can influence organisational outcomes in addition to those associated with a leader's qualities and behaviour.

Figure 6.2

Situational influences on leadership effectiveness

Therefore, in contrast to theories of leadership which argue for a universal view of what traits and/or behaviours leaders should have, other theories maintain that a leader's behaviour should be contingent upon the organisational situation prevailing.

Behaviour along a continuum

One of the best known theories of leadership, which takes into account situational factors, is that of Tannenbaum and Schmidt (1973) which arranges leadership behaviour along a continuum not dissimilar to the 'directive' and 'participative' leadership styles which contribute to the dimensions of the Ohio State and Michigan studies discussed above.

At the 'boss-centred leadership' extreme, which assumes a high level of leader power, leaders *tell* subordinates what to do. At the other, 'subordinate-centred leadership' extreme, leaders and subordinates *jointly* make decisions. Moving along the continuum between these two positions, from the area of greatest freedom for leaders to the area of greatest freedom for subordinates, the leadership style becomes increasingly less authoritative and more participative. To this extent, the styles of leadership suggested are little different from those identified by the Ohio State and Michigan University studies, except in the degree of independence of the dimensions. What is different from the 'one best way' theories is that Tannenbaum and Schmidt do not support one preferred leadership style. On the contrary, they suggest that a leader should move along the continuum, selecting the style that is most appropriate to the situation prevailing, for which they use a threefold categorisation according to the 'forces' which they say should determine the style of leadership to use. These three forces are:

Forces in the manager – each manager will have his or her own combination of personality characteristics, skills and knowledge, values and attitudes which predisposes the adoption of one particular style of leadership or another.

Forces in the subordinate – subordinates vary in their characteristics such as the degree of support needed, experience in and knowledge of the work, commitment to organisational goals, expectations as to how leaders will behave, previous experience of different leadership styles. As Smith (1991, p. 212) says: 'Inexperienced, immature and uncommitted subordinates may force even the most participative manager to adopt an autocratic, telling, style.'

Forces in the situation – these divide into two categories: first, the nature of the task or problem itself, and second, the general context in which the leadership activity takes place. This can include: the time available to make a decision, the organisational culture and power balances between the different participants in the situation, and general opportunities and constraints arising from organisational structures and processes as well as environmental and societal influences. A simple example is that should a fire break out (a well-defined problem with an objective criterion of success), an appropriate leadership style would *not* be to call a meeting to discuss what should be done. A more relevant example is the case of new government regulations which must be adhered to and over which there is little opportunity for flexibility in implementation. In some cases, changes in the organisational environment are so sudden and severe that a more authoritative leadership style is the only one relevant to the situation. In other cases, the prevailing organisational structure and culture may force a more participative style of leadership. Illustration 6.5 is an example of the application of these concepts to leadership in a situation facing the Beautiful Buildings Company (BB Company) in one of its ventures to build luxury apartments in Japan.

Illustration 6.5
LITTLE ROOM TO MANOEUVRE

Jayne was pleased that she had been put in charge of BB Company's latest building venture, the second of its kind to take place in Japan. She had limited experience of working in this country but had spent some time talking to staff working on the other Japanese site about how to approach the management of those employed on the building works. She knew, therefore, that there were a number of factors she would need to take into account when deciding on her own leadership approach.

The diagram below illustrates the situation Jayne faced.

The length of rules on the diagram indicate the degrees of freedom available to Jayne in the situation which faced her. The line indicating her own leadership style shows her preferences were for a more consultative/participative style which she had been accustomed to using with staff in Britain. However, most of the Japanese employees were accustomed to a more formal management–subordinate relationship, and were likely to work in this type of relationship, given the fact that Jayne was a woman. The task of building the apartments was complex but, in many ways, defined. Much of what was required had been worked out beforehand. However, as with all building works, unknown factors such as the weather and possible unexpected problems with the ground, let alone any industrial relations problems which could arise, contributed to there being certain unstructured elements to the situation. If any two of these factors combined, some extensive negotiations might need to be held between management and workers or their representatives. The BB Company prided itself on its care for its workers, so the organisational context was one which veered more towards a human-relations type of approach than an authoritarian one. Even so, profit was profit and the industry was a very competitive one. The organisation did not want anything to go wrong.

What the diagram shows is that Jayne has not much room for manoeuvre in deciding what approach to take as a leader in this situation. The overlap between all the forces is not large. If she cannot influence any of the factors associated with the subordinates, the task and the context, she must make sure to adopt a leadership style which tends towards the directive end of her preferences.

Fiedler's contingency model of leadership

The task-oriented/people-oriented continuum of leadership styles is also the centre-piece of Fiedler's (1967) contingency theory of leadership. In this case, however, the three situational variables said to determine the style of leadership to be adopted are:

Leader–member relations – the extent to which a leader has the support of her or his group members. To determine this, questions might be asked about the willingness of group members to do what the leader tells them, the degree of trust existing between the leader and the followers and the extent to which followers will support the leader's decisions.

Task structure – the extent to which the task or purpose of a group is well defined and the outcomes can be seen clearly to be a success or failure. To determine this, questions about the measurability of the outcomes might be asked. In other words, is it possible to judge 'success' objectively or might there be different views on how the outcomes should be assessed?

Position power – the amount of power (particularly reward power) which the leader can use to accomplish his or her, and the group's, purposes. The issue here is whether leaders have the support of higher management for the way they deal with subordinates.

A comparison of Fiedler's variables with those of Tannenbaum and Schmidt (1973) shows the 'task structure' variable to be similar in both cases. However, the other variables are different one from another. The underlying 'contingency' argument, though, remains the same. Consequently, according to Fiedler, the style of leadership adopted should take account of particular situational conditions in terms of the three variables identified and the subsequent degree of favourability or otherwise of the total situation. What is different about Fiedler's findings is that the relationship of leadership style to the favourableness/unfavourableness of the situation is a curvilinear one. In other words, when the situation is very favourable or very unfavourable, the most effective leadership style is said to be a task-oriented, more directive one, rather than a person-oriented one. When the situation is of moderate favourability to the leader, the style recommended is a person-oriented one. Table 6.1 illustrates this in a simplified form. Of course, in reality, the relationship is not as simple as this. However, the argument that a more consultative and participative style is necessary in situations of confusion and maybe suspicion seems logical. When the situation is very favourable to the leader, he or she can probably take a more directive style, given the trust and support to be expected from group members. In very unfavourable situations, the leader must emphasise the need for task accomplishment in order to push the group towards its goals. This requirement, in turn, dictates a more directive, task-oriented approach.

Implicit in Fiedler's contingency theory is that leaders can adapt their leadership styles to the prevailing situation. However, Fiedler believes this to be difficult – as the allusions in Illustration 6.1 show – and, therefore, suggests that either leaders should be chosen so that their management style fits the situation or elements of the situation need to be modified. However, neither strategy seems easy, thus confirming the existence of certain difficulties in 'matching' leaders and leadership situations.

Table 6.1
Fiedler's contingency theory of leadership

	Leader–Member Relationships	Task structure	Position power	Leadership style
1	good	structured	high	Task-oriented
2	good	structured	low	style
3	good	unstructured	high	recommended
4	good	unstructured	low	Person-oriented
5	poor	structured	high	style
6	poor	structured	low	recommended
7	poor	unstructured	high	Task-oriented
8	poor	unstructured	low	style recommended

Hersey and Blanchard's situational theory

Another difficulty with contingency theories is the question of how much importance should be attached to each contingency factor. Clearly the task and the amount of power held by the leader are important, but it seems logical that the characteristics and expectations of group members or subordinates are more important in deciding what style of leadership to adopt – after all it is these people who must carry out the task.

This would appear to be the case with Hersey and Blanchard's (1993) situational leadership theory which puts greatest stress on one major situational factor – the readiness of what they term the leader's 'followers'. According to this theory, a leader's behaviour should depend on the readiness of followers to accept responsibility and to be willing to make their own decisions. As with the other theories already discussed, the leadership behaviour is defined by Hersey and Blanchard in terms similar to those used for the initiating structure and consideration behaviours identified by the Ohio State researchers. The theory agrees with these researchers that these two behaviours are independent of one another. Therefore, a leader could be low on both task and relationship behaviour, high on both or high on one and low on another. As a result any leader's behaviour may fall into one of four quadrants – which go from 'telling' through 'selling' and 'participating' to 'delegating'. The readiness of followers also falls into four categories, each of which, in an ideal world, should trigger one of the four types of leadership behaviour. Gordon (1993) refers to this theory as a 'life-cycle' model of leadership, presumably because the followers move from being both unable and unwilling (or too insecure) to take on responsibility for their own actions, to being either unable but willing (or confident) or willing but unable, to the highest state of readiness where they are both able and willing to take responsibility for decisions and actions.

Figure 6.3 shows how a leader's behaviour should change according to the quadrant into which the followers' readiness falls.

An examination of Figure 6.3 shows the similarity of the four quadrants to the four corners of Blake and McCanse's (1991) leadership grid. This is not surprising given the two leadership styles and the combinations available. However, while Blake and McCanse argue for a 'one best way' of leader (the 9,9 way) for all occasions, Hersey and Blanchard argue that a leader's style should be contingent upon the characteristics and attitudes of those who are led. In contrast to, for instance, Fiedler's views, both

Figure 6.3

Hersey and Blanchard's theory of situational leadership

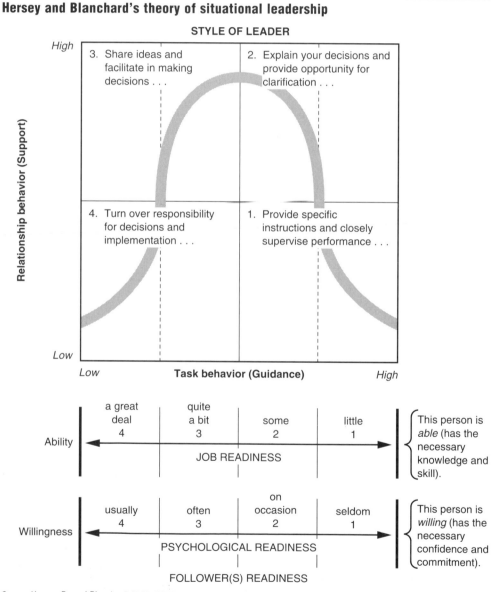

Source: Hersey, P., and Blanchard, K. H. (1993), *Management of Organizational Behavior: Utilizing Human Resources* (6th edn.), Englewood Cliffs, NJ, Prentice-Hall, p. 197.

theories assume a leader's style is flexible enough to change according to the prevailing situation and, in Hersey and Blanchard's case, that it can presumably change in the presence of different groups and as the followers 'mature' through the cycle referred to by Gordon. Illustration 6.6 is a good example of how forces in the leader, the subordinates and the situation could be said to influence the leadership style to be adopted.

Illustration 6.6
WORLD BANK CHIEF'S CRY FROM THE HEART

World Bank chief's cry from the heart

Michael Holman and Patti Waldmeir on Wolfensohn's passionate appeal to senior management

Seldom if ever can a World Bank president have made a speech as impassioned and as critical as the one Mr James Wolfensohn made to senior management at a meeting in Washington on March 12.

It was a cry from the heart of a man who seeks to inspire as much as to lead, but who has seen that inspiration blocked by cynicism and distrust. For 90 minutes before 300 senior colleagues, Mr Wolfensohn fought that cynicism with the rhetorical weapons he uses so well: frankness, sincerity, passion and hyperbole.

He concluded on a high note, adopting the tone of enthusiasm he hopes will infect the work of his subordinates around the world: 'I am . . . talking about a new atmosphere of change and a new atmosphere of hope and a new dream . . . where we can say we are affecting the lives of people in the world (more) positively than anyone else, and we are doing it brilliantly.'

He spoke of a 'humanised' Bank, of a future when 'we can say that we care, that we can cry about poverty, that we can laugh when people have a good time, that we can embrace our clients, that we can feel part of them, where we can tell our kids we made a difference.' He had even invited two of his own children to earlier inspirational sessions, 'because I want them to be proud of me, I want them to think that what I am doing is different'.

But these comments came at the end of an extraordinarily critical session in which the new Bank chief, reviewing progress after nine months as head, alternately cajoled, chastised, implored and berated his listeners. Participants say the atmosphere was by turns subdued, and electric.

The issues were wide-ranging. But again and again, Mr Wolfensohn hammered home one central message with a vivid metaphor: there was a 'glass wall' which was standing in the way of his efforts to ensure that the Bank was more efficient as a development agency.

The Bank chief's frustration was palpable: he has staked his reputation on revolutionising the internal culture of the organisation, as an essential prerequisite to improving the Bank's ability to deliver development worldwide.

Among other things, Mr Wolfensohn wants success in the Bank to be judged by the performance of projects rather than the number of loans approved.

At times, his tone bordered on despair: 'I don't know what else we can do, in terms of standard or even non-standard approaches, to try to bring change in the institution. I just don't know what else to do.

'How can we get a new basis for working inside the bank? How can we change the atmosphere? How can we move from cynicism, distrust and distance, to risk-taking and involvement? . . . there is so much baggage. There is a need, somehow, to break through this glass wall, this unseen glass wall, to get enthusiasm, change and commitment,' he said.

'I cannot have a situation where we as a group don't have that sense of excitement, commitment, and trust. I don't expect it overnight, but I have to tell you we have got to change this, and I don't know how to do it. I just don't know how to do it.'

Bank insiders say his comments were partly designed to shock his audience – the managers whose past performance has inspired wide-spread distrust among the staff. They say Mr Wolfensohn does not believe his experiment in more effective management is in peril.

Illustration 6.6 continued

But the evidence from internal Bank studies of personnel, cited by him in the meeting, is grim. Results of Bank 'focus' (study) groups 'undeniably show that there is a lack of trust in management, a huge sense of cynicism and there is some distance which I cannot get my hands on between expressed desire to move forward for change, and commitment in the organisation . . . there is a palpable reservation in the air.'

The distrust is hampering efforts to restructure the organisation. Mr Wolfensohn is keen to improve the Bank's relationships with its clients by creating posts for 'country managers' who would be the main point of contact for governments. These country managers would then draw on specialist skills within the Bank through an internal market.

Senior officials say that staff support the principle of this plan, but fear that it will be exploited by the chosen managers, who will exercise favouritism and patronage in the way they use resources elsewhere in the organisation.

This sometimes operates among people of the same nationality and sometimes under 'fiefdoms' which have developed over time, officials say.

The studies show that 40 per cent of Bank employees do not trust management. Bank insiders believe this is partly the result of past personnel policies: 'When good people don't always get promoted and those promoted are not always good, then the management responsible for that does not engender trust,' said one participant in the meeting.

Such a personnel issue was high on the agenda at the meeting: senior staff were unhappy about alleged favouritism on the part of Mr Wolfensohn and his top aides in the choice of individuals for a new training initiative. But questioners soon moved on to other issues. One senior manager took the opportunity to complain: 'Up to now, I've had the impression that you thought you had all the answers, and that the message was "get on board, or get off the ship".'

Others spoke of a 'culture of approval, a culture where people don't express their opinions forthrightly' for fear of jeopardising career prospects. For his part, Mr Wolfensohn said he was astonished at 'the lack of interpersonal generosity (and) the lack of a team, a sense of team'.

He appealed to his colleagues to do their own independent thinking about change: 'I do not have a monopoly on the ideas . . . I am enfranchising every one of you . . . to come up with some ideas of how we can bring about the change,' he said, adding, 'there is just something here which the surveys show, and which I can feel, which is inhibiting us . . . and I just beg you to think about it.'

Source: Holman, M., and Waldmeir, P. (1996), *Financial Times*, 29 March, p. 4.

ACTIVITY 6.4

Using any of the theories discussed above, carry out an analysis of the situation facing James Wolfensohn in his new role at the World Bank.

If you were James Wolfensohn, what leadership style would you adopt to help gain the objectives he mentions? (see Illustration 6.6).

Path-goal theory of leadership

The assumption of a flexible style of leadership in Hersey and Blanchard's (1993) theory is also true of what has come to be called the 'path-goal' theory of leadership, which also argues that leadership style (directive, supportive, participative or achievement oriented) is contingent upon various situational factors. Originally developed by House (1971), path-goal theory maintains that the leader should use the style of leadership which is most effective in influencing subordinates' perceptions of the goals they need to achieve and the way (or path) in which they should be achieved. The theory relates directly to expectancy theories of motivation in that a leader will be judged successful if she or he can help subordinates reach their goals. In other words effective leadership will help subordinates turn effort into appropriate and high-level performance.

Two dominant situational factors are relevant to this theory. These are, first, the characteristics of the team or group members, that is the subordinates; and second, the nature of the task or job and the immediate context in which it takes place. The task of the leader is, therefore, to use a style which is congruent with the skills, motivation and expectations of subordinates and with the goals to be achieved, the design of the jobs and the resources and time available. Figure 6.4 is a generalised diagram of these factors which are presumed to intervene between the effort put into doing a job and the subsequent performance.

The subordinate characteristic of 'locus of control' in Figure 6.4 is of interest as it has not appeared in any of the other main leadership theories considered above. In the same way as leaders may, characteristically, veer towards one style more than another, subordinates also have preferences for the way they are managed and this is influenced by their locus of control, that is, their beliefs about who controls their lives. Smith (1991, p. 220) describes the concept of locus of control as follows:

> The locus of control concerns a person's beliefs about who controls their life. People with an internal locus of control believe that they control their own lives. People with an external locus of control believe other people control their lives. According to path-goal theory of leadership non-directive styles of leadership should be used with 'internals' and a directive style should be used with externals. Internals like to be asked, externals like to be told.

Figure 6.4

Factors intervening between effort and performance

NATURE OF TASK AND ITS CONTEXT

Robbins (1996, p. 428) gives the following hypotheses connecting leadership style with path-goal theory situational factors:

Directive leadership leads to greater satisfaction when tasks are ambiguous or stressful than when they are highly structured and well laid out.

Supportive leadership results in high employee performance and satisfaction when subordinates are performing structured tasks.

Directive leadership is likely to be perceived as redundant among subordinates with high perceived ability and with considerable experience.

The more clear and bureaucratic the formal authority relationships, the more leaders should exhibit supportive behaviour and deemphasise directive behaviour.

Directive leadership will lead to higher employee satisfaction when there is substantive conflict within a work group.

Subordinates with an internal locus of control (those who believe they control their own destiny) will be more satisfied with a participative style.

Subordinates with an external locus of control will be more satisfied with a directive style.

Achievement-oriented leadership will increase subordinates' expectancies that effort will lead to high performance when tasks are ambiguously structured.

Robbins refers to the work of Keller (1989) and Wofford and Liska (1993) as examples of support for path-goal theory, saying (pp. 428–9): 'The evidence supports the logic underlying the theory. That is, employee performance and satisfaction are likely to be positively influenced when the leader compensates for things lacking in either the employee or the work setting.' While this is likely to be true, effective leaders are also those who can match their leadership approach to the strategic focus and values of the organisation in which they operate.

Matching organisational models and leadership roles

The discussion above has identified a number of situational variables which might be said to influence the style and behaviour of leaders. These are: leaders' predispositions to one style rather than another; the strength of their power base to deliver rewards to their followers; the expectations and skills of the followers and their preparedness for different degrees of autonomy in their own actions; the nature of the task to be achieved; and the many factors (e.g. organisational structure, culture, time and resources available) which make up the organisational context in which leadership operates.

With respect to the latter, it could be argued that an organisation's strategic focus together with preferred forms of control will determine many of the other factors and, therefore, the particular leadership style adopted. Two different pieces of research pick up on these ideas to suggest links between different organisational models and different approaches to leadership.

The first of these is that of Quinn (1988) who proposes four organisational models distinguished on the basis of two bi-polar dimensions. These are:

Table 6.2
Summary of Quinn's (1988) four organisational models

Human Relations Model (adaptable and internally focused)	Open Systems Model (adaptable and externally focused)	Rational Goal Model (stable and externally focused)	Internal Process Model (stable and internally focused)
Towards: • Flexibility • Decentralisation • Differentiation • Maintenance of the sociotechnical system	Towards: • Flexibility • Decentralisation • Differentiation • Expansion • Competitive position of overall system	Towards: • Centralisation • Integration • Maximising output • Competitive position of overall system	Towards: • Centralisation • Integration • Consolidation • Continuity • Maintenance of sociotechnical systems
Values: • Human Resources • Training • Cohesion • Morale	Values: • Adaptability • Readiness • Growth/Acquisition • External support	Values: • Productivity • Efficiency • Planning • Goal setting	Values: • Information • Management • Communication • Stability • Control
THE TEAM	THE ADHOCRACY	THE FIRM	THE HIERARCHY

Source: Based on Quinn, R. E. (1988), 'Beyond Rational Management: Mastering the Paradoxes and Competing Demands of High Performance', San Francisco, Jossey-Bass, p.48.

(a) the adaptability and flexibility of the way organisations operate as opposed to the desire for stability and control; and

(b) whether organisations are outward looking (towards the environment and the competition) or internally focused towards the maintenance of systems and procedures.

Table 6.2 summarises the different characteristics of the four organisational models which result from combining these four different organisational orientations. Quinn uses the terms 'the hierarchy', 'the firm', 'the adhocracy' and 'the team' as a shorthand way of describing the internal process, rational goal, open systems and human relations organisational models respectively.

What is interesting about the framework illustrated in Figure 6.5 is Quinn's linking of different dimensional positions with leadership style and the roles leaders should play. An examination of Figure 6.5 shows leadership styles positioned around the outer edge of the framework with the leadership roles inside them. From this, it can be seen that different leadership styles and behaviour 'fit' different organisational models.

A second piece of research, by Farkas and Wetlaufer (1996), came to similar conclusions to Quinn about the dependence of leadership style and behaviour on the needs of the organisation and the business situation at hand. On the basis of interviews with 160 chief executives around the world, these researchers found five distinctive approaches to leadership, each of which was associated with different emphases in terms of strategic planning, research and development (R&D),

Figure 6.5

Competing values framework of leadership roles

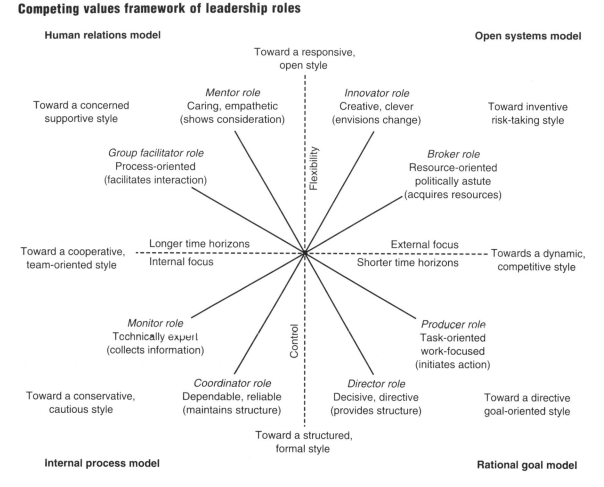

Human relations model

Open systems model

Toward a responsive,
open style

Mentor role
Caring, empathetic
(shows consideration)

Innovator role
Creative, clever
(envisions change)

Toward a concerned
supportive style

Toward inventive
risk-taking style

Group facilitator role
Process-oriented
(facilitates interaction)

Broker role
Resource-oriented
politically astute
(acquires resources)

Flexibility

Toward a cooperative,
team-oriented style

Longer time horizons
Internal focus

External focus
Shorter time horizons

Towards a dynamic,
competitive style

Monitor role
Technically expert
(collects information)

Producer role
Task-oriented
work-focused
(initiates action)

Control

Toward a conservative,
cautious style

Coordinator role
Dependable, reliable
(maintains structure)

Director role
Decisive, directive
(provides structure)

Toward a directive
goal-oriented style

Toward a structured,
formal style

Internal process model

Rational goal model

Source: Quinn, R. E. (1988), *Beyond Rational Management: Mastering the Paradoxes and Competing Demands of High Performance* (San Francisco, Jossey-Bass, p. 86.

recruitment and selection practices, matters internal to the organisation or matters external to it and with whom, and how, they spent their time. According to Farkas and Wetlaufer (p. 111) the leadership approach to be adopted depends on answering questions such as: 'Is the industry growing explosively or is it mature? How many competitors exist and how strong are they? Does technology matter and, if so, where is it going? What are the organisation's capital and human assets? What constitutes sustainable competitive advantage, and how close is the organisation to achieving it?' To these questions, one could also add: 'What kind of changes is the organisation facing and what do these mean for the role of leadership?'

LEADERSHIP IN TIMES OF CHANGE

The discussion so far suggests a number of conclusions, not all compatible, about leadership in times of organisational change. The first, which relates to the 'one best way' of leading, is that most of the characteristics presumed necessary for successful leadership by the trait theorists appear relevant to leaders of change. However, Kirkpatrick and Locke's (1991) identification of drive, leadership motivation, honesty and integrity, self-confidence, cognitive ability and knowledge of the business seem most relevant – along with the trait of general intelligence. The second is that, given these characteristics, there might be a particular type of leadership behaviour which is most appropriate to leading change. This is the development-oriented behaviour which the researchers Ekvall and Arvonen (1991) and Lindell and Rosenqvist (1992a, 1992b) claim to have found. The third is that transformational leadership seems almost tailor-made for leading change. For instance, in their book entitled, *The Transformational Leader*, Tichy and Devanna (1990) put forward a dramatic analogy of transformational leadership when they propose triggers for change emerging from what they call 'the prologue' of the new global playing field. Acts I (Recognising the need for revitalisation), II (Creating a new vision) and III (Institutionalising change) all follow on from this prologue. The 'epilogue' of 'History repeating itself' serves to emphasise the continuous nature of change and, therefore, the necessity for continuous transformation of organisations and the people in organisations having the continuing need for transformational leadership.

If these conclusions are accepted, the search for leaders of change could stop here. However, as the contingency theories of leadership show, leadership style and behaviour can vary according to the different characteristics of different organisational situations. In addition to those described above, these situations also include an organisation's stage of development, the nature of the change process itself, and the forces for or against any change, including individuals' and groups' resistance to change.

Leadership and the organisational life-cycle

The stages through which an organisation goes, as it forms, develops and matures (and maybe disappears) were discussed in Chapter 2 with particular reference to the work of Greiner (1972). However, Greiner, as well as identifying these phases in an organisation's evolution, also sets out the different organisational practices required during each evolutionary phase. One of these practices is the style which top management should adopt according to an organisation's growth phase (*see* Table 6.3).

Clarke (1994, p. 12) elaborated on the phases and styles propounded by Greiner to suggest the following management styles:

Phase 1 – individualistic, creative, entrepreneurial, ownership
Phase 2 – strong directive
Phase 3 – full delegation and autonomy

Table 6.3
Matching top management style to organisational growth phases

Organisational growth phases	Phase 1 Growth through CREATIVITY	Phase 2 Growth through DIRECTION	Phase 3 Growth through DELEGATION	Phase 4 Growth through CO-ORDINATION	Phase 5 Growth through ELABORATION
Top management style	Individualistic and entrepreneurial	Directive	Delegative	Watchdog	Participative

Source: Derived from Greiner, L. (1972), 'Evolution and revolution as organizations grow', *Harvard Business Review*, July–August, p. 45.

Phase 4 – watchdog
Phase 5 – team oriented, interpersonal skills at a premium, innovative, educational bias

Greiner's suggestions are helpful in drawing attention to the need for change in the management style of top management and other organisational leaders, as organisations evolve and mature. This need is supported by suggestions by Clarke and Pratt (1985) who identify four different styles of managerial leadership required at different stages in the life of an organisations life. These are:

- the *champion* to fight for and defend the new business;
- the *tank commander* to take the business into its next stage of growth, someone to develop a robust team and direct the business into exploitable parts of the market;
- the *housekeeper* to keep the business on an even keel as it enters the mature stage to provide efficiency as well as effectiveness;
- the *lemon-squeezer* to get the most out of the business as it is in danger of decline.

The idea that organisations at different stages of growth need different leadership approaches has also been taken up by Quinn (1988) whose work has already been discussed above (*see* Table 6.2 and Figure 6.5). For instance, Quinn argues that an organisation will start its life-cycle positioned predominantly in the open systems (the 'adhocracy') quadrant of the framework (*see* Figure 6.5). As it grows and develops, it will include the elements of the human relations model (the 'team') and a focus on productivity and accomplishment from the rational goal model (the 'firm'). As it reaches the stage of formalisation, it will become less oriented to the open systems and human relations models and will take on more of the characteristics of the internal process model (the 'hierarchy'). Finally, in its elaboration of structure stage, it will use elements of all the organisational models, but will re-focus, in particular, back to the open systems model. The implications of this life-cycle for any organisation's management and its leadership approach are shown in Table 6.3. This implies that an inventive risk-taking style – typified by innovative, broker type behaviour – is most appropriate in the early stages of an organisation's development. As the organisation develops towards an established collectivity, this should be tempered with a style more supportive of employees and more group oriented – in other words leaders should behave as mentors and group facilitators. As growth and development continue, and the organisation enters a more formalised stage, a more conservative, cautious style is suggested, and so the roles of monitor and co-ordinator become most important. Finally, in an organisation's most elaborated stage, leadership styles are required which are flexible enough to change orientation according to the complex, changing situations within the organisation itself, but with an emphasis on resource acquisition and innovation in anticipation of further change.

ACTIVITY 6.5

Compare and contrast the leadership styles and behaviours described by Greiner, Clarke and Quinn in terms of their relationship to, and usefulness for, managerial leadership during the different phases or stages of an organisation's development.

How do these leadership styles and behaviours accord with your own experience of effective and ineffective leadership at different organisational growth stages?

The results of completing Activity 6.5 may reveal some differences in the three classifications of leadership styles and behaviours surveyed. However, an issue which arises from all three descriptions is that of whether the same leaders can take the organisation through all these phases. Theories such as those of Hersey and Blanchard (1993) and path-goal theory (House, 1971) would say 'Yes'. However, Fiedler (1967), in his exposition of a contingency theory of leadership, would advise caution in this respect. This is also the view of Clarke and Pratt (1985) and is further supported by evidence that, because different people have different thinking styles (Kirton, 1976) and preferred behavioural roles (Belbin, 1993), they will have different preferences for the way they interpret and cope with change. Care should be taken, therefore, not to assume that the same leader can be 'all things to all situations'. In addition, it may be that one style of leadership may be appropriate to a particular type of change while another may be appropriate to a different type of change.

Leadership and the nature of change

In Chapter 2, a range of different ways of defining change were reviewed. Table 6.4 shows how different typologies of change might relate one to another and to the environmental conditions giving rise to them.

There is little in the literature to suggest which leadership styles and behaviours are most associated with each type of change. Two exceptions stand out. The first is the assumption that transformational leadership is associated with transformational or frame-breaking change. The second is the work of Dunphy and Stace (1993) who have, specifically, linked styles of leadership to types of change. Figure 6.6 shows the results of these linkings.

Table 6.4
Environmental conditions and types of change

ENVIRONMENTAL FORCES FOR CHANGE			TYPES OF CHANGE			
Ansoff and McDonnell (1990)	Strebel (1996a)	Stacey (1996)	Tushman et al. (1988)	Dunphy and Stace (1993)	Grundy (1993)	Stacey (1996)
Predictable Forecastable by extrapolation	Weak	Close to certainty	Converging (fine-tuning)	Fine-tuning	Smooth incremental	Closed
Predictable threats and opportunities	Moderate	Close to certainty	Converging (incremental)	Incremental adjustment		Contained
					Bumpy incremental	
Partially predictable opportunities Unpredictable surprises	Strong	Far from certainty	Discontinuous or frame-breaking	Modular transformation Corporate transformation	Discontinuous	Open-ended

Figure 6.6

The Dunphy and Stace change matrix

Source: Dunphy, D., and Stace, D. (1993) 'The strategic management of corporate change', *Human Relations*, Vol. 46, No. 8, p. 908.

An examination of Figure 6.6 shows that any style of management can be used with any type of change. However, Dunphy and Stace's research with 13 service-sector organisations which had gone through large-scale environmental change indicates that, for transformational change at the corporate level, a directive/coercive style of leadership is likely to be most successful. What is interesting, though, is Dunphy and Stace's (p. 917) statement that: 'once this basis for organisational renewal is in place, there is a choice to be made at the corporate level as to the mix of directive and consultative strategies needed to keep the momentum of change'. With regard to accompanying change at the business (operational) level, they suggest a more consultative style to win commitment of employees at that level.

Logic suggests that a more consultative style of management is more appropriate to converging, incremental types of change which are, in turn, likely to be associated with environmental forces for change which are predictable and of moderate strength, as shown in Table 6.4. However, Strebel (1996a) proposes a model which not only links leadership style and approach to environmental forces for change, but also links these to the degree to which an organisation is open to change initiatives. Consequently, any discussion of the leadership of change must take account of the capability and willingness of any organisation to remain either closed or open to the prospects of change. Leading change, therefore, will almost certainly be concerned with overcoming resistance to change.

Obstructing and facilitating processes for change

For the management of any organisation which is reacting to, or planning for, change there will be forces acting to facilitate the change and forces acting against it. Although these forces are important for any type of change, they become particularly important in the context of frame-breaking or transformational change. Newton (1996) discusses a number of processes which, she says, obstruct or facilitate change. Some of these factors and others are given in Illustration 6.7.

The forces *for* change listed in Illustration 6.7 are categorised into external and internal forces (in relation to the organisation). The forces *against* change are categorised into individual responses and organisational responses. Yet another distinction which could be made is between those forces which: (a) prevent a new perspective being formed, and (b) prevent implementation of change once the intentions for change are known (Ginsberg and Abrahamson, 1991).

External and internal forces associated with change

Forces for change originating in the external environment of an organisation were discussed in Chapters 1 and 2 as part of the PETS description of the organisational environment. These, together with internal forces, such as the need for new product development or restructuring to accommodate new technological processes, are likely to facilitate change in that they are the triggers for change. However, these forces may be counteracted by other forces which resist change; for instance, those listed in

Illustration 6.7

FORCES FOR AND AGAINST CHANGE

Driving forces for change	Driving forces against change
1. External forces	*1. Individual resistance*
● role of the State	● fear of the unknown
● social pressures	● dislike of the uncertainty and ambiguity surrounding change
● changing technology	
● constraints from suppliers	● potential loss of power base
● stakeholder demands	● potential loss of rewards
● competitor behaviour	● perceived lack of skills for new situation
● customer needs	● potential loss of current skills
2. Internal forces	*2. Organisational resistance*
● organisational growth	● inertial forces deriving from the systemic nature of organisations
● pressures for increased performance	
● managerial aspirations	● interlocking aspects of structure, control systems, rituals and routines, signs and symbols
● political coalitions	
● redesign of jobs	● inertial forces deriving from group norms
● restructuring	● potential loss of group power bases
	● entrenched interests of stakeholders
	● lack of organisational capability
	● lack of resources
	● threat to resource allocations

Illustration 6.7 which, themselves, may be externally or internally generated. However, the role of leading change is more likely to be concerned with resistance from inside the organisation (which can be from individuals or be organisationally generated), this being the type of resistance most immediately manageable.

It is clear from an inspection of the factors listed in Illustration 6.7 that, for specific change situations, some forces will be stronger than others. One technique for depicting the range and strength of forces for and against change is that of *Force Field analysis*. Developed in the 1960s, force field analysis is based on the idea that, in any change situation, there are forces supporting change and forces opposing change. The theory, upon which the technique is based, implies that when the balance of the two sets of

Figure 6.7

A force field diagram

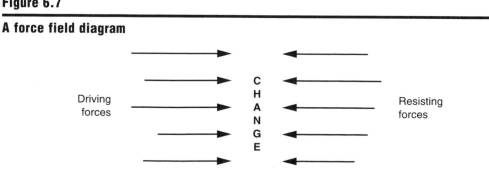

forces is equal, no change will occur. Thus, it is argued that, if change is desired, the forces supporting change need to be strengthened and those opposing change weakened. Figure 6.7 is a generic representation of a force field diagram, while Illustration 6.8 (drawing on the advice of Carnall (1990) and Huczynski and Buchanan (1994)) outlines the steps necessary for carrying it out.

McCalman and Paton (1992) suggest that force field analysis, as well as operating as a technique in its own right, can be incorporated into other change situation analyses such as the TROPICS test which is discussed in Chapter Two. The results of such analyses help in deciding the extent to which an organisation is open or closed to change. In this respect also, Strebel (1992, p. 67) offers the following advice.

1. Look for closed attitudes by examining what processes are in place for bringing new ideas into the industry, company, or business unit, especially at the highest levels; and by probing whether management is aware of the change forces.
2. Look for an entrenched culture by examining what processes are in place for reflecting on values and improving behaviour and skills; and by enquiring to what extent behaviour and skills are adapted to the forces of change.
3. Look for rigid structures and systems, by examining when the organisation, business system, the stakeholder resource base, and the industry last changed significantly; and by enquiring to what extent the structures and systems are capable of accommodating the forces of change.
4. Look for counterproductive change dynamics by examining whether historical forces of change are driving the business; and by enquiring to what extent the historical forces of change have become the new force of resistance.
5. Assess the strength of the overall resistance to change by examining to what extent the various forces of resistance are correlated with one another; and by describing the resistance threshold in terms of power and resources needed to deal with the resistance.

Illustration 6.8
FORCE FIELD ANALYSIS

Step 1: Define the problem in terms of the present situation, with its strengths and weaknesses, and the situation you would wish to achieve. Define the target situation as precisely and unambiguously as possible.

Step 2: List the forces working for and against the desired changes. These can be based on people, resources, time, external factors, corporate culture.

Step 3: Rate each of the forces for and against change in terms of *strength*: high, medium or low. Give the strength ratings numerical values: 5 for high, 3 for medium, and 1 for low; this allows totals for driving and resisting forces to be calculated.

Step 4: Using a diagram such as that in Figure 6.8, draw lines of different lengths to indicate the different strengths of the forces.

Step 5: Label each line to indicate whether that force is

very important (VI), important (I) or not important (NI).

Step 6: For each very important (VI) and important (I) force supporting the change, indicate how you would attempt to strengthen the force. Then do the same for those forces opposing the change, but in this case indicate how you would weaken the force.

Step 7: Agree on those actions which appear most likely to help solve the problem of achieving change.

Step 8: Identify the resources that will be needed to take the agreed actions and how these resources may be obtained.

Step 9: Make a practical action plan designed to achieve the target situation which should include:
● timing of events
● specified milestones and deadlines
● specific responsibilities – who does what.

Figure 6.8 Contrasting change paths

Resistance	PROACTIVE	REACTIVE	RAPID	
Closed to change	Radical leadership	Organizational realignment	Downsizing and restructuring	Discontinuous paths
Can be opened to change	Top-down experimentation	Process reengineering	Autonomous restructuring	Mixed paths
Open to change	Bottom-up experimentation	Goal cascading	Rapid adaptation	Continuous paths
	Weak	Moderate	Strong	Change force

Source: Strebel, P. (1996a), 'Choosing the right change path', *Mastering Management*, Part 14, *Financial Times*, p. 7.

Assuming assessments such as these can be done, Strebel's (1996a) juxtaposition of the level of intensity of forces for change (which he designates as weak, moderate or strong and which could be calculated from use of force field analysis) with the degree of resistance expected (that is, whether an organisation is closed to change, can be opened to change, or is open to change) is useful for determining the leadership behaviour and overall management approach to implementing change (*see* Figure 6.8).

The role of leadership in Strebel's model is most clearly spelt out in the case of weak environmental change forces in an organisational situation of being closed to change. Of this situation, Strebel says that weak change forces imply proactive change; in an organisation unused to and closed to change, this implies radical leadership. By this, Strebel means an approach which will break the dominant culture of resistance by starting with top management and continuing through a process of shaking up others in the organisation. The proposed behaviour of change leaders (or, as Strebel refers to them, change agents) in this and the other situations shown in Figure 6.8 is summarised by Strebel as follows (1996a, p. 6):

> It is useful to distinguish between the different levels of 'change-force' intensity. Weak change forces are difficult to discern and require skill in communications and in identifying the value creating idea – but there is time for experimentation. Moderate change forces are those which have started to affect performance but do not threaten survival: getting people's attention is easier and multi-disciplinary teams should be employed.
>
> Those organisations with high resistance have very few 'change agents' and require a radical approach to break the dominant culture. The process should start with resistors at the top, can benefit from headstrong leadership (though can equally end in a disastrous ego trip), and requires some form of reorganisation. In organisations that can be opened to change, management has to help the change agents, and top-down experimentation is desirable. In organisations that are already open to change there is usually little risk in leaving the resistors until last. Bottom-up experimentation and goal cascading should be possible.

Strebel's model of paths to change is quite complex and, as this discussion is focused on leadership, the paths to change identified in the final column are only tangentially relevant – they are discussed further in Part Three of the book. What is important, here, is to note Strebel's comment (p. 5) that: 'Change leaders cannot afford the risk of blindly applying a standard recipe and hoping it will work. Successful change takes place on a path that is appropriate to the specific situation.'

Responding to resistance to change

Leadership can be conceptualised in terms of its three main functions within a group or organisation (Open University, 1991, p. 48). These are:

- the *strategic* function – developing a sense of direction in the group or organisation;
- the *tactical* function – identifying and choosing the most appropriate means to pursue the group's or the organisation's chosen path;
- the *interpersonal* function – maintaining the morale, cohesion and commitment of the group or organisation.

It is important to note that these functions do not, necessarily, divide themselves among leaders at the top, middle and other parts of organisations. All the functions are carried out by all leaders whatever their status. However, it is reasonable to suggest that the strategic and tactical functions will feature more prominently in the planning and early stages of change, with the tactical and interpersonal functions featuring more prominently during the change process and when the change is in place.

Reducing or overcoming resistance to change depends on identifying the sources of resistance, as discussed above. It also depends on a leader's ability to be task oriented (both strategically and tactically) when the time requires it, but also relationship oriented to address the more individualised resistances to change. A first step is to recognise the conclusions of a number of writers (e.g. Rashford and Coghlan, 1989; Clarke, 1994; Nortier, 1995) that individuals faced with change often go through a traumatic process of shock and denial before they come to acknowledge and adapt to it. What must not be forgotten, however, is that change can be exciting and can bring new and positive opportunities for all. The notion of a vision and communicating that vision is important in this context, as exemplified by Clarke (1994, p. 124) when she says: 'It is a vision of a new future which provides the pull-through and momentum for change.' This view is reinforced by two articles (Beer, Eisenstat and Spector, 1990; Kotter, 1995) in the *Harvard Business Review*, both of which refer to the need for a vision to guide the change. This is, however, clearly not sufficient, as the other points of advice from these authors show (*see* Illustrations 6.9 and 6.10).

The advice on what to do given by Beer *et al.* (1990) and that on what *not* to do given by Kotter (1995) clearly overlaps in content and intent, and each element of advice is offered as relevant for all situations. By contrast, an earlier article by Kotter and Schlesinger (1979) is more circumspect in detailing a range of different approaches for dealing with resistance to change. These are:

- education and communication
- participation and involvement
- facilitation and support
- negotiation and agreement
- manipulation and co-optation
- explicit and implicit coercion.

In detailing the advantages and disadvantages of each method, Kotter and Schlesinger explain the particular set of circumstances where each approach might be used. For instance, if the change initiators possess considerable power, and change must come quickly, some form of coercion would be appropriate. On the other hand, an approach associated with negotiation (or more collaboratively, participation) is more likely to succeed where the change initiators do not have complete information and where others have power to resist.

Illustration 6.9
SIX STEPS TO EFFECTIVE CHANGE

1. Mobilise commitment to change through joint diagnosis of business problems.

2. Develop a shared vision of how to organise and manage for competitiveness.

3. Foster consensus for the new vision, competence to enact it, and cohesion to move it along.

4. Spread revitalisation to all departments without pushing it from the top.

5. Institutionalise revitalisation through formal policies, systems and structures.

6. Monitor and adjust strategies in response to problems in the revitalisation process.

Source: Beer, M., Eisenstat, R. A., and Spector, B. (1990), 'Why change programmes do not produce change', *Harvard Business Review*, November–December.

Illustration 6.10
WHY TRANSFORMATION EFFORTS FAIL

[handwritten annotation: link to project management ?]

According to Kotter (1995), transforming organisations fail through:

1. Not establishing a great enough sense of urgency

2. Not creating a powerful enough coalition

3. Lacking a vision

4. Undercommunicating by a factor of ten

5. Not removing obstacles to the new vision

6. Not systematically planning for and creating short-term wins

7. Declaring victory too soon

8. Not anchoring changes in the corporation's culture

The value of Kotter and Schlesinger's analysis lies in the way it can help managers understand specific instances of opposition to change in order to work out an approach relevant to a particular situation. This, together with Illustrations 6.9 and 6.10, bring this chapter's discussion back to the beginning when the question was posed as to what leadership approach works best in situations of organisational change. Taken together, these illustrations show how leaders of change need to have certain attitudes and behaviours which are of benefit regardless of the prevailing situation, but they also need to understand that some behaviours are more effective in some situations and other behaviours more effective in other situations. Leadership, together with the other aspects of organisational life discussed in this Part of the book, comprise the context in which change takes place. With the description of this context now completed, we can proceed to the more practical considerations of how to design, plan and implement change, discussed in Part Three.

DISCUSSION QUESTIONS AND ACTIVITIES

1 Drawing on your own experience of organisational change, describe:

   (a) a situation where, in Reich's (1991) terms, someone acted as 'hero';
   (b) a situation where the notion of the leader as hero was less evident than Reich's concept of the 'team as hero'.

   What were the advantages and disadvantages of these two different leadership situations?

2 In the context of the discussion of different types of change posed in Chapter 2, debate the advisability of seeking managers of change who will act as transformational leaders.

3 Examine the concept of 'leaders of change' as it might apply across different societies and organisations.

REFERENCES

Ansoff, I. H., and McDonnell, E. J. (1990), *Implanting Strategic Management*, Englewood Cliffs, NJ, Prentice-Hall.

Bartol, K. M., and Martin, D. C. (1994), *Management*, McGraw-Hill.

Bass, B. M. (1990), 'From transactional to transformational leadership: Learning to share the vision', *Organizational Dynamics*, Winter, pp. 19–31.

Beer, M., Eisenstat, R. A., and Spector, B. (1990), 'Why change programmes do not produce change', *Harvard Business Review*, November–December.

Behling, O., and McFillen, J. (1996), 'A syncretical model of charismatic/transformational leadership', *Group & Organization Management*, Vol. 21, No. 2, June, pp. 163–91.

Belbin, M. (1993), *Team Roles at Work*, Oxford, Butterworth Heinemann.

Blake, R. R., and McCanse, A. A. (1991), *Leadership Dilemmas: Grid Solutions*, Houston, TX, Gulf Publishing.

Blake, R. R., and Mouton, J. S. (1964), *The Managerial Grid*, Houston, TX, Gulf Publishing.

Carnall, C. (1995), *Managing Change in Organizations* (2nd edn.), London, Prentice-Hall.

Clarke, C., and Pratt, S. (1985), 'Leadership's four-part progress', *Management Today*, March, pp. 84–6.

Clarke, L. (1994), *The Essence of Change*, Hemel Hempstead, Prentice-Hall.

Coleman, J. C. (1969), *Psychology and Effective Behaviour*, Glenview, IL, Scott Foresman.

Dulewicz, V., and Herbert, P. (1996), 'Leaders of tomorrow: how to spot the high-flyers', *Financial Times*, 20 September, p. 16.

Dunphy, D., and Stace, D. (1993), 'The strategic management of corporate change', *Human Relations*, Vol. 46, No. 8, pp. 905–20.

Ekvall, G., and Arvonen, J. (1991), 'Change-centred leadership: an extension of the two-dimensional model', *Scandinavian Journal of Management*, Vol. 7, No. 1, pp. 17–26.

Farkas, C. M., and Wetlaufer, S. (1996), 'The ways chief executive officers lead', *Harvard Business Review*, May–June, pp. 110–22.

Fayol, H. (1949), *General and Industrial Management*, London, Pitman.

Fiedler, F. E. (1967), *A Theory of Leadership*, McGraw-Hill.

Fiedler, F. E. (1989), 'The effective utilisation of intellectual abilities and job relevant knowledge in group performance: cognitive resource theory and an agenda for the future', *Applied Psychology: An International Review*, Vol. 38, No. 3, pp. 289–304.

Gastil, J. (1994), 'A definition and illustration of democratic leadership', *Human Relations*, Vol. 47, No. 8.

Ginsberg, A., and Abrahamson, E. (1991), 'Champions of change and strategic shifts: the role of internal and external change advocates', *Journal of Management Studies*, Vol. 28, No. 2, pp. 173–90.

Gordon, J. R. (1993), *A Diagnostic Approach to Organizational Behaviour*, London, Alleyn and Bacon.

Greiner, L. (1972), 'Evolution and revolution as organizations grow', *Harvard Business Review*, July–August.

Grundy, T. (1993), *Managing Strategic Change*, London, Kogan Page, pp. 24–6.

Handy, C. (1993), *Understanding Organizations*, London, Penguin.

Hersey, P., and Blanchard, K. H. (1993), *Management of Organizational Behavior: Utilizing Human Resources* (6th edn.), Englewood Cliffs, NJ, Prentice-Hall.

Holman, M., and Waldmeir, P. (1996), 'World Bank chief's cry from the heart', *Financial Times*, 29 March, p. 4.

House, R. J. (1971), 'A path-goal theory of leader effectiveness', *Administrative Science Quarterly*, September, pp. 321–38.

Huczynski, A., and Buchanan, D. (1994), *Organizational Behaviour. Student Workbook* (2nd edn.), Hemel Hempstead, Prentice-Hall

Kenter, R. M. (1991), 'Change-motor skills: what it takes to the be creative', in Henry J., and Walker, D. (eds.), *Managing Innovation*, London, Sage.

Keller, R. T. (1989), 'A test of the path-goal theory of leadership with need for clarity as a moderator in research and development organizations', *Journal of Applied Psychology*, April, pp. 208–12.

Kirkpatrick, S. A., and Locke, E. A. (1991), 'Leadership: do traits matter?', *Academy of Management Executive*, May, pp. 48–60.

Kirton, M. J. (1976), 'Adaptors and innovators: a description and a measure', *Journal of Applied Psychology*, Vol. 61, pp. 622–9.

Kotter, J. P. (1990), *A Force for Change: How Leadership Differs from Management*, New York, Free Press.

Kotter, J. P. (1995), 'Leading change: why transformation efforts fail', *Harvard Business Review*, March–April.

Kotter, J. P., and Schlesinger, L. A. (1979), 'Choosing strategies for change', *Harvard Business Review*, March–April.

Likert, R. (1961), *New Patterns of Management*, McGraw-Hill.

Lindell, M., and Rosenqvist, G. (1992a), 'Is there a third management style?', *Finnish Journal of Business Economics*, Vol. 3, pp. 171–98.

Lindell, M., and Rosenqvist, G. (1992b), 'Management behavior dimensions and development orientation', *Leadership Quarterly*, Winter, pp. 355–77.

Lord, R. G., De Vader, C. L., and Alliger, G. M. (1986), 'A meta-analysis of the relation between personality traits and leadership perceptions: An application of validity generalization procedures', *Journal of Applied Psychology*, Vol. 71, pp. 402–10.

Luthans, F., and Lockwood, D. L. (1984), 'Toward an observation system for measuring leader behavior in natural settings', in Hunt, J. H., Hosking, D. M., Schriesheim, C. A., and Stewart, R. (eds.), *Leaders and Managers: International Perspectives on Managerial Behavior and Leadership*, New York, Pergamon.

McCalman, J., and Paton, R. A. (1992), *Change Management. A Guide To Effective Implementation*, London, P.C.P.

Mann, R. D. (1959), 'A review of the relationship between personality and performance in small groups', *Psychological Bulletin*, Vol. 56, No. 4, pp. 241–70.

Mintzberg, H. (1979), *The Nature of Managerial Work*, Englewood Cliffs, NJ, Prentice-Hall.

Mullins, L. J. (1996), *Management and Organisational Behaviour*, London, Pitman.

Newton, J. (1993), 'Obstructing and facilitating processes in strategic change: a research approach', Proceedings of the British Academy of Management Conference, 20–22 September.

Nortier, F. (1995), 'A new angle on coping with change: managing transition', *Journal of Management Development*, Vol. 14, No. 4, pp. 32–46.

Quinn, R. E. (1988), *Beyond Rational Management, Mastering the Paradoxes and Competing Demands of High Performance*, San Francisco, Jossey-Bass.

Rashford, N. S., and Coghlan, D. (1989), 'Phases and levels of organisational change', *Journal of Managerial Psychology*, Vol. 4, No. 3, pp. 17–22.

Reich, R. B. (1991), 'The team as hero', in Henry, J., and Walker, D., *Managing Innovation*, London, Sage.

Robbins, S. P. (1996), *Organizational Behavior, Concepts, Controversies, Applications* (7th edn.), Englewood Cliffs, NJ, Prentice-Hall.

Smith, M. (1991), 'Leadership and supervision', in Smith, M. (ed.), *Analysing Organizational Behaviour*, New York, Macmillan.

Stacey, R. (1996), *Strategic Management and Organisational Dynamics*, London, Pitman.

Stodgill, R. M. (1948), 'Personal factors associated with leadership: a survey of the literature', *Journal of Psychology*, Vol. 25, pp. 35–71.

Stodgill, R. M., and Coons, A. E. (1957), *Leader Behavior: Its Description and Measurement*, Columbus, Ohio State University Bureau of Business Research.

Strebel, P. (1992), *Breakpoints, How Managers Exploit Radical Business Change*, Cambridge, MA, Harvard Business Press.

Strebel, P. (1996a), 'Choosing the right path', Mastering Management, Part 14, *Financial Times*, pp. 5–7.

Strebel, P. (1996b), 'Breakpoint: How to Stay in the Game', Mastering Management, Part 17, *Financial Times*.

Tannenbaum, R. and Schmidt, W. H. (1973), 'How to choose a leadership pattern', *Harvard Business Review*, Vol. 51, May–June, pp. 162–80.

Tichy, N. M., and Devanna, M. A. (1990), *The Transformational Leader* (2nd edn.), New York, Wiley.

Tichy, N. M., and Ulrich, D. O. (1984), 'The leadership challenge – a call for the transformational leader', Sloan Management Review, Fall, pp. 59–68.

Tushman, M. L., Newman, W. H., and Romanelli, E. (1988), 'Convergence and upheaval: managing the unsteady pace of organizational evolution', in Tushman, M. L., and Moore, W. L. (eds.), *Readings in the Management of Innovation*, New York, Ballinger Publishing Company.

Useem, M. (1996), 'Do leaders make a difference?', Mastering Management, Part 18, *Financial Times*, pp. 5–6.

Watson, C. M. (1983), 'Leadership, management and the seven keys', *Business Horizons*, March–April, pp. 8–13.

Wesley, F., and Mintzberg, H. (1989), 'Visionary leadership and strategic management', *Strategic Management Journal*, Vol. 10, pp. 17–32.

Westley, R. (1996), 'Mrs Beeton, management guru,' *Financial Times*, 26 April, p. 15.

Woffard, J. C., and Liska, L. Z. (1993), 'Path-goal theories of leadership: a meta-analysis', *Journal of Management*, Winter, pp. 857–76.

Wright, P. (1996), *Managerial Leadership*, London, Routledge.

Part Three

STRATEGIES FOR MANAGING CHANGE

Introduction to Part Three

Two major themes have emerged from the discussions in Parts One and Two of the book which have a bearing on the practical issues of preparing for, designing and implementing change in organisations. These can be grouped broadly into the categories of the content of change and the context in which it happens. Part One of the book concentrated on the content of organisational change and what causes it, while Part Two explored the formal and informal aspects of organisational life which influence the process of change and within which change happens.

This part of the book turns to the practicalities of *doing* change in the sense of designing, planning and implementing change – in other words concentrating on the processes through which change comes about. Two different approaches to change, each encompassing various methodologies, are discussed respectively in Chapters 7 and 8. These approaches relate directly back to the types of change discussed in Chapter 2, in particular, the concepts of hard and soft problems, that is, difficulties and messes. Consequently, Chapter 7 concentrates on change approaches which are based on rational-logical models of change which are most appropriate for situations of hard complexity where the 'people' issues are low. In contrast, Chapter 8 recognises that many change situations involve issues of organisational politics, culture and leadership (as discussed in Part Two of the book) which dictate an approach to change which can deal more easily with situations characterised by soft complexity.

Finally, Chapter 9 seeks briefly to pull together a number of themes and strands of discussion to assemble a group of factors which, together, are more likely to help organisations succeed through change than otherwise.

CHAPTER 7

Hard systems
models of change

There are a number of models for handling change in situations of hard complexity. This chapter describes one and, in order to demonstrate its use, applies it to a particular change situation. The limitations of this type of model are discussed.

Objectives

To:

- recognise change situations (problems/opportunities) characterised mainly by hard complexity, where the use of hard systems methodologies are appropriate;

- describe the main features of hard systems methodologies for defining, planning and implementing change;

- explain the Hard Systems Model of Change (HSMC) as representative of hard systems methodologies of change;

- discuss the limitations of hard systems methodologies of change and, therefore, the need for other change methodologies more suited to situations of soft complexity.

SITUATIONS OF CHANGE

In Chapter 2, a number of different ways of categorising organisational change were discussed. These ranged from changes which happen incrementally, and which may affect only one part of an organisation, to the more radical, frame-breaking or discontinuous changes which pervade almost every aspect of an organisation's functioning. As Chapter 2 also showed, expectations with respect to the ease with which change happens vary according to its perceived complexity. Consequently, change in situations which are characterised by hard complexity is more likely to be enacted easily and speedily than change in situations which show soft complexity, that is, where issues are contentious and there is a high level of emotional involvement on the part of those likely to implement the change and those who will be affected by it.

There are many approaches to planning and implementing change. Some are more appropriate to situations of hard complexity – which Chapter 2 also described as 'difficulties' – while others are more appropriate to situations of soft complexity or, as Chapter 2 characterised them, 'messy' situations. Flood and Jackson (1991), using a systems perspective, classify various methodologies in a similar way but use the terms 'simple system' and 'complex system' instead of difficulties and messes. What is of more interest, though, is that Flood and Jackson also classify these methodologies according to their appropriateness of use in situations characterised by different ideological viewpoints. Three ideological viewpoints representing three types of relationships between people, are defined. Two of these (the unitary and pluralist viewpoints) have been discussed already in Chapter 5 (see Illustration 5.8); all three are described in Illustration 7.1.

Using an extensive list of different methodologies for problem-solving and change, Flood and Jackson suggest which ones are most appropriate in situations characterised as simple or complex systems but modified by whether relationships between people tend to be of a unitarist, pluralist or coercive nature. It is not the purpose here to consider all the possibilities. What is important, for this discussion, is to note that different logics dominate each possibility in terms of suggesting a particular approach to change. Consequently, in situations of hard complexity (e.g. where simple systems and a unitarist ideology of relationships prevails), a particular type of change approach will be appropriate, whereas in situations of soft complexity (e.g. where complex systems and a pluralist ideology of relationships prevails), a different type of change approach should be used. This chapter concentrates on the first of these situations, to describe an approach to change which is representative of those approaches which are best applied in the relatively bounded situations described variously as difficulties, simple/unitarist systems or, in more straightforward terms, 'hard' situations.

Illustration 7.1

CHARACTERISTICS OF UNITARY, PLURALIST AND COERCIVE RELATIONSHIPS

Unitary

People relating to each other from a unitary perspective:

- share common interests
- have values and beliefs which are highly compatible
- largely agree upon ends and means
- all participate in decision-making
- act in accordance with agreed objectives

Pluralist

People relating to each other from a pluralist perspective:

- have a basic compatibility of interest
- have values and beliefs which diverge to some extent
- do not necessarily agree upon ends and means, but compromise is possible
- all participate in decision-making
- act in accordance with agreed objectives

Coercive

People relating to each other from a coercive perspective:

- do not share common interests
- have values and beliefs which are likely to conflict
- do not agree upon ends and means and 'genuine' compromise is not possible
- coerce others to accept decisions

Source: Based on Flood, R. L., and Jackson, M. C. (1991), *Creative Problem Solving: Total Systems Intervention* (Chichester, Wiley, pp. 34–5).

SYSTEMATIC APPROACHES TO CHANGE

Most people have the capacity to think logically and rationally. Indeed, some would say this is the only way to approach problem-solving or responding to opportunities and, therefore, there can be one basic way of planning and implementing change. It is upon this premise that the more systematic approaches to managing change are based. Derived from earlier methods of problem-solving and decision-making such as systems engineering methods and operational research (Mayon-White, 1993), these 'hard' approaches rely on the assumption that clear change objectives can be identified in order to work out the best way of achieving them. What is more, a strict application of these approaches dictates that these objectives should be such that it is possible to quantify them, or at least be sufficiently concrete that one can know when they have been achieved. For instance, consider the situation described in Illustration 7.2.

Illustration 7.2 provides an example of what appears to be a difficulty about which most people could agree – it appears to have fairly defined boundaries. There are clearly some problems with the way IT faults are reported to the IT support service

---

Illustration 7.2

DISSATISFACTION WITH THE SYSTEM FOR PROVIDING IT SUPPORT SERVICES

Vernabelle, a member of staff of the Faculty of Art and Design at Singleton University, was making a telephone call to the office of the IT support service to report that the computer link from her office to the library was not working. As usual, there was no one there – she supposed the two staff employed in the office were somewhere in the Faculty of Art and Design seeing to someone else's computer. She decided, therefore, to send a memo but knew that, because of the time the internal post took, it would not get to the IT support office before the next day. Even then, from past experience, she suspected that when it was received, she would not receive a response without at least one reminder and perhaps two. Overall, she took a particularly dim view of the quality of IT support service provided and was sure that, if she were responsible for this service, she could improve its effectiveness without too much effort and resources.

---

and the way they are responded to when received. It is also clear that some quantitative indices could be devised on which to judge the system and which might give evidence of improvement if this were to take place. What follows is, first, a generalised description of a model of change which is most suited to situations such as that described in Illustration 7.2 – that is, in situations which are more of a difficulty than a mess and, second, a more fully worked out example of its use to plan and implement change in the Beautiful Buildings Company (BB Company).

THE HARD SYSTEMS MODEL OF CHANGE

Some of the clearest expositions of methods for planning and implementing change in 'hard' situations are those found in Open University course materials (1984, 1994) and the writings of Flood and Jackson (1991) and McCalman and Paton (1992). The methodology for change described here draws on all these sources. To avoid confusion with the Open University's latest model, the 'Systems Intervention Strategy' and McCalman and Paton's 'Intervention Strategy Model', the approach described here is referred to as simply the 'Hard Systems Model of Change' (HSMC).

Change in three phases

The HSMC is a method which has been developed for designing and managing change. Its roots lie in methods of analysis and change associated with systems engineering, operational research and project management, that is, where there is an emphasis on means and ends – in other words, on the means with which particular set goals are to be achieved. The HSMC is particularly useful when dealing with situations which lie towards the 'hard' end of the hard–soft continuum of change situations. It provides a rigorous and systematic way of determining objectives (or goals) for change; this is followed by the generation of a range of options for action; the last step is testing those options against a set of explicit criteria. The method is particularly useful where quantitative criteria can be used to test options for change. However, it is also possible to use qualitative criteria – a possibility which is discussed later in the chapter. The process can be thought of as falling into three overlapping phases.

- The *description* phase (describing and diagnosing the situation, understanding what is involved, setting the objectives for the change).
- The *options* phase (generating options for change, selecting the most appropriate option, thinking about what might be done).
- The *implementation* phase (putting feasible plans into practice and monitoring the results).

Within these three phases a number of stages can also be identified. These are shown in Illustration 7.3. What follows describes the stages in more detail.

Illustration 7.3
STAGES WITHIN THE HARD SYSTEMS METHODOLOGY OF CHANGE

Phases	Stages	Actions appropriate for each stage
Description	1. Situation summary	● Recognise need for change either to solve a problem or take advantage of an opportunity. ● Test out others' views on the need for change. ● Using appropriate diagnostic techniques, confirm the presence of hard complexity and a difficulty rather than a mess.
	2. Identify objectives and constraints	● Set up objectives for systems of interest. ● Identify constraints on the achievement of the objectives.
	3. Identify performance measures	● Decide how the achievement of the objectives can be measured.
Options	4. Generate options	● Develop ideas for change into clear options for achievement of the objectives. ● Consider a range of possibilities.
	5. Edit options and detail selected options	● Describe the most promising options in some detail. ● Decide, for each option, what is involved, who is involved and how it will work.
	6. Evaluate options against measures	● Evaluate the performance of the chosen options against the performance criteria identified in stage 3.
Implementation	7. Develop implementation strategies	● Select preferred option(s) and plan how to implement.
	8. Carry out the planned changes	● Involve all concerned. ● Allocate responsibilities. ● Monitor progress

The stages

Illustration 7.3 shows how the stages relate to the phases and provides an indication of likely actions at each stage. An important point to note, however, is that, although Illustration 7.3 presents the phases and stages as a series of sequential steps which follow logically on, one from another, this rarely happens so neatly in real life. There will, almost certainly, be times when there is a need for iteration or 'backtracking', from one stage to earlier stages, as insights generated at later stages reveal the requirement for modifications to previous ones.

Phase 1: Description

Stage 1: Situation summary

The basic idea in Stage 1 is to start by describing the system within which change is going to be made. This stage includes the following.

- Stating the commitment to the analysis and the reason for doing it. For example, statements like the following might be made:

  a commitment to ensuring the current product range is maintained after the takeover.

  a commitment to developing new markets while maintaining market share for existing services.

  a commitment to reducing the amount of floor space occupied by merchandise not achieving at least a 25 per cent profit margin.

- Describing, in words and with diagrams, the situation within which changes will be set.

At the end of this stage the scope of the study will be defined as will the range of problems and issues to be addressed.

Stage 2: Identification of objectives and constraints

In the context of stage 2, an objective can be defined as something which is desired; a constraint is something which inhibits or prevents achievement of an objective. In reality, objectives are likely to be things over which members of organisations may have some control. Constraints are frequently things in an organisation's environment (whether this is internal or external to the organisation) over which it has little control. This stage addresses both objectives and constraints. It involves being clear about where the decision-makers want to go and which ways might be impassable or perhaps temporarily blocked. This stage involves the following.

- Listing objectives which are consistent with the themes which emerged from the diagnostic stage.
- Arranging the objectives into a hierarchy of objectives – an objectives tree. An example of a generalised objectives tree is shown in Figure 7.1. This shows how the high-level objective comes at the top, with lower-level objectives (sub-objectives)

Figure 7.1

The structure of an objectives tree

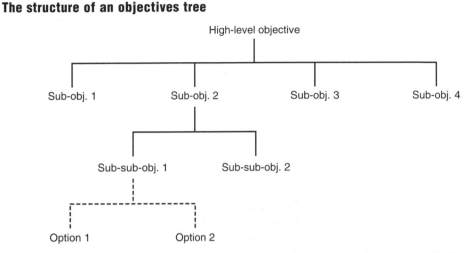

Note: Some objectives may not be compatible – achieving one may mean sacrificing another. In other cases, some objectives may be linked to others – achieving one or more may be necessary in order to achieve another.

arranged in descending order. Lower-level objectives 'lead to' or help the achievement of higher-level objectives.

● Listing constraints in terms of those which: (a) are inviolable and (b) may be modified.

Stage 3: Identification of performance measures

The question to be answered in identifying performance measures is: 'How will I know whether or not I have achieved my objective?' If at all possible, use quantifiable measures, e.g. costs (in monetary terms), savings (in monetary terms), time (years, days, hours), amount of labour, volume etc. This stage includes:

● Formulating measures of performance which can be put against the objectives on the objectives tree.

It is possible that some objectives cannot be quantified. In this case, some form of rating or ranking can be used as a measure of performance. Figure 7.2 is an example of an objectives hierarchy for improving the effectiveness of an organisation's information technology support service. The measures of performance for each of the main objectives are in brackets.

Phase 2: Options

Stage 4: Generation of options (routes to objectives)

The setting up of objectives to be achieved is based on the concept of *what* needs to be done to bring about change. By contrast, the generation of options stage is the stage of finding out *how* to achieve the objectives. If the objectives tree is well developed, as Figure 7.1 shows, some of the lower-level objectives may actually be options. There

Figure 7.2

An objectives tree for improving the IT support services

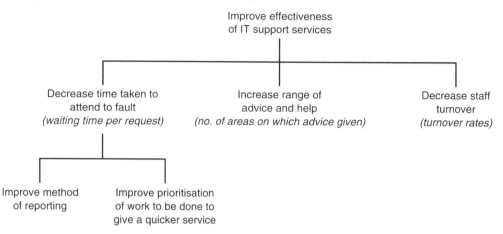

will, however, almost certainly be more. In addition, therefore, to any options which 'creep into' the objectives tree, this stage involves the following.

- Drawing up a list of options. This can be done by making use of any number of creative thinking techniques such as:
  - Brainstorming
  - Ideas writing
  - Questioning others
  - Focus groups
  - Interviews
  - Research
  - Meetings

At the end of this stage, a set of specific ideas should have been generated which will help the problem or opportunity – in the sense that they will further the achievement of the objective(s), rather than that they will break the constraints, and lead to beneficial changes to the situation described in stage 1. Figure 7.3 gives a list of options for the sub-sub-objective of 'Improve prioritisation of work to be done to give a quicker service' – which is one of the objectives in an objectives hierarchy for improving the effectiveness of the service given by an organisation's IT department in support of those who use computer-based programs to help with their work.

Stage 5: Editing and detailing selected options

At the stage of editing and detailing some options, it may be necessary to sort the options, in terms of those which are likely to be feasible given the particular situation described in stage 1 and the constraints identified in stage 2. The selected options should then be described in more detail – or 'modelled' – in terms of what is involved, who is involved and how it will work. It may be that some options cluster together

Figure 7.3

An objectives tree for improving the IT support services, with options generated for the two sub-sub-objectives

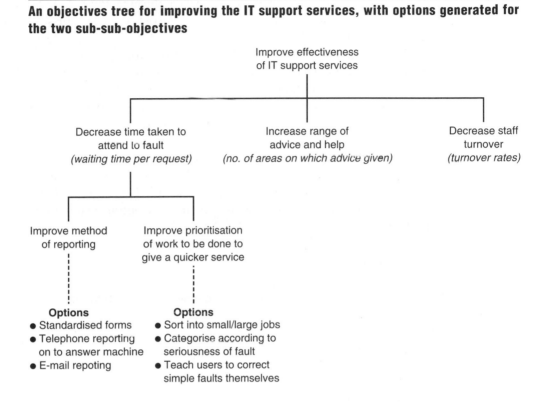

and are better considered as a group. Other options will stand independently and must, therefore, be considered in their own right. There are many ways of testing how an option might work. The following are some possibilities drawn from a comprehensive list produced by the Open University (1994, pp. 35–6).

(a) Physical models (architectural models, wind-tunnel test pieces, etc.).

(b) Mock-ups (make mock-ups of new products – sewing machines, aircraft, clothes dryers, etc.).

(c) Computer simulation models (for complex production systems, financial systems, etc.).

(d) Cashflow models (either manually produced or computer driven).

(e) Experimental production lines, or laboratory-scale plant.

(f) Scale plans and drawings (alternative office layouts, organisational structures, etc.).

(g) Cost/benefit analyses (as models of the likely trade-offs which would take place if a particular option were exercised; can be qualitative as well as quantitative).

(h) Corporate plans or strategies (any one plan or proposal represents a 'model' of how the corporation or organisation could develop its activities in the future).

(i) Organisation structure plans and proposals (for example, a chart of a new organisation structure would show how the formal communication links or reporting channels would work if the structure were adopted).

(j) Organisational culture analyses (methods of describing organisational cultures as the means of identifying effects of different options on the culture of the organisation).

Clearly, some of these processes can be time-consuming and expensive. However, many options can be described or modelled through the use of diagrams (e.g. of different organisational structures, of input-output processes) or some form of cost-benefit analysis.

It is at this stage of the HSMC that each of the options generated for the objectives in Figure 7.3 would be explored in more detail, using the questions listed above about who would be involved, how it would work and what financial and other resources would be required for it to work. Some form of cost-benefit analysis could be used with costs and benefits being those of time as well as money.

Stage 6: Evaluating options against measures

The evaluation stage of the change process is a decision area. It allows choices of options to be made against the criteria identified in stage 3. Figure 7.4 shows a generalised evaluation matrix which compares one option against another on the basis of the measures set during stage 3.

Fig 7.4 An evaluation matrix

Objectives and related measures of performance	Option A	Option B	Option C	Option D
Objective 1, measure 1				
Objective 2, measure 2				
Objective 3, measure 3				

Before making your recommendation you should:

- Check that the model you have used is an accurate representation of the system.
- Consider whether the model seems to contain any bias or mistaken assumptions.
- Evaluate each option, or combination of options, according to how well it meets the performance measures. Rating the options overall on a scale (say of 1 for very good and 5 for very bad) is a useful guide.

Figure 7.5 is a rough estimate of the desirability of some of the options generated from the objectives in Figure 7.3.

A more detailed examination of each option in Figure 7.5 would show more precisely the impact, in terms of the performance criteria, on each objective listed. For the purposes of this example, however, an estimate has been made. On the basis of these, it is clear from the evaluation matrix in Figure 7.5 that some of these options could be combined. For instance, the best method of reporting should be combined with the best method for prioritising work to be done. On this basis, option 2 combined with option 3 seem to contribute most to the main objective. However, if

Figure 7.5 An evaluation matrix for some options to improve the effectiveness of the IT support services

Objectives and related measures of performance	Options			
	Telephone reporting on to answer machine	E-mail reporting	Categorisation according to seriousness of fault	Use of written standardised reporting form
Sub-objective Decrease time taken to attend to fault (*waiting time per request*)	Low cut in waiting time.	Medium cut in waiting time.	High cut in time for serious faults; low cut for simple faults.	Low cut in time – delays through need to post.
Sub-sub-objective Improve method of reporting (*fault reporting received more quickly and accurately*)	High increase in speed of reporting.	High increase in speed and some increase in accuracy of reporting.	No effect.	High increase in accuracy of reporting.
Sub-sub-objective Improve prioritisation of work to be done (*serious faults dealt with first*)	Difficult to estimate.	Small improvement.	High improvement.	Some improvement.

an E-mail standard format of reporting were to be used, this would also help speed and accuracy in reporting faults. It could also include space for indicating urgency in terms of lack of access to the particular program affected. The only problem with an E-mail solution is that this relies on this function not being the one which is at fault! If this is the case, written or telephone communication must be resorted to.

Phase 3: The implementation phase

Stage 7: Implementation

In problems of a definite 'hard' nature, implementation will rarely be a problem. With problems tending towards 'softness', implementation will be a test of how much people involved in the change have participated in its design.

There are three strategies for implementation:

(a) pilot studies leading to eventual change;
(b) parallel running;
(c) big bang.

Pilot studies help sort out any problems before more extensive change is instituted, but they can cause delay – a factor that is particularly important in a fast-moving dynamic situation.

Parallel running applies most frequently to the implementation of new computer systems, but can be applied to other kinds of change. The new system is run, for a time, alongside the old system, until confidence is gained that the new system is reliable and effective.

Big bang implementation maximises the speed of change, but can generate the greatest resistance to change. Big bang implementations carry a high risk of failure unless planned very carefully.

Often implementation involves a blend of all three strategies.

Stage 8: Consolidation – 'carry through'

It takes time for new systems to 'bed in'. It is at this stage that there tends to be a decline in concentration on the need to support the change, nurture it and the people involved. Yet this is one of the most crucial stages if the change is to be accepted and successful. Even after the implementation process, further changes can be forced on the situation at any time if the imbalance between the system and the environment becomes too great. There is no justification for 'sitting back'!

USING THE HARD SYSTEMS MODEL OF CHANGE

Illustration 7.4 describes concerns about the way large plant and machinery is acquired and maintained for use on the building sites of the Beautiful Buildings Company (BB Company). What follows is a description of the process Gerry Howcroft went through to identify a number of options for improving this situation, to put before the senior managers meeting. The description takes the form of notes made by Gerry, interspersed with comments on the method he used.

Illustration 7.4

FINANCIAL SAVINGS ON THE PROVISION AND MAINTENANCE OF PLANT FOR USE ON BUILDING SITES

'The next item on the agenda is the issue of the increasing costs of providing and maintaining major items of plant on the UK building sites. At our last meeting, we saw an earlier draft of this paper. We must now come to some decision as to which option to follow and how it will be implemented.'

So spoke Gillian Lambeth, the managing director of the Beautiful Buildings Company which was having one of its regular senior managers meetings. The next item on the agenda was the increasing costs of purchasing and maintaining large items of plant (such as cranes, diggers and earth-moving equipment) used on the various UK building sites. The item had come to the fore because of the latest rises in the cost of purchasing and maintaining some of these large items of plant which were necessary components in any building project. What was more, in the case of plant breakdowns, getting the specialist maintenance services to effect speedy repairs was always problematical.

Gerry Howcroft, who was responsible for overseeing management of all the UK sites, had prepared a number of options for change which he believed would reduce these costs and improve the maintenance problems. These had already been discussed in rough form at a previous meeting. He had now gained more information on costs etc. of following the different options and had distributed the latest version of these to the managers before the meeting. The meeting now settled down to discuss what to do.

Change at the BB Company

Gerry Howcroft's Note 1   *19 May*

Need to think back to that course on managing change.

Is this a difficulty or a mess?

Application of criteria discussed in the book they gave us (Senior, 'Organisational Change' – Chapter 2 – Illustrations 2.9 and 2.10) ... situation is: bounded in terms of problem definition, people involved, timescale and resources available.

Plus – situation is like Stacey's conditions of 'close to certainty' rather than conditions of 'far from certainty' (also mentioned in Senior's book – Chapter 2).

Think, therefore, that this is more of a difficulty than a mess.

So – think will have a go at using the HSMC.

Stage 1: Summarising the BB Company's concerns

As overall sites manager, Gerry was responsible for the acquisition and maintenance of plant and equipment deemed necessary for carrying out the complex activities which take place on any building site. In this role, he had to make sure that large plant such as cranes and diggers were fit to carry out the work required of them. This entailed his finding the best suppliers in terms of cost and service back-up and ensuring proper maintenance of the plant. Recently, however, the costs of maintaining two large cranes and a digger, which were currently being used on two different sites, had begun to escalate and it seemed as if costs generally for using plant such as this were going up. Gerry wondered whether the equipment had been ill-used or not maintained well or whether it was simply beginning to wear out. As part of the first stage of applying the HSMC, he decided to visit the sites in question and talk to the site manager and any others who had views about the provision, use and maintenance of this type of plant. On his return he summarised his findings in another note (*see* Note 2).

Gerry Howcroft's Note 2   *21 May*

Visited Karen (site manager) at the Three Towers site who said cranes such as these should last 'forever' if looked after. Think this far-fetched given the way the guys use them. Didn't seem to be anyone personally responsible for servicing and maintaining them – one of the men got some overtime each week to hose them down – if they broke down and the operator couldn't fix it, the service agent was sent for. On the other hand, Jed (who operated the crane all the time at the Riverside site) said his crane was just so old that, in spite of good maintenance it had 'had its day' - this in spite of Jed's obvious feelings of 'ownership' towards the crane!

Think there are many contributions to rising costs – a couple of diagrams might help – see Note 3.

Gerry Howcroft's Note 3   23 May

Looking at these diagrams, think I am dealing with a 'system for providing and maintaining plant for use on UK building sites' ... which is different from what I first thought, which was 'a system for provision of plant for UK building sites'. The new definition includes the way plant is used as well as the way it is provided and maintained – as Karen reminded me when she saw the diagrams when she visited the office!

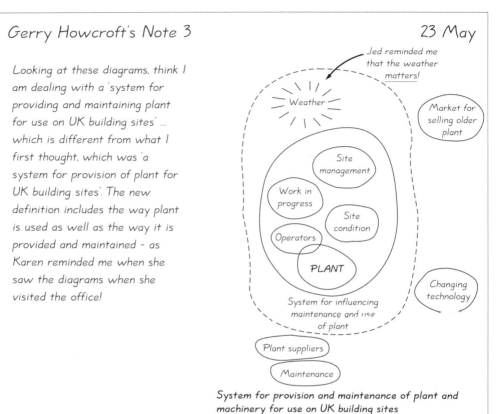

System for provision and maintenance of plant and machinery for use on UK building sites

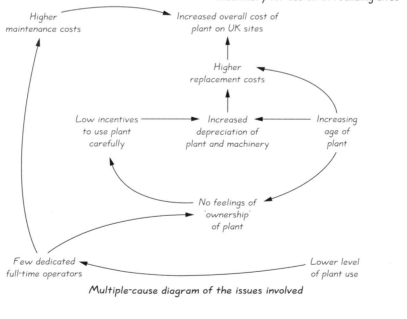

Multiple-cause diagram of the issues involved

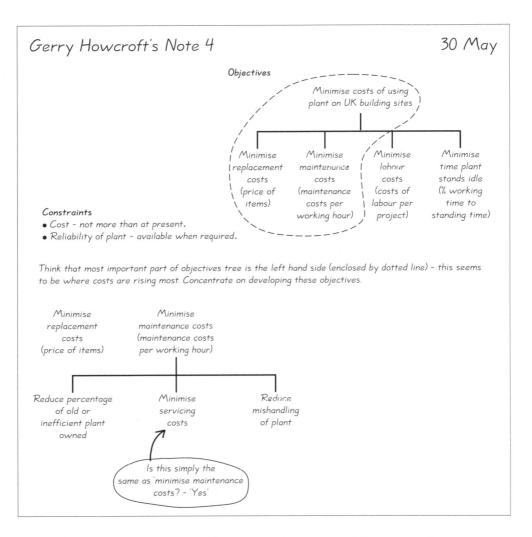

Stage 2: Setting up objectives to be achieved and recognising constraints

Having summarised the situation regarding the issue of plant costs, Gerry's next step was to build a hierarchy of quantifiable objectives. His Note 4 shows the results of this activity. Gerry did not find this activity particularly easy, given the requirement of the HSMC methodology that lower-level objectives should logically contribute to higher-level objectives and contribute overall to the top objective, in this case of 'minimising the costs associated with the use of plant on UK building sites'. However, he recognised that some confusion of objectives was inevitable before a clear system of objectives began to emerge. Even so, he reminded himself that the characteristics of a good objective are that:

1. It should address the problem to be solved.
2. It must be relevant to the issues identified.

3. It should provide a guide on what needs to be done to make the change from the current situation to the desired situation.
4. It must be something which can feasibly be acted upon.

It can be seen from Gerry's Note 4 that he did not develop all the higher-level objectives into more detailed sets of sub-objectives. Given his knowledge of his management colleagues and their way of thinking, he made a decision to concentrate on the objective 'Minimise maintenance costs' to develop sub-objectives for further consideration, but also to consider the objective 'Minimise replacement costs'. With regard to the objectives 'Minimise labour costs' and 'Minimise time plant stands idle', he kept these 'in reserve' in case of need for further exploration of the issue.

Having developed his objectives hierarchy as far as he could in a direction thought feasible and achievable, the next step for Gerry was to develop further the measures of performance for the objectives identified (in brackets) in Note 4.

Stage 3: Identify performance measures

Note 5 shows the table Gerry compiled to ensure he had some idea of how he would tell if and when an objective had been achieved. From Gerry's Note 5, it can be seen that some objectives are more difficult to quantify, in *practice*, even if, theoretically, measures can be put upon them. In addition, the simple measure of 'price of items' for the objective 'minimise replacement costs' was not sufficient. The cost needed to be expressed for a certain period of time which could be related either to (say) a number of years or the period of a particular project. The measure for reducing mishandling of plant could, perhaps, have been formulated in monetary terms but, for the present, Gerry decided to use a scale to judge the likely effects of any option on this objective.

Gerry Howcroft's Note 5	*2 June*
Objective	*Measure*
1. *Minimise replacement costs*	*Cost of replacing item of plant over a specified period of time averaged out per year (assume cost of new plant for now).*
2. *Minimise maintenance costs*	*Cost of maintenance (includes servicing and repair) averaged out on a working hourly basis – i.e. does not include time standing idle.* *Will need to get accounts to get these figures.*
3. *Reduce percentage of old/ inefficient plant*	*Say no plant to be more than eight years old.*
4. *Reduce mishandling of plant*	*Difficult to measure. May have to look at training given – assuming training improves standard of plant handling. Another measure might be cost of maintenance per operator – easier to do when operator full-time on plant.* *For now using a scale of 1 (low) to 5 (high) according to effect on plant might be okay.*

Stage 4: Generate options for change

Having set up some objectives to be achieved – hopefully, to improve the situation, Gerry's next step was to generate a range of options which would enable the objectives to be achieved. He did this by asking Kerry, one of the site managers, and the accounts manager to help in 'brainstorming' ideas for change. The results of this brainstorm are shown in Note 6.

Gerry Howcroft's Note 6   6 June

Options for change

Objective:	Minimise replacement costs
Options:	Find cheapest supplier
	Stop buying plant
	Increase replacement time
	Get someone else to replace the plant
	Hire not buy
	Lengthen life of plant
	Buy secondhand
Objective:	Reduce percentage of old/inefficient plant owned
Options:	Sell everything over a certain number of years old
	Sell everything not used on a regular basis and hire occasionally as required
	Replace old plant with new plant more frequently
	Don't own any plant
	Borrow plant from others
Objective:	Minimise servicing costs
Options:	Reduce number of services per period of time (say operating hours)
	Obtain cheaper provision of services
	Don't service at all
	Operators do all servicing rather than just basics
	Use other people's plant and which they service
	Contract out servicing to lowest bidder
Objective:	Reduce mishandling of plant
Options:	Train operators in plant handling
	Institute operator gradings (linked to pay) based on handling performance
	Contract out operating to operators employed by specialist agencies

---

Stage 5: Edit options and detail selected options

Gerry considered all these options in the light of the constraint of maintaining a high level of reliability of plant. It seemed that the options might reduce to a few main themes. At this point, Gerry decided to try out the options list on a couple of colleagues (one of whom was the company accountant) to see which they thought might be feasible. He also used his own judgement. He eventually arrived at a list which included some options as they stood, amalgamated others, and eliminated others (*see* Note 7).

Gerry Howcroft's Note 7   9 June

Themes emerging from options list

- Finding a cheaper source for buying plant (either new or secondhand)
- Don't buy plant - hire or borrow
- Use only plant which is less than eight years old (or whatever period seems appropriate considering rise in repair and maintenance as age increases).
- Increase the period of time before replacement
- Service plant less frequently than at present
- Train operators to do all servicing and maintenance
- Contract out operating to specialist firms
- Offer incentives for better operating practices

Comments

Some of these options contradict each other, so if one is taken up another might be automatically cancelled - e.g. 'Increase time before replacement' conflicts with 'Use plant eight years old or younger'.

Given the importance the MD attaches to safety on sites, I am going to go for options which are in line with her concerns and which meet the constraint of 'reliability of plant'.

For the time being, therefore, I am going to turn an objective into a constraint and work to have plant which is no older than eight years.

Within these constraints, the following seem worthy of further consideration:

1. Continue buying own plant (search for cheapest deals) with maintenance outsourced.
2. Continue buying own plant with maintenance done by own staff.
3. Continue buying plant which is used continuously and hire other for occasional use: maintenance of own plant done by own staff.
4. Continue buying plant which is used continuously and hire otherwise but outsource maintenance of own plant.
5. Hire all plant with maintenance as part of the deal.
6. Offer incentives for good performance in plant handling.

I guess there are more permutations but, depending on how the costings come out on these we can look at those later.

As Note 7 indicates the options available seemed to range from, at the one extreme, the BB Company's owning and maintaining all plant to, at the other extreme, hiring (or leasing) plant which was maintained entirely by the suppliers. A number of possibilities were clearly possible between these two. The options listed as 1 to 5 are a mix of these. What is evident from the range of possible options is that some quite detailed information is required before one option can be evaluated against another. In addition, option 6 might only be relevant if one of options 1 to 4 were chosen. If option 5 were chosen, incentives to operate the plant well might not be thought relevant if all maintenance costs were included in the hire contract.

Stage 6: Evaluate options against measures

The method of evaluating options against the measures of performance associated with each of the objectives to be reached varies according to the type of options generated. For example, if the options are different production systems, not only would these have to be evaluated on cost measures, but they might also involve evaluation through building some simulations of the different systems. These could, of course, be physical models but they could also be computer models. For Gerry's purposes, it was possible to construct an evaluation matrix which allowed comparison of options one against another in terms of the measures of performance for the defined objectives. Note 8 is a record of Gerry's first attempt, on very limited information, at an evaluation matrix.

Gerry Howcroft's Note 8   *16 June*

Options

Objectives and related measures of performance.	1. Continue buying own plant with maintenance outsourced.	2. Continue buying own plant with maintenance by own staff.	3. Continue buying continuously used plant and hire plant which is used only occasionally; maintenance of own plant done by own staff.	4. Continue buying continuously used plant and hire otherwise; outsource maintenance of own plant.	5. Hire all plant with maintenance as part of the deal.	6. Offer incentives for good plant-handling performance.
Minimise replacement costs (£ per year)	High cost	Medium cost	Medium cost	Medium cost	Medium cost	Low cost
Minimise maintenance costs (£ per working hour)	High cost	Medium cost	Medium cost	Medium-high cost	Medium cost	Low cost
Reduce mishandling of plant (scale of 1 to 5 - 1 being least effect; 5 being most effect)	1	3	2	1	1	4

Need to give some information on this to the senior managers meeting on 23 June - only a week away!

Have only got limited information on options - still can make some guesses at this point and will take the views of colleagues as to which options to pursue - then must get better information on hiring etc.

Gerry took copies of the first draft of the evaluation matrix to the senior managers meeting. The outcome of the discussion of what he had prepared was that he should get more information on options 3, 4 and 5 which involved different levels of hiring plant instead of purchasing it. What Gerry had, in effect, to do was to go back to stage 5 to get more detail about these options before preparing a final evaluation matrix. This took some time, what with getting information from the finance department (only to discover that it was not kept in a 'user friendly' form!) and from companies which hired out plant and equipment. Eventually, however, having gathered as much information as he could, he prepared a final evaluation matrix for discussion at the meeting referred to in Illustration 7.4.

The outcome of that discussion is recorded in Gerry's Note 9.

Gerry Howcroft's Note 9   5 August

What a long discussion which went round and round in circles – difficult to decide between one option and another – the evaluation matrix was very helpful but then decisions are not always perfectly logical!

Eventually, decided on the hiring option with maintenance all-in – however we could not change overnight to this from where we are at present – just purchased a new digger on the Blackton site.

Will need to do a thorough survey of the state of plant on all the sites to determine when to make the change-over to hiring.

Interesting that the meeting decided to retain our own operators for now (even though could get an agency to supply these) – so will start talks with Personnel as to how we might give extra training and/or offer incentives to improve operator performance – after all, the maintenance costs part of the hiring contract is dependent on the amount of maintenance needed – large repairs will incur extra cost.

Seems an implementation strategy is required!

Stage 7: Develop implementation strategy

Gerry realised that the 'big bang' strategy for implementing change was not viable for his situation. Some of the plant had only recently been purchased, while other items were some years old. Overall, plant on the various sites was in different states of repair. Therefore, Gerry decided to go for the 'parallel running' implementation strategy where older and/or poorly maintained plant was replaced first. This would also offer the opportunity of monitoring the costs of hiring against owning *in reality* as against the theoretical case which the options had presented. If, after all, the savings proved negligible or negative, another evaluation of options could be done.

One good thing about retaining the company's own operators was that there were likely to be few problems from the workforce on the changeover. What might happen, however, was the occasional hiring of plant plus operator when it was required for a limited short period. This would give a chance to see how such hirings were received generally.

Stage 8: Carrying out the planned changes

For Gerry and the other senior managers, the changes, when implemented, will need monitoring. Changing from purchasing plant to hiring it may not mean much change in the way plant is operated on the building sites. However, the changes in the way maintenance and repairs are done will require operators and site managers to learn a new system of reporting and getting these done.

One of the benefits of going through the processes involved in applying the HSMC methodology was that Gerry realised how little monitoring of the costs of plant usage had been done up to the change. When trying to obtain the costs of the different ways of providing and maintaining plant, he became very much aware of the diffuse nature of much of the information he wanted. From now on, he was going to make sure that the finance department arranged its systems so that monitoring of large expenditures such as this could be monitored. This would, of course, mean yet more change but in a different part of the organisation. Gerry wondered whether this was another case of applying the HSMC!

ISSUES IN USING THE HARD SYSTEMS MODEL OF CHANGE

The HSMC has been posed as a methodology for change which is most appropriately used in situations of hard complexity, or what have been termed difficulties. The case study involving Gerry Howcroft and the BB Company illustrates this use. In Gerry Howcroft's case, there is reason to believe that resistance to the planned changes will not be high. However, this is not always the case, as the discussion in Chapter 6 showed. Whenever and wherever possible, therefore, those people who are likely to be affected by the change should be consulted as early as possible. In addition, support from senior management is essential for any but the most localised, operational types of change.

It was clear, in Gerry's case, that the information he needed to construct an informative evaluation matrix was not easily obtainable – particularly with regard to that which he required from his own organisation. This stage of the methodology can, therefore, be quite long if a realistic evaluation of options is to be done. On the other hand, it is possible to go through the stages of the methodology quite quickly to address key factors associated with the change situation. A small group of people could quickly drive a way through this methodology to suggest at least a tentative solution in a situation requiring change. In addition, as McCalman and Paton (1992, p. 67) point out:

> A Q & D (quick and dirty) analysis can be a useful starting point for the change agents tackling a more complex problem. It will indicate key factors and potential barriers to change, it will highlight the principal players and give an indication of resource requirements. Such an analysis will at an early stage set the scene for things to come and provide the change agents with a valuable insight into the complexities of the transition process.

An example of using the HSMC as a starting-point to an analysis of a more messy situation is given in Illustration 7.5. This demonstrates the early stages in considering how to expand the provision and delivery of open and resource-based learning in the further education colleges run by the local education authority of 'Shire County'.

Illustration 7.5

CHANGE IN THE FURTHER EDUCATION COLLEGES OF 'SHIRE COUNTY'

Existing stage of affairs

- Falling numbers of 16–19 year olds coming into further education (FE)

- Only small percentage of adults participating in FE

- Current FE provision not always accessible to needs of adults in terms of content, qualifications and mode of delivery

GAP

Desired state of affairs

- Increase proportion of 16–19 year olds in FE

- Signficant increase in number of adults in FE

- Improve accessibility for all learners, but for adults in particular, i.e. greater choice of content, qualifications and mode of delivery relevant to educational and training needs

This state of affairs brought forth the following commitment statement:

In an environment of decreasing numbers of 16–19 year olds and limited numbers of adults participating in further education, the aim for the future is to make it possible for more people to participate in education and training through the expansion of open and resource-based learning (O&RBL) both as an integral part of mainstream provision as well as an alternative but equally credible way of facilitating and accrediting learning.

A causal-loop diagram (*see* Figure 7.6) was constructed to provide further information about the forces operating for and against the desire to expand O&RBL. From this a range of objectives were formulated, together with a list of possible measures of performance.

An initial attempt at an objectives hierarchy is shown in Figure 7.7.

Possible measures of performance (not particularly attached to specific objectives):

- Establish O&RBL centres by ? (date)

- Extend availability of provision to 48 weeks per year by ? (date)

- Achieve *x* % of open and resource-based learners by ? (date)

- ? (number) of companies using O&RBL by ? (date)

- ? (number) of staff trained in the delivery of O&RBL by ? (date)

- ? (number) of students gaining qualifications through O&RBL by ? (date)

- Complete changeover to providing mathematics instruction in modules by ? (date)

- ? % increase in use of O&RBL in all mainstream provision by ? (date)

Figure 7.6

Causal-loop diagram of the situation facing 'Shire County' further education service

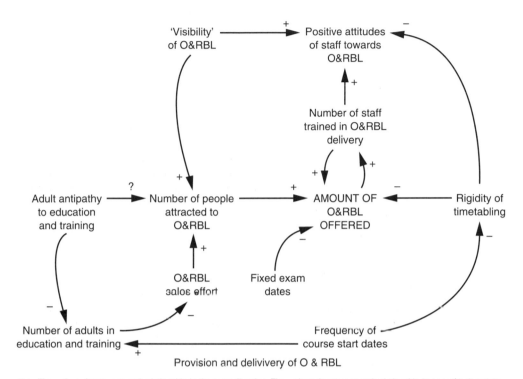

Note: The + signs denote a causal relationship in the same direction. The – signs denote a causal relationship in opposite directions.

Using the HSMC, in the case of Shire County, was useful for setting out the commitment to change, carrying out (with the help of diagrams) a situational analysis of the forces for and against the change, and formulating some objectives and measures of performance in preparation for planning and implementing the change. What this methodology was less good at doing, was identifying the political issues surrounding the implementation of radical change of this kind. In addition, current organisational, professional and institutional cultures were clearly going to work to make changes of this kind difficult to achieve.

This was a case where the changes desired were going to take some time to come to fruition and these would involve changes, not only to the buildings and teaching areas (i.e. physical changes) but also in people's attitudes and behaviours – changes which would include both staff and students (present and potential students). The changes being proposed here were more in line with what has been described as 'organisational development', that is, change which is ongoing, which involves most parts of the organisation and most of its members and which will not succeed without the involvement of all concerned at all stages in the change process. The next chapter describes in more detail a change process more relevant to situations of soft complexity – in other terms, situations known as messes.

Figure 7.7

Hierarchy of objectives for expanding O&RBL provision in 'Shire County'

Routes to objectives
- Staff development
- Senior management 'edicts'
- Set up working groups on modularisation

- Get exam bodies to be more flexible
- Publicise provision
- Purchase OL materials

DISCUSSION QUESTIONS AND ACTIVITIES

1 From your's or other people's experiences, identify three change situations where application of the HSMC could prove useful. Then identify three situations where it would 'run into difficulties'. Justify your categorisation.

2 As far as is feasible, apply the HSMC to a change situation with which you are familiar.

REFERENCES

Flood, R. L., and Jackson, M. C. (1991), *Creative Problem Solving: Total Systems Intervention*, Chichester, Wiley.

McCalman, J., and Paton, R. A. (1992), *Change Management. A Guide to Effective Implementation*, London, P.C.P.

Mayon-White, B. (1993), 'Problem-solving in small groups: team members as agents of change', in Mabey, C., and Mayon-White, B. (eds.), *Managing Change*, London, P.C.P.

Open University (1984), Block III, 'The hard systems approach', in *Complexity, Management and Change: Applying a Systems Approach*, Course T301, Milton Keynes, Open University.

Open University (1994), 'Managing the change process', in *Managing Development and Change*, Course B751, Milton Keynes, Open University.

Stacey, R. (1996), *Strategic Management and Organisational Dynamics*, London, Pitman.

CHAPTER 8

Soft systems models for change

Through a revision of the concept of soft complexity, this chapter begins by challenging the notion of rationality as applied to organisational change. This is followed by a short description of Lewin's three-phase model of change as a prelude to a more detailed description and discussion of organisational development as an approach to change. Some limitations of organisational development as a change philosophy and as a change approach are discussed.

Objectives

To:

- recognise that some change situations (problems/opportunities), by nature of their complexity and particular characteristics, require soft rather than hard systems approaches to change;

- consider the philosophy, value orientation and theoretical underpinnings of Organisation Development (OD) as a generalised example of soft systems models for change;

- outline and describe the processes and practices which comprise most OD approaches to designing and implementing organisational change;

- discuss the limitations of OD approaches to managing change.

MANAGING CHANGE IN SITUATIONS OF SOFT COMPLEXITY

The previous chapter ended with an example of the need for change for which the HSMC had limited applicability. This was because the situation which gave rise to the requirement to expand open and resource-based learning in further education colleges in 'Shire County' was characterised by elements of both hard and soft complexity. As Chapter 7 showed, it was possible, using the HSMC, to build an objectives hierarchy with measurable performance criteria and to generate some options for bringing about the necessary changes. However, while this was fine in theory, other factors – the organisational culture, entrenched power bases and established leadership styles, as well as the simultaneous reorganisation of the county education service which was driving the change – combined to make the process of change much more complex, diffuse and confused than it appeared at first sight. In summary, what faced those charged with bringing about the changes was much more of a mess than a difficulty, implying that a different approach to planning and implementing change was required.

In an article aptly named, 'The art and science of mess management', Ackoff (1993) identifies three different 'kinds of things' that can be done about problems. He says (p. 47): 'They can be *resolved*, *solved* or *dissolved*'.

According to Ackoff, 'to resolve a problem is to select a course of action that yields an outcome that is good enough, that *satisfices* (satisfies and suffices)'. This is an approach which relies on common sense, based on previous experience as to what might work or not and, to some extent, on trial and error. People who use this approach (and Ackoff says most managers are problem-resolvers) do not pretend to be objective in their decision-making. They use little specially collected data, either of a quantitative or qualitative nature, justifying their conclusions by citing lack of time or lack of information or too complex a situation for anything other than minimising risk and maximising the likelihood of survival. Ackoff calls this the 'clinical' approach to dealing with messes, a metaphor which emphasises different people preoccupied with different aspects of the problem situation, but coming together to reach some consensus on how to proceed with resolving the problem. However, while this approach is likely to keep most people satisfied and 'on board' with the change, a major criticism is that, because of its commitment solely to qualitative-type thinking based on past experience and hunch, it lacks analytical rigour in its formulation of objectives and the means of evaluating their attainment. Therefore, it is never quite clear how far the objectives of the change have been met.

This criticism can certainly not be levelled at the 'solvers' of problems. By contrast with resolvers of problems, rather than using simple common sense and what might have been successful in the past, solvers of problems use approaches to problems which are much more heavily reliant on research-based scientific methods, techniques and tools. This means they eschew qualitative models in favour of quantitative models in their aspirations to be completely objective. Ackoff calls this the 'research' approach to mess management. It is much more likely to be used by management scientists and technologically oriented managers. This approach is akin to hard systems models of change in its emphasis on quantitative methods of analysis, objective setting and generation of options for change as demonstrated in the description of the HSMC in the previous chapter. However, while addressing the lack of 'hard' data in the clinical approach to mess management, the research approach is limited in that its techniques are more applicable to mechanistic systems (which lend themselves to performance definition and measurement) than to purposeful human behaviour (which includes many unmeasurable elements). In addition, given that a mess is not just one problem but a complex of problems interacting one with another, decomposing the mess to deal with one problem at a time (as this approach would suggest) loses the essential properties of the larger more complex whole. This is summarised well by Ackoff when he says (p. 51):

> Therefore, when a research-orientated planner decomposes a mess by analysis, he loses its essential properties. . . . As a consequence, what he perceives as the hard facts of the mess are really soft fictions of his imagination, abstractions only loosely related to reality.

From the above, it seems that both resolvers, with their clinical approaches to bringing about change, and solvers of problems, with their research approaches to change, are limited in their capacity to plan and implement change in unbounded soft situations characterised as messes. Consequently, Ackoff suggests a third approach based on the concept of *dissolving* problems. Of this approach to problem-solving, he says (p. 48):

> To *dissolve* a problem is to change the nature, and/or the environment, of the entity in which it is embedded so as to remove the problem. Problem dissolvers *idealise* rather than satisfice or optimise because their objective is to change the system involved or its environment in such a way as to bring it closer to an ultimately desired state, one in which the problem cannot or does not arise.

He calls this approach the 'design' approach in that problem-dissolvers, in addition to using the methods and techniques of problem-resolvers and problem-solvers, seek to redesign the characteristics of the larger system containing the problem (for instance, changing the organisational culture, structure, systems and/or processes). Thus, they look for dissolution of the problem in the wider containing system rather than looking for solutions in the contained parts. Ackoff (p. 48) maintains that only a minority of managers use this approach and they are those, 'whose principal organisational objective is *development* rather than growth or survival, and who know the difference'. Of the concept of development he says (pp. 48–9):

> To develop is to increase and desire to improve one's quality of life and that of others. Development and growth are not the same and are not even necessarily related.

As an example of this, he refers to the fact that a heap of rubbish can grow without developing and a person can develop without growing.

As the situation for change unfolded in the further education system in 'Shire County', it became evident that this was not a problem to be resolved or solved, but a complex of problems which was likely to require the wider system containing it to be redesigned, if progress was to be made towards achieving the stated objectives. These objectives themselves were, incidentally, somewhat unclear and by no means shared by all.

It is not usual, in the literature on change, to find reference to 'dissolving' problems. Yet most of the change models associated with 'soft' situations and systems (i.e. those characterised by soft complexity) imply a need for redesigning systems at many levels of the organisation. These include issues associated with individuals and the groupings they form, as well as with organisational strategy, structure and processes. This means not only an emphasis on the *content* and *control* of change (as the hard systems models of change dictate), but also an emphasis on the *process* by which change comes about, or as Buchanan and Boddy (1992, p. 27) maintain, a need for 'backstaging' as well as 'public performance'. In other words, there is a need to be concerned with what Buchanan and Boddy (p. 27) call 'the exercise of "power skills", with "intervening in political and cultural systems", with influencing negotiating and selling, and with "managing meaning"'.

The consequences of this are that designing change in messy situations must also include attention to issues such as problem ownership, the role of communication and the participation and commitment of the people involved in the change process itself. It also means, as evidenced below, challenging the notion that planning and implementing change can be wholly rational, a notion that the majority of hard systems models of change assume.

The challenge to rationality

For some time, the literature on corporate strategy and strategic change (*see*, for instance: Carnall, 1995; Johnson, 1990; Kirkbride, Durcan and Obeng, 1994; Stacey, 1996) has put forward arguments challenging the idea that people make decisions and choices according to some rational model of decision-making. For instance, Johnson (1993) argues strongly that rational models of change, with their associated scientific management techniques, overlook the significance of the cultural, political and cognitive dimensions of organisational life. The discussion, in Chapter 4, of Johnson and Scholes' (1997) cultural web is a strong indictment of the contention that managers and implementers of change always (or even frequently) act according to some abstract formulation of what is rational in any particular situation.

This is not to say, however, that people do not act rationally. It is to say, as Carnall (1995) would maintain, that they act according to their own view of what is rational for them. This will include their particular perspective of the causes, consequences and need for change, moulded by their values, culture, attitudes and political position within the organisation. Any case for change will not, therefore, be accepted according to some (supposedly) objective rational analysis. Change, in this scenario, will only be possible and effective if it is accompanied by processes which address, in particular, the feelings, needs and aspirations of individuals, the group processes which bind them together and the structures and systems which are forces for stability rather than change. Added to these are the cultural, political and symbolic processes which act to maintain the current organisational paradigm or 'the way things are done around here'.

Given all of the above, it appears that hard systems models of change, although necessary in some defined and agreed situations, are not sufficient to explain organisational messes and are extremely limited in providing a model for planning and implementing change in these situations. In summary, therefore, what the above discussion leads to is an argument for an approach to change which can cope more effectively with situations of soft complexity – in other words, some type of soft systems model for change.

There is neither the space nor the necessity to illustrate here all the different variants of models for bringing about change in soft, messy situations. What follows, therefore, is a generalised description of 'organisation development' (more commonly known as the OD approach) – an umbrella term for a set of values and assumptions about organisations and the people within them which, together with a range of concepts and techniques, are thought useful for bringing about long-term, organisation-wide change; that is, change which is more likely to dissolve problems than to resolve or solve them.

ORGANISATION DEVELOPMENT – PHILOSOPHY AND UNDERLYING ASSUMPTIONS

According to French and Bell (1990, p. 17), in their book entitled *Organization Development, Behavioral Science Interventions for Organizational Improvement*, organisation development (OD) is:

> A top-management-supported, long-range effort to improve an organization's problem-solving and renewal processes, particularly through a more effective and collaborative diagnosis and management of organization culture – with special emphasis on formal work team, temporary team, and inter-group culture – with the assistance of a consultant-facilitator and the use of the theory and technology of applied behavioral science, including action research.

Cummings and Worley (1993, p. 1) in their book entitled, *Organization Development and Change*, say organisation development is:

> a process by which behavioural knowledge and practices are used to help organizations achieve greater effectiveness, including improved quality of life, increased productivity, and improved product and service quality. . . . the focus is on improving the organization's ability to assess and to solve its own problems. Moreover, OD is oriented to improving the total system – the organization and its parts in the context of the larger environment that impacts upon them.

An examination of these definitions confirms some distinguishing characteristics of the OD approach to change. These are:

1. It emphasises goals and processes but with a particular emphasis on processes – the notion of organisational learning (Argyris and Schon, 1978) as a means of improving an organisation's capacity to change, is implicit in OD approaches.
2. It deals with change over the medium to long term, that is, change which needs to be sustained over a significant period of time.

3. It involves the organisation as a whole as well as its parts.
4. It is participative, drawing on the theory and practices of the behavioural sciences.
5. It has top-management support and involvement.
6. It involves a facilitator who takes on the role of a change agent (Buchanan and Boddy, 1992).
7. It concentrates on planned change but as a process that can adapt to a changing situation rather than as a rigid blueprint of how change should be done.

The significance of people

The OD approach to change is, above all, an approach which cares about people and which believes that people at all levels throughout an organisation are, individually and collectively, both the drivers and the engines of change. Consequently, one underlying assumption is that people are most productive when they have a high quality of working life. In addition, there is an assumption that, in many cases (and perhaps the majority), workers are under-utilised and are capable, if given the opportunity, of taking on more responsibility for the work they do and of contributing further to the achievement of organisational goals.

McCalman and Paton (1992, p. 94) offer three 'fundamental' concepts with respect to the management of people and gaining their commitment to their work and organisation. These are:

1. Organisations are about people.
2. Management assumptions about people often lead to ineffective design of organisations and this hinders performance.
3. People are the most important asset, and their commitment goes a long way in determining effective organisation design and development.

These assumptions are not new. Even so, many managers continue to believe in Taylorism and scientific management – which in Matsushita's (1988) words means: 'executives on one side and workers on the other, on one side men [sic] who think and on the other men [sic] who can only work'. Yet, Matsushita, drawing on his experience as head of the Sony organisation, went on to say:

> We are beyond the Taylor model; business, we know, is so complex and difficult, the survival of firms so hazardous in an environment increasingly so unpredictable, competitive and fraught with danger, that their continued existence depends on the day-to-day mobilisation of every ounce of intelligence.

The OD approach to change is entirely in line with these sentiments. What is more, these sentiments extend to a number of assumptions regarding people in groups. The first of these is that people are in general *social* beings. They will, therefore, form groups – whether these are legitimised by the organisation in terms of formal work teams or whether they are the more 'informal' groupings which form part of every organisation's functioning. French and Bell (1990, p. 45) reinforce this assumption by saying that: 'one of the most psychologically relevant reference groups for most people is the work group, including peers and superiors'. Consequently, the work group becomes increasingly important in any attempt at change. Yet, in many cases, work groups do not utilise effectively resources for collaboration. For instance, the formal leader of any group cannot perform all the leadership functions at all times and in all situations. Thus, for a group to become effective, all group members must share in problem-solving and in working to satisfy *both* task and group members' needs. If work groups are managed in such a way as to engender a climate of mistrust and competition between participants, then any change will be seen as a threat rather than an opportunity and all the negative aspects of group functioning will come to the fore to work against the change. OD approaches to change assume, therefore, that work groups and teams are an essential element in the process of designing and implementing change. However, as individuals interact to form groups and other collective working relationships, so do groups interact and overlap to form larger organisational systems which, in their turn, influence an organisation's capacity to learn and change.

The significance of organisations as systems

One of the characteristics of OD approaches to change mentioned earlier in the chapter is that it involves the organisation as a whole as well as its parts – a characteristic which is exemplified by Pugh (1993, p. 109), when he refers to organisations as 'coalitions of interest groups in tension'. Chapter 1 introduced the idea that organisations are systems of interconnected and interrelated sub-systems and components which include more formal organisational structures and processes, as well as the more informal aspects of organisational life such as culture, politics and styles of leadership which are closely bound up with the values and attitudes people bring to their work places.

This idea is one of the most important assumptions of OD as a process of facilitating change. This is because, first, it reinforces the systemic nature of organisational life and the fact that changes in one part of the organisation will inevitably impact on operations in another part. For instance, the multiple-cause diagrams used in previous chapters to depict a number of different change situations are good illustrations of the *interconnectedness* of causes and consequences of complex messy situations.

Second, and related to this, it challenges the assumption that a single important cause of change with clear effects can be found, as well as the assumption that any cause and its effects are necessarily closely related in space and time. This is most clearly stated by Carnall (1995, p. 55) when he says:

> [The] causes of a problem may be complex, may actually lie in some remote part of the system, or may lie in the distant past. What appears to be cause and effect may actually be 'coincidental' symptoms.

Third, any organisation is a balance of forces built up and refined over a period of time. Consequently, proposed change of any significance will inevitably change this balance and will, therefore, almost certainly encounter resistance. Consequently, OD approaches assume that no single person or group can act in isolation from any other. For instance, if win-lose strategies are common to the behaviour of management, this way of dealing with conflict will permeate other workers' attitudes to settling disputes and disagreements. On the other hand, if managers openly discuss problems and take views on how these might be addressed, then this culture of trust and co-operation will reach into other parts of the organisation's functioning – hence the belief that OD activities need to be led by top management if they are to succeed in bringing about successful change.

Fourth, because organisation development as a concept is assumed to operate throughout an organisation, the OD process is most definitely not a 'quick fix' to the latest management problem. This is articulated by French and Bell (1990, p. 48), who say that change 'takes time and patience, and the key movers in an OD effort need to have a relatively long-term perspective'.

Finally, OD approaches to change are essentially processes of facilitating *planned* change. Consequently, an effective manager of change:

anticipates the need for change as opposed to reacting after the event to the emergency; *diagnoses* the nature of the change that is required and carefully considers a number of alternatives that might improve organisational functioning, as opposed to taking the fastest way to escape the problem; and *manages* the change process over a period of time so that it is effective and accepted as opposed to lurching from crisis to crisis. (Pugh, 1993, p. 109.)

The mind-map in Figure 8.1 summarises the philosophy and underlying assumptions of OD as a process for facilitating organisational change. The remainder of this chapter attempts to spell out in more detail the nature of the OD process itself.

THE OD PROCESS

OD is at heart a process of facilitation of organisational change and renewal. It operates at all levels of the organisation – individual, group and organisational. It is a relatively long-term process for initiating and implementing planned change. It takes into account the messy nature of many organisational problems which involve unclear goals and differing perspectives on what constitutes the problems, let alone how to solve them. It recognises organisations as social entities where political as well as intellectual responses to change can be expected. It agrees with Benjamin and Mabey's (1993, p. 181) statement that: 'While the primary stimulus for change in organisations remains those forces in the external environment, the primary motivator for *how* change is accomplished resides with the people in the organisation.'

On the basis of these assumptions, organisation development as a process for instigating and implementing change has two important characteristics. The first is that it is a process of change which has a framework of recognisable phases which take the organisation from its current state to a new more desired future state. Second, within and across these steps, the OD process can be perceived to be a collection of activities and techniques which, selectively or accumulatively, help the organisation

Figure 8.1

Basic assumptions of OD as a model for change

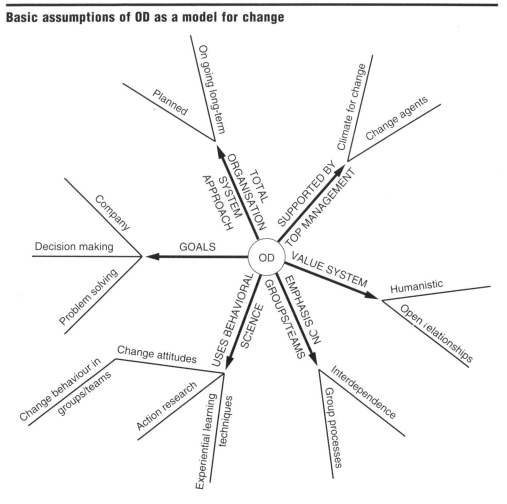

and/or its parts to move through these phases. The idea of phases can be most clearly demonstrated through a consideration of Lewin's (1951) three-phase model of change. This is followed by a more detailed description of OD as it has developed in more recent times.

Lewin's three-phase model of change

As mentioned above, most OD models of change consist of a series of phases (or steps/stages, depending on nomenclature). One such model, although based on work done many decades ago, is still referred to extensively in the literature on change. This is Lewin's (1951) model of the change process as one consisting of the three phases of: *unfreezing*, *moving* and *refreezing*.

Unfreezing

The first of these phases – unfreezing – concerns the 'shaking up' of people's habitual modes of thinking and behaviour to heighten their awareness of the need for change. This would probably include the introduction of information showing discrepancies between desirable goals and modes of operating and what is currently happening. According to Goodstein and Burke (1993), it might even include selectively promoting or terminating employees. For instance, in the case of the largest college 'Pitford College', in 'Shire County' (see Illustration 7.5), a member of staff was promoted to be Director of Open and Resource-Based Learning (O&RBL). Other staff had their responsibilities changed to include 'tutoring' (rather than teaching) students working mainly in a self-service type of learning environment. All staff received news that a new O&RBL centre was to be built and that the timetables of all full-time students would be altered so that at least 20 per cent of their time would be spent learning in the new centre, using multi-media materials on a 'pick and mix' basis according to their needs. Part of this unfreezing process was the extensive consultation with heads of departments and other decision-makers to discuss the new developments – which were seen as challenging the prevailing wisdom of how education and training in the further education sector should happen.

Moving

The second phase of Lewin's change process – moving – is essentially the process of making the actual changes that will move the organisation to the new state. As well as involving new types of behaviour by individuals, this includes the establishment of new strategies and structures, with associated systems to help secure the new ways of doing things. In 'Shire County', this involved a number of different activities. First, a series of staff seminars on the concept and operation of O&RBL were carried out. As a result, staff were concerned with redesigning their courses to include at least 20 per cent delivery of learning on O&RBL principles. In fact, some staff planned to deliver certain learning programmes as *predominantly* O&RBL programmes.

In addition, in 'Pitford College' and one of the other two colleges in 'Shire County', large new O&RBL centres were built with multi-media teaching and learning facilities. Dignitaries representing education, industry and commerce were invited to the opening ceremonies which were used as a symbol for change as well as advertising the facilities to those who might support them. The inclusion of local employers' representatives emphasised the importance of providing for the needs of adult learners as well as those of the youngsters who had, traditionally, been the main 'customers' of these colleges. What is more, in the redefinition of teaching as 'facilitating learning' it was recognised that the managers of these new O&RBL centres did not necessarily have to be academics. This was further reinforced by associating the new centres very closely with existing library and computer services whose staff were not classed as academics.

Refreezing

Lewin's final phase in the change process – refreezing – involves stabilising or institutionalising the changes. This requires securing the changes against 'backsliding' and may include recruitment of new staff who are 'untainted' by the old habits. The continuing involvement and support of top management is crucial to this step. All of the elements of Johnson and Scholes' (1997) cultural web (*see* Chapter 4) are important in establishing new ways of doing things. Once strategy, structure and systems have been changed, it is equally important to reinforce the changes through symbolic actions and signs such as a change of logo, forms of dress, buildings design and ways of grouping people to get work done. The use of continuous data collection and feedback is essential to keep track of how the change is progressing and to monitor for further change in the light of environmental changes.

As an example of Lewin's three-phase change process, Goodstein and Burke (1993) make reference to the change British Airways (BA) made, from being a government-owned enterprise to being a privately owned one – a change which involved moving from what was basically a bureaucratic and militaristic culture to a service-oriented and market-driven one. Regarding the refreezing step, they mention how the continued involvement and commitment of top management helped ensure that the changes were 'fixed' in the way BA did business. Promotion was given to those employees who displayed commitment to the new values with a 'Top Flight Academy' being established to train senior management according to the new way of doing things. In addition, Goodstein and Burke (pp. 169–70) say: 'Attention was paid to BA's symbols as well – new, upscale uniforms; refurbished aircraft; and a new corporate coat of arms with the motto "We fly to serve".'

In the case of the colleges in 'Shire County', although the move to a culture of open and resource-based learning continued to some degree, it was constrained by a slackening off of commitment from top management as the environment in which the colleges operated changed yet again and brought new imperatives. Included in this were changes in the economic environment which brought changes in the political environment. These were increasing unemployment rates among young people and, as a result, a commitment on the part of government to increase training opportunities through funding further education provision for the 16–19 age group. In addition, there was an increase in training opportunities for adults. These opportunities operated outside the further education system, thereby, perhaps, lessening the requirement for more flexible provision within the further education colleges themselves. Consequently, the phase of 'moving' the current situation to the desired future one was never fully completed and the follow-through of refreezing – absorbing the change into the culture of the organisation – was thus put in jeopardy.

Lewin's three-phase model of organisational change can be criticised mainly for its concept of refreezing, that is, the idea of cementing the changes into place to create a new organisational reality. While this aim to prevent the backsliding mentioned above is laudable, it tends to ignore the increasingly turbulent environment within which many modern organisations operate and the need for *continuous* change. However, this should not detract from the debt which current OD approaches owe to the work of Lewin and his colleagues. This debt is summarised by French and Bell (1990, p. 25) when they say: 'Lewin's field theory and his conceptualizing about group dynamics, change processes, and action research were of profound influence on the people who were associated with the various stems of OD'. This remains the case to the present time.

Lewin's concept of organisational change as a *process* dominates much of OD theory. In addition there is widespread recognition that organisations must carry out an assessment of where they are now, where they want to be in the future and how to manage the transition from the one state to the other. Where current theories of OD are leading, however, is to a realisation that change is a process which is not linear and which is itself complex and messy, including many loops back and forth from one stage in the process to another. The following description tries to capture the essence of this. However, because of the limitations of the written word to describe something that is so dynamic in action, the process may appear more mechanistic than it is in reality. It should be remembered that what is being proposed is only a framework within which many variations may occur.

OD: AN ACTION-RESEARCH BASED MODEL OF CHANGE

According to McCalman and Paton (1992, p. 135), 'change is a continuous process of confrontation, identification, evaluation and action'. They go on to say that the key to this is what OD proponents refer to as an action-research model. French and Bell (1990) give a detailed description of action research. Briefly, it is a collaborative effort of data gathering, data discussion, action planning and action between the leaders and facilitators of any change and those who have to enact it. Therefore, action research is, as its name suggests, a combination of research and action. This means collecting data relevant to the situation of interest, feeding back the results to those who must take action, collaboratively discussing the data to formulate an action plan, and finally, taking the necessary action.

A number of elements distinguish this approach from the hard systems model of change discussed in Chapter 7. First, it is not a 'one-off' event which ends when a change has been completed. In their article describing the application of OD in an American electricity utility, Alpander and Lee (1995) illustrate this by saying: 'Organisations which are successful in maintaining their competitiveness have learned to view change not as a one-time event, but an ongoing process necessary to remain on the cutting edge in meeting customer needs'. Second, it is an iterative or cyclical process which is continuous and which, if OD is taken as part of an organisation's philosophy of action, continues as part of everyday organisational life. Third, each of the components of the model (diagnosis, data gathering, feedback to the client group, data discussion and work by the client group, action planning and action) may be used to form each of the phases which make up a typical OD process. On the other hand, these components may, collectively, form cycles of activity *within* each stage of the OD process. Finally, the OD approach to change is firmly embedded in the assumption that all who are or who might be involved in any change should be part of the decision-making process to decide what that change might be and to bring it about. It is not, as some hard systems models of change suggest, a project planned and implemented by senior managers or some designated project manager, with the assumption that other workers in the organisation will automatically go along with it.

Figure 8.2

The OD model for change

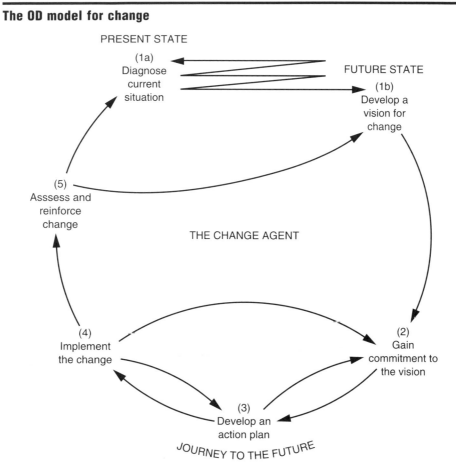

Building on the concept of action research, Figure 8.2 shows the stages of the OD model. These are described in more detail below. However, it is important to note that change on the scale involved in most OD efforts does not succeed without some established facilitation function. Hence, the emphasis on the role of the change agent, as evidenced by positioning this person or group in the centre of the diagram. The role of the facilitator or change agent, is discussed later in the chapter. What follows first is a more detailed description of the stages which make up the OD model itself.

Stages 1a and 1b: The present and the future

An examination of Figure 8.2 shows two stages strongly linked together in a symbiotic relationship. Hence the labelling of them as 1a and 1b – that is, two processes which are, in effect, intertwined and which could be regarded as one. The reason for this is that it is never clear whether a change process should start with the development of a vision for change (that is, where the organisation wants to be), followed by a diagnosis of where the organisation is at present; or whether a start should be made with diagnosing 'what is', followed by statements about 'what could be'. For instance, Buchanan and McCalman (1989), in their four-step model of perpetual transition management, pose the 'trigger layer' (which examines environmental opportunities and threats) before the 'vision layer' (which defines the future). On the other hand, Mabey and Pugh (1995) put as the first stage the process of agreeing the organisation's purpose/mission. This is followed by an assessment of the organisation's external and internal environments.

In reality, as the zigzag arrow in Figure 8.2 shows, these two processes act in parallel, with each process feeding the other as it proceeds until some idea of a future direction is achieved. However, for ease of description, stages 1a and 1b are discussed separately.

Stage 1a: Diagnose current situation

This stage is where the concept of PETS (political, economic, technological and socio-cultural factors) and the metaphor 'winds of change' (*see* Chapter 1) are useful as tools for diagnosing triggers for change that emanate from the external environment of the organisation. In addition the temporal and internal environments must be assessed. In an ideal world, this would be done on an ongoing basis (a) to detect strategic drift (*see* Chapter 2) and (b) to gather data on the organisation's capacity to respond to a change in direction or ways of operating. However, sometimes it takes a crisis to trigger this type of diagnosis. For instance, individuals in a newly created UK university (previously a polytechnic) had been pressing for several years for an increase in research activity supported by appropriate resources. It was only when the university lost valued government grant money that senior managers declared: 'something must be done' and a major investigation was instigated to ascertain what this might be and how it could happen.

Diagnostic processes such as these clearly call upon the data-gathering component of the action-research aspects of the OD model and the feedback of the results for discussion and verification by those concerned with, and involved in, the subsequent change. As mentioned above, in addition to data-gathering about the organisation's external environment, there is also a need for a more detailed examination of such things as:

- individuals' motivation and commitment to their work and organisation;
- recruitment practices, career paths and opportunities;
- prevailing leadership styles;
- employee training and development provision;
- intra- and inter-group relationships;
- organisational structure and culture.

Data-gathering, therefore, is done at the individual, group and organisational levels and should include those things which form barriers to organisational performance as well as those which contribute to organisational success.

ACTIVITY 8.1

Consider your own organisation or one with which you are familiar.

If you were appointed as a change consultant to this organisation, what data would you want to collect and how would you go about doing this – without alienating the people concerned from the process?

Methods of collecting data include questionnaires, individual and 'focus-group' interviews, observation and examination of organisational documents. Price (1987) suggests collecting data on what people *think*, *feel* and *do* in terms of the *tasks* they perform, their *ways of working*, and the *relationships* they have with each other. Many of the illustrations and activities in the chapters in Part Two are useful diagnostic tools for use at this stage in the change process.

ACTIVITY 8.2

Go back to Part Two of the book and list those illustrations and activities which you think might be useful for the process of carrying out a diagnosis of the current state of your organisation, or one with which you are familiar.

It is clear that data collection and analysis is crucial to this stage in the OD process. It is important to note, however, the necessity for giving feedback on the findings to those from whom the data came, for further discussion and verification – a process particularly important in the case of data gained from the administration of questionnaires and through observation, where there is little interaction between questioner and questioned. This feedback process also serves the purpose of developing a vision for change – that is, where the organisation wants to be in the future.

Stage 1b: Develop a vision for change

An organisation's sense of what needs to change comes out of the process of organisational diagnosis and creative thinking. However, as mentioned above, this does not happen only when the diagnosis is complete. As the diagnosis proceeds and problem and success areas emerge, theories of what should be changed begin to form. These, in turn, bring demands for new information which will eventually move the process towards some definition of what the future should look like.

One way of looking at this stage of activity is to perceive it as a *creative* phase, in the sense that 'something new' is being looked for. This might imply a different strategy in terms of products, services or markets. It might also imply a change in structure and culture – including the way people are managed and led. Flood and

Jackson (1991) suggest the use of metaphors as organising structures to help people think about their organisations. The examples given are: organisations as machines, organisms, brains, cultures, teams, coalitions and prisons. Thus, stage 1a would be concerned with identifying what metaphor most matched the current organisation and stage 1b would identify a metaphor to which its members might aspire.

Pat Snelson (1996), of RS Components (*see* Illustration 4.8 in Chapter 4), says that a vision must:

- drive the business forward;
- inspire;
- yield sustainable advantage.

Burnside (1991, p. 193) says:

> A vision can be described as a living picture of a future, desirable state. It is living because it exists in the thoughts and actions of people, not just in a written document. It is a picture because it is composed not of abstractions but of images.

On the concept of 'images', he quotes Lievegoed (1983, p. 75) as saying: 'Images are more meaningful than abstract definitions. Images always have a thought content, an emotional value, and a moral symbolic value' and goes on to say: 'A vision is thus integrative because it brings these dimensions together'. According to Burnside, there are two main aspects to visions – the strategic picture, which he calls the 'head' side, and the relational picture, which he calls the 'heart' side.

The charter and mission statements of the Body Shop reflect closely the views and ideals of its owners. In addition, considerable effort is put into spreading the messages they contain to everyone throughout the 1210 shops located in some 45 countries (as at February 1995). Indeed, the development of an extended Body Shop Charter was achieved through groups of employees from all levels of the organisation meeting off-site at intervals for many months (*see* Activity 8.3).

This example of employee involvement in the development of an organisation's vision underlines the close linking of stages 1a and 1b and their combined outputs in identifying an organisation's present and desired states in terms of two aspects of its functioning. These outputs are: first, the gap which represents the difference between an organisation's current strategy and goals and those to which it must aspire in order to respond to the forces and circumstances of the external environment; second, the gap between what Benjamin and Mabey (1993, p. 182) call: 'the core values as related internally to the ethos of the organisation'.

Stage 2: Gain commitment to the vision and the need for change

It is at the second stage of the process that feedback from the results of stages 1a and 1b are most important. Unless those concerned and involved with the change have been consulted and have participated in the process to this point, there will be little incentive for them to 'buy into' the new vision and the change process which will follow it.

ACTIVITY 8.3

How far do you think the following statements made by the Body Shop go towards meeting the definitions of a vision given above?

THE BODY SHOP'S TRADING CHARTER

We aim to achieve commercial success by meeting out customers' needs through the provision of high quality, good value products with exceptional service and relevant information which enables customers to make informed and responsible choices.

Our trading relationships of every kind – with customers, franchisees and suppliers – will be commercially viable, mutually beneficial and based on trust and respect.

THE BODY SHOP'S MISSION STATEMENT – OUR REASON FOR BEING

- To dedicate our business to the pursuit of social and environmental change.

- To CREATIVELY balance the financial and human NEEDS of our stakeholders: employees, customers, franchisees, suppliers and shareholders.

- To COURAGEOUSLY ensure that OUR business is ecologically sustainable, meeting the needs of the *present* without compromising the *future*.

- To MEANINGFULLY contribute to local, national and international communities in which we trade, by adopting a code of conduct which ensures *care, honesty, fairness* and *respect*.

- To PASSIONATELY campaign for the protection of the environment and human and civil rights, and *against animal testing* within the cosmetics and toiletries industry.

- To TIRELESSLY work to narrow the gap between principle and practice, while making fun, *passion* and *care* part of our daily lives.

Source: The Body Shop case study (1995), Kellogg School of Management, Northwestern University, Evanston, IL, USA and The Body Shop International Plc, West Sussex, UK.

This stage is akin to the 'conversion layer' of Buchanan and McCalman's (1989) model of perpetual transition management – the one which follows the trigger and vision layers which were mentioned above. However, gaining recruits for the change is not easy, as Pugh's (1993) four principles for understanding the process of organisational change show (*see* Illustration 8.1 and Activity 8.4). These principles in turn draw attention to the need for managers to use many different and interacting ways to gain the commitment and involvement of all concerned in the change programme.

Pugh's four principles draw attention to the need for, not just two-way, but many-way communication as part of the process of gaining commitment to the vision and the need for change. This is one of the reasons why most descriptions of OD-type models of change emphasise the importance of managing resistance through discussion, negotiation and active participation of those likely to have to make the

> ## Illustration 8.1
> ## PUGH'S PRINCIPLES AND RULES FOR UNDERSTANDING AND MANAGING ORGANISATIONAL CHANGE
>
> **Principles for understanding organisational change**
>
> *Principle 1: Organisations are organisms*
> This means the organisation is not a machine and change must be approached carefully with the implications for various groupings thought out. Participants need to be persuaded of the need for change and be given time to 'digest' the changes after implementation.
>
> *Principle 2: Organisations are occupational and political systems as well as rational resource-allocation ones*
> This means that thought must be given to how changes affect people's jobs, career prospects, motivation and so on. It also means paying attention to how change will affect people's status, power and the prestige of different groups.
>
> *Principle 3: All members of an organisation operate simultaneously in the rational, occupational and political systems*
> This means that all types of arguments for change must be taken seriously. It is not sufficient merely to explain away different points of view. Rational arguments for change are as important as those which involve changes in occupational and political systems.
>
> *Principle 4: Change is most likely to be acceptable with people who are successful and have confidence in their ability and the motivation to change*
> This means ensuring an appropriate place (or set of people) from which to start the change and to ensure the methods used are relevant to those who are 'first in line' in accepting the change.
>
> *Source*: Based on Pugh, D. S. (1993), 'Understanding and managing change', in Maybey, C. and Mayon White, B. (eds.) *Managing Change* (2nd edn.), London, P.C.P.

changes. Established work groups and teams become particularly important at this stage, as is evidenced by French and Bell's (1990, pp. 126–7) statement that:

> Collaborative management of the work team culture is a fundamental emphasis of organisation development programmes. This reflects the assumption that in today's organisations much of the work is accomplished directly or indirectly through teams. This also reflects the assumption that the work team culture exerts a significant influence on the individual's behaviour. . . . Teams and work groups are thus considered to be fundamental units of organisations and also key leverage points for improving the functioning of the organisation.

Consequently, the process of gaining commitment to change must include working at the group level of the organisation and recognising the strength of influence of both formal and informal group leaders. In addition, it is more efficient of time and effort to communicate with individuals as groups than with them solely as individuals – even though this should not be the only means of communicating with them. It is not, however, sufficient merely to inform people of the vision and the necessity for change.

ACTIVITY 8.4

Identify a major change in an organisation with which you are familiar – preferably one in which you have been involved.

Consider each of Pugh's principles and make notes regarding the following in terms of gaining people's commitment to the need for a new vision and associated change.

Principle 1
- *Were the implications for different groupings thought out?*
- *What (if any) methods were used to persuade people of the need for change?*

Principle 2
Was thought given to how the changes might impact on people's:
- *positions and prospects?*
- *status?*
- *power?*

Principle 3
Were the comments (supportive or otherwise) of different people and groups taken seriously and acted upon?

Principle 4
- *How much effort was made to increase people's confidence in the new vision?*
- *How much effort was made to identify those people and groups who were most likely to 'spearhead' the change?*

This is because visions for change are rarely so clearly structured that information from all levels of the organisation can be ignored. As Smith (1995, p. 19), writing on the realities of involvement in managing change, says: 'no top manager can know at the outset [of any change] exactly what needs doing, what information is needed, or where it is located'.

Jones (1994, p. 49), a colleague in the same consultancy practice as Smith, talks of 'listening to the organisation'. Reporting research with top management on the reasons why large-scale programmes of change often fail, Smith says that nearly all the managers interviewed reported on how much they had underestimated the importance of communication. However, as Jones says, this is not simply a question of senior management shouting louder from the top. This will not identify and bring to the surface the doubts that people have and their fears of what change might mean for them. Neither will it bring to the surface any problems with implementing the vision which top management may not be able to see for themselves.

Far from shouting from the top, the action-research cycle of collecting and analysing data, and feeding back the results should be maintained here, as in the previous stages, so as to avoid widespread alienation of the workforce from the need to change and the vision to which it relates. Lloyd and Feigen (1997, p. 37) neatly summarise the dangers of not doing this when they say: 'Vision statements only work when the needs of those at the bottom of the organisation are integrated upwards with the needs of the market'.

Accomplishing this means being sensitive, not only to people's worries about the way tasks and structures may be affected by the change, but also to what Mabey and Pugh (1995, p. 36) term the 'emotional readiness for change, the quality of existing relationships and the latent commitment to new ways of working'. Otherwise, any plan for action has little chance of being successfully implemented.

Stage 3: Develop an action plan

The development of an action plan can be thought of as beginning the phase of managing the transition from an organisation's current state to its desired future state, as shown by the 'JOURNEY TO THE FUTURE' label in Figure 8.2. However, it also continues the process of gaining commitment to the vision but with a somewhat changed emphasis on *how* that vision can come about.

A number of issues are important in this stage of the OD process. One is the issue of *who* is to guide the planning and, later, the implementation of the change. Another is the issue of precisely *what* needs to change to achieve the vision, while a third is *where* any intervention should take place. The following explores these issues in more detail.

The role of a change agent

The success of using an OD approach to facilitate change rests on the qualities and capabilities of those who act as the facilitators of change. Moving organisations from current to future changed states is not easy and requires knowledge and skills which some managers do not possess. In addition, many managers are so close to the day-to-day issues and problems of managing that they are unable to stand back from the current situation to take a long look at how things might be different. For these and other reasons, such as a need for managers themselves to learn how to manage change, the use of a change agent is usually deemed desirable in most OD approaches to change. However, the change agent as facilitator of change does not necessarily have to be from outside the organisation – he or she might very well come from another part of the organisation, not the one which is the focus of the change. Indeed, some large organisations have departments or divisions which are specifically set up to act as OD consultants to the rest of the organisation.

Buchanan and Boddy (1992) devote a complete book to the subject of the change agent. In it they give a helpful list of the competencies of effective change agents, based on research on how managers deal with change (*see* Illustration 8.2). For instance, Selfridges the large London department store, has a Director of Strategic Change.

The list in Illustration 8.2 is a useful one and is reminiscent of the characteristics of 'transformational' leaders discussed in Chapter 6. However, this list must be considered in the context of how it came about. The evidence for constructing the list came mainly from questioning project managers – that is *internal* change agents who were concerned with changes in their own project areas. Perhaps, because of this, it emphasises more the *content* of the change and how to get ideas accepted, rather than the *process* skills of consultation and participation which form an essential part of the

---

Illustration 8.2

COMPETENCIES OF AN EFFECTIVE CHANGE AGENT

Goals

1. Sensitivity to changes in key personnel, top management perceptions, and market conditions, and to the way in which these impact the goals of the project in hand.
2. Clarity in specifying goals, in defining the achievable.
3. Flexibility in responding to changes outwith the control of the project manager, perhaps requiring major shifts in project goals and management style, and risk taking.

Roles

4. Team building activities, to bring together key stakeholders and establish effective working groups, and clearly to define and delegate respective responsibilities.
5. Networking skills in establishing and maintaining appropriate contacts within and outside the organisation.
6. Tolerance of ambiguity, to be able to function comfortably, patiently, and effectively in an uncertain environment.

Communication

7. Communication skills to transmit effectively to colleagues and subordinates the need for changes in project goals and in individual tasks and responsibilities.
8. Interpersonal skills, across the range, including selection, listening, collecting appropriate information, identifying the concerns of others, and managing meetings.
9. Personal enthusiasm, in expressing plans and ideas.
10. Stimulating motivation and commitment in others involved.

Negotiation

11. Selling plans and ideas to others, by creating a desirable and challenging vision of the future.
12. Negotiating with key players for resources, or for changes in procedures, and to resolve conflict.

Managing up

13. Political awareness, in identifying potential coalitions, and in balancing conflicting goals and perceptions.
14. Influencing skills, to gain commitment to project plans and ideas from potential sceptics and resisters.
15. Helicopter perspective, to stand back from the immediate project and take a broader view of priorities.

Source: Buchanan, D., and Boddy, D. (1992), *The Expertise of the Change Agent* (Hemel Hempstead, Prentice-Hall, pp. 92–3).

---

facilitation role. In this respect it can be compared with McCalman and Paton's list of the roles taken on by effective change agents. These are:

1. To help the organisation define the problem by asking for a definition of what it is.
2. To help the organisation examine what causes the problem and diagnose how this can be overcome.
3. To assist in getting the organisation to offer alternative solutions.
4. To provide direction in the implementation of alternative solutions.
5. To transmit the learning process that allows the client to deal with change on an ongoing basis by itself in the future. (McCalman and Paton, 1992, p. 147.)

In contrast to the concept of a change agent, Kotter (1996) uses the concept of a 'guiding coalition' and suggests four key characteristics as being essential for it to be effective. These are (Kotter, 1996, p. 57):

1. **Position power:** Are enough key players on board, especially the main line managers, so that those left out cannot easily block progress?
2. **Expertise:** Are the various points of view – in terms of discipline, work experience, nationality, etc. – relevant to the task at hand adequately represented so that informed, intelligent decisions will be made?

3. Credibility: Does the group have enough people with good reputations in the firm so that its pronouncements will be taken seriously by other employees?

4. Leadership: Does the group include enough proven leaders to be able to drive the change process?

It is clear, however, that the guiding coalition cannot, by itself, cause widespread change to happen. What it can do is to set targets for change which, collectively, will move the organisation and its members much closer to realising the vision which was developed in stage 1b and further refined in stage 2. Having done this, the issue becomes: '*Who is do what, with what kind of involvement by others?*'

Responsibility charting 🐝

Beckhard and Harris (1977, pp. 104–8) have developed a technique called 'responsibility charting' which assesses the alternative behaviours for each person or persons involved in a series of actions designed to bring about change. They describe the making of a responsibility chart as follows:

> Responsibility charting clarifies behaviour that is required to implement important change tasks, actions, or decisions. It helps reduce ambiguity, wasted energy, and adverse emotional reactions between individuals or groups whose interrelationship is affected by change. The basic process is as follows:
>
> Two or more people whose roles interrelate or who manage interdependent groups formulate a list of actions, decisions, or activities that affect their relationship (such as developing budgets, allocating resources, and deciding on the use of capital) and record the list on the vertical axis of a responsibility chart [*see* Figure 8.3]. They then identify the people involved in each action or decision and list these 'actors' on the horizontal axis of the form.

The actors identified can include:

R = The person who has the *responsibility* to initiate the action and who is charged with ensuring it is carried out.

A = Those whose *approval* is required or who have the power to *veto* the decision. This could be the responsible person's superiors.

S = Those who can provide *support* and resources to help the action to take place.

I = Those who merely need to be *informed* or consulted but who cannot veto the action.

Certain ground rules are set out when making a responsibility chart. French and Bell (1990, p. 137) summarise these as follows:

> First, assign responsibility to only one person. That person initiates and then is responsible and accountable for the action. Second, avoid having too many people with an approval-veto function on an item. That will slow down task accomplishment or will negate it altogether. Third, if one person has approval-veto involvement on most decisions, that person could become a bottleneck for getting things done. Fourth, the support function is critical. A person with a support role has to expand resources or produce something that is then used by the person responsible for the action. This support role and its specific demands must be clarified and clearly assigned. And, finally, the assignment of functions (letters) to persons at times becomes difficult. For example, a person may want A-V (approval-veto) on an item, but not really need it; a person may not want S (support) responsibility on an item, but should have it; or two persons each want R (responsibility) on a particular item, but only one can have it.

Figure 8.3

Example of a responsibility chart

Actors → Actions ↓															

Key:
R = Responsibility (not necessarily authority)
A = Approval (right to veto)
S = Support (put resources towards)
I = Inform (to be consulted before action but with no right ot veto)

ACTIVITY 8.5

Identify a change initiative in which you have been involved (or one with which you are familiar). You may find it helpful to use the example identified in completing Activity 8.4.

To give you practice in using a responsibility chart, list some of the actions associated with that change and assign the people involved according to their responsibility role(s).

Consider whether Beckhard and Harris's ground rules for assigning roles were adhered to. If not, did this cause confusion of responsibilities and/or impede action?

This discussion of responsibility charting illustrates the 'chicken and egg' nature of planning organisational change. While it is right to consider *who* will lead and participate in implementing change, this has to be done in conjunction with *what* it is that needs to change.

The what and where of change

Pugh (1986) has devised a matrix of possible change initiatives based on the different issues which can hamper change and the level at which they occur. Figure 8.4 is a reproduction of what has become known as the 'Pugh OD matrix'.

Figure 8.4

The Pugh OD matrix

	Behaviour (What is happening now?)	Structure (What is the required system?)	Context (What is the setting?)
Organisational level	General climate of poor morale, pressure, anxiety, suspicion, lack of awareness of, or response to, environmental changes. *survey feedback, organisational mirroring*	Systems goals – poorly defined or inappropriate and misunderstood; organisation structure inappropriate – centralisation, divisionalisation or standardisation; inadequacy of environmental monitoring mechanisms. *change the structure*	Geographical setting, market pressures, labour market, physical condition, basic technology. *change strategy, location, physical condition, basic technology*
Inter-group level	Lack of effective co-operation between sub-units, conflict, excessive competition, limited war, failure to confront differences in priorities, unresolved feelings. *intergroup confrontation (with third party consultant), role negotiation*	Lack of integrated task perspective; sub-unit optimisation, required interaction difficult to achieve. *redefine responsibilities, change reporting relationships, improve co-ordination and liaison mechanism*	Different sub-units' values, life style; physical distance. *reduce psychological and physical distance; exchange roles, attachments, cross-functional groups*
Group level	Inappropriate working relationships, atmosphere, participation, poor understanding and acceptance of goals, avoidance, inappropriate leadership style, leader not trusted, respected; leader in conflict with peers and superiors. *process consultation, team building*	Task requirements poorly defined; role relationships unclear or inappropriate; leader's role overloaded, inappropriate reporting procedures. *redesign work relationships (socio-technical systems), self-directed working groups*	Insufficient resources, poor group composition for cohesion, inadequate physical set-up, personality clashes. *change technology, layout, group composition*
Individual level	Failure to fulfil individual's needs; frustration responses; unwillingness to consider change, little chance for learning and development. *counselling, role analysis, career planning*	Poor job definition, task too easy or too difficult. *job restructuring/modification, redesign, enrichment, agree on key competencies*	Poor match of individual with job, poor selection or promotion, inadequate preparation and training, recognition and remuneration at variance with objectives. *personnel changes, improved selection and promotion procedures, improved training and education, bring recognition and remuneration in line with objectives*

The matrix reproduced in Figure 8.4 can be used to help with action planning (as represented by the initiatives listed in italics) about: (a) the type of intervention required to facilitate change in line with the organisation's vision (represented by the columns), and (b) the level at which it should take place (represented by the rows). For instance, at the level of the individual, problems may be occurring because there are few opportunities for promotion from the job of factory floor supervisor to higher levels of management, sales people see no reason to change given their current bonus plan and many middle managers have made their jobs to suit their own needs rather than those of the organisation. Problems at the inter-group level might include marketing and production arguing about the feasibility of setting up a new production line to satisfy what the marketing staff consider to be a market opportunity. Intervention is frequently required at the organisational level when an organisation's structure prevents the emergence of, let alone action upon, initiatives which could be beneficial to the organisation as a whole.

Beckhard and Harris (1987, p. 73) suggest the following organisational subsystems – any of which can be considered as a starting point for change:

- *Top management*: the top of the system
- *Management-ready systems*: those groups or organisations known to be ready for change.
- *'Hurting' systems*: a special class of ready systems in which current conditions have created acute discomfort
- *New teams or systems*: units without a history and whose tasks require a departure from old ways of operating
- *Staffs*: subsystems that will be required to assist in the implementation of later interventions
- *Temporary project systems*: ad hoc systems whose existence and tenure are specifically defined by the change plan.

ACTIVITY 8.6

What similarities and differences can be found between Pugh's levels of analytical focus and Beckhard and Harris's list of subsystems for intervention?

In addition to the issue of where change interventions might take place, the planning of OD interventions must also take account of the degree of change needed, that is, the scope of the change activities. In terms of the Pugh OD matrix, this means considering whether: (a) people's *behaviour* needs to change, and/or (b) the *organisation's structure and systems* need to change and/or (c) the *context or the setting* needs to change. According to Mabey and Pugh (1995, pp. 40–1):

> The first (left-hand) column is concerned with current behaviour symptoms which can be tackled directly. Since it suggests methods and changes which address the symptoms without intervening into the required system or setting, this column comprises the least radical of the

development strategies. Indeed in some cases the results may not be recognised as change at all – merely as overcoming some difficulties in the proper workings of the current system. Thus in one application, as the result of a team-building exercise with a Ward Sister and her staff, the functioning of the ward, the morale of staff, and the standard of patient care all improved. The Hospital Management Committee regarded this process not as a change, but one of getting the organisation to work properly.

But it may be that this degree of intervention is not sufficient to achieve the required aims. It could be that, however improved the group atmosphere and leadership style, the group will not function well because it is not clear what the organisation requires of it, adequate information to carry out the group task is not available at the appropriate time, and the tasks are inappropriately divided and poorly allocated to the members of the group. In these circumstances, the second column, concerned with organising the required system, is the appropriate degree of intervention. This is a greater degree of intervention because it may require change in the structure, systems, information flows, job design, etc., which inevitably affects a much wider range of the 'organisational environment' of the particular group.

Even this degree of intervention may be insufficient. The problems may lie in the contextual setting (changing market pressures, physical distance, poor group composition, poor promotion procedures, etc.). Then the degree of intervention in the third (right-hand) column is appropriate. This is a still greater degree of intervention requiring strategy changes, considerable expenditure of resources (both financial and human), and carrying with it greater likelihood of disruption with its attendant costs. It is not, therefore, to be undertaken lightly.

Mabey and Pugh go on to say that, as action moves from the left through to the right-hand column, a greater degree of intervention and commitment is required. Consequently, they suggest starting at the left column of the matrix and moving towards the right only as it becomes necessary because of the dictates of the problem. Activity 8.7 offers an opportunity to become more familiar with the content of the matrix and how it might be used in planning change.

As stated above, the process of developing an action plan for change should be done through consultation and collaboration with those who will implement the change, thus reinforcing commitment to change. Beckhard and Harris's (p. 72) concept of the action plan being a 'road map' for the change effort is a useful one. In addition, they say that an effective action plan should have the following characteristics:

- *Relevance:* activities are clearly linked to the change goals and priorities.
- *Specificity:* activities are clearly identified rather than broadly generalised.
- *Integration:* the parts are closely connected.
- *Chronology:* there is a logical sequence of events.
- *Adaptability:* there are contingency plans for adjusting to unexpected forces.

The last of these characteristics is particularly important. As anyone knows, it is all well and good, setting out on a journey with the route well defined beforehand. However, because of the many things which exist to thwart the best laid plans (for instance in the case of the road map and journey: traffic, passenger sickness, road works, accidents and so on), the plan must be flexible enough to adapt to the changing circumstances of not only *what* needs to change, but also possible changes in the

---

ACTIVITY 8.7

The best way to understand the Pugh OD matrix is to apply its different 'cells' to a real organisational example.

Choose a situation from your own experience where a need for change has been established.

Go through the matrix and note which cells are appropriate for starting interventions which will help in the change process.

If you find this too difficult to start with, look at the following list of organisational problems and activities and note in which of the Pugh matrix cell(s) you would place them.

1 *The accounts department who 'lived' on the top floor always seemed to be at logger-heads with the research and development team who were 'housed' in an outside annex.*

2 *Since the redundancies, which were mentioned wherever you went in the organisation, people were moaning about the amount of work they had to do and the lack of recognition of this by senior management.*

3 *The staff in the post room appeared bored with their jobs. Admittedly the work was rather repetitive.*

4 *It took so long to get an answer to queries, because the boss had always to be informed.*

5 *The members of the project group felt abandoned and without leadership.*

---

transition process itself. Consequently, as Figure 8.2 shows, the development of an action plan must always be linked closely to its subsequent implementation.

Stage 4: Implement the change

Any text dealing specifically with organisation development as a change methodology contains details of different techniques and methods for initiating and implementing change (*see*, for instance, French and Bell, 1990; Cummings and Worley, 1993). For the present purposes, the activities in italics in the Pugh OD matrix in Figure 8.4 can be used to illustrate ways of initiating organisational change. As the matrix illustrates, these relate to the different levels of analytical focus and the scope of the change activities. The following gives additional details of those activities which require further explanation. It should be noted however that, because these activities are mainly concerned with the behaviour column of the matrix, it *does not mean* that they are, necessarily, any more important than the activities concerned with structure and context. They are selected for further explanation simply because they may not be as familiar as some of the others.

Survey feedback

Surveys can be used to assess the attitudes and morale of people across the organisation and are used at different stages in the OD process. At the implementation stage, they are important for the effective management of the change. Feedback from these surveys to those involved in the change activities helps stimulate discussion of what is working and what is not and should result in modifications to the action plan or the way it is being implemented or, sometimes, to a reorientation of the vision.

For example, in 1994, Lloyds of London, one of the city's prestigious financial institutions, carried out an employee opinion survey on the progress of a large-scale change programme, the results of which were fed back to the staff involved for further discussion and appropriate action. Clarke, Hooper and Nicholson (1997, p. 29), writing about this, say:

> The process was designed to demonstrate to people that the corporation was not just saying: 'Your views are important', but that it actually meant it. Not only was the management team prepared to listen; it would also distribute the results openly and honestly. More importantly it would act on the views expressed. Sophisticated timetabling, communications, objective-setting and measurement ensured that this happened.

The survey was repeated 18 months later to identify progress on actions resulting from the first survey.

Organisational mirroring

'The organisation mirror is a set of activities in which a particular organisational group, the host group, gets feedback from representatives from several other organisational groups about how it is perceived and regarded' (French and Bell, 1990, p. 147). Organisational mirroring is different from interventions at the inter-group level, being concerned with relationships between three or more groups. It is a technique which benefits from the services of a change consultant who is not connected with any of the groups involved in the process. A 'fishbowl' technique is frequently used as part of organisational mirroring. This is where the group asking for feedback (the host group) first sits and listens to what the other group representatives have to say (without interruption). The representatives of the host group and the other group then exchange places to allow the host group to have their say (ask for clarification, information etc.) without interruption. Finally, the representatives of both groups are divided into small sets to work together on problems which emerge before all coming together to devise action plans, assign people to tasks and set target dates for improvements to be completed.

The techniques of survey feedback are most frequently associated with gaining information on people's attitudes and behaviour. It should not be forgotten, however, that other types of information-gathering will be just as important – for instance with regard to progress against financial and other quantifiable measures of organisational performance.

Intergroup confrontation (with third-party assistance)

Although a technique of 'confrontation' sounds alarming, it enables two groups, which have their unique specialities, to confront organisational issues which go beyond their particular expertise. Mabey and Pugh suggest that an exercise such as this might require two days of work away from distractions and helped by a 'neutral' facilitator. The objective is to help the members of the two groups increase their awareness of the importance of each other's activities to the overall organisational performance and thus reduce a sense of 'them and us'.

Both French and Bell, and Mabey and Pugh suggest a process where each group is asked to produce two lists. The first is: the complaints 'we' have against 'them'. The second is: the complaints that 'we' think 'they' would have about 'us'. Lists are then shared between the two groups. According to Mabey and Pugh, two characteristics usually emerge. First, some of the complaints can be dissolved fairly quickly, being the result of simple misunderstandings or lack of communication. Second, the lists of both groups show a surprising degree of congruency; in other words 'we' know what they think about 'us' and 'they' know what we think about 'them'. The lists form the basis for further discussion and exploration of how conflict can be resolved and more positive working relationships established.

Role negotiation

Role negotiation is a technique developed by Harrison (1972). Basically, it involves individuals or groups negotiating to 'contract' to change their behaviour on a quid pro quo basis. In general, it requires the help of a facilitator and, (typically) during a day's workshop session, each set of participants is asked to say what they want the others to *do more of*, *do less of*, or *maintain unchanged*. A follow-up meeting a month or so later assesses progress and, if necessary, renews or sets up new contracts. It is important to note that this *does not* involve probing people's likes and dislikes about each other. It concentrates solely on the roles they play and their behaviour as part of these.

Process consultation

This is rather more than a technique in that Schein (1987) has written a book entitled *Process Consultation*. From Schein's point of view, process consultation is a central part of organisational development. According to French and Bell (1990, p. 152): 'the crux of this approach is that a skilled third party (consultant) works with individuals and groups to help them learn about human and social processes and learn to solve problems that stem from process events'. The kinds of interventions which are part of process consultation are: agenda-setting interventions, feedback of observational data, coaching and counselling of individuals and suggestions about group membership, communication and interaction patterns and allocation of work, responsibilities and lines of authority. French and Bell say (p. 153):

> The process consultation model is similar to team-building interventions and intergroup team-building interventions except that in PC greater emphasis is placed on diagnosing and understanding process events. Furthermore there is more emphasis on the consultant being more nondirective and questioning as he or she gets the groups to solve their own problems.

Team building

Team building is an essential part of the OD process. Team-building techniques can be used for established long-term groups as well as for special, shorter-term, project groups. Processes included in team building are: (a) diagnosis of the task together with individuals' and group needs; (b) diagnosis and negotiation of roles; (c) responsibility charting; (d) understanding and managing group processes and culture. Usually, a change agent or independent consultant/facilitator is used to help in team building.

Life and career planning

There are a number of exercises which can help in career planning, which is part of life planning. One is to draw a life line representing the past, present and future. Past events are positioned according to important things which have happened in life, including things done well and things done not so well – 'ups' as well as 'downs'. Future desired events are also recorded on the line, and some indication is given of time of achievement. Another exercise is to write one's obituary as if death were to occur now and then as if death was some years in the future. The latter exercise is intended to give some idea of what is hoped for in the near and far future.

ACTIVITY 8.8

Think back to the change which you identified for Activity 8.5.

Which of the techniques (at any level or scope) in Pugh's OD matrix were used as the change was implemented?

Were they appropriate?

The role of short-term wins

Implementing change which will ultimately transform an organisation is a *long-term process* and it is understandable if commitment to the vision becomes somewhat weakened on the way. Consequently, the achievement of 'short-term wins' (Kotter, 1996) is important, both as a motivating factor and as a mechanism for tracking the progress towards the longer-term goals. However, Kotter goes further than this in identifying six ways in which short-term wins can help organisational transformations. These are:

- *Provide evidence that sacrifices are worth it*: Wins greatly help justify the short-term costs involved.
- *Reward change agents with a pat on the back*: After a lot of hard work, positive feedback builds morale and motivation.
- *Help fine-tune vision and strategies*: Short-term wins give the guiding coalition concrete data on the viability of their ideas.
- *Undermine cynics and self-serving resisters*: Clear improvements in performance make it difficult for people to block needed change.
- *Keep bosses on board*: Provides those higher in the hierarchy with evidence that the transformation is on track.
- *Build momentum*: Turns neutrals into supporters, reluctant supporters into active helpers, etc. (Kotter, 1996, p. 123.)

Short-term wins do not, however, happen automatically as part of the change process. They have to be planned *deliberately* so that they become much more probabilities than possibilities. According to Kotter (pp. 121–2), a short-term win has three characteristics:

1. It's visible; large numbers of people can see for themselves whether the result is real or just hype.
2. It's unambiguous; there can be little argument over the call.
3. It's clearly related to the change effort.

An example of a short-term win is when a company reduces delivery time on one of its 10 main products by a pre-determined percentage in a pre-determined time; or when the number of customer complaints reduces by (say) 50 per cent during the first half of the year; or when the jobs of a group of employees become easier to do because they are getting more relevant information in a more timely way. Short-term wins are not those of the type: 'We expect to increase our sales in the next couple of months'; nor is the fact that two previously sworn enemies are now talking pleasantly to each other a short-term win, unless the outcome is some further improvement in morale and organisational performance.

The setting and assessment of short-term wins links the implementation stage of the OD process to the more all-embracing assessment of the organisation's progress towards its vision and the continuing reinforcement of the change process itself.

Stage 5: Assess and reinforce the change

Assessing change

In organisational situations of hard complexity, it is relatively easy to assess the extent to which change has been achieved. The setting of 'hard' objectives and quantifiable performance measures makes this a more straightforward process. However, in the softer, more 'messy' situations where change methodologies of the OD type tend to be used, change is an evolving process concerned not only with changes in quantifiable performance objectives, but more frequently with changes in attitudes, behaviours and cultural norms where measurement is bound to be less precise. Even so, measurement of these things is possible. It is also desirable in terms of its role in providing positive feedback that the change process is 'working' and in testing how far the organisation has moved towards achievement of its vision.

A number of ways are available for measuring the softer issues associated with change. These are:

1. *A survey or cultural audit*, which can potentially cover all staff. Its results can be quantified and quickly disseminated. The audit can be done at regular intervals to provide repeated snapshot measures of an organisation's progress towards its change objectives. The Nationwide Building Society is an example of an organisation which uses such a system as part of its commitment to continuous improvement.

2. *Interviews with individuals or focus groups*, which allow the collection of more qualitative, in-depth information. An example of testing what a company's vision and values statement meant to staff was the exercise carried out by the Body Shop just after a public challenge to its integrity regarding its stance of being socially responsible in its policies and practices. The Body Shop called it 'gazing into the mirror'. It consisted of 44 meetings each with 20 different staff and managers from all parts of the organisation. All the meetings were attended by a board member and a moderator who later summarised the discussions to produce a report of the main themes arising and subsequent recommendations for action.

3. *An examination of turnover and absenteeism rates* as an indication of general morale and well-being.

4. *An analysis (through observation or questionnaire) of group performance* in terms of task achievement, but also in terms of the quality of meetings (including number of meetings and length) and leader performance.

5. *'Picturing the organisation'*, that is, asking staff to present their perception of the organisation in graphical or image terms rather than in words. This might include the use of metaphors in line with those suggested by Morgan (1986) in Chapter 4 or Flood and Jackson (1991) (*see* stage 1b above). Alternatively, it might be in the form of a 'Rich Picture' (Checkland, 1981), that is, a collage of images represented by drawings and symbols connected by other symbols depicting the relationships between them. Illustration 8.3 is an example of a rich picture depicting a situation of change from a centrally run service for people with learning disabilities. This meant a change from mainly hospital-based provision to provision which was in line with a 'care in the community' concept – that is, devolving care to a myriad of much smaller units, the management of which had to 'sell' their services (in competition with others) to the national health authority which was charged with 'buying' them on behalf of the users.

When the rich pictures about an organisation start to resemble images closely related to the vision, management can have some confidence that the change has been successful in respect of how employees feel about it.

Reinforcing and consolidating change

Farquhar, Evans and Tawadey (1989, p. 49) say: 'A real danger in the process of organisational change is the failure to carry it through sufficiently far. Companies may be tempted to relax when the immediate crisis recedes while they still have not addressed the deeper organizational problems which generated the crisis.' The lesson from this is that the new order resulting from any change needs to be institutionalised. This is well put by Mabey and Pugh (1995, p. 50) when they say:

> Individuals need to be held personally accountable for prescribed initiatives; new working relationships and boundaries between different working groups need to be negotiated; ways of recognising and rewarding desirable behaviours and attitudes need to be devised to demonstrate that the organisation is serious about the change strategies that have been set.

It is pointless expecting people's behaviour to change if this is not reinforced by concomitant changes in personnel policies and practices, including appraisal, career

Illustration 8.3
RICH PICTURE OF CHANGES IN THE ORGANISATION OF SERVICES FOR PEOPLE WITH LEARNING DISABILITIES

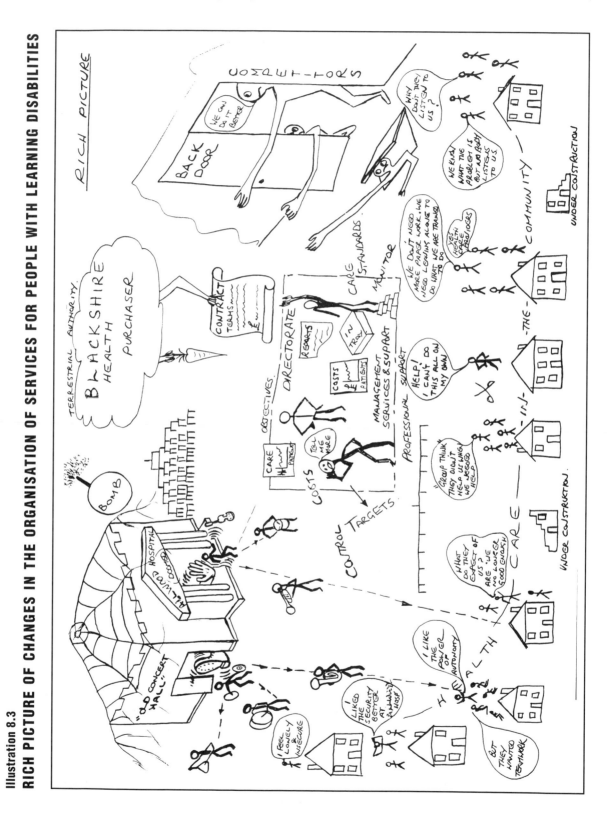

development and reward systems. In addition, staff training and development needs to re-orient itself to the needs of the new vision and the changes which help guide its attainment. According to Farquhar *et al.*, this is particularly important with regard to middle managers. While change can happen fast at the top (often through bringing in new people) and be accepted at the lower levels of an organisation (particularly if the rewards for change are clear), middle managers, who perform the bridging function between the two, may be slower to accept new cultures, policies and practices. Yet it is middle management which must make change work. They must, therefore, be given the new skills they will need – particularly when structures and cultures are expected to change.

More generally, the action-research model of data collection, data analysis and feedback for action is just as important at this stage of OD as at any other. Any change programme is stressful, but if employees continue to *own* change this stress will become, not negative stress, but positive pressure to accept that change can be the norm, with the adoption of innovative, change-oriented behaviour.

AN ASSESSMENT OF THE OD MODEL FOR CHANGE

The model of OD presented here departs to some extent from early OD models which emphasised mainly the attitudinal and behavioural aspects of organisational life and gave insufficient attention to aspects such as strategy, structure, technology and, in particular, the needs of customers or clients, let alone shareholders, and the financial environment within which most organisations operate. Not only has it drawn from these earlier models, but it has used elements of other more directive change models such as Kotter's (1996) eight-stage change process and Buchanan and McCalman's (1989) model of perpetual transition management.

Even so, organisation development as a philosophy and a process can be critiqued according to a number of criteria. The following are examples.

OD does not always face up to harsh realities of change

Almost all models of change include, in one form or another, the underlying concept of unfreezing. From an OD point of view this would be achieved through a typical action-research process of data-collection, analysis and feedback as part of a participatory process of education for change. Yet, authors such as Clarke (1994) and Johnson (1990) describe this process of unfreezing in much harsher terms.

Thus, Clarke (pp. 147–8) talks of 'speeding up the unfreezing process' through *destabilising* people to detach then from the old order. She quotes the example of Centraal Beheer, an insurance company in The Netherlands, 'creating an anxiety greater than the risk of doing something different'. She goes on to say (p. 149): 'Pent-up anger and discontent are the motivators for change; no significant change is possible without them.' Clarke talks the language of crisis and even of engineering a crisis in order to speed up the unfreezing process.

Johnson (p. 190) goes further than Clarke with his talk of 'symbolic acts of questioning or destruction' to start the unfreezing process. He gives examples of John de Lorean trying to change his division of General Motors by promulgating stories to ridicule the dominant culture and of Lee Iacocca firing 33 out of 35 vice-presidents within three years of taking over at Chrysler. Johnson continues this line of thinking by saying (p. 190): 'As conflict and debate grows, managers may actually foster it by symbolic acts of conflict, destruction and degradation.'

However, care must be taken that crisis is not seen merely as a threat and, as Ferlie and Bennett (1993) point out, paradoxically reduces energy, creativity and flexibility. From an OD point of view crisis would be seen as an opportunity which, in Ferlie and Bennett's (p. 270) words, 'forces awkward issues up the agendas [when] we are likely to see continuing pressure from pioneers, the formation of special groups who evangelise the rest of the organisation, high energy and commitment levels, and a period of organisational plasticity in which anything seems plausible'.

Alternatively, as Farquhar et al. (19.., p. 37) point out: 'Not all companies see crisis as a prerequisite for major organisational change. The World Bank, for example, believes that a trigger of another kind may be sufficient. This could range from the aspirations of top management, through anxiety about an uncertain future, to a downturn in results.' Monitoring the internal and external organisational environments on a regular basis can detect potential crises in their early and most treatable phases. What needs to be recognised is that change without crisis is most frequently incremental and time is needed to build the momentum for larger-scale, more radical change.

OD is limited when change situations are 'constrained'

OD has been promoted as a change model for coping with situations of soft complexity where goals and also the means of achieving them are unclear. However, there are situations which have many of the characteristics of soft complexity yet are constrained in the sense that the goals are pre-determined and the means of achieving them are to some extent set. In other words, change is dictated by top management or the precise requirements of some part of the organisation's external environment. For instance, health care is proscribed by the need to safeguard the public against malpractice and legislation regarding the use of treatments and drugs. Setting up a new doctor's practice must adhere to many different forms of regulatory requirement. Franchisees must often run their businesses according to the dictates of the franchiser.

It may be, of course, that, when change is desirable, a Hard Systems Model of Change is most appropriate. However, 'dictated' change is likely to bring resistance from those who must implement it. Therefore, although the earlier stages of the OD model may not be applicable, there is still the requirement to develop an action plan, implement, assess and reinforce change. In addition, gaining commitment to, and participation in, this part of the change process by those who must make the change is of the utmost importance. Consequently, even in highly constrained situations of change, implementation must be as carefully executed as in any other OD process.

OD in the public sector

Chapter 3 discussed the work of Burns and Stalker (1961) and illustrated the differences between mechanistic and organic organisational structures (*see* Illustrations 3.15 and 3.16). A consideration of these shows how an organic structure, rather than a mechanistic structure, is more suited to organisations embracing an OD model of change. Consequently, the application of OD in the mechanistically structured, bureaucratic organisations which are typical of governmental and publicly accountable organisations is a difficult undertaking. Writing on organisational development in the public sector, McConkie (1993, pp. 634–42), writing from a North American perspective but one which applies generally, discusses a number of reasons why the application of OD in public sector organisations is likely to give rise to problems. These, together with others, are:

1. The basic philosophical differences between the assumptions and values of OD and those of the bureaucratic model (which is typical of most public sector organisations) are significant because public sector organisations typically reflect strong adherence to bureaucratic norms and behaviour patterns – forms and patterns foreign to those of OD – therefore making OD application difficult and sensitive, though not impossible.

2. Public sector organisations have multiple authoritative decision-makers and multilevel accountability and reporting relationships. They are also 'supervised' by many interests, such as the general public, other government agencies, interest groups, the media and so on. All these make it difficult first, to get support and gain approvals for an OD initiative, and second, to guide OD designs to fruition because so many people and interests 'get in the way'.

3. Financial support is difficult to obtain for OD work in public sector organisations. This is because, first, funding for consultancy (i.e. external change agents) is limited compared with that available in the private sector, and, second, so many different people have to agree to the spending of funds.

4. In public sector organisations, the large variety of different and frequently conflicting interests, different political allegiances, reward structures and values make OD, as a system-wide effort, difficult to apply. OD interventions are, therefore, more likely to be of a small-scale nature in single departments or work groups.

5. McConkie (p. 640), on the writings of Golembiewski (1969), says: 'five aspects of the public "habit background" . . . make it an inhospitable host for OD: public patterns of delegation, the legal habit, the need for security, the procedural regularity and caution, and the slowly developing image of the "professional manager"'.

6. Decision-making in public sector organisations tends to be pushed upwards towards the top. This contrasts with OD objectives which seek to increase self-control and self-direction of organisation members, something which is difficult if decisions must always be passed to upper levels of management. What is more, deciding where the 'top' is can be confusing. It might be the highest level of the administration, but it may be necessary also to take account of elected and appointed political interests –

which may be at both local and national level. The generally accepted assumption that OD-type interventions should have the support of top management and, frequently, should be led by them, sits uneasily with the realisation that, in some instances, for political reasons the top may not want to be seen to be involved.

These points paint a depressing picture for the likelihood that any OD model for change could succeed in public sector organisations. However, as the public sector (in the UK for example, the health service, local authorities, some government departments) has become more privatised in its outlook and with regard to outcomes, the OD model for change becomes more realistic and easier to apply. Indeed, because of the extreme complexity of these organisations and the massive changes which they are having to face, change models which do not take account of the soft, messy situations they face have little likelihood of succeeding. What OD practitioners must realise is that they need to be very flexible in the way they apply their models for change in these particular types of change scenario.

DISCUSSION QUESTIONS AND ACTIVITIES

1 Debate the pros and cons of using external change agents compared to internal ones.

2 Compare and contrast the HSMC and the OD approach to change.

3 Draw a rich picture of life as experienced by you in your organisation.

REFERENCES

Ackoff, R. L. (1993), 'The art and science of mess management', in Mabey, C., and Mayon-White, B. (eds.), *Managing Change*, London, P.C.P.

Alpander, G. G., and Lee, C. R. (1995), 'Culture, strategy and teamwork, the keys to organizational change', *Journal of Management Development*, Vol. 14, No. 8, pp. 4–18.

Argyris, C., and Schon, D. A. (1978), *Organizational Learning: A Theory of Action Perspective*, Reading, MA, Addison-Wesley.

Beckhard, R., and Harris, R. T. (1987), *Organizational Transitions, Managing Complex Change* (2nd edn.), Reading, MA, Addison-Wesley.

Benjamin, G., and Mabey, C. (1993), 'Facilitating radical change: a case of organization transformation', in Mabey, C., and Mayon-White, B. (eds.), *Managing Change* (2nd edn.), London, P.C.P.

The Body Shop Case Study (1995), Kellogg School of Management, Northwestern University, Evanston, IL, USA and The Body Shop International Plc, West Sussex, UK.

Buchanan, D., and Boddy, D. (1992), *The Expertise of the Change Agent, Public Performance and Backstage Activity*, Hemel Hempstead, Prentice-Hall.

Buchanan, D., and McCalman, J. (1989), *High Performance Work Systems: The Digital Experience*, London, Routledge.

Burns, T., and Stalker, G. M. (1961), *The Management of Innovation*, London, Tavistock.

Burnside, R. M. (1991), 'Visioning: building pictures of the future', in Henry, J., and Walker, D. (eds.), *Managing Innovation*, London, Sage.

Carnall, C. (1995), *Managing Change in Organizations*, Hemel Hempstead, Prentice-Hall.

Checkland, P. (1981), *Systems Thinking, Systems Practice*, Chichester, Wiley.

Clarke, J., Hooper, C., and Nicholson, J. (1997), 'Reversal of fortune', *People Management*, 20 March, pp. 22–6, 29.

Clarke, L. (1994), *The Essence of Change*, Hemel Hempstead, Prentice-Hall.

Cummings, T. G., and Worley, C. G. (1993), *Organization Development and Change* (5th edn.), St. Paul, MN, West Publishing Company.

Farquhar, A., Evans, P., and Tawadey, K. (1989), 'Lessons from practice in managing organizational change', in Evans, P., Doz, E., and Laurent, A. (eds.), *Human Resource Management in International Firms: Change, Globalization, Innovation*, London, Macmillan.

Ferlie, E., and Bennett, C. (1993), 'Patterns of strategic change in health care: district health authorities respond to AIDS', in Hendry, J., Johnson, G., and Newton, J. (eds.), *Strategic Thinking, Leadership and the Management of Change*, Chichester, Wiley.

Flood, R. L., and Jackson, M. C. (1991), *Creative Problem Solving: Total Systems Intervention*, Chichester, Wiley.

French, W. L., and Bell, C. H., Jun. (1990), O*rganization Development, Behavioral Science Interventions for Organization Improvement*, Englewood Cliffs, NJ, Prentice-Hall International.

Goodstein, L. D., and Burke, W. W. (1993), in 'Creating Successful Organization Change', Mabey, C., and Mayon-White, B. (eds.), *Managing Change*, London, P.C.P.

Harrison, R. (1972), 'When power conflicts trigger team spirit', *European Business*, Spring, pp. 27–65.

Johnson, G. (1990), 'Managing strategic change; the role of symbolic action', *British Journal of Management*, Vol. 1. pp. 183–200.

Johnson, G. (1993), 'Processes of managing strategic change', in Mabey, C., and Mayon-White, B. (eds.), *Managing Change*, London, P.C.P.

Johnson, G., and Scholes, K. (1997), *Exploring Corporate Strategy. Texts and Cases* fourth edition, Hemel Hempstead, Prentice-Hall International.

Jones, P. (1994), 'Which lever do I pull now? – the role of "emergent planning" in managing change', *Organisations & People*, Vol. 1, No. 1, January, pp. 46–9.

Kirkbride, P. S., Durcan, J., and Obeng, E. D. A. (1994), 'Change in a chaotic post-modern world', *Journal of Strategic Change*, Vol. 3, pp. 151–63.

Kotter, J. P. (1996), *Leading Change*, Boston, MA, Harvard Business School Press.

Lewin, K. (1951), *Field Theory in Social Science*, New York, Harper & Row.

Lievegoed, B. (1983), *Man on the Threshold*, Driebergen, p. 75.

Lloyd, B., and Feigen, M. (1997), 'Real change leaders: the key challenge to management today', *Leadership & Organization Development Journal*, Vol. 18, No. 1, pp. 37–40.

Mabey, C., and Pugh, D. (1995), Unit 10, 'Strategies for managing complex change', Course B751, *Managing Development and Change*, Milton Keynes, Open University.

McCalman, J., and Paton, R. A. (1992), *Change Management. A Guide to Effective Implementation*, London, P.C.P.

McConkie, M. L. (1993), 'Organization development in the public sector', in Cummings, T. G., and Worley, C. G., *Organization Development and Change* (5th edn.), St. Paul, MN, West Publishing Company.

Matsushita, K. (1988), 'The secret is shared', *Manufacturing Engineering*, March, pp. 78–84.

Morgan, G. (1986), *Images of Organization*, London, Sage.

Price, C. (1987), 'Culture change – the tricky bit', *Training and Development*, October, pp. 20–2.

Pugh, D. (1986), 'Planning and Managing Change', Block 4: *Organizational Development*, Milton Keynes, Open University.

Pugh, D. (1993), 'Understanding and managing change', in Mabey, C., and Mayon-White, B. (eds.), *Managing Change* (2nd edn.), London, P.C.P.

Schein, E. (1987), *Process Consultation Volume II: Lessons for Managers and Consultants*, Reading, MA, Addison-Wesley.

Smith, B. (1995), 'Not in front of the children: the realities of "involvement" in managing change', *Organisations & People*, Vol. 2, No. 2, pp. 17–20.

Snelson, P. (1996), 'How to "Deep Six" Strategic Planning', Nene College of Higher Education/University of Leicester, MBA Speakers' Day.

Stacey, R. (1996), *Strategic Management and Organisational Dynamics*, London, Pitman.

CHAPTER 9

Factors for success

The material in this chapter takes the form of revision and extension of some major themes discussed in the book, in order to suggest pointers to understanding and managing change successfully. The following themes are addressed: the multiple paths to change; the challenge of diversity; empowerment and control; creativity and innovation.

Objective

● Through a revision of issues discussed elsewhere in the book, together with additional argument and discussion, to suggest a number of factors which contribute to successful organisational change.

INTRODUCTION

The two chapters in Part One, together, gave a picture of organisations functioning in multiple environments and responding to environmental disturbances of greater or lesser intensity by planned or forced change in one or all of their parts. This picture was elaborated in Part Two by addressing aspects of organisational life which intervene to influence change outcomes in one direction or another. During this discussion, a variety of contrasting ideas on the nature of change and how it should be responded to and managed were advanced. Finally, in Part Three, two major methodologies of change were described. Given all this, it would be ideal if the overall outcome was an all-embracing, widely accepted theory of change with agreed guidelines on how to 'do it'. Unfortunately, this is not the case. There are, however, some themes which have emerged as being particularly important in any discussion of change. The purpose of this final chapter is, therefore, to identify these for further discussion, with a view to emphasising their role in the pursuit of successful organisational change. Four have been chosen.

The first is that there is no 'one best approach' to change. The second is that organisational life and change take place in a cultural context. The third relates to the importance of people and the issues of empowerment versus control. Finally, the argument that creativity and innovation are necessary attributes of change is discussed.

THE MULTIPLE PATHS TO CHANGE

In May 1996, the journal *Human Relations* brought out a special issue entitled 'Organizational Change in Corporate Settings' which is recommended reading for anyone interested in investigating further different theories of change and their relationship to each other. What is interesting in the context of the present discussion is that all the articles, taken together, suggest there are many ways of understanding and managing change.

This is a view which has surfaced throughout the book and particular reference was made to it in Chapters 2 and 6 in the discussion of the work of Dunphy and Stace (1993) and Strebel (1996) who argue that different change contexts require different change policies and practices. In a later article, Stace (1996) refers to organisational contingencies and paths to change, concepts which chime with Strebel's advice on how to choose the right path to change, depending on the change context. Thus, for these scholars and others, provided the various contingent factors can be identified, *choosing* a path to change becomes uncontentious.

However, the idea of *choice* may not be what it seems. This is because contingency approaches to change assume, in the main, that change can be *planned*. However, as the discussion of Quinn's (1980) and Wilson's (1992) work, in Chapter 2, shows, this is not always the case, as change emerges in ways that are frequently unexpected. In addition, even if one particular path has been chosen, a multitude of influences can arise to deflect both its end point and the means of getting there. What is more, the issue of planned change does not necessarily include the issue of whether change should progress incrementally or take place through more radical transformational means. Much depends on whether the world is seen as reasonably predictable, unpredictable or verging on chaos – in other words, whether the world is seen through the eyes of what Kirkbride, Durcan and Obeng (1994) term the modernist, sophisticated modernist or post-modernist views of change.

Briefly, a *modernist* view of the world would see change as incremental, evolutionary, constantly developing, following a linear path and worked out according to a known recipe about what should change and how. Thus modernists tend to believe in change models based on simple cause and effect: if the right levers are pulled in relation to desired outcomes, those outcomes should surely follow. It is unlikely that processes of change adopted by modernists would result in anything more than transitional change, that is, change that might influence the structure and systems elements of the cultural web (*see* Chapter 4) but leave the underlying organisational paradigm untouched.

A *sophisticated modernist* view of the world would see change as transformational, revolutionary, periodic, following a circular path (i.e. 'moving in a complex and dynamic fashion from emerging strategy to deliberate strategy and back again' (Kirkbride *et al.*, p. 157)), and one where the end point can change as the change process unfolds. As a result, this view recognises that the world does not stand still for long, hence the requirement for an approach to change which, according to Mintzberg (1990), creates change in response to emerging strategy.

The *post-modernist* view of change is best summed up in the words of Kirkbride *et al.* (pp. 158–9):

> The post-modern world can . . . be seen as one characterised by randomness and chaos, by a lack of certainty, by a plethora of competing views and voices, by complex temporalities, and where organisations are unable to produce recipes for dealing with the unstable environment.
>
> In essence, the post-modernist approach rejects the notions of progress, linearity and regular patterning. Change can occur in any direction at any time, which itself could be conceived of in new ways such as 'spiral time'. (Burrell, 1992; Filicove and Filipec, 1986.)

A cursory examination of some of today's organisations will show that there is 'truth' in all of these views of change – the 'trick' is to know when and where one or the other is current. For instance, in limited, constrained situations, a modernist view of change may be most appropriate and might be linked, loosely, to the Hard Systems Model of Change which implies transition rather than transformation and planned rather than emergent change.

The version of an OD model of change presented in the previous chapter is more congruent with a sophisticated modernist view of the world – provided the presence of continuous feedback loops is stressed, and it is recognised that the vision and its associated change goals are not fixed – in the sense that the change process is never complete.

The post-modernist view of change does not easily attach itself to any recognisable model of change. What it does point towards, however, is a model of organisation which is organic, flexible, niche market oriented, where jobs are highly de-differentiated, de-demarcated and multi-skilled in a context of employment relationships based on subcontracting and networking (*see* Clegg, 1990 and the discussion of network and virtual organisations in Chapter 3). Change, in this context, could take on any number of faces and forms.

Success factors: information, knowledge and flexibility as constituents of change

Given the above, successful change is more likely if the following happens. First, there is the need for continuous surveillance of the internal and external organisational environments as well as the temporal environment for, as pointed out in Chapter 1, time itself is a cause for change. Second, there is the need for change managers and facilitators to understand the characteristics of change situations and be familiar with the different characteristics of change so as not to think incremental change is appropriate when nothing but transformational change will do and vice versa. Finally, planning is all well and good, but success is more likely when plans remain flexible even to the extent of contemplating changes of vision, mission or purpose as time unfolds.

In summary, although change can be planned, it quite frequently simply emerges. Whether planned or emergent, it takes a number of different forms, each of which requires a different type of action. While there is no one best way to achieve successful organisational change, making efforts to understand the wide variety of change situations and to be familiar with the different characteristics of change itself will help organisations and their members negotiate appropriate paths to change and, therefore, increase the likelihood of successful change outcomes.

THE CHALLENGE OF DIVERSITY

The discussion in Chapter 4 identified issues associated with differences between people from different societal cultures. It also touched upon diversity of gender and race within national groupings. It is not difficult to find many organisations, large and small, which operate across the world. However, even in organisations which would not be labelled 'global', diversity is both an issue of concern, but also an issue of hope. It is an issue of concern because many think that too much diversity of outlook among workforces constrains the development of a shared sense of purpose and commitment to organisational goals. However, it is also an issue of hope in that today's organisations need people who can bring varied perspectives to ways of doing things and solving problems. In times of organisational change, this is particularly important. Two aspects of diversity are addressed here. The first is international diversity, that is, difference at the societal level. The second is intranational diversity, that is, differences between individuals and groupings within a particular organisation's workforce. The first is discussed mainly in the context of change methodologies. The second is discussed more briefly – given its overlap with the theme of creativity and innovation, which is dealt with at the end of this chapter.

Change methodologies and national culture

The previous two chapters have described at least three ways of designing and implementing organisational change. In addition, ways of dealing with resistance and conflict have been addressed. What must be recognised, however, is the predominantly Western bias of much that is written about organisations and change. Consequently, writers such as Jaegar (1986), and more recently Adler (1997), do well to warn that not all change methods and techniques are transportable across national boundaries to other parts of the world, or even to different ethnic groupings within single countries. This is particularly the case with the range of techniques associated with OD as a philosophy and a methodology for bringing about change.

In an extensive discussion of organisational development and national culture, Jaegar links typical OD values with each of Hofstede's (1980) dimensions of culture and concludes that they have a low correspondence with high power distance, high uncertainty avoidance, high masculinity and moderate individualism. Consequently, some OD-type interventions are unlikely to gain easy acceptance in societies which score high on these dimensions. This is confirmed by Cummings and Worley (1993) who give an example of people from Scandinavian countries as being sympathetic to OD change methods, which is in line with their scores on Hofstede's dimensions. They contrast this with people from Latin American countries (who score high on power distance, uncertainty avoidance and masculinity) who are unlikely to be comfortable with some of the OD ways of effecting change.

The OD philosophy of people-centred leadership and employee participation in the change process is unlikely to find favour in countries such as France and Italy where managers subscribe to ideals of hierarchy and formalised organisational systems (*see* Laurent, 1983). The title of Jack's (1997) article in the *Financial Times* – 'Caste in Stone' and his comment, 'Challenge French corporate hierarchies at your peril' – say much of French managers' attitudes to the participative styles of leadership which are typical of OD approaches to change.

Even with these reservations, there remain many OD techniques which can be used in spite of there existing less than propitious attitudes and beliefs on the part of those involved. Citing Harrison (1970), French and Bell (1990) use the concept of 'depth of intervention' to distinguish those techniques which interact mainly with the more formalised organisational systems (such as job enrichment, management by objectives, role analysis and attitude surveys) and those which go deeper into exploring the informal and more personal organisational systems – for instance, team building, encounter groups and interpersonal relationship explorations. Depth of intervention is a useful concept for deciding how 'deep' to go in the use of OD-type interventions as part of the process of change which involves people from different cultures. It is particularly relevant for those organisations which operate outside their home country environment.

Operating worldwide

Many organisations operate across national boundaries, and doing so has implications for managers and their staff. However, the implications are likely to differ depending on whether an organisation operates in what Keegan (1989) terms an *ethnocentric, polycentric* or *geocentric* way.

Organisations with an ethnocentric orientation are those which tend to offer a standard product across the world and which operate with centralised decision-making from the home country base. Managers, wherever they are located, are usually chosen from the home country nationals on the basis that operations and ways of managing 'abroad' should mirror those in the home base.

By contrast, organisations with a geocentric orientation accept that things might be done differently in different countries. Consequently, although there is still a degree of overall centralised co-ordination of activities, products, operations and methods of management are tailored to the different conditions in each country. In this type of organisation, instead of managers being 'sent out' (e.g. as expatriates) from the home country, the organisation trains and develops host country managers to operate in a decentralised, mainly autonomous way. Organisations subscribing to a polycentric view of business fit somewhere between these two.

At least two issues arise from these distinctions. First, there is what Robbins (1996) calls the 'culture shock cycle'. This consists of the stages which newcomers to foreign countries go through as they adjust to living and working in a foreign culture – stages which can take up to six months to complete. The culture shock cycle is particularly relevant to managers from ethnocentrically orientated organisations as they struggle to manage workforces which are very different from those in their home country. It is less of a problem for organisations with a polycentric or geocentric orientation, given the practice of developing host country nationals to become managers.

The second issue is that of choosing techniques to help facilitate organisational change according to whether an organisation operates in an ethnocentric, polycentric or geocentric way. Cummings and Worley (1993) suggest that the choice of techniques which are typical of OD approaches to change should vary according to different organisational characteristics, in terms of the three orientations described above. For instance, ethnocentrically orientated organisations (which Cummings and Worley call 'global' organisations) are likely to make good use of career planning, role clarification, senior management team-building and conflict-management techniques. At the other extreme, geocentrically orientated organisations (designated by Cummings and Worley as 'transnational' organisations), which operate a much more devolved policy, need to tailor their techniques according to each of the countries in which they operate. They must also be aware of the issues involved in the workings of multicultural teams. According to Adler (1997), while such teams have every potential for reaping the benefits of diversity, they also face problems arising from culturally different ways of communicating, negotiating and decision-making, let alone culturally different assumptions about what motivates people and how they should be led.

Workforce diversity

Diversity within the workforce occurs not only across national boundaries, where organisations operate on a global, multinational or transnational basis, but also inside organisations (or parts of them) located in a single country. As well as varying according to race or ethnicity, individuals working together also vary in terms of gender, age, sexual preference and able-bodiness – characteristics which, like race or ethnicity, are fairly well unalterable. What is more, the proportions of people who vary according to these criteria are changing, with consequences for workplace practices and procedures. Two accounts, with different emphases, illustrate this.

The first is a recent *Labour Market and Skills Trends* report (that for 1997/1998) from the UK Department for Education and Employment. This says that the number of women in the workforce will continue to grow but that they are still under-represented at management levels. The report also points out the continued discrimination against appointing older people and the very young to jobs. In addition, people from ethnic minority groupings have lower economic activity rates than the white population. Unemployment rates for disabled people are high. This is not a very optimistic picture for those who are not white, male and aged between 25 and 50 years old.

This picture can, however, be set against another account of workforce changes which is best reported in the words of Robbins (1996, pp. 61–2):

> During the next decade, new worker growth in the United States will be occurring most rapidly among women and Hispanics. This is going to result in reshaping the overall labour force. By the year 2005, women will likely hold 50 percent of all jobs in the United States. . . . minorities will hold more than one out of four jobs. Whilst these small percentage changes may not seem important, they are! They indicate that the white-male working population is aging and the younger faces in organisations will belong to women, African-Americans, Latinos, and Asian-Americans.

Robbins goes on to say that this is happening not just in the United States but across the world. To quote:

> Take Western Europe as an example. Eight million legal immigrants and an estimated 2 million illegal immigrants now live in 15 nations of the European Union. A particularly large influx of Muslims and Africans in recent years has been changing the religious and racial composition of these countries. And in Asia, the big challenge in organisations is adjusting to the rapid increase in the number of women employees, especially in the managerial ranks. Although a distinct minority, women are making significant inroads into managerial positions throughout Asia. . . . even in Japan, long hostile to corporate women, females are increasing their presence in management.

Workforce diversity, which seems set to increase, has implications for the management of change. Managing effectively such diversity is a significant component in the successful management of change.

Success factor: using diversity as a constituent of change

Organisational managers who think they can achieve successful organisational change without recognising the differences among the members of their workforces are heading for problems and possibly disasters. The discussion above suggests a number of things. First, people at all levels in organisations must recognise that difference is not to be feared. This means recognising that difference is something which can be used to enhance organisational performance rather than be a matter for regret. Second, recognising difference does not mean that interacting with people from other cultures will be easy. Successful intercultural exchange requires tolerant understanding of other people's attitudes and beliefs as well as appreciating the underlying values by which they live. Third, if organisations are to change to increase organisational performance, the gifts, talents and living/behaviour patterns of all their members must be used. This impinges substantially on how organisations arrange their affairs in order to take account of widely differing expectations, patterns of working and power relationships.

In summary, recognising and accepting diversity of any kind is the first step to using differences among employees to the greater satisfaction of everyone and the better good of the organisation. Managers are constantly faced with expressions of the tension between uniformity and diversity. Effective management uses this tension to promote new ways of organising work in order to give everyone equal treatment and equal opportunity. People are an organisation's most precious resource. Managers cannot afford to ignore the diversity of this resource. Valuing diversity affirms people's uniqueness at the same time as recognising their capacity to work collectively for the benefit of themselves and the organisation. This is even more true during times of change than it is at any other time.

EMPOWERMENT AND CONTROL

People know a game is being played, but they don't know what the rules are.

(From a talk by Wendy Hirsh, Associate Director of the Institute of Employment Studies, at the Institute of Personnel Development's Human Resource Development Week, 4–6 March 1997)

The quotation above is a good example of the situation which prevails in many organisations. Yet common sense seems to say that change will not happen unless those concerned understand the reasons for it and are prepared to 'will' it. On the other hand, as the discussion in Chapters 2 and 6, on the nature of change and ways of leading it, show, there may be occasions when directive (and even coercive) rather than participative approaches are appropriate. This raises an issue which pervades the theory and practice of organisational change – that of empowerment versus control.

The meaning of empowerment

Empowerment can mean many things to many people. It can have a political emphasis which implies certain types of social, economic and political relationships in the context of who gains and who loses in any society. On the other hand, it can be restricted to how individuals, in a personal capacity, grow and develop to become more autonomous and take more responsibility for their own actions. Empowerment can also describe how certain people might band together to achieve particular collective goals. However, in the context of the management of organisations, empowerment is more likely to focus on the second of the views described above. In line with this, Burdett (1996, p. 33) offers the following definition:

> 'Empowerment' is the voluntary transfer of ownership of a task or situation to an individual or group having the ability and willingness appropriate to that situation, in an enabling environment.

This definition, while short and to the point, is particularly helpful in its emphasis on the concepts of *ownership*, *ability*, *willingness* and an *enabling environment*. Empowerment is, therefore, a multi-dimensional concept implying a process which is complex and an outcome which is not easily accomplished, even in the most propitious of circumstances. Even so, the ideal of empowering employees with respect to decision-making about, and the doing of, work has gained strength in conjunction with the belief that organisations must operate in increasingly turbulent, unpredictable environments.

Given this assumption, there are a number of conditions which must be satisfied if those who work in organisations are not to feel and believe that this is merely the latest ploy to get them to work harder for the same reward. The main condition is that managers must learn how to share power.

Empowering managers

In a review of previous research, Gratton and Pearson (1993, p. 1) say that:

> Empowerment processes have been achieved by a movement from hierarchical layers to team based activities; from narrow, single task jobs to whole process, multiple tasks; from a management role of directing and controlling to one of coaching and facilitation; from top down leadership to sharing with the team; and from job processes based on management planning and control to team planning and learning.

From this review, they identify six clusters of characteristics which are typical of empowering mangers. In summary these are:

1. *Management style*
   - maintaining an open and collaborative approach;
   - fostering opportunities for subordinate participation in decision-making;
   - creating teams whose members are joined by common purposes;
   - ensuring employees have the knowledge and understanding to contribute.

2. *Delegation and involvement*
- establishing a process whereby power is shared with subordinates;
- working hard to enable rather than simply delegate;
- ensuring team members have autonomy from bureaucratic constraints.

3. *Giving recognition and feedback*
- motivating by expressing confidence in team members;
- ensuring employees feel they are making a difference;
- rewarding followers informally with personal recognition.

4. *Interpersonal empathy*
- building relationships with other people;
- dealing with emotions through humour and symbolism;
- having reached a highly mature stage of personal and emotional development.

5. *Communication*
- having the capability to manage complex interdependencies;
- networking;
- establishing credible communication channels with their boss, peers and subordinates.

6. *Vision*
- having a vision;
- articulating a set of values;
- creating inspirational and meaningful goals.

These characteristics are interesting in the light of what Williams (1996) calls the 'deficit' model of leadership in which 'the leader leads from behind, assessing the resources available within the team and defining the contribution required from the leader according to the areas of weakness – plugging the gaps' (p. 40). This model of leadership is consistent with one which seeks to develop subordinates and involve them fully in decisions about the way work is done. However, as the results of Gratton and Pearson's research show, in the light of subordinate perceptions, many managers do not demonstrate strengths in these areas. Particular weaknesses are in the areas of showing recognition and feedback and particularly in the area of interpersonal sensitivity. A number of reasons have been suggested to explain why this is so.

Hierarchy versus empowerment

In spite of the emphasis put on network forms of organisation and the emergence of the virtual organisation, many large organisations continue to conform to hierarchical principles of structure and accountability as described in Chapter 3. This is particularly so with regard to rule-governed public institutions. The skills which managers need to be successful in this type of organisation are not those which comfortably agree with the principles of empowering subordinate levels of staff. Even if empowering abilities are developed, they are unlikely to be rewarded or acknowledged. Behaving in empowering ways does not support the culture and processes which make these managers successful. Many of the characteristics – such as showing determination, drive/energy, leading from the front, objective decision-making and personal achievement – are not among the key empowering characteristics.

A good example of the way some senior managers think about the issues of staff involvement in decision-taking comes from research done by Smith (1995). He talked to chief executives and top managers of organisations going through change to try to find out what goes wrong and what might make change programmes successful. The title of the article, 'Not in front of the children' says a lot! What he found was that (p. 18):

> CEOs talk a good game about involvement, but what they mean is that they will involve staff only at the *implementation* stage of change. CEOs and top managers made it quite clear that an essential element of their jobs in times of change is to design and present to their organisations a workable strategy for managing the change. They – and only they – determine the right way forward. . . . Their attitude seems to be, 'not in front of the children'. As one CEO said to us: 'I read what is going on, decide what to do, and develop the package. Staff are fully involved in the implementation.'

The issue of loss of control is very real for many managers when they are contemplating empowerment processes and behaviours. Furze and Gale (1996) say some of the common concerns of managers focus around the questions: 'How will I know what is happening?', 'Will I look weak and unable to manage?', 'Can I trust them?', 'Will they do the things the way I have done them?'

From the other side of the coin, it is quite feasible that some employees do not want to be empowered. The introduction of flatter organisational structures has frequently brought more work and responsibility without a commensurate increase in reward. In addition, because many employees have been conditioned to accept a degree of 'learned helplessness' they become nervous at the thought of a reduction in the security of established rules and procedures.

Empowerment assumes that employees share organisational goals, but this is not always true. As Chapter 5 discussed, pluralist organisations have plural goals, and the 'trick' is to manage among these. Furthermore, empowerment assumes collective decision-making and team-working. Collective approaches in these areas are more difficult than they appear, given the individualistic nature of much of management in the Western world. Interacting with this difficulty is the problem of communicating constantly and consistently to achieve the sharing of power which empowerment demands. Ultimately, it must be recognised that employee empowerment is intended to serve the purposes of the organisation in its quest to achieve high levels of performance and to meet the challenges of competitors. In doing this, it can, however, also enhance organisational members' working lives.

Given the above, and accepting that a management use of the term empowerment is one based on the notion of personal development, there is still every reason to believe that:

> Organisations that implement empowerment programmes can provide a certain measure of employee satisfaction and organisational empowerment if managers adapt to individual

employees' learning styles, and use control in a manner that does not sap employees' energies. Coupled with the use of techniques for improving organisational effectiveness (such as job design, open communication, etc.) employee participation may be increased and feelings of self-efficacy may be enhanced. (Leiba and Hardy, 1994, p. 268.)

Success factor: empowerment as a constituent of change

On balance, change is more likely to be successful if all those concerned are willing collaborators in the process of bringing it about. Putting empowerment into action requires a number of things. First, managers must decide whether empowerment extends to the goals as well as the means; that is, are they willing to transfer ownership of *what* should be done as well as how it should be done? Is the vision negotiable as well as how to enact it? Second, an intention to operate on empowerment principles needs to be followed by a deliberate action plan of training and development for all employees, starting with the managers. It cannot be assumed that managers know how to empower unless they have been sufficiently trained and educated to do so. Third, the behaviours relevant to having an empowered workforce must be the behaviours which are rewarded as part of a philosophy that can learn from failures rather than condemn and look for scapegoats for them.

In summary, empowerment as an aim and a process is not the answer to accomplishing organisational change in all circumstances. However, organisational change is likely to be more successful if employees are involved in all stages of its design and implementation. The actions required for achieving this are serious and far-reaching. Managers, themselves, need to reach a mature stage of personal development in order to empower their staff in ways which do not exploit them, while at the same time being truthful that employee empowerment also means organisational empowerment. Managers must 'model' the behaviour they wish to see in their subordinates. Subordinates must also be provided with relevant training and education to give them the skills and the confidence they need to work in an empowered way. Finally, empowerment as an aim and a process has much more chance of succeeding if the structures and procedures of organisations are designed to facilitate employee involvement rather than to enforce employee control.

CREATIVITY AND INNOVATION

Organisational change does not come from nothing. There is always some precipitating event – which can be quite small, so as to be almost unnoticeable, or cataclysmic in its size and impact. Whichever is the case, the response almost always involves some creative thinking and, particularly, in the case of more radical transformational change, some innovative result.

The concept of creativity is particularly apt for the change situations which in Part One of the book are described as 'messes'. Examples of such situations are those where the problem (or problems) is not even understood, let alone any possible solution, and those where individuals and groups each have their own interpretation of what is 'wrong' and what might be done about it. In other words, these are situations which have all the characteristics of soft complexity.

Of creativity and innovation, Henry (1991, p. 3) says:

> Creativity is about the quality of originality that leads to new ways of seeing and novel ideas. It is a thinking process associated with imagination, insight, innovation, ingenuity, intuition, inspiration and illumination. However, creativity is not just about novelty: for an idea to be truly creative it must also be appropriate and useful. The related term innovation is usually used to describe the process whereby creative ideas are developed into something tangible, like a new product or practice.

Of interest here is the question of how to harness the creative process to the change process so as to achieve increased organisational performance – which is the aim of most change programmes. Two issues need to be considered. The first is the issue of the creative *person*. The second is the issue of the creative *organisation*.

Creative styles and creative behaviour

A number of scholars have suggested a range of characteristics typical of what they regard as creative people. For example, McAleer (1991) cites having: a personal aesthetic, problem-finding ability, mental mobility, risk-taking, objectivity and inner motivation. Guildford (1959) identifies problem sensitivity, idea fluency, flexibility, originality and problem redefinition. Henry (1994) summarises these characteristics to come up with four which seem to be important. These are:

- *Positivity*, which implies tolerance and the capacity for taking hold of opportunities;
- *Playfulness*, which includes having independence of thought and a leaning towards risk-taking;
- *Passion*, that is, being motivated and committed;
- *Persistence* based on experience and sensitivity to the problem.

Categorising people in this way seems to suggest that there are some people who are creative and others who are not. However, creativity should not be seen as something of which individuals can have a lot or a little. In an extensive review of the literature on cognitive style as a description of the way people acquire, store and use knowledge, Hayes and Allison (1994) support the contention that people differ in their approaches to problem-solving and decision-making, but that there is no style which is 'the best': one creative style may be useful in some situations while a different one is useful in others.

Kirton's adaption–innovation theory

There are many categorisations of creative thinking styles (Hayes and Allison list 22). One which is relatively easy to understand and which has a well-validated way of measuring someone's creative style, is that of Kirton (1976, 1984), based on his adaption–innovation theory. Briefly, the adaption–innovation theory defines and measures two styles of decision-making which lie at different poles of a bi-polar scale. According to Kirton, everyone can be located on a continuum ranging from highly adaptive to highly innovative according to their scores on his creative style measure – the Kirton Adaption–Innovation Inventory (KAI).

Kirton starts from the premise that everyone is creative but that people are creative in different ways. Describing the extremes of the continuum, Kirton (1984, p. 137) says:

> *Adaptors* characteristically produce a sufficiency of ideas, based closely on, but stretching, existing agreed definitions of the problem and likely solutions. They look at these in detail and proceed within the established mores (theories, policies, practices) of their organisations. Much of their effort in change is in improving and 'doing better'. . .

> *Innovators*, by contrast, are more likely in the pursuit of change to reconstruct the problem separating it from its enveloping accepted thought, paradigms and customary viewpoints, and emerge with much less expected, and probably less acceptable solutions. They are less concerned with 'doing things better' than with 'doing things differently'.

Each of these styles has its strengths and weaknesses. Words and phrases which are seen as typical of each style are:

1. *Adaptors*: precise, reliable, efficient, methodical, prudent, disciplined, conforming, sound, stability, dependable, high accuracy, cautious, continuity, analytical, sensitive to people, high boredom tolerance, maintains group cohesion and co-operation, provide a safe base for innovators' riskier operations.

2. *Innovators*: indiscipline, tangential thinking, queries problems, manipulates problems, irreverent, abrasive, creates dissonance, impractical, challenge rules, delegate routine tasks, intuitive, low self-doubt, little respect for custom, threaten group cohesion and co-operation, provide the dynamics to bring about periodic radical change.

Clearly, any of these characteristics can be viewed as a strength or a weakness depending on the demands of the situation and the characteristics of others involved. Whichever is the case, the adaptor–innovator distinction appears to mirror other dichotomous descriptions of cognitive style such as convergent–divergent thinking, and left brain–right brain thinking. What is more, although individuals can learn to *behave* in ways different to their creative thinking style, evidence for a link between thinking style and personality reinforces Kirton's claim that the adaptor–innovator styles of thinking represent fairly stable *preferences* with regard to an individual's creative thinking style.

The implications of this for organisational change are that few organisations will thrive for long if they are staffed by individuals who are all innovators or who are all adaptors. While innovators are relevant in situations of radical, transformational change, adaptors are required to assist in the ongoing incremental modifications to strategy, structure and processes which are part of the continuous life of all organisations. Organisations, and groups within them, need both adaptors and innovators to be effective.

Care needs to be taken, however, to manage the gap between innovators and adaptors. Given a scale of scores ranging between 46 and 146 (with scores from the general population normally distributed with a mean of 95), Kirton (1994) says that there are noticeable differences in preferred ways of behaving between individuals where KAI scores are 10 points or more apart. What is more, a difference of 20 points can lead to difficulties in communication and collaboration – an important point given the necessity for most people to work with others (often not of their choice), frequently in groups or teams. Even so, groups need both adaptors and innovators to be most effective. What they also need is someone who can take the role of 'bridger', that is, someone whose KAI score is intermediate between others whose scores are such that they are unlikely to see the world from the same point of view.

Whether those involved work individually or in teams, change projects benefit from the presence of both innovators and adaptors. For instance, different stages of a project require different ways of thinking and behaving. In the initial stages, where the emphasis is on generating new ideas, the innovators can be relied on to push the boundaries of thinking beyond the conventional. At the same time, diagnosis of an organisation's current situation is something which adaptors do well, given the requirement for detailed information-gathering. As the project moves on, innovators can help in the generation of ideas for action while the adaptors work out implementation strategies. What is most important, however, is that innovators and adaptors learn to value the strengths of each other.

A creative organisational climate

It is one thing to try to use the talents of people with creative thinking styles appropriate to the task in hand, whether this is ongoing organisational business or the design and implementation of change. Although necessary, this is not sufficient. For individuals and groups to operate in creative ways, organisations must offer what Ekvall (1991) calls a 'creative climate' (climate being defined as the manifestation at the observable level of organisational culture – *see* Chapter 4). He defines this in more detail through identifying a number of dimensions such as: challenge, freedom, idea-support, trust, dynamism, playfulness, debates, conflicts, and risk-taking. Two extreme types of organisation are identified. One, he calls 'innovative' (in terms of its record of product innovation) and the other, he terms 'stagnated'. In relation to the organisational climate dimensions, Ekvall's research shows that, except for conflict, innovative organisations score highly on each of the dimensions while stagnated organisations score significantly lower.

The concept of a creative climate is taken further by Ekvall with his discussion of an 'idea-handling' system. This links up with the concept of creative thinking, in that some mechanism is required if ideas are not to become lost, and to help them through to fruition. However, he puts three provisos on this, saying (p. 77):

● No idea-handling system can work successfully without a supportive climate in terms of the dimensions . . . referred to.

- An idea-handling system can make a good climate even better.
- An idea-handling system which is set up in an organisation where the climate is bad tends to make that climate still worse. The system becomes another area of conflict and distrust.

These sentiments echo those of Majaro (1988) who suggests that a creative organisation has three characteristics:

- a climate conducive to creative thinking;
- an effective system for communicating ideas;
- procedures for managing innovation.

Ekvall is uncompromising in his contention that a bureaucratically structured organisation, operating on scientific management lines, is unlikely to offer a supportive environment for creative thinking and innovation. In contrast, Kuratko (1995) is more optimistic that, through the process of *intrapreneurship*, bureaucratic environments can help an atmosphere of innovation to prosper. He cites Sathe (1988), who has suggested a number of areas on which organisations should focus in order to facilitate a more creative environment. These are:

1. To encourage, not mandate entrepreneurial activity within the organisation.
2. To keep managers in positions long enough to allow them to learn an industry and a particular division; third, to sustain a commitment to innovative projects long enough for momentum to occur.
3. To emphasise people as much as the project.

Kuratko says that ultimately, to create an intrapreneurial strategy, the ethos of bureaucracy will need to change. This might be towards what Ekvall calls the 'bureaucracy with a human face', but more effectively towards Ekvall's notion of organisations which combine an ethos of change together with care about people – a theme which links up with the discussion of empowerment above and the OD methodology described in Chapter 8.

Success factor: creativity and innovation as constituents of change

Creativity and innovation will be part of change only if attention is given to: (a) the characteristics of the people involved and the way differences in cognitive styles can contribute to the creative design and implementation of change; and (b) the issue of a creative organisational climate in which people of all creative thinking styles can flourish and find support for the ways in which they work best. Neither of these conditions is easy to meet. They require attitudes and actions on the part of managers who are themselves constrained in their thinking. However, an open mind will go further than anything else in enabling people to come to view those who differ from them, not as wrong-headed, or even dangerous, but as complementary assets. In addition, managers and others need to maintain a questioning attitude regarding the structures and processes which can constrain creativity. So long as they can maintain this attitude, they should be able to provide the idea-handling systems which, at the least, will ensure that no useful ideas are lost and, at the most, will steer them through to provide enhanced organisational performance.

In summary, the close connection between creativity, innovation and change is evidenced by the number of books and articles which consider these, in many ways, to be inseparable. The conclusion here is that responding to, or planning, change involves forms of creative thinking which are varied in focus and means. All people are creative, but creative in different ways. The challenge for all members of organisations is to understand further these differences and to value the strengths of those who are different from themselves. Looking for complementary ways of thinking rather than only for those which match one's own is a way of ensuring appropriate innovation as a component of any change. However, encouraging creativity of outlook is not sufficient in today's changeable turbulent environments. Constructing an organisational climate which is conducive to creative thinking and idea-handling is important if the full benefits of a creatively oriented staff are to be felt.

TO CONCLUDE . . .

Change is about nothing if it is not about persistence. This means persisting in the face of an ultra-unstable environment; persisting in the face of systems which are built for stability rather than change; persisting in the face of plans which are out of date as soon as they are formed. It means applying the same principles to people as are applied to 'things' – that is, the knowledge that nothing is perfect. This means recognising that people will act in infuriating and annoying ways but that, when necessary, will bring the genius of their humanity to solve apparently unsolvable problems. Change is not easy but it can be interesting. It is certainly worth the journey even if the place of arrival is surprising.

REFERENCES

Adler, N. J. (1997), *International Dimensions of Organizational Behavior* (3rd edn.), Cincinnati, OH, South Western College Publishing, ITP.

Burdett, D. (1996), '"Empowerment" defined', *Occupational Psychologist*, No. 28, April, pp. 33–4.

Burrell, G. (1992), 'Back to the future: time and organization', in Reed, M., and Hughes, M. (eds.), *Rethinking Organization: New Directions in Organization Theory and Analysis*, London, Sage.

Clegg, S. R. (1990), *Modern Organization: Organization Studies in the Postmodern World*, London, Sage.

Cummings, T. G., and Worley, C. G. (1993), *Organization Development and Change* (5th edn.), St Paul, MN, West Publishing Company.

Department for Education and Employment, *Labour Market & Skills Trends 1997/1998*, Department for Education and Employment, SEN 287, Crown Copyright.

Dunphy, D., and Stace, D. (1993), 'The Strategic Management of Corporate Change', *Human Relations*, Vol. 46, No. 8, pp. 905–20.

Ekvall, G. (1991), 'The organizational culture of idea-management: a creative climate for the management of ideas', in Henry, J., and Walker, D. (eds.), *Managing Innovation*, London, Sage.

Filicove, B., and Filipec, J. (1986), 'Society and concepts of time', *International Social Sciences Journal*, Vol. 107, pp. 19–32.

French, W. L., and Bell, C. H. (1990), *Organization Development: Behavioral Science Interventions for Organization Improvement*, Englewood Cliffs, NJ, Prentice-Hall International.

Furze, X., and Gale, X. (1996), Jack (1997), 'Caste in Stone', *Financial Times*,

Gersick, C. J. G. (1991), 'Revolutionary change theories: a multilevel exploration of the punctuated equilibrium paradigm', *Academy of Management Review*, Vol. 16, pp. 10–36.

Gratton, L., and Pearson, J. (1993), 'Empowering leaders: are they being developed?', Occupational Psychology Conference, January.

Guildford, J. P. (1959), 'Traits in creativity', in Anderson, H. H. (ed.), *Creativity and its Cultivation*, New York, Wiley.

Harrison, R. (1970), 'Choosing the depth of organizational intervention', *Journal of Applied Behavioral Science*, Vol. 6, pp. 181–202.

Hayes, J., and Allison, C. W. (1994), 'Cognitive style and its relevance for management practice', *British Journal of Management*, Vol. 5, pp. 53–71.

Henry, J. (1991), 'Making sense of creativity', in Henry, J. (ed.), *Creative Management*, London, Sage.

Henry, J. (1994), Block 1, 'Perspective', in *Creative Management*, Milton Keynes, Open University.

Hofstede, G. (1980), *Culture's Consequences: International Differences in Work-related Values*, London and Beverly Hills, Sage.

Jaegar, A. M. (1986), 'Organization development and national culture: Where's the fit?', *Academy of Management Review*, Vol. 11, No. 1, pp. 178–90.

Keegan, W. J. (1989), 'International-Multinational-Global Marketing: a typology', Chapter 1 in Keegan, W. J. (ed.), *Global Marketing Management* (4th edn.), Englewood Cliffs, NJ, Prentice-Hall International.

Kirkbride, P. S., Durcan, J., and Obeng, E. D. A. (1994), 'Change in a chaotic world', *Journal of Strategic Change*, Vol. 3, pp. 151–63.

Kirton, M. (1976), 'Adaptors and innovators: a description and measure', *Journal of Applied Psychology*, Vol. 61, No. 5, pp. 622–9.

Kirton, M. (1984), 'Adaptors and innovators – why new initiatives get blocked', *Long Range Planning*, Vol. 17, No. 2, pp. 137–43.

Kluckhohn, J. P., and Strodtbeck, F. L. (1961), *Variations in Value Orientations*, Evanston, IL, Row, Peterson.

Kuratko, D. F. (1995), 'Developing entrepreneurship within organizations is today's challenge', *Entrepreneurship, Innovation and Change*, Vol. 4, No. 2, pp. 99–104.

Laughlin, R. C. (1991), 'Environmental disturbances and organizational transitions and transformations: some alternative models', *Organization Studies*, Vol. 12, No. 2, pp. 209–32.

Laurent, R. C. (1991), 'Environmental disturbances and organizational transitions and transformations: some alternative models', *Organization Studies*, Vol. 12, No. 2, pp. 209–32.

Leiba, S., and Hardy, C. (1994), 'Employee empowerment: a seductive misnomer?' in Hardy, C. (ed.), *Managing Strategic Action: Mobilizing Change: Concepts, Readings and Cases*, London, Sage.

McAleer, N. (1991), 'The roots of inspiratiton', in Henry, J. (ed.), *Creative Management*, London, Sage.

Majaro, S. (1988), *The Creative Gap*, London, Longman.

Mintzberg, H. (1990), 'Strategy formation: schools of thought', in Frederickson, J. (ed.), *Perspectives on Strategic Management*, New York, Harper Business, pp. 105–235.

Quinn, J. B. (1980), 'Managing strategic change', *Sloan Management Review*, Vol. 21, No. 4, pp. 3–20.

Rajagopalan, N., and Rasheed, A. M. A. (1995), 'Incremental models of policy formulation and non-incremental changes: critical review and synthesis', *British Journal of Management*, Vol. 6, No. 4, pp. 289–302.

Robbins, S. P. (1996), *Organizational Behavior: Concepts, Controversies, Applications*, Englewood Cliffs, NJ, Prentice-Hall International.

Sathe, V. (1988), 'From surface to deep corporate entrepreneurship', *Human Resource Management*, Winter, pp. 389–411.

Smith, B. (1995), 'Not in front of the children: the realities of "involvement" in managing change', *Organisations & People*, Vol. 2, No. 2, pp. 17–20.

Stace, D. (1996), 'Dominant ideologies, strategic change, and sustained performance', *Human Relations*, Vol. 49, No. 5, pp. 553–70.

Strebel, P. (1996), 'Choosing the right path, Mastering Management, Part 14, *Financial Times*.

Williams, H. (1996), *The Essence of Managing Groups and Teams*, Hemel Hempstead, Prentice-Hall.

Wilson, D. (1992), *A Strategy of Change, Concepts and Controversies in the Management of Change*, London, Routledge.

Author index

(Please note that the page numbers in brackets indicate end of chapter reference pages)

Subject index